T0214129

Lecture Notes in Artificial Intelligence   12228

Subseries of Lecture Notes in Computer Science

Series Editors

Randy Goebel
  University of Alberta, Edmonton, Canada
Yuzuru Tanaka
  Hokkaido University, Sapporo, Japan
Wolfgang Wahlster
  DFKI and Saarland University, Saarbrücken, Germany

Founding Editor

Jörg Siekmann
  DFKI and Saarland University, Saarbrücken, Germany

More information about this subseries at http://www.springer.com/series/1244

Abdelkhalick Mohammad ·
Xin Dong · Matteo Russo (Eds.)

Towards Autonomous Robotic Systems

21st Annual Conference, TAROS 2020
Nottingham, UK, September 16, 2020
Proceedings

 Springer

Editors
Abdelkhalick Mohammad 🆔
Faculty of Engineering
University of Nottingham
Nottingham, UK

Xin Dong 🆔
Faculty of Engineering
University of Nottingham
Nottingham, UK

Matteo Russo 🆔
Faculty of Engineering
University of Nottingham
Nottingham, UK

ISSN 0302-9743   ISSN 1611-3349   (electronic)
Lecture Notes in Artificial Intelligence
ISBN 978-3-030-63485-8   ISBN 978-3-030-63486-5   (eBook)
https://doi.org/10.1007/978-3-030-63486-5

LNCS Sublibrary: SL7 – Artificial Intelligence

© Springer Nature Switzerland AG 2020, corrected publication 2021
This work is subject to copyright. All rights are reserved by the Publisher, whether the whole or part of the material is concerned, specifically the rights of translation, reprinting, reuse of illustrations, recitation, broadcasting, reproduction on microfilms or in any other physical way, and transmission or information storage and retrieval, electronic adaptation, computer software, or by similar or dissimilar methodology now known or hereafter developed.
The use of general descriptive names, registered names, trademarks, service marks, etc. in this publication does not imply, even in the absence of a specific statement, that such names are exempt from the relevant protective laws and regulations and therefore free for general use.
The publisher, the authors and the editors are safe to assume that the advice and information in this book are believed to be true and accurate at the date of publication. Neither the publisher nor the authors or the editors give a warranty, expressed or implied, with respect to the material contained herein or for any errors or omissions that may have been made. The publisher remains neutral with regard to jurisdictional claims in published maps and institutional affiliations.

This Springer imprint is published by the registered company Springer Nature Switzerland AG
The registered company address is: Gewerbestrasse 11, 6330 Cham, Switzerland

Preface

This book constitutes the proceedings of the 21st Annual Conference Towards Autonomous Robotic Systems (TAROS 2020), held in Nottingham, UK, on September 16, 2020.

As the longest running UK-hosted international conference on robotics and autonomous systems, TAROS is aimed at the presentation of the latest results and methods in autonomous robotics research and applications. It provides researchers from the UK, Europe, or worldwide with opportunities to engage and discuss cutting-edge robotics technologies. TAROS offers a friendly environment for academia and industry to take stock and plan future progress, welcoming senior researchers and research students alike, and specifically provides opportunities for students and early-career scientists to discuss their work with a wider scientific community.

TAROS 2020 was organized by the Rolls-Royce University Technology Centre in Manufacturing and On-wing Technology at the University of Nottingham, UK, and it took place virtually on September 16, 2020. We were delighted to be able to attract world-renowned experts in robotics to deliver keynote lectures: Prof. Ian D. Walker from Clemson University, USA; Dr. James Kell from Rolls-Royce, UK; Mr Xingxing Wang, Founder and CEO of Unitree Robotics, China; and Dr. Fumiya Iida from the University of Cambridge, UK.

The conference program included an oral presentation of each full paper and a poster presentation for short papers. The finalists of the Queen Mary UK Best PhD in Robotics Award also presented their work, and the winner was announced during the conference.

The 43 papers were carefully reviewed and selected from 63 submissions, which present and discuss significant findings and advances in autonomous robotics research and applications. Furthermore, two additional papers were reviewed and selected for publication by the UK-RAS 2020 senior programme committee. The proceedings are organized in the following topical sections: soft and compliant robots; mobile robots; learning, mapping and planning; human-robot interaction; and robotic systems and applications.

We would like to thank all the authors for submitting their work to TAROS 2020, and all the participants for their contributions. We would also like to thank all the reviewers and the conference sponsors, including the RAIN Hub, the IET, UK-RAS Network, the University of Nottingham, and Springer.

September 2020

Xin Dong
Abdelkhalick Mohammad
Matteo Russo

Organization

General Chair

Dragos Axinte   University of Nottingham, UK

Program Chairs

Xin Dong   University of Nottingham, UK
Abdelkhalick Mohammad   University of Nottingham, UK
Matteo Russo   University of Nottingham, UK

Web Chair

Cecilia Flores   University of Nottingham, UK

Steering Committee

Chris Melhuish   Bristol Robotics Laboratory, UK
Mark Witkowski   Imperial College London, UK

Program Committee

Akram Alomainy	Queen Mary University of London, UK
Andres Gameros Madrigal	University of Nottingham, UK
Andy Weightman	The University of Manchester, UK
Barry Lennox	The University of Manchester, UK
Charlie Yang	University of the West of England, UK
Christos Bergels	King's College London, UK
David Branson	University of Nottingham, UK
Dongbing Gu	University of Essex, UK
Dongdong Xu	University of Nottingham, UK
Elizabeth Sklar	University of Lincoln, UK
Guowu Wei	University of Salford, UK
Hareesg Godaba	Queen Mary University of London, UK
Helge A. Wurdemann	University College London, UK
Kaspar Althoefer	Queen Mary University of London, UK
Ketao Zhang	Queen Mary University of London, UK
Lorenzo Jamone	Queen Mary University of London, UK
Marc Handeide	University of Lincoln, UK
Matteo Russo	University of Nottingham, UK
Mingfeng Wang	University of Nottingham, UK
Mini Saaj	University of Lincoln, UK

Nan Ma	University of Nottingham, UK
Nicolas Rojas	Imperial College London, UK
Roderich Gross	The University of Sheffield, UK
Sanja Dogramadzi	University of the West of England, UK
Sen Wang	Heriot-Watt University, UK
Shan Luo	The University of Liverpool, UK
Stefan Poslad	Queen Mary University of London, UK
Thrishantha Nanayakkara	Imperial College London, UK
Venky Dubey	Bournemouth University, UK
Yan Jin	Queen's University Belfast, UK
Zhirong Liao	University of Nottingham, UK

Contents

Mobile Robots

Learning, Mapping and Planning

Human-Robot Interaction

Robotic Systems and Applications

Soft and Compliant Robots

A Scalable Variable Stiffness Revolute Joint Based on Layer Jamming for Robotic Exoskeletons

Matthew Shen$^{(\boxtimes)}$, Angus B. Clark , and Nicolas Rojas

REDS Lab, Dyson School of Design Engineering, Imperial College London,
25 Exhibition Road, London SW7 2DB, UK
{matthew.shen17,a.clark17,n.rojas}@imperial.ac.uk
http://www.imperial.ac.uk/reds-lab

Abstract. Robotic exoskeletons have been a focal point of research due to an ever-increasing ageing population, longer life expectancy, and a desire to further improve the existing capabilities of humans. However, their effectiveness is often limited, with strong rigid structures poorly interfacing with humans and soft flexible mechanisms providing limited forces. In this paper, a scalable variable stiffness revolute joint is proposed to overcome this problem. By using layer jamming, the joint has the ability to stiffen or soften for different use cases. A theoretical and experimental study of maximum stiffness with size was conducted to determine the suitability and scalablity of this technology. Three sizes (50 mm, 37.5 mm, 25 mm diameter) of the joint were developed and evaluated. Results indicate that this technology is most suitable for use in human fingers, as the prototypes demonstrate a sufficient torque (0.054 Nm) to support finger movement.

Keywords: Variable stiffness · Layer jamming · Exoskeleton

1 Introduction

Robotic exoskeletons have been a recent focus of robotics research due to rise of areas such as power augmentation and rehabilitation robotics. Robotic exoskeletons are advantageous as they combine the strength of robots and dexterity and control of humans to create a man-machine system which is more intelligent than a robot, but also more powerful than a human [8]. In recent years, the majority of research into robotic exoskeletons has focused on creating a rigid frame which the user is strapped onto to reduce the strain on the user when a large torque is applied by the exoskeleton [7]. Although a rigid exoskeleton can provide extra structural integrity to the man-machine system, multiple rotary joints may also cause loss of degrees of freedom (DOF) in certain configurations [13]. Misalignment of the exoskeleton and human joints can also result in inaccuracies in measurements as well as applying unergonomic forces upon the user.

© Springer Nature Switzerland AG 2020
A. Mohammad et al. (Eds.): TAROS 2020, LNAI 12228, pp. 3–14, 2020.
https://doi.org/10.1007/978-3-030-63486-5_1

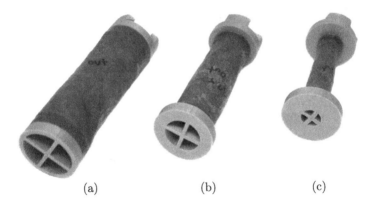

(a)   (b)   (c)

Fig. 1. The developed variable stiffness joints based on layer jamming technologies at three radii:(a) 25 mm, (b) 18.75 mm, and (c) 12.5 mm.

Solutions to these problems have already been proposed, but are at the cost of increased mechanical complexity [4,16].

An alternative approach is to utilise soft wearable robotics which are less bulky and do not need to be aligned to each user as accurately as their rigid counterparts. In general, soft exoskeletons are used in cases where the user requires assistance to carry out daily tasks which are not intensive. Researchers have developed different forms of wearable exoskeletons to suit different purposes [9,15]. Soft exoskeletons can also no longer be actuated using motors that require a rigid framework, instead, tendons and artificial muscles are most commonly used in these devices. A downside of soft exoskeletons are that they are inherently controlled by tension, which loses the ability of holding a certain position rigidly. This is a necessary function to protect joints of the user in cases of rehabilitation.

A solution to this is to improve current soft wearable exoskeletons by using elements from continuum robots, which are variable stiffness limb segments that can be reconfigured to suit the user's needs [6,12]. If a variable stiffness element can be incorporated into designs of current soft exoskeletons, advantages of a soft exoskeleton can be preserved while ensuring sufficient protection to the joints when required. Currently, the most reliable continuum robots achieve variable stiffness using one of two mechanical methods: layer-jamming and granular-jamming [5,10,11]. Both of the above-mentioned technologies rely on applying pressure to increase friction between mechanical objects to control the stiffness of the overall limb. However, layer-jamming is advantageous over granular-jamming due to a smaller volume required, a lighter weight as well as being hollow [6]. In the case of an exoskeleton, the layer-jamming technology could be set up around the user's joints, in which its advantages allows it to be more suitable in creating a comfortable interface with human users.

Kim et al. [11] described a design of a variable stiffness joint based on layer-jamming and activated using a vacuum pump, successfully demonstrating the

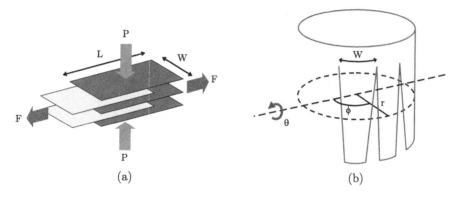

Fig. 2. (a) Layer jamming principle: With a pressure applied over stacked layers, force F is required to separate the layers and (b) schematic diagram outlining Eq. 2 parameters of the variable stiffness joint in relation to the revolute axis.

effectiveness and feasibility of layer-jamming technologies. In their research, the 1 DOF variable stiffness joint was used as a proof of concept in the development of a snake-like manipulator with variable stiffness. In this paper, we leverage this design principle to implement a scalable variable stiffness joint by applying negative pressure to contract layers of Mylar films. We present a novel 1 DOF variable stiffness exoskeleton joint, differing from previous research which has focused on continuum robot implementations. As shown in Fig. 1, three proto-types were produced to measure the capabilities of the layer jamming technology at different scales. By investigating the operation of the variable stiffness joint under varying conditions, scaling of stiffness can be calculated. These results are useful to improve the design of soft exoskeletons to be used on joints of varying sizes on the human body.

The rest of this paper is organised as follows. In Sect. 2, the expected forces and stiffness of the joints are calculated and compared against scale. In Sect. 3, development and manufacturing details are discussed, with inclusion of consideration of specific design aspects. In Sects. 4 and 5, results and trends are analysed and feasibility of use in soft exoskeletons are reviewed. Finally, conclusions and practicalities are discussed in Sect. 6.

2 Theoretical Analysis

When looking at the effectiveness of a variable stiffness joint, the maximum stiffness of the joint is a good indicator. To evaluate the maximum stiffness in terms of a maximum resistive torque, the tensile strength of the layers must be considered, which can be expressed as the maximum static friction between the layer jamming layers:

$$F = \mu n P W L, \tag{1}$$

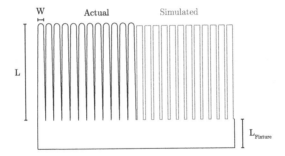

Fig. 3. Unwrapped singular Mylar layer, with actual design of the Mylar layer (left, black) and simulated Mylar layer used in calculation of total resistive torque (right, red).(Color figure online)

where μ is the static coefficient of friction, n is the number of contact surfaces, P is the applied pressure in the normal direction, and W and L are the width and length of the layer jamming flaps respectively. This is shown in Fig. 2a.

It is to be noted that this is an approximation of the tensile strength which assumes that all the contact areas of the layers will 'slip' at exact the same moment. As the kinetic coefficient of friction is lower than the static coefficient of friction, this approximation will lead to an estimation of the tensile strength that is greater than reality.

Now, the maximum resistive torque can be considered. It is important to realise that the resistive torque that each of the flaps provides is dependent on the orientation of the flaps with respect to the rotational axis of the joint. The motion of overlapping flaps with normal axis parallel to the axis of rotation is purely rotational, while flaps with normal axis perpendicular have purely transnational motion. Flaps in between will naturally have contributions from both translational and rotational motion, resulting in challenging calculations.

Instead of considering both motions separately, Kim et al. has carried out the calculation through analysing the motion of a infinitesimal segment of the layers [11]. From this, Kim et al. was able to derive the maximum resistive torque as:

$$\tau(\phi) = p\mu w \left(\frac{L}{4} \sqrt{(L\cos\phi)^2 + (2r\sin\phi)^2} \right.$$

$$\left. + \frac{(r\sin\phi)^2}{\cos\phi} \ln\left(\frac{L}{2r}\cot\phi + \sqrt{(\frac{L}{2r}\cot\phi)^2 + 1} \right) \right).$$

where r is the radius of the jamming cylinder. It is seen from Eq. (2) that the resistive torque of each flap is a function of ϕ, which is defined as the angle between the normal axis of the flaps and the axis of rotation of the joint, shown in Fig. 2b.

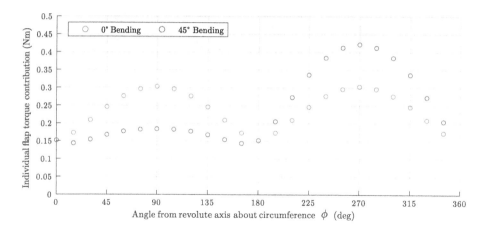

Fig. 4. Simulated torque contribution of the flaps at each orientation at bending angles of 0° (red) and 45° (blue) of the joint.(Color figure online)

To extend this calculation to include the bending orientation of the joint, a modification of the effective overlapping length of the flaps can be imposed:

$$L'(\phi) = L + \Delta L_\theta(\phi) = L - \theta r \sin(\phi),\tag{3}$$

where θ is the angle that defines the orientation of the joint. By replacing L with L' in Eq. (2), the resistive torque of a flap at any bending angle of the joint can be determined. From here, the total resistive torque can be calculated through summing the contributions of each flap in Eq. (2) to define a theoretical value of maximum resistive torque of the layer jamming joint.

The theoretical results of the individual flap contribution to the total torque with respect to the angle at which the flap is situated is modelled using the structure shown in Fig. 3 and results are shown in Fig. 4. The parameters used in this analysis are equivalent to the design parameters used in designing the largest prototype, namely $r = 25$ mm, $L = 40$ mm, $p = 80$ kPa, $\mu = 0.4$ and $w = 5$ mm. A total of 10 layers were used with 24 flaps in each layer. From Fig. 4, a symmetric contribution of torque can be seen as expected at 0° bending of the joint. On the other hand, at 45° bending, an asymmetric contribution is observed as a result of the modifications in effective overlapping length around the joint. Between angles 0° and 180°, a significant decrease in torque is the direct result of a decreased L', whereas the opposite effect is observed between angles 180° and 360°.

Interestingly, the modification of an bending orientation as introduced by the inclusion of consideration of effective overlap in Eq. (3) has no effect on the total resistive torque, which remains a constant with varying θ. This can be explained as the increase in overlap of a flap is exactly equivalent to the decrease of overlap in the flap directly opposite, resulting in a zero net effect on the total torque.

Table 1 shows the results of the simulation of total torque and maximum rotational force that can be applied to the end of the joints. It would be expected

Table 1. Design parameters of the variable stiffness joints

Radius (mm)	Length (mm)	L (mm)	W (mm)	τ_{total} (Nm)	Force (N)
25	160	50	4.9	34.09	426.09
18.75	140	22.5	3.4	6.60	82.55
12.5	120	15	2.0	1.68	20.97

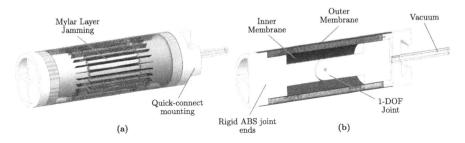

(a)   (b)

Fig. 5. CAD drawing of the designed variable stiffness joint (25 mm design): (a) Outer view showing overlapping layers and (b) cross sectional view showing internal structure.

that the scaling of the total force would be quadratic due to the quadratic scaling of surface area of the flaps with radius. However, the total torque seems to scale exponentially instead. This is non-physical and highlights the failures in simplifications of the model at large scales. A suggestion to improve this model is to derive the net torque based on each infinitesimal surface area instead of flap segment.

3 Development of Joint

The development of the joint was based off previous designs of layer jamming proposed by other authors [11,12]. The basic setup consisted of circular layers of flaps which overlapped, encapsulated by two layers of membrane as seen in Fig. 5. By using a vacuum pump to generate a negative pressure between the layers, atmospheric pressure compresses the layers together to achieve layer jamming which stiffens the overall structure. Variable friction can then be fine tuned through control of the applied negative pressure, with a theoretical maximum of -101.3 kPa.

In this paper, three prototypes at different scales are presented, each with 24 flaps in each of the 10 Mylar (polyethyleneterephthalate film) layers, manufactured using a laser cutter. The end housing were 3D printed in acrylonitrile butadiene styrene (ABS) material, and connected to a vacuum pump via a 6 mm PVC tubing. The latex membrane were cut to required size by hand from a large sheet and formed into a tubular shape with adhesive; once dried, they were then attached to the end housing to create the vacuum chamber. Specific design parameters of each prototype can be found in Table 1, where the smallest

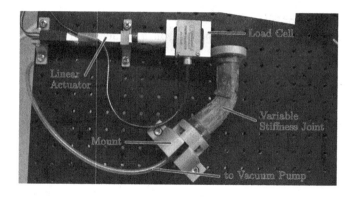

Fig. 6. Experimental setup for evaluating maximum resistive torque of the joint.

prototype of radius 12.5 mm was a limit as prototypes with smaller radius were too difficult to manufacture. The prototypes were created such that they shared the same base radius, ensuing fair and comparable results when mounting onto a test bed.

During development of the prototypes, design parameters were specified with respect to the chosen radius of the central joint and a desired maximum bending angle ($45°$). All parameters follow the principle of minimising the overall structure without compromising functionality. By defining the central radius and maximum bending angle, the overall length of the joint is determined by considering the amount of room required for the Mylar layers to slide across each other with a minimum overlap of $2r$ for each flap at the maximum bending angle. Following this calculation, the minimum length of the Mylar flaps are $2r + \frac{3}{2}\theta_{max}r$, which defines the minimum length of the whole joint to be $2(r + \theta r)$. The radius of the inner membrane was also chosen with consideration of the thickness of each layer to ensure they can be contained within the membranes.

4 Experimental Evaluation

4.1 Experimental Setup

To evaluate the performance of the layer jamming joints at varying operational parameters, the test setup shown in Fig. 6 was used. The test-bed was based on an optical bench with threaded holes 6 mm diameter spaced in a square lattice of 25 mm separation between adjacent holes. Housing for each of the components were created and 3D printed in ABS material to match the spacing on the bench.

The tests conducted focused solely on the stiffness of the joint, which was measured using a load cell(DBBSM 5 kg) connected to a linear actuator (Actuonix L12-100-100-12-I). Each test would consist of the linear actuator pressing the load 10 mm into the end of the variable stiffness joint to measure the maximum resistive force. From the force experienced by the load cell, the length of the joint was used to calculate the resistive torque exerted by the joint. Readings were acquired using a NI DAQ (LabView 6211), from which the maximum reading of force was extracted from the measured data.

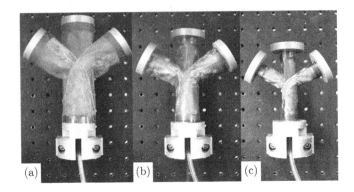

Fig. 7. Bending capabilities of the developed variable stiffness joints of radius 25 mm (**a**), 18.75 mm (**b**), and 12.5 mm (**c**).

For each of the three joints created, tests were conducted in 3 orientations: clockwise push at 0° (upright) and −45°, and anticlockwise push at 45°. The three positions for each of the joints are shown in Fig. 7. Negative pressure levels of 0–80 kPa were tested in increments of 20 kPa for each joints at each orientation. It is noted that due to the natural springiness of the joints, tests at 0 kPa could only be conducted at the 0° orientation as the joints cannot hold its orientation at 45° and −45° when no pressure is applied. To ensure reliable results, the pressure and orientation of the joints were reset between each repeat measurement by turning off the vacuum pump and moving the joint across its whole range before setting it into the desired orientation.

4.2   Results

The results of the experiment are shown in Fig. 8, confirming the increase of stiffness with pressure in most scenarios. The 9 sets of data do not show a clear linear trend between pressure and total torque as predicted, and fluctuations indicate large margin of errors in the collected data. The maximum torques observed for the 25 mm, 18.75 mm and 12.5 mm were 0.216 Nm, 0.138 Nm and 0.054 Nm respectively.

Results also indicate an overall increase in stiffness with radius as expected. However, no conclusive trend of stiffness against scale can be observed from the results gathered.

Comparing the three orientations, it is seen that the 0° orientation provided the highest stiffness out of the three examined orientations, which differs from the simulated results where bending angle does not result in a net effect. Further comparing results from the −45° and 45° orientation, it is observed that the two

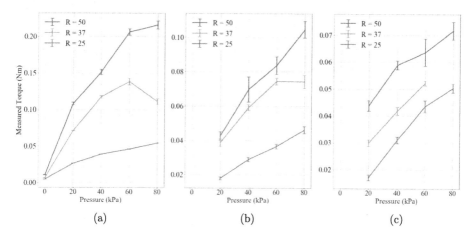

Fig. 8. Maximum resistive torque of the variable stiffness joints under different vacuum pressures and orientations: **(a)** 0° pushing clockwise, **(b)** −45° pushing clockwise, and **(c)** 45° pushing anticlockwise.

sets of data do not correlate well. This is unexpected as the joints were designed to be symmetric, which suggests that the results should also be symmetric across bending angles.

The measurement of the anticlockwise push at −80 kPa is not measured due to a leakage in the $r = 18.75$ mm joint which prevents the vacuum pump from reaching the desired pressure. The other points of the $r = 18.75$ mm joint at −80 kPa also exhibit unexpected results, with a decrease of stiffness at 0° and −45° orientations from its previous point.

Comparing the measured results with the simulated values, the simulated values are all substantially higher than the measured values, with the simulated value at $r = 25$ mm being 2° of magnitude higher than the measured value. This discrepancy is discussed further in the section below.

In Fig. 9, an implementation of the joint used as a restrictive elbow exoskeleton is seen. This use case would be most suitable for users with injured elbows, biceps or triceps, in which the stiffening capabilities will support the user's muscles in maintaining a desired elbow orientation.

5   Discussion

Specific trends cannot be extracted from the measured results, and correlation between measured datasets at different radii are not observed across the pressure range. This emphasises the great margin of systematic error seeing as the standard error of the measurement does not encompass the range of fluctuation of the measured data. There are three potential causes of systematic error and their effects are discussed below.

Firstly, structural deformation of the layer jamming structure due to high pressures will cause the recorded stiffness of the structure to decrease. This

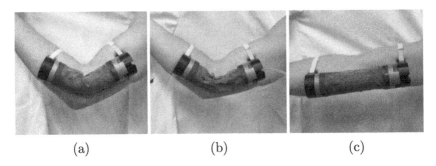

(a)   (b)   (c)

Fig. 9. The developed variable stiffness joint implemented as a restrictive elbow exoskeleton: **(a)** Variable stiffness off with arm bent, **(b)** Variable stiffness on with arm bent, and **(c)** Variable stiffness off with arm straight.

occurs when the pressure applied by the membranes on the Mylar layers causes them to buckle and lose structural integrity, which allows the joint to bend without the Mylar layers sliding across each other at all. The effect of this is most clearly seen for the $r = 18.75$ mm joint, where an increase in pressure from 60 kPa to 80 kPa has not increased the stiffness at the tested orientations.

Another source of significant systematic error is the inconsistencies in the manufacturing process. To ensure that results are comparable, the joints are designed to scale proportionally. However, during the lengthy process of manufacturing, alignment of each of the parts with respect to another cannot be ensured to perfection. This results in an increase in the spread of the measured results, and also provides an explanation to the observed asymmetry in results of the clockwise and anticlockwise orientations.

A persistent source of error may be caused by leakages of the inner membrane. As maximum reachable pressures of each of the joints decrease over the experimental process, it is clear that punctures in the outer membrane are developing. Leakages in the outer membrane do not affect measured results as long as the barometer indicates the desired pressure reading. However, leakages in the outer membrane also indicate the possibility of punctures in the inner membrane, which could be problematic. This is because in the design of the joints, the volume within the inner membrane is also sealed air-tight, if a leakage exists, the effective vacuum would extend to within the inner membrane. As a result, only the outer membrane would provide pressure onto the layers, which would substantially decrease the observed resistive torque of the joints.

Discrepancies between the simulated values and the measured values can be explored in three respects. At non-zero bending angles, the Mylar cylinders deform and are no longer exactly circular, which causes structural deformation that causes a reduction of torque. This may explain to how the bending angle influences overall torque. Next, the simulation assumes that all of the layers slip at the same time. Since static friction is larger than kinetic friction, this assumption will cause the force estimated to be greater by up to a factor of $\mu_{static}/\mu_{kinetic} \approx 2$. Lastly, the model supposes that bending of the joint can only be allowed through slipping of the layers, which is not always the case. If the structural strength of the Mylar cylinder is weaker than the resistive strength of the Mylar friction, the structure may bend under buckling of the layers, which will cause a lower observed torque.

Relating the measured results to physical parameters of the human body. The average human finger (middle) has a diameter of 23.2 mm (male) and 20.4 mm (female), wrist with a diameter of 55.7 mm (male) and 49.0 mm (female) [1]. These values are comparable to the 12.5 mm and 12.5 mm joints presented in this paper. In activities of daily living, the amount of force required by the proximal interphalangeal (PIP) joint in the finger ranges from ~1.8–43.5 N [3]. This corresponds to a minimum torque of 0.004 Nm, which is within the range of resistive torque the 12.5 mm joint can provide at 80 kPa [2]. This comparison suggests that the design is suitable for use in robotic finger exoskeletons in its current state.

On the other hand, torque required by the wrist for activities of daily living are estimated to be 8.62 Nm (male) and 5.20 Nm (female) [14]. This is significantly higher than the maximum torque of 0.22 Nm supplied by the 25 mm joint, making this version of the variable stiffness joint unsuitable for use in the wrist.

6   Conclusion

In this paper three variable friction joints at radii of 12.5 mm, 18.75 mm and 25 mm were manufactured to explore the scalability of layer jamming joints and their uses in soft robotic exoskeletons. The maximum stiffening capabilities of the joints were measured in three orientations: 0° and −45° bending angle pushing clockwise, and at 45° bending angle pushing anticlockwise. At each orientation, the joints were measured at pressures of 0–80 kPa in increments of 20 kPa to investigate the overall trend.

The joints demonstrated maximum resistive torques of 0.216 Nm, 0.138 Nm and 0.054 Nm for the 25 mm, 18.75 mm and 12.5 mm joints, respectively. Algebraic trends of the prototypes are not observed with respect to scale or pressure from the results due to large margin of systematic errors. From comparing the maximum resistive torques, this technology in its current form is most suited for use in robotic exoskeletons for the human finger joint for support and protection for activities of daily living. Future work may explore manufacture techniques to further optimise the product as well as methods to increase resistive torque to enable usage in soft exoskeletons that support other joints of the human body.

References

1. Bolton, C.F., Carter, K.M.: Human sensory nerve compound action potential amplitude: variation with sex and finger circumference. J. Neurol. Neurosurg. Psychiatry **43**(10), 925–928 (1980)

2. Bundhoo, V., Park, E.J.: Design of an artificial muscle actuated finger towards biomimetic prosthetic hands. In: Proceedings of 12th International Conference on Advanced Robotics, ICAR 2005, pp. 368–375. IEEE (2005)
3. Butz, K.D., Merrell, G., Nauman, E.A.: A biomechanical analysis of finger joint forces and stresses developed during common daily activities. Comput. Methods Biomech. Biomed. Eng. **15**(2), 131–140 (2012)
4. Carignan, C., Tang, J., Roderick, S.: Development of an exoskeleton haptic interface for virtual task training. In: 2009 IEEE/RSJ International Conference on Intelligent Robots and Systems, pp. 3697–3702. IEEE (2009)
5. Clark, A.B., Rojas, N.: Assessing the performance of variable stiffness continuum structures of large diameter. IEEE Robot. Autom. Lett. **4**(3), 2455–2462 (2019)
6. Clark, A.B., Rojas, N.: Stiffness-tuneable limb segment with flexible spine for malleable robots. In: 2019 International Conference on Robotics and Automation (ICRA), pp. 3969–3975. IEEE (2019)
7. Frey, M., Colombo, G., Vaglio, M., Bucher, R., Jorg, M., Riener, R.: A novel mechatronic body weight support system. IEEE Trans. Neural Syst. Rehabil. Eng. **14**(3), 311–321 (2006)
8. Gopura, R., Kiguchi, K., Bandara, D.: A brief review on upper extremity robotic exoskeleton systems. In: 2011 6th International Conference on Industrial and Information Systems, pp. 346–351. IEEE (2011)
9. In, H., Kang, B.B., Sin, M., Cho, K.J.: Exo-Glove: a wearable robot for the hand with a soft tendon routing system. IEEE Robot. Autom. Mag. **22**(1), 97–105 (2015)
10. Jiang, A., Xynogalas, G., Dasgupta, P., Althoefer, K., Nanayakkara, T.: Design of a variable stiffness flexible manipulator with composite granular jamming and membrane coupling. In: 2012 IEEE/RSJ International Conference on Intelligent Robots and Systems, pp. 2922–2927. IEEE (2012)
11. Kim, Y.J., Cheng, S., Kim, S., Iagnemma, K.: Design of a tubular snake-like manipulator with stiffening capability by layer jamming. In: 2012 IEEE/RSJ International Conference on Intelligent Robots and Systems, pp. 4251–4256. IEEE (2012)
12. Langer, M., Amanov, E., Burgner-Kahrs, J.: Stiffening sheaths for continuum robots. Soft Robot. **5**(3), 291–303 (2018)
13. Lo, H.S., Xie, S.Q.: Exoskeleton robots for upper-limb rehabilitation: state of the art and future prospects. Medical Eng. Phys. **34**(3), 261–268 (2012)
14. Morse, J.L., Jung, M.C., Bashford, G.R., Hallbeck, M.S.: Maximal dynamic grip force and wrist torque: the effects of gender, exertion direction, angular velocity, and wrist angle. Appl. Ergon. **37**(6), 737–742 (2006)
15. Park, Y.L., Santos, J., Galloway, K.G., Goldfield, E.C., Wood, R.J.: A soft wearable robotic device for active knee motions using flat pneumatic artificial muscles. In: 2014 IEEE International Conference on Robotics and Automation (ICRA), pp. 4805–4810. IEEE (2014)
16. Stienen, A.H., Hekman, E.E., Van Der Helm, F.C., Van Der Kooij, H.: Self-aligning exoskeleton axes through decoupling of joint rotations and translations. IEEE Trans. Robot. **25**(3), 628–633 (2009)

A Universal Stiffening Sleeve Designed for All Types of Continuum Robot Systems

Yihua Fang[✉], Christopher Bishop, Weiming Ba, Jorge Barrientos Díez, Abd Mohammad, and Xin Dong

RR-UTC: Manufacturing and on-Wing Technology, University of Nottingham, 522 Derby Rd, Nottingham NG8 1BB, UK
Yihua.Fang@nottingham.ac.uk

Abstract. Continuum robots have been utilized for several light-duty applications, such as minimally invasive surgery in the medical field and inspection in the industry. However, the existing design solutions do not offer system stiffness adaptability through a modular attachment. To overcome this disadvantage, in this paper, a low-cost sleeve is developed to 'rigidize' an existing continuum robot. The sleeve enables systems to withstand greater torques when undertaking tasks while al-lowing robots' flexibility to navigate into a confined space. This 'stiffening sleeve' is made of heating elements (Nichrome wires) and thermoplastics (polymorph), which have the advantages of low manufacturing costs, simplicity of assembly/disassembly, and universal compatibility with various types of continuum robots. In a further experiment, a small sleeve is demonstrated to decrease the unwanted displacement of a slender continuum robot tip by 20%–69% under a load of 200–450 g.

Keywords: Continuum robot · Stiffness adjustment

1 Introduction

Continuum robots have been investigated by many researchers for industrial, medical, and security applications, due to their unique features and advantages such as high flexibility, high dexterity, obstacle-avoidance capability, and so on [1–3]. However, compared with rigid link robots, the main drawback of continuum robots is low stiffness, which limits the capability for carrying efficient end load/force. To overcome this drawback, some solutions for adjustable backbone stiffness have been developed, they allow continuum robots to move freely when in a relatively low stiffness state and to lock the arm when in a relatively high stiffness state.

One widely utilized approach is to use granular material, such as dry sand, to lock/unlock the backbone mechanism by applying a vacuum [4–6]. For instance, in the research of Nadia et al., ground coffee was deployed to fill the Lumen of a spring-based backbone. By applying a vacuum to squeeze grains via the chamber, the grains switch from liquid-like state to solid-like state, which makes the backbone have controllable backbone stiffness. However, this approach requires a relatively large volume for reaching an appropriate stiffness, making it difficult to be miniaturized.

© Springer Nature Switzerland AG 2020
A. Mohammad et al. (Eds.): TAROS 2020, LNAI 12228, pp. 15–24, 2020.
https://doi.org/10.1007/978-3-030-63486-5_2

Electro-rheological (ER) fluids also have been exploited for a novel variable stiffness worm robot. By applying an electric field, ER fluids can transform into a 'gel' phase from the liquid-like one. Based on this concept, each section of the worm robot can be blocked at an arbitrary configuration when a voltage is applied. However, the drawback of this concept is that high voltage (500 V) and a large volume of ER fluids need to be applied for blocking a large-scale construction [7].

The phase-change material is a more feasible approach. In a worm robot developed by Cheng et al., the solder-alloy mixture is integrated into the joint mechanism, which can be thermally activated to selectively "lock" or "unlock" the joint, thereby modulating the overall robot stiffness [8–10].

The other main approach is to control the friction between rigid links for varying stiffness [11]. The friction is controlled by adjusting wire tension, so the mechanisms can switch between rigid and flexible modes rapidly. However, the stiffness is dependent on the friction which is determined by the size of the contact area between the adjacent links, the links must be large enough to sustain the load and generate enough friction to lock the system. Hence, it is difficult to create a long and compact manipulator based on this approach.

More recently, a novel approach is presented which utilizes a "layer jamming" mechanism to obtain variable stiffness [12]. The backbone of a "layer jamming" continuum robot consisting of multiple coupled rubber layers, which is wrapped in a latex rubber skin. The friction between layers can be enhanced significantly by applying vacuum pressure, rendering the backbone rigid. But the mechanism still needs a large contacting area between layers for generating appropriate friction to interlock the elements of the backbone.

Another mechanical 'rigidizing' solution is to employ an interlocking mechanism [13], which can generate greater 'locking' force. In this type of design, toothed links are the key features to lock the mechanism. Controlled by a pneumatic driver, it could engage/disengage with each other.

The shape memory polymer joint is also a new solution [14]. In this prototype, the joint of each section of a snake robot was made of shape memory layers containing a heating sheet inside. By adjusting temperature via the heating element, the stiffness of SMP layers could be controlled. Through this method, they can easily select active sections and block inactive sections.

In summary, several efficient solutions have been developed, which can be divided into two main categories:

Phase-changing materials: Electro-rheological (ER) fluids and thermally activated material (e.g. solder-alloy mixture)

Mechanical approaches: granular material, pneumatic, and mechanical locking mechanism (e.g. cable locking and toothed link mechanisms).

However, it seems most of them require a relatively large volume for generating enough stiffness, making it difficult to miniaturize. Among these solutions, the approach of thermally activated material seems more promising, since it can provide relatively higher stiffness at smaller dimensions. However, there is a need to identify a lightweight material that can switch between rigid and soft states at a low temperature (between 40°

and 100°). The material needs to provide efficient stiffness in a rigid state and be flexible in the soft state.

In this paper, a 'stiffening sleeve' designed for the continuum robot system which consists of heating elements (Nichrome wires) and thermoplastics (polymorph) is introduced. The rest of the paper is structured as follows: Sects. 2 discusses the theory behind the design in detail. Section 3 presents several prototypes of the proposed rigidizing system, followed by Sect. 4 that demonstrates the experiment as well as the results which validate this idea. Finally, Sect. 5 concludes this paper and gives out some advice for further research work.

2   Methodology

The basic concept is to utilize stiffening material, which can repeatadly switch between relatively low and high stiffness, to allow continuum robot to have variable stiffness.

The two candidate classes of stiffening material are thermoplastic material and low-melting-point alloys, which can melt at a low temperature (below 100 °C) and get solidified above room temperature. Table 1 shows the specifications of several stiffening materials.

Table 1. Melting Temperature for candidate material

Material	Melting temperature (°)
Polymorph	60
Field's alloy (Bi 32.5, In 51.0, Sn 16.5)	62
Wood's metal (Bi 49.5, Pb 27.3, Sn 13.1, Cd 10.1)	70

2.1   Concept of a Two-DOFs Variable Stiffness Joint/System Design

The two-DOFs variable stiffness joints are the building block of a rigidizing system. The principle is shown in Fig. 1. This structure (one segment) is composed of three disks, two orthogonal groups of compliant joints, heating elements (Nichrome wire), and stiffening material (thermoplastic), which fills the gaps between adjacent disks. Nichrome wire can generate heat when a current flow through it, which can heat up and melt the thermoplastic material. When the current is turned off the material cools and returns to the rigid state.

When integrated with a continuum robot, the variable stiffness system (comprised of multi two DOF segments) is mounted to the outside of the robot, as shown in Fig. 2(a). Specifically, in the soft state, the system can be bent to an arbitrary configuration due to the movement of the continuum robot. The thermoplastic material is constrained by a rubber tube from outside, and the rubber covered continuum robot from inside.

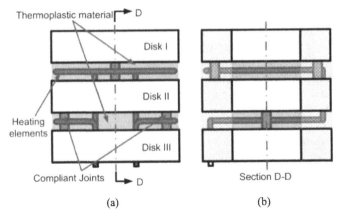

Fig. 1. Two DOFs variable stiffness joint

Hence, the thermoplastic material can be moved inside the tube when in the compliant state to conform to the motion of the snake, as shown in Fig. 2(b), which allows the stiffness of the system to be kept constant. Subsequently, when the power is turned off, the thermoplastic material gets cooled and solidified, as shown in Fig. 2(c). By switching between the soft and rigid states, the continuum robot can bend and get rigidized at an arbitrary configuration.

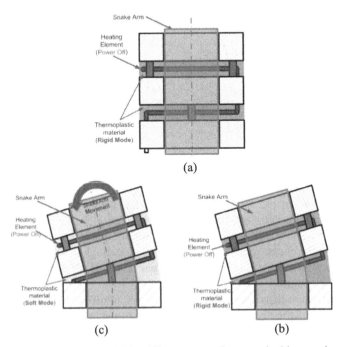

Fig. 2. Work principle of the variable stiffness system (integrated with a continuum robot)

However, the structure of this variable stiffness system (i.e. contains many rings, pins, and wires) makes it uneasy to be manufactured and installed on a snake robot. In the following chapter, another solution named 'stiffening sleeve' will be proposed with lower cost, better processability, and greater compatibility.

2.2 Concept of a Variable Stiffness Sleeve System Design

As shown in Fig. 3, This 'sleeve' is mainly made of thermoplastics and heating element (Nichrome wires) inside. By controlling the inputted current to heating elements, the stiffness of the thermoplastics could be adjusted. An alternative way is to add a steel spring to make the whole system stiffer.

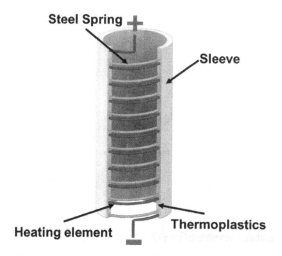

Fig. 3. schematic of the variable stiffness sleeve system

The variable stiffness sleeve has a simpler structure and fewer limitations than the previous concept comprised of variable stiffness joints. Thus, it is easy to make a prototype with different diameters/shapes to integrate with various types of continuum robots.

In the next section, several prototypes will be presented to evaluate these concepts, and a final solution will be selected to apply on a real continuum robot system.

3 Prototypes

For evaluating the stiffening concept, several variable stiffness systems have been built and tested. The stiffening system can be added to a continuum manipulator to give variable-stiffness capability. These non-articulated, tubular constructions consist of:

- A power supplier (up to 24 V).
- Heating elements (Nichrome wires).

- Thermoplastics (polymorph: liquid-like, when melting).
- External & internal sleeve (rubber/Kevlar tube) for constraining the thermoplastics.
- The 2-DOF-joint-structure (described in Sect. 2.1) also contains aluminum disks and steel pins.

3.1 The Prototype of a Two-DOFs Variable Stiffness Joint/System

Figure 4 shows a prototype of this concept. By heating it, the snake arm unit could be easily softened and bent, while it is comparatively rigid under room temperature.

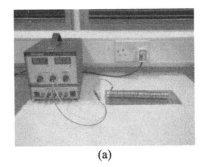

(a)

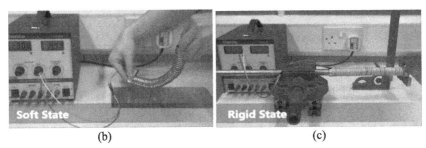

(b)   (c)

Fig. 4. Demonstration of a stiffening continuum robot. (a) the single-section prototype; (b) the soft state of variable stiffness system; (c) the rigid state of variable stiffness system.

3.2 The Prototypes of the Variable Stiffness Sleeve System

Two prototypes with & without steel springs are made to compare the performance of a variable stiffness sleeve system.

Prototype (1): As shown in Fig. 5(a), the system comprises a compression steel spring in polymorph covered by Kevlar sleeve. The system can be heated up by activating NiCr wire and softens at a temperature of 60 °C. However, it was found that the max bend of the continuum robot (approx. 30°) is limited by the spring stiffness (a larger force is required to bend the spring) and Kevlar tube (low elongation ratio).

Prototype (2): This system is constructed with the same principles but with alternative sleeve material (rubber, which has a greater elongation ratio) and does not use a

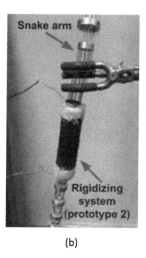

(a)   (b)

Fig. 5. Variable stiffness system prototypes: (a) prototype 1; (b) prototype 2;

steel spring for increasing the stiffness. The demonstrator was built and integrated with the continuum robot to test the bending capability of the variable-stiffness system, as shown in Fig. 5(b). It was found that compared with prototype 1, this system allows the continuum robot to generate a larger bending angle in the soft state while still having good stiffness in the rigid state.

According to the above tests, it can be seen that: 1) the 2-DOF-joint structure adds too much weight and thickness to a continuum robot; and if we want to apply it to a different robot, it will take a long time to re-manufacture a unit. 2) The prototype 1 of stiffening sleeve restricts the bending of a continuum robot too much. 3) The spring-less stiffening sleeve may be the best solution to apply on a real continuum robot among these candidates. The main elements of the system (thermoplastic: polymorph; heating element: NiCr wire; sleeve: rubber) are also determined and utilized in the next prototype.

4 Experiment and Results

Next, a two-section variable stiffness system was mounted on the base of two sections of the arm (Fig. 6) to minimize the deflection caused by end loads. This system can reach a soft state in 3 min by applying a 2A current via a NiCr wire (0.4 mm in diameter) and get rigid in 20 min after turning off the power of the heating element.

As shown in Fig. 7, the continuum arm was tested with initial shape (with both bending angle and direction angle are equal to 0°). A load within the range of 40–450 g was attached to the tip, by comparing tip-displacements of the arm when equipped with/without the variable stiffness system (also named as rigidizing system, RS system), the performance of the system could be evaluated. The data in Table 2 are the averaged results for several tests under the same working condition.

Table 2 and Fig. 8 demonstrate the experiment results. Column 2 and column 3 of Table 2 list tip-displacement under loads when the robot is in soft and rigid state

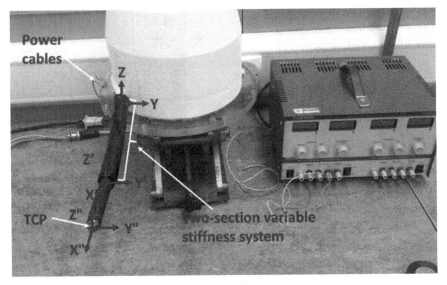

Fig. 6. A 2-section variable stiffness continuum robot

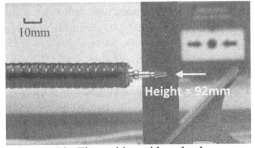

(a) Tip-position with no load

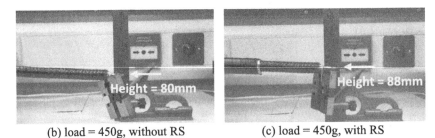

(b) load = 450g, without RS   (c) load = 450g, with RS

Fig. 7. Payload test of the snake arm with/without rigidizing system

respectively. By comparison, it can be found that the unwanted tip-displacement was largely eliminated by the variable stiffness system, up to 69 percent when added 450 g weight, we have demonstrated a variable stiffness system that can significantly increase the stiffness of existing continuum robots by enhancing compliant joints.

Table 2. Displacements of the variable stiffness continuum robot versus end loads

Mass of the end load (g)	The displacement of tip (mm) (Soft state)	The displacement of tip (mm) (Rigid state)	Percentage of the displacement decrease
50	0.5	0.3	40%
100	1.0	0.7	30%
150	1.4	1.1	21%
200	2.0	1.4	30%
250	3.3	1.7	48%
300	5.3	2.0	43%
350	7.7	2.6	66%
400	8.8	3.0	65%
450	11.9	3.6	69%

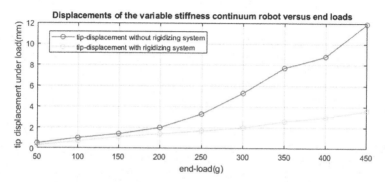

Fig. 8. Displacements of the variable stiffness continuum robot versus end loads

5   Conclusion and Further Work

In conclusion, we have successfully demonstrated the thermo-polymorph based stiffening concept, which greatly improves the load capacity of a continuum robot. The experiment results presented indicate that under relatively large load (up to 450 g), the unwanted displacement of snake-tip was significantly eliminated by the variable stiffness system (up to 69%).

In the future work, a more detailed test of the stiffening property of the thermoplastic material could be conducted, thus we could select optimal material (even mixed material) to improve performance of this 'stiffening sleeve' as well as building a numeric model for the softening/hardening process to develop a more powerful robot controller. More efficient heating methods could also be explored to fasten the softening/hardening process.

Acknowledgment. This research was supported by the EPSRC project (EP/P027121/1 Through-life performance: From science to instrumentation).

References

1. Axinte, D., et al.: MiRoR—miniaturized robotic systems for holisticin-siturepair and main-tenance works in restrained and hazardous environments. IEEE/ASME Trans. Mechatron. **23**(2), 978–981 (2018)

2. Wang, M., Palmer, D., Dong, X., Alatorre, D., Axinte, D., Norton, A.: Design and development of a slender dual-structure continuum robot for in-situ aeroengine repair. In: 2018 IEEE/RSJ International Conference on Intelligent Robots and Systems (IROS), pp. 5648–5653. IEEE (2018)

3. Dong, X., Palmer, D., Axinte, D., Kell, J.: In-situ repair/maintenance with a continuum robotic machine tool in confined space. J.f Manufact. Process. **38**, 313–318 (2019)

4. Brown, E., et al.: Universal robotic gripper based on the jamming of granular material. Proc. Natl. Acad. Sci. **107**(44), 18809–18814 (2010)

5. Cheng, N.G., et al.: Design and analysis of a robust, low-cost, highly articulated manipulator enabled by jamming of granular media. In: 2012 IEEE International Conference on Robotics and Automation, pp. 4328–4333. IEEE (2012)

6. Jiang, A., Xynogalas, G., Dasgupta, P., Althoefer, K., Nanayakkara, T.: Design of a variable stiffness flexible manipulator with composite granular jamming and membrane coupling. In: 2012 IEEE/RSJ International Conference on Intelligent Robots and Systems, pp. 2922–2927. IEEE (2012)

7. Sadeghi, A., Beccai, L., Mazzolai, B.: Innovative soft robots based on electro-rheological fluids. In: 2012 IEEE/RSJ International Conference on Intelligent Robots and Systems, pp. 4237–4242. IEEE (2012)

8. Cheng, N.G.: Design and analysis of active fluid-and-cellular solid composites for control-lable stiffness robotic elements. Doctoral dissertation. Massachusetts Institute of Technology (2009)

9. Cheng, N., et al.: Design and analysis of a soft mobile robot composed of multiple ther-mally activated joints driven by a single actuator. In: 2010 IEEE International Conference on Robotics and Automation, pp. 5207–5212. IEEE (2010)

10. Telleria, M.J., Hansen, M., Campbell, D., Servi, A., Culpepper, M.L.: Modeling and imple-mentation of solder-activated joints for single-actuator, centimeter-scale robotic mechanisms. In: 2010 IEEE International Conference on Robotics and Automation, pp. 1681–1686. IEEE (2010)

11. Transport® Endoscopic Access Device - Retroflex.: http://usgimedical.com/eos/components-transport.htm. Accessed on 13 Dec 2019

12. Kim, Y.J., Cheng, S., Kim, S., Iagnemma, K.: A novel layer jamming mechanism with tunable stiffness capability for minimally invasive surgery. IEEE Trans. Rob. **29**(4), 1031–1042 (2013)

13. Yagi, A., Matsumiya, K., Masamune, K., Liao, H., Dohi, T.: Rigid-flexible outer sheath model using slider linkage locking mechanism and air pressure for endoscopic surgery. In: International Conference on Medical Image Computing and Computer-Assisted Intervention, pp. 503–510. Springer, Berlin, Heidelberg (2006)

14. Firouzeh, A., Salehian, S.S.M., Billard, A., Paik, J.: An under actuated robotic arm with adjustable stiffness shape memory polymer joints. In: 2015 IEEE International Conference on Robotics and Automation (ICRA), pp. 2536–2543. IEEE (2015)

A Passively Compliant Idler Mechanism for Underactuated Dexterous Grippers with Dynamic Tendon Routing

Jinhong Wang[⊠][iD], Qiujie Lu[iD], Angus B. Clark[iD], and Nicolas Rojas[iD]

REDS Lab, Dyson School of Design Engineering, Imperial College London,
25 Exhibition Road, London SW7 2DB, UK
{jinhong.wang17,q.lu17,n.rojas}@imperial.ac.uk
http://www.imperial.ac.uk/reds-lab

Abstract. In the field of robotic hands, tendon actuation is one of the most common ways to control self-adaptive underactuated fingers thanks to its compact size. Either differential or direct drive mechanisms are usually used in these systems to perform synchronised grasping using a single actuator. However, synchronisation problems arise in underactuated grippers whose position of proximal joints varies with time to perform manipulation operations, as this results in a tendon-driven system with dynamic anchor pulleys. This paper introduces a novel passively compliant idler mechanism to avoid unsynchronisation in grippers with a dynamic multi-tendon routing system, such that adequate grasping contact forces are kept under changes in the proximal joints' positions. A re-configurable palm underactuated dexterous gripper is used as a case study, with the performance of the proposed compliant idler system being evaluated and compared through a contact force analysis during rotation and translation in-hand manipulation tasks. Experiment results clearly demonstrate the ability of the mechanism to synchronise a dynamic tendon routing gripper. A video summarising experiments and findings can be found at https://imperialcollegelondon.box.com/s/hk58688q2hjnu8dhw7uskr7vi9tqr9r5.

Keywords: Dynamic tendon-driven system · Underactuated hands · In-hand manipulation

1 Introduction

The dexterous in-hand manipulation capability of grippers has drawn lots of research attention due to its importance in enhancing the adaptability of robotic systems. It remains an open problem whose complexity emerge from the fact that fingers often need to change their orientations, relative positions, and contact forces to perform in-hand manipulation tasks. Indeed, the optimised actuation method for robot fingers is also an open research question. For the majority of hands, the actuation of separate fingers is done using separate actuators. For

© Springer Nature Switzerland AG 2020
A. Mohammad et al. (Eds.): TAROS 2020, LNAI 12228, pp. 25–36, 2020.
https://doi.org/10.1007/978-3-030-63486-5_3

example, the GCUA Hand has two geared DC motors to actuate each finger by pulling different tendons [4]. Other cases include the JLST hand [14], the DLR-Hand II [3] and the OLYMPIC prosthetic hand [9], just to name some, which all actuate each finger with its own actuator. This solution provides higher dexterity compared to solutions based on combined underactuation [1], but is more expensive and complex to control due to the increased number of actuators.

Underactuation, that is, the control of more degrees of freedom that actuators are available [7], has been frequently leveraged for robot hand design. For instance, avoiding the use of a tendon, Cheon et al. [5] used differential gear mechanisms for underactuation, where the differential gear ratio is determined by the length of phalanges. Ma et al. [11] used a differential-driven pair in their gripper, where two fingers were connected with a single tendon and actuation was achieved by pulling a pulley in the centre. Similarly, Rossi et al. [13] used a force distribution system with a cascade of floating pulley systems, where the primary pulley is in-turn connected to another two secondary pulleys. When the primary pulley is pulled by the actuator, a quarter of the force from the motor goes to each of the four fingers connected to the secondary pulleys. Additionally, Gosselin et al. [8] attached an additional tendon to the primary pulley to actuate the thumb, and the force from thumb is hence different from the other fingers.

Alternatively, Niestanak et al. [12] proposed the closed loop tendon mechanism for multi-finger actuation where all the fingers are controlled by a single loop of the tendon. The tendon is fixed at the fingertips and different joints of the finger with pins and tubes. With a single motor winding up the tendon, the total length of the tendon loop decreases leading to the flexion of the desired joints. However, the contact forces for each finger are uneven due to the mix of directly and indirectly connected tendons to fingers. Baril et al. [2] looked into a few tendon driven systems that have single-input/multiple-output underactuated mechanisms as described above, and their combination was claimed to be most compact and efficient mechanism due to low friction and evenly distributed forces. For reconfigurable hands such as that developed by X. Cui et al. [6], the tendon length for each finger differs, thus the constant force and tendon length models mentioned previously are not longer suitable. Lu et al. [10] provided one solution to this problem by routing the tendon through the five-bar-mechanism based reconfigurable palm, ensuring the length of the tendon is independent of the palm configuration. However, this constant tendon system requires a high actuation force due to the complex routing design.

In this paper, a novel passively compliant idler mechanism for managing unsynchronised multi-tendon actuation in underactuated grippers is proposed. By maintaining the tension in the tendons, the force provided by the fingers on an object is sufficient to keep the object in a stable grasp during dexterous in-hand manipulations. In Sect. 2, we discuss the design and development of the introduced idler system. We then demonstrate the design of the reconfigurable hand used for testing the idler system in Sect. 3. Next, in Sect. 4 and 5, we evaluate and discuss the idler performance in in-hand manipulation tasks. Lastly, we conclude in Sect. 6.

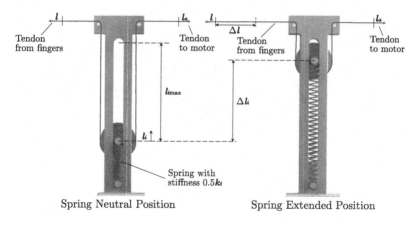

Fig. 1. Schematic of the proposed passively compliant idler mechanism

2 Development of the Idler System

Idlers are usually used in flexible mechanical transmissions such as belt or chain drive systems. The main purpose of including idlers in the system is to increase the wrap angle on the smaller pulley/sprocket so that the force-transfer capacity can be maximised. In addition, to ensure the performance of the flexible drive, the belts or chains must be kept in tension during operation. However, in practice belts or chains are purchased at fixed lengths and it is common to have them with excess length. With the addition of adjustable idlers, the excess slack length can be taken up and the additional tension improves the transmission efficiency.

A similar concept can be applied to the tendon actuation for grippers. When the tendon is routed, the total length is fixed. For robot hands with reconfigurable palms, it is common for finger positions to change relative to the actuators, which means the fixed tendon lengths would either become too long or too short for the same finger posture, hence the fingers might lose contact with the grasped object. This is further complicated in underactuated grippers that only use a single actuator for multiple fingers as different tendons can have different slack lengths. To prevent this, a passively compliant idler pulley system (schematics shown in Fig. 1) was implemented before connecting tendons to the actuator to keep all the tendons in tension and maintain the necessary contact force between the finger tip and the object.

2.1 Static Modelling of the Idler System

As shown in Fig. 1, the idlers are free to move linearly with a range of $l_{i_{max}}$ and they hold each tendon in tension with springs pulling them downwards with a total stiffness of k_t. Since the idler system is connected between the fingers and the actuator, the forces applied to the fingers are provided by the springs until the idlers have reached their top-most position. The force applied by the springs

 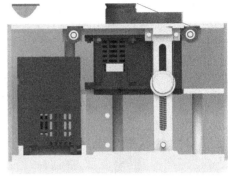

Fig. 2. Left: Single idler structure view. **Right:** Sectional CAD view of the idler system with tendon routing (red). (Color figure online)

to the pulley is given by Hooke's law $F = k_t \times \Delta l_i$ where Δl_i is the extended length of the springs. Since each idler is a moving pulley, the tension force is hence $F_t = \frac{1}{2} k_t \times \Delta l_i$. In addition, the actuated tendon length l_a is twice of the spring extension length l_i. When the finger has grasped an object, and then the tendon is loosen by a length of Δl, the following equation must be satisfied in order to keep the grasp:

$$F_{grasp} \leq \frac{1}{4} k_t (l_a - \Delta l) + f_{static} - F_{restore} \tag{1}$$

where F_{grasp} is the minimum grasping force required, f_{static} is the total static friction in the tendon system and $F_{restore}$ is the restoring force by the fingers. Therefore, when actuating the fingers, extra tendon length would be wound in order to compensate for the potential tendon slack during manipulation.

The minimum spring extension to ensure a grasp can be derived:

$$l_{i_{min}} = \frac{2(F_{grasp} + F_{restore} - f_{static})}{k_t} \tag{2}$$

Thus, the actual range for idlers to move during manipulation is $l_{i_{max}} - l_{i_{min}}$. For each specific tendon, Δl_{max} is constant and is determined by the design of the gripper. Therefore, it is important to make sure that

$$\Delta l_{max} \leq 2(l_{i_{max}} - l_{i_{min}}) \tag{3}$$

For unsynchronised multi-tendon systems, there would be different Δl_{max} for each tendon and there would be different Δl during manipulations as well. Each tendon was connected to the actuator pulley separately based on corresponding Δl_{max} and when actuating the tendons for a grasp, the maximum Δl among all tendons should be used in calculation to make sure that all the fingers will not lose contact with the object.

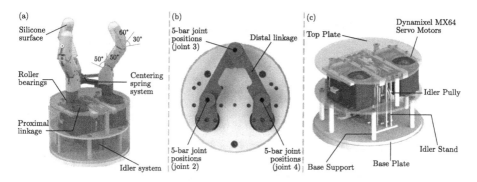

Fig. 3. (a) CAD model showing the overall gripper structure with the idler base. Finger joint angle limits are also shown. **(b)** CAD Model showing the palm. **(c)** CAD model shows the idler system structure in the base of the tested reconfigurable hand

2.2 Implementation of the Idler System

Three idler stands are used in the case study, namely a robotic hand with reconfigurable palm. The design of this robot hand is detailed in the Sect. 3. Figure 2 shows the single idler structure and the tendon routing, in which all three tendons pass through a small hole on the top plate and are routed through several tendon pulley. When the palm is reconfigured during manipulation, the tendon can loosen or tighten such that the idlers would move up or down for compensation. In the implemented prototype, the idler stands have a minimum range of $l_{i_{max}} = 50$ mm , which fully utilised the spaces between top and base plate. The Δl_{max} is calculated to be approximately 60 mm for the reconfigurable palm. Therefore, the relationship stated in Eq. 3 is satisfied. The sum of restoring forces $F_{restore}$ and static friction f_{static} was measured to be 7.075 N. Two springs with stiffness of 1000 N/m were used for each idler. The tendons were fixed to the tendon actuator pulley when palm is at the closest position (minimum tendon length) with reference to Eq. 2 for relative idler positions. During manipulation, the tendon actuator is set based on Eq. 1 in order to provide enough force to maintain a stable grasp.

3 Design of the Gripper

The gripper that was implemented with the idler system has a five-bar linkage with three underactuated fingers located at its moving joints. Therefore, when re-configuring the five-bar linkage, which is the gripper's palm, the fingers would move relative to the base where the tendon actuator is mounted. The length of the tendons would hence need to be adjusted in order to maintain the grasp forces. In addition, the tendon length change of each finger is different from each other which provides more problems for the actuation. The idler system introduced in Sect. 2 is therefore incorporated with the gripper and the final prototype is shown in Fig. 3(a).

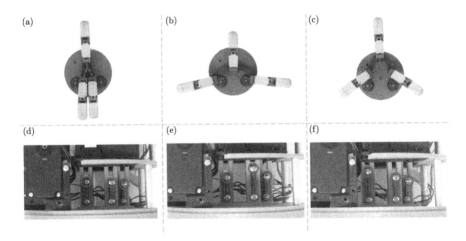

Fig. 4. Different types of grasps achievable with the reconfigurable gripper: (**a**) Parallel, (**b**) T-shape, and (**c**) Trigonal planar. (**d–f**) indicate the positions of the idler pulleys (indicated by red circles) corresponding to each of the grasping configurations. (Color figure online)

3.1   Five-Bar Reconfigurable Palm

With the five-bar linkage as the palm of the gripper shown in Fig. 3(b), dexterous in-hand manipulation can be performed. By actuating two proximal linkages, the relative positions of the fingers can be changed and different configurations can be achieved (Fig. 4), e.g.. parallel, T-shape, trigonal grasping etc. A symmetrical structure with two proximal bars and two distal bars having the same length was used for the five-bar linkage. In addition, the motor separation (the fixed link in the five-bar palm system) was set to have the same length of the distal linkage, which is 70 mm, so that fingers can easily grasp objects in a equilateral triangle (trigonal) configuration. When selecting the length of proximal bars, the avoidance of singularities and collision during operation became the main considerations. The proximal bar lengths were hence set to be 20 mm. A caster wheel was used in the palm to support the gripper during operation. Roller bearings (20 mm) were added between the faces of the links to reduce the friction and improve the performance of the five-bar linkage.

3.2   Underactuated Fingers

6 mm machine screws were used to affix three identical fingers with two pha-langes which were fixed at the joints of the five-bar linkage that allowing the rotation of the fingers. For each finger, the proximal phalanx has $\pm50°$ and the distal phalanx has $+60°/-40°$ range of motion as shown in Fig. 3(a). The linear springs with stiffness of 65 N/m were fixed at the back of the fingers in order to provide the restoring forces for the underactuated fingers. To enhance the

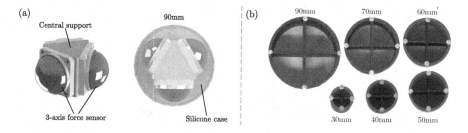

Fig. 5. Objects used to evaluate the performance of the gripper with and without the idler system. **(a)** A soft cylindrical object with embedded trigonal 3-axis force sensors and **(b)** regular cylindrical objects in various sizes.

contact friction force between the fingers and the objects, the fingertips and the proximal phalanges were coated in textured silicone (SmoothOn Eco-Flex 00–10).

To maintain the grasp capabilities of the gripper, ideally fingers must face towards to the centre of the triangle formed by the three finger base positions (joints 2, 3 and 4 shown in Fig. 3(b)) in the x-y plane. To achieve this, three high stiffness springs were attached to the base of each fingers and the other end is connected to each other, where the holding point of all three springs is located at the centre of the triangle. Therefore, no matter how the five-bar linkage system is reconfigured, the springs would always adjust the finger position, turning them towards to the centre of the palm.

3.3 Design of the Prototype

The prototype is mainly constructed from the 3D printed parts on a single nozzle desktop printer. Polylactic Acid (PLA) was used to print the mounting plates, motor supports and the fingers. To increase the rigidity of the structure, the five bar linkages were printed using Polyethylene Terephthalate Glycol (PETG). Three Dynamixel MX 64 servo motors were used to control the gripper, two for five bars and one for all three underactuated fingers. An Arduino Nano micro-controller was used to control the gripper by using a software serial connected tristate buffer (74LS241N) to communicate using half-duplex UART protocol with motors.

4 Performance Evaluation

4.1 Experimental Setup

The sensors used for the experiments are shown in Fig. 5(a). Three OMD-30-SE-100N force sensors were fixed to the central support block. A silicone case was then made to provide the housing for the sensors and also made the testing object easier to grasp. The sensors log the data with a frequency 100 Hz and

Fig. 6. Illustration of the experimental trajectories by highlighting the starting and ending positions of the testing object.

the compression force in vertical direction of each sensor were taken and plotted against time for comparison. Moreover, testing objects with a variety of sizes, 30–90 mm as shown in Fig. 5(b), were employed to prove the gripper's capability for in-hand manipulation.

In the experiments, two trajectories were performed as shown in Fig. 6. Namely, an equilateral triangle co-planar movement and a pure rotational movement. The actuation of the equilateral triangle co-planar movement was achieved by keeping the proximal bars parallel (hence keeping the fingers at equilateral triangle configuration) and rotate 180°, from positive x to negative x direction, with the same speed. The rotation trajectory ideally can rotate the object around 68°. The rotation range of the proximal bars are based on the inverse kinematic values output from the simulation of the gripper manipulation workspace. Each experiment was repeated three times to provide reliable results and another set of data was obtained for the same gripper but using a direct drive mechanism (i.e. without the idler system—routing the tendons straight from the fingers to the actuation motor) for comparison.

4.2   Idler Performance

Figure 7 presents the data taken by the three sensors for two different trajectories. For each trajectory, first three rows of graphs show the variation of compression forces received by each sensor during manipulation of the gripper with idler system incorporated, while the last row of data shows that of the gripper without the idlers. Sensors 1, 2 and 3 correspond to the finger at joint 4, 2 and 3, (as labelled in Fig. 3(b)) respectively. Three data sets shared a similar trend of force variation and at the end position of the trajectory, all the fingertips were still in contact with the sensor assembly and the sensors were still held in place.

From the data for both of the trajectories, it is obvious that the gripper with idler system is able to maintain a higher average grasping force during the manipulation than the gripper which the tendons are directly connected to the actuator. In addition, during the experiments for the comparison group, we found out that without the idler system, the gripper is impossible to grasp an

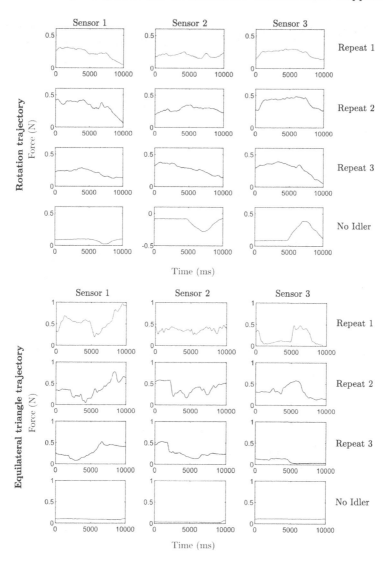

Fig. 7. Sensor data for both movements. Each column indicates each sensor's reading. Each movement has three trials of results with idler system and one trial without the idler system (last row).

object with different grasping configurations, let alone to perform in-hand manipulations. During the rotation trajectory experiments for gripper without idlers, finger 2's tip lost contact with the object completely and the sensor assembly was only supported by the proximal phalanx of the finger in vertical direction. Therefore, the sensor did not experience the vertical compression but has lateral deformation, leading to a negative value in the result (Fig. 7).

For the grasping tests for smaller testing objects (<90 mm), the gripper with the idlers successfully maintained the object for both trajectories while the gripper without idlers failed to perform the grasping at the position and the object could only sit on the proximal phalanges. The detailed implementation of the experiments can be found in the video (link provided in the abstract).

5   Discussion

According to the experimental results in Fig. 7, although there are fluctuations in the forces provided, the idler system successfully maintained the contact forces that is necessary for the grasp whereas the comparison group failed to perform the manipulation. In fact, the general trend and the fluctuations were expected for the idler system and can be explained by the mechanism of the system.

As explained in Sect. 2, the idler positions would change actively according to the change in tendon length Δl during manipulation. Therefore, the tendon tension would be slightly different due to changes in l_i, so does the force for the grasp F_{grasp}. It is then easy to deduce that if the tendon actuator is held constant, when the fingers move further away from the centre hole on the top plate, which means the ideal tendon length is larger than the actual tendon length, the idlers would then move upwards for compensation. Although the finger posture remains the same, the actual grasping force F_{grasp} has increased due to a raise in l_i, and vice versa.

With this understanding, the fluctuations can thus be explained. For the rotation trajectory, in average, sensor 3's reading increases at the beginning and drop back to its starting position during the manipulation. It is because the distance between the joint 3 of the five-bar linkage and the centre hole firstly increases and then drops back to the initial distance during this trajectory. Similarly, sensor 2 experiences least fluctuation because in the five-bar linkage system, the distance change between position of joint 2 and the centre point during the manipulation is trivial. Additionally, during the rotation trajectory, the triangle formed by joint 2, 3 and 4 of the five-bar linkage was not maintained constant. When the geometry of this triangle changes, the contact points of the fingers would change at the same time because the fingers were designed to have spherical tips so that it has local rolling at the contact surface with the object to prevent the slipping. Therefore, the force applied by the fingertip is no longer perpendicular and at the centre of the sensors, which lead to a drop in sensor reading during the manipulation.

As for the equilateral triangle trajectory, since the geometry of the triangle formed by fingers was always maintained as equilateral, there was not any changes in the contact points that have occurred. The trend was consistent for the data set. Different from the previous trajectory, this co-planar trajectory would require much larger initial tendon actuation length because between the movement between 90° and 270°, the tendon length change Δl is the largest for the finger located at joint 3 of the five-bar linkage because it passes the furthest point. Similar to the other two fingers, the tendon length change Δl is relatively large compare to the rotation trajectory; therefore, the force reading varies more significantly.

The initial contact points between the fingers and the sensor assembly also affected the sensor reading. For instance, the reading of sensor 3 is close to zero for the third set of data, but the forces from other two fingers were providing enough force to support the sensor assembly so that it was not falling off. In addition, if the sensor assembly was not placed horizontally at the initial point, it would lead to an un-evenly distributed force among three contact points and hence lead to the deviation in the data retrieved. The other source of the experimental error could be from the sensor assembly where as the deformation of the silicone shell would lead to a change in the force readings as it is effectively acting as a spring in the system. The silicone shell is used to create a stable grasping situation when the contact points are changing. This could be improved by using other types of force sensors which can detect the force no matter the contact points or add tactile sensors in the fingertips.

According to the results, it has been proven that by satisfying a few criteria for the spring selection, the idler system is capable to synchronise a dynamic tendon routing system to perform different grasping configurations and in-hand manipulation. However, the current idler system design is not robust enough to provide 100% successful rate. The structure rigidity, tendon routing method for fingers and system, and the spring selection criterion could be further developed for better performance and adaptability.

6   Conclusion

In this paper, a concept of passively compliant idler system was developed for unsynchronisation-prone multi-tendon systems. We presented the design, construction, and evaluation of the idler system on a reconfigurable underactuated gripper, which makes the actuation of multiple tendons with a single motor possible by incorporating an spring system. Through the use of a five-bar linkage as the palm of the gripper, the tendon system becomes unsynchronised and the routing system is then dynamic. The proposed idler system is capable of controlling the tendon length for different grasping configurations and in-hand manipulations. We experimentally evaluated the idler system by in-hand manipulating various objects with sensors. From the force sensor readings we see that with the proposed idler system, the gripper is able to maintain the grasping force for the fingers during the manipulation. Moreover, the idlers can also perform precise grasps and manipulations of small objects (30 mm diameter) without losing or dropping them. Therefore, this demonstrates that by satisfying a few criteria for spring selection, it is possible to have a single actuator adjusting different forces for each of the tendon stream. This provides a simple but efficient solution for tendon-actuated multi-finger gripper whose positions of proximal joints vary with time. Regarding future work, an optimisation of the spring selection criterion could be further developed by incorporating further considerations about friction for instance. The routing optimisation can also be improved to reduce friction and to reduce the effects of sudden change in tendon lengths, thus minimising the fluctuations of the force provided by the fingers.

References

1. Bai, G., Rojas, N.: Self-adaptive monolithic anthropomorphic finger with teeth-guided compliant cross-four-bar joints for underactuated hands. In: 2018 IEEE-RAS 18th International Conference on Humanoid Robots (Humanoids), pp. 145–152. IEEE (2018)
2. Baril, M., Guay, F., Gosselin, C., et al.: Static analysis of single-input/multiple-output tendon-driven underactuated mechanisms for robotic hands. In: ASME 2010 International Design Engineering Technical Conferences and Computers and Information in Engineering Conference, pp. 155–164. American Society of Mechanical Engineers Digital Collection (2010)
3. Butterfaß, J., Grebenstein, M., Liu, H., Hirzinger, G.: Dlr-hand ii: next generation of a dextrous robot hand. In: Proceedings 2001 ICRA. IEEE International Conference on Robotics and Automation (Cat. No. 01CH37164), vol. 1, pp. 109–114. IEEE (2001)
4. Che, D., Zhang, W.: Gcua humanoid robotic hand with tendon mechanisms and its upper limb. Int. J. Soc. Robot. **3**(4), 395–404 (2011)
5. Cheon, S., Choi, W., Oh, S.R., Oh, Y.: Development of an underactuated robotic hand using differential gear mechanism. In: 2014 11th International Conference on Ubiquitous Robots and Ambient Intelligence (URAI), pp. 328–334. IEEE (2014)
6. Cui, X., Sun, J., Zhang, X.S., Xu, S.J., Dai, J.S.: A metamorphic hand with coplanar reconfiguration. In: 2018 International Conference on Reconfigurable Mechanisms and Robots (ReMAR), pp. 1–7. IEEE (2018)
7. Dollar, A.M., Howe, R.D.: The highly adaptive SDM hand: design and performance evaluation. Int. J Robot. Res. **29**(5), 585–597 (2010)
8. Gosselin, C., Pelletier, F., Laliberte, T.: An anthropomorphic underactuated robotic hand with 15 dofs and a single actuator. In: 2008 IEEE International Conference on Robotics and Automation, pp. 749–754. IEEE (2008)
9. Liow, L., Clark, A.B., Rojas, N.: Olympic: a modular, tendon-driven prosthetic hand with novel finger and wrist coupling mechanisms. IEEE Robot. Autom. Lett. **5**(2), 299–306 (2019)
10. Lu, Q., Baron, N., Clark, A.B., Rojas, N.: The ruth gripper: systematic object-invariant prehensile in-hand manipulation via reconfigurable underactuation. Under review
11. Ma, R.R., Dollar, A.M.: An underactuated hand for efficient finger-gaiting-based dexterous manipulation. In: 2014 IEEE International Conference on Robotics and Biomimetics (ROBIO 2014), pp. 2214–2219. IEEE (2014)
12. Niestanak, V.D., Moshaii, A.A., Moghaddam, M.M.: A new underactuated mechanism of hand tendon injury rehabilitation. In: 2017 5th RSI International Conference on Robotics and Mechatronics (ICRoM), pp. 400–405. IEEE (2017)
13. Rossi, C., Savino, S., Niola, V., Troncone, S.: A study of a robotic hand with tendon driven fingers. Robotica **33**(5), 1034–1048 (2015)
14. Song, J., Zhang, W.: JLST hand: a novel powerful self-adaptive underactuated hand with joint-locking and spring-tendon mechanisms. In: Agah, A., Cabibihan, J.-J., Howard, A.M., Salichs, M.A., He, H. (eds.) ICSR 2016. LNCS (LNAI), vol. 9979, pp. 492–501. Springer, Cham (2016). https://doi.org/10.1007/978-3-319-47437-3_48

An Inhomogeneous Structured Eversion Actuator

Taqi Abrar$^{(\boxtimes)}$ (ID), Ahmed Hassan (ID), Fabrizio Putzu (ID), Hareesh Godaba (ID),
Ahmad Ataka (ID), and Kaspar Althoefer (ID)

Centre for Advanced Robotics @ Queen Mary (ARQ), Queen Mary University
of London, Mile End Road, London E1 4NS, UK
{t.abrar,ahmed.hassan,f.putzu,h.godaba,a.rizqi,k.althoefer}@qmul.ac.uk

Abstract. Soft actuators are free from any rigid, bulky, and hard components. This is greatly beneficial towards achieving compliant actuation and safe interactions in robots. Inspired by the eversion principle, we develop a novel soft actuator of the inhomogeneous cross-section that can linearly extend and achieve a large payload capability. The proposed soft actuator is a hollow sleeve, made from an airtight fabric, and features a top part of cylindrical shape and a bottom part of a conical shape. Unlike conventional eversion robots that extend unilaterally from the tip, in this proposed actuator the top cylindrical part and the bottom conical part are partially folded inwards so that the two tips are attached together. When pneumatic pressure is applied, the cylindrical part everts increasing in length while the conical section reduces in length folding inwards. The actuator achieves linear strains of 120% and can generate a force 84 N at a low pressure of 62 kPa. We develop a theoretical model to describe the force and strain characteristics of the actuator during eversion from conical shape to cylindrical shape. The results showcase a step towards large strain, high force actuators for safe and compliant robots.

Keywords: Eversion actuator · Inflatable structure · Soft actuators · Design parameters

1 Introduction

Soft robotics has gained enormous attention from the researchers resulting in developments of new kinds of soft actuators and robots in the recent era. These soft actuators overcome the barriers of their rigid counterparts in aspects such as safety, adaptability, and low cost. They have made a mark in many application areas including grasping of delicate and fragile objects [1], wearable robots [2,3], and exploration of extreme environments that are not accessible by humans [4–6].

This work was supported in part by the EPSRC National Centre for Nuclear Robotics project (EP/R02572X/1) and the Innovate UK WormBot project (104059).

© Springer Nature Switzerland AG 2020
A. Mohammad et al. (Eds.): TAROS 2020, LNAI 12228, pp. 37–48, 2020.
https://doi.org/10.1007/978-3-030-63486-5_4

One of the main enablers of soft robots is the linear actuator that can generate translatory motion. Many linear actuators contract when pressurized by air such as pouch motors [7], McKibben muscles [8], and bio-inspired actuator [9,10], or extend in length such as the vine inspired actuator and robots [11,12], bio-inspired inflatable actuator [13] and fiber reinforced actuator [14]. These actuators generally have a fixed end while the other end translates depending upon the actuation pressure causing the change in length of the actuator. The most important considerations of these expanding/contracting linear actuators are the actuation strain and the payload capability.

Eversion actuators are soft pneumatic actuators that are bio-inspired and perform linear actuation. They are generally cylindrical shaped and made from soft materials like plastics and fabrics [11]. The distal part of the cylindrical sock-like structure is folded inside itself and the proximal opening is connected to a pneumatic input. When the air is pressurized inside the actuator, the previously folded part unfolds with the cylindrical structure gradually everting from the tip. This mechanism has led to achieving unprecedented extension ranges spanning tens of meters in length. Moreover, the lack of stretching in the material allows the optimal generation of axial forces due to an applied pressure [15].

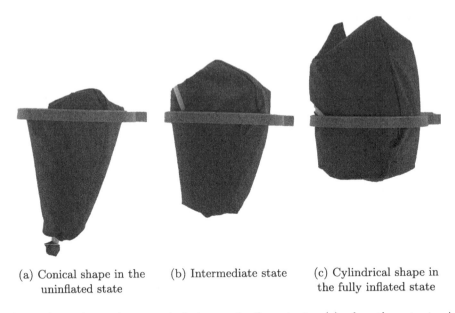

(a) Conical shape in the   (b) Intermediate state   (c) Cylindrical shape in
    uninflated state   the fully inflated state

Fig. 1. Actuation and geometrical changes in the actuator (a) when the actuator is uninflated, it is conical in shape, (b) when actuated, the cylindrical part everts and the conical tip draws in towards the centre of the actuator, (c) cylindrical part is completely everted and the cone is completely inverted.

In this paper, we propose a new kind of soft pneumatic actuator inspired by the eversion mechanism (Fig. 1). The actuator has an inhomogeneous structure, the bottom half has a conical shape (Fig. 1a) while the top half part of the actuator has a cylindrical shape (Fig. 1c). The actuation mechanism of the actuator is based on the eversion principle. This design allows the actuator to achieve stroke length of up to 100% tip displacement which is higher than the actuation strains in many of the existing pneumatic soft actuators such as pouch actuators and McKibben's muscles. Furthermore, there are minimal energy losses due to stretching of material or due to friction, as the outer segment of the eversion actuator does not slide against the external environment.

The remainder of this paper is organized as follows: The geometry and fabrication of the actuator are discussed in Sect. 2. In Sect. 3, we develop an analytical model that can predict the actuation characteristics. Experimental results and simulation studies are presented in Sect. 4, followed by discussion and future work in Sect. 5.

2   Hardware Design

An actuator that extends its length by everting out its body from the center when pressurised can be categorised as an eversion actuator [16]. They are made from soft materials and are lightweight, compliant in nature, and can squeeze through narrow regions [10]. They also have low energy losses due to the friction and can grow from a very small size to multiple times of their initial length [12,16].

The traditional eversion-based actuators or robots in the literature have a uniform cylindrical cross-section with one side connected to the air source for pressurizing the actuator [12]. In an attempt to develop a fully self-contained actuator based on the eversion principle, both ends of the cylindrical tube can be folded inwards and connected at the center. However, in this configuration, a pressure applied to the inner chamber of the structure will only cause it to stiffen without producing any displacement. To solve this problem, we create the actuator from a profile of inhomogeneous cross-section. This will enable the actuator to produce eversion (unfolding of material) on one end and inversion (folding of the material) at the other end of the actuator, thereby causing a displacement and actuation force. The design and the construction of such an inhomogeneous eversion actuator is presented in this section.

2.1   Design of the Actuator

The actuator consists of two different geometrical shapes combined together. The top part is cylindrical and the bottom part is conical, which makes the whole structure of the actuator inhomogeneous. For the construction of the actuator, an airtight fabric sheet (Breathable Coated Microfibre from UKfabrics Online) is cut in the desired shape (Fig. 2). As shown in the figure, the cross-section of the actuator is made to be inhomogeneous by attaching the top of the cone to the bottom of the cylindrical shape. The two adjacent longitudinal sides are sewn

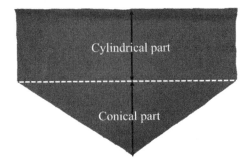

Fig. 2. Fabrication of the actuator: a flat sheet is cut into the shape shown above to form a cylindrical and a conical part.

to construct the desired shape of the actuator. To ensure that there is no air leakage, all the seams and closures are sealed using a cyanoacrylate super glue. Once the sealing is done, the structure is turned inside out, moving the created seams to the inside of the actuator.

2.2 Eversion in the Proposed Inhomogeneous Actuator

To complete the fabrication process, the tip of the cone (which is at the bottom) is folded inward and attached to the closed end of the cylinder (which is at the top). Once the tip of the cone and the cylinder are joined together and sealed, the tip is pulled back such that the cylinder now rests inside the conical structure. As a result, the shape of the visible actuator becomes conical with the cylindrical part folded inside. When pneumatic pressure is applied during actuation, the previously folded part moves in the direction away from the bottom (the tip of the cone), achieving a movement based on the principle of eversion (Fig. 1b).

As illustrated in Fig. 3, the tip of the cone is attached to the top of the cylindrical shape. When the previously folded part unfolds while everting from the top of the cone, the top of the cylinder pulls the tip of the cone. In other words, when the cylindrical part of the actuator is everting, the conical part inverts and folds into the actuator. This results in an increase in the length of one (cylindrical) side and simultaneously, reduction in the length of the other (conical) side. As a consequence, the total length of the actuator remains fixed, but the tip of the actuator is displaced across the whole length of the actuator.

3   Analytical Model

We now develop an analytical model to describe the forces and actuation strains in the actuator when it is actuated by pneumatic pressure. At the initial unactuated state (also called the reference state), the geometry of the actuator is given by dimensions of the cone- radius, r_{co} and height, h_{co}. At any given state of the actuator, its geometry can be represented by the everted length, h_{cy}, the

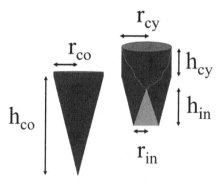

Fig. 3. Geometry of the inhomogeneous eversion actuator in the reference (unactuated) state and an actuated state.

inverted length, h_{in}, and the radius of the cross-section at the bottom tip in the conical part, r_{in} as shown in Fig. 3.

The bottom of the actuator is composed of conical shape and when the actuator is not inflated, the shape of the actuator will be conical, therefore the volume of the actuator at the beginning can be defined as;

$$V_{co} = \frac{\pi r_{co}^2 h_{co}}{3}, \tag{1}$$

Where V_{co} is the volume of the cone, r_{co} is the radius of the cone, and h_{co} is the height of the cone. While on the other hand, when fully-inflated, only the top part (which is cylindrical in shape) is visible, therefore the volume of the actuator when it is fully extended can be defined as

$$V_{cy} = \pi r_{cy}^2 h_{cy}, \tag{2}$$

Where V_{cy} is the volume of the cylinder, r_{cy} is the radius of the cylinder, and h_{cy} is the height of the cylinder. While the top part is everting, at the same time, the tip of the cone (bottom of the actuator) starts inverting. The volume of the cone V_{in} inverted at any state can be defined as

$$V_{in} = \frac{\pi r_{in}^2 h_{in}}{3}, \tag{3}$$

Where r_{in} is the radius of the cone and h_{in} is the height of the cone folded back due to the eversion at the top part of the actuator. Since the volume and shape of the actuator is changing from conical to cylindrical, therefore the volume of the actuator V_a any point of time can be defined as

$$V_a = V_{co} - 2V_{in} + V_{cy} \tag{4}$$

By substituting the values in above the Eq. 4, the new Eq. 5 will be

$$V_a = \frac{\pi r_{co}^2 h_{co}}{3} - \frac{2\pi r_{in}^2 h_{in}}{3} + \pi r_{cy}^2 h_c \tag{5}$$

The above Eq. 5 contains 2 types of parameters, constant dimensions and variable parameters.

Constant dimensions	Variable parameters
r_{co}	r_{in}
h_{co}	h_{in}
r_{cy}	h_{cy}

Based on the geometry,

$$r_{co} = r_{cy} = r_a, \tag{6}$$

$$h_{cy} = h_{in} = h_e, \tag{7}$$

Where r_a is the radius of the actuator and h_e is the height of the eversion. Therefore the proposed actuator has two knowns (fixed) and two unknowns (variable) parameters.

Fixed parameter	Variable parameters
r_a	r_{in}
h_{co}	h_e

From the geometry of the cone, we can also estimate the relationship between the conical shape of the actuator and the cone which goes inside the actuator during eversion.

$$\frac{h_e}{r_{in}} = \frac{h_{co}}{r_a} \tag{8}$$

With this relationship the Eq. 5 will become

$$V_a = \frac{\pi}{3}(r_a^2 h_{co} - 2r_{in}^2 h_e + 3r_a^2 h_e) \tag{9}$$

$$V_a = \frac{\pi}{3}(r_a^2 h_{co} - 2\frac{r_a^2 h_e^2 h_e}{h_{co}^2} + 3r_a^2 h_e) \tag{10}$$

$$V_a = \frac{\pi r_a^2}{3}(h_{co} - 2\frac{h_e^3}{h_{co}^2} + 3h_e) \tag{11}$$

$$V_a = \frac{\pi r_a^2 h_{co}}{3}\{1 - 2(\frac{h_e}{h_{co}})^3 + \frac{3h_e}{h_{co}}\} \tag{12}$$

$$V_a = V_{co}\{1 - 2(\frac{h_e}{h_{co}})^3 + \frac{3h_e}{h_{co}}\} \tag{13}$$

Differentiating Eq. 13 with respect to h_e, we get;

$$\frac{dV_a}{dh_e} = (-\frac{6V_{co}h_e^2}{h_{co}^3} + \frac{3V_{co}}{h_{co}}) \tag{14}$$

Due to the conservation of energy, the work done by the actuator by the virtual displacement of a load is equal to the work done by the air pressure through a change in volume of the actuator. This relation is given as;

$$W = -Fdh = Pdv. \tag{15}$$

So, the actuating force is given by;

$$F = -P\frac{dV_a}{dh_e} \tag{16}$$

Substituting the value of dV_a/dh_e from Eq. 14 in above Eq. 16, we get:

$$F_{h_e} = -\frac{3PV_{co}}{h_{co}}\{1 - 2(\frac{h_e}{h_{co}})^2\} \tag{17}$$

4   Results

We conduct experiments to understand the payload capabilities of the actuator at different isometric strains. The pressure applied to the actuator is regulated via an electro-pneumatic regulator (SMC-ITV2050-212BL4). The actuator is in the state where the top part is folded inside (see Fig. 1a) and attached to the bottom part (the tip of the cone) as shown in Fig. 3. The bottom of the cone is attached to the Z-axis of the RFT Force Torque sensor (ROBOTOUS RFT40-SA01-D) to measure the force exerted by the actuator on an object at zero actuation strain.

An actuator with the following representative dimensions was built. The conical part has a length 100 mm while having a radius 37.5 mm and the cylindrical part has the same radius 37.5 mm and the same active length of 100 mm.

4.1   Blocked Force Test

In this section, the experiment was conducted to measure the maximum force generation capability of the actuator. The actuator is attached to a rigid 3d printed structure which is firmly affixed to a support. The tip of the cone of the actuator in the reference configuration (Fig. 1a) is attached to a fixed force sensor. This configuration also corresponds to the zero strain configuration of the actuator. Different pneumatic pressures ranging from 0 to 69 kPa in increments of 6.9 kPa were applied to the actuator and the forces measured by the FT sensor are noted. The maximum test pressure is limited to 69 kPa to prevent fracture of the actuator. When pressure is applied, the cylindrical fabric inside the conical region tries to evert and applies force on the tip which pulls on the force sensor. Consequently, a force is recorded by the FT sensor. From Fig. 4, we see that as the pressure increases, the force increases almost linearly with pressure showing a piston type behaviour.

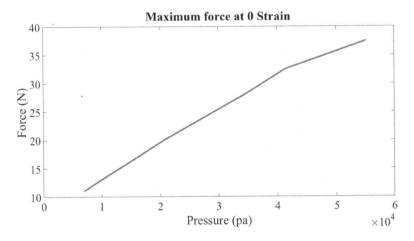

Fig. 4. Blocked force test results. Force exerted by the actuator when attached to a fixed FT (force-torque) sensor

In the proposed model (Eq. 17), the force has a linear relationship which agrees well with the experimental measurements for the force generated by the actuator (Fig. 4). Further increase in the pressure can increase the force generated by the actuator but may cause a fracture when the stresses in the fabric reach the yield strength of the material. The seams sealed by adhesive are also prone to leakage at high pressures.

4.2 Actuation Force at Different Strains

Unlike a piston in a cylinder, when the eversion actuator is undergoing actuation, the effective cross-section area of the everting tip keeps changing due to the varying cross-section caused by the cylinder in cone design. Hence, the payload capability of the actuator varies with the actuation strain. To understand this variation, we conduct experiments to measure the force output of the actuator under a fixed pressure at varying strains. The frame to which the base of the actuator (seen as the blue annular frame in Fig. 5) is mounted on the Instron universal testing machine (UTM) fitted with a 2 kN load cell as shown in Fig. 5. The load cell is attached to the tip of the cone via a fishing line acting as an inextensible thread. The Instron head is programmed to translate 100 mm stroke length with a speed of 1 mm/s.

Fig. 5. Inhomogeneous eversion actuator mounted on a universal testing machine (UTM) for characterizing the generated forces

Three different pressures are applied to the actuator and the pull tests are conducted. Figure 6a shows that the response of the actuator. When the input pressure is increased, the magnitude of force generated by the actuator also increases. At a pressure of 62 kPa, force as high 80 N is produced. We can see that, as the strain increases to the maximum, the force in all three pressure cases reduces to zero. The scaling of the forces for a given strain is nearly proportional to the pressure reinforcing observation noted in the analytical model.

4.3 Theoretical Results

We now utilise the model developed in Sect. 3 to calculate the actuation force at different strains and compare them to the experimental results. Figure 6b illustrates the force required by the actuator to create a specified strain for a given input pressure. As the strain increases to the maximum, the force decreases to zero linearly. This is qualitatively similar to the experimental results in Fig. 6a. The predicted values for the force are higher than the experimental values due to several reasons. We assume no pressure loss due to leakage while in the experiments, there is slight leakage from the seams and the actuator is considered to be made of an ideal cylinder and a cone that may deviate from the experiments.

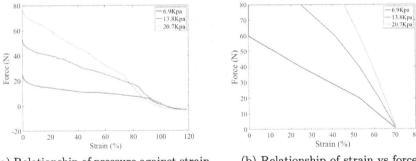

(a) Relationship of pressure against strain   (b) Relationship of strain vs force

Fig. 6. Performance of the actuator. (a) Measured force as a function of strain for different applied pressures.(b) Modelled Force as a function of strain for different applied pressures.

In a practical scenario, when the actuator is used as an artificial muscle, it sometimes needs to pull or push the constant load, for example, lift a mass suspended from the tip of the actuator. To model this scenario, the effect of the payload on the actuation strain at a given pressure in the previously discussed pressure range of 0–69 kPa with increments of 6.9 kPa, is calculated. Different loads ranging from no load to a load 30 N with increments 5 N are considered. Figure 7 shows the strain achieved as a function of pressure with different constant loads applied at the tip. This is analogous to the practical case in which a load is attached to the tip of a vertically aligned actuator and pressure is applied to the actuator to lift the load. We can see that when the load is small, the actuator can lift the load to its maximum stroke length at a low pressure. However, when the load is increased it requires higher pneumatic pressure to lift the load to its maximum strain level. The non-linear nature of the pressure-strain curve is attributed to the geometry of the actuator and the non-linear nature of change of the volume of the actuator with the tip displacement.

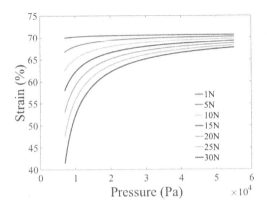

Fig. 7. Modelling result. Strain as a function of pressure for different applied constant loads.

5 Conclusion

The actuator based on the eversion of an inhomogeneous structure is presented in this paper. The inhomogeneous eversion actuator is capable of displacement up to 100% of its length from its original position. During the eversion and displacement of its tip, it can generate a significant payload. The actuator is constructed from fabric ensuring the actuator remains soft in nature. The inhomogeneous structure of the actuator is divided into two sections; the top portion which is initially folded inside is cylindrical in shape and everts from the bottom part which is conical in shape. Even made from soft material, this eversion based inhomogeneous actuator can fully actuate for a range of loads. A theoretical model to explain the mechanism of actuation is developed and the results are qualitatively consistent with the experiments. The actuator achieves a high force of 80 N at a low pressure of 62 kPa. In future work, this actuator will be integrated into articulated mechanisms to achieve low weight and high payload compliant robots.

Acknowledgment. This work was supported in part by the EPSRC National Centre for Nuclear Robotics project (EP/R02572X/1), the Innovate UK WormBot project (104059).

References

1. Hassan, A., Godaba, H., Althoefer, K.: Design analysis of a fabric based lightweight robotic gripper. In: Althoefer, K., Konstantinova, J., Zhang, K. (eds.) TAROS 2019. LNCS (LNAI), vol. 11649, pp. 16–27. Springer, Cham (2019). https://doi.org/10.1007/978-3-030-23807-0_2
2. Abrar, T., Putzu, F., Althoefer, K.: Soft wearable glove for tele-rehabilitation therapy of clenched hand/fingers patients. In: Annual Conference on New Technologies for Computer and Robot Assisted Surgery, pp. 93–94 (2018)
3. Putzu, F., Abrar, T., Althoefer, K.: Development of a soft inflatable structure with variable stiffness for hand rehabilitation. In: Annual Conference on New Technologies for Computer and Robot Assisted Surgery, pp. 103–104 (2018)
4. Coad, M.M., et al.: Vine robots: design, teleoperation, and deployment for navigation and exploration. arXiv preprint arXiv:1903.00069 (2019)
5. Luong, J., et al.: Eversion and retraction of a soft robot towards the exploration of coral reefs. In: 2019 2nd IEEE International Conference on Soft Robotics (RoboSoft), pp. 801–807. IEEE (2019)
6. Ataka, A., Stilli, A., Konstantinova, J., Wurdemann, H.A., Althoefer, K.: Kinematic control and obstacle avoidance for soft inflatable manipulator. In: Althoefer, K., Konstantinova, J., Zhang, K. (eds.) TAROS 2019. LNCS (LNAI), vol. 11649, pp. 52–64. Springer, Cham (2019). https://doi.org/10.1007/978-3-030-23807-0_5
7. Niiyama, R., Rus, D., Kim, S.: Pouch motors: printable/inflatable soft actuators for robotics. In: 2014 IEEE International Conference on Robotics and Automation (ICRA), pp. 6332–6337. IEEE (2014)
8. Tondu, B., Lopez, P.: The McKibben muscle and its use in actuating robot-arms showing similarities with human arm behaviour. Ind. Robot Int. J. **24**(6), 432–9 (1997)

9. Maghooa, F., Stilli, A., Noh, Y., Althoefer, K., Wurdemann, H.A.: Tendon and pressure actuation for a bio-inspired manipulator based on an antagonistic principle. In: 2015 IEEE International Conference on Robotics and Automation (ICRA), pp. 2556–2561. IEEE (2015)

10. Stilli, A., Wurdemann, H.A., Althoefer, K.: Shrinkable, stiffness-controllable soft manipulator based on a bio-inspired antagonistic actuation principle. In: 2014 IEEE/RSJ International Conference on Intelligent Robots and Systems, pp. 2476–2481. IEEE (2014)

11. Abrar, T.A., Putzu, F., Konstantinova, J., Althoefer, K.: EPAM: Eversive pneumatic artificial muscle. In: 2019 2nd IEEE International Conference on Soft Robotics (RoboSoft), pp. 19–24. IEEE (2019)

12. Hawkes, E.W., Blumenschein, L.H., Greer, J.D., Okamura, A.M.: A soft robot that navigates its environment through growth. Sci. Robot. **2**(8), eaan3028 (2017)

13. Cianchetti, M., et al.: Soft robotics technologies to address shortcomings in today's minimally invasive surgery: the STIFF-FLOP approach. Soft Robot. **1**(2), 122–31 (2014)

14. Hawkes, E.W., Christensen, D.L., Okamura, A.M.: Design and implementation of a 300% strain soft artificial muscle. In: 2016 IEEE International Conference on Robotics and Automation (ICRA), pp. 4022–4029. IEEE (2016)

15. Godaba, H., Putzu, F., Abrar, T., Konstantinova, J., Althoefer, K.: Payload capabilities and operational limits of eversion robots. In: Althoefer, K., Konstantinova, J., Zhang, K. (eds.) TAROS 2019. LNCS (LNAI), vol. 11650, pp. 383–394. Springer, Cham (2019). https://doi.org/10.1007/978-3-030-25332-5_33

16. Putzu, F., Abrar, T., Althoefer, K.: Plant-inspired soft pneumatic eversion robot. In: 2018 7th IEEE International Conference on Biomedical Robotics and Biomechatronics (BioRob), pp. 1327–1332. IEEE (2018)

Resistance Tuning of Soft Strain Sensor Based on Saline Concentration and Volume Changes

Joanna Jones[✉], Zachary Gillett, Eduardo Perez-Guagnelli, and Dana D. Damian[✉]

Automatic Control and Systems Engineering Department, University of Sheffield, Sheffield S1 3JD, UK
{jjones8,d.damian}@sheffield.ac.uk

Abstract. Soft sensors have a wide potential in augmenting the functionality of soft robots for healthcare, by providing information without compromising the mechanical compliance. Soft sensors that are based on ionic solutions are of particular interest, as they can be used for in-the-body medical applications due to their biocompatibility. In this paper, we present a soft strain sensor whose resistance is tuned by varying its volume and its ionic concentration. The study opens up the possibility of creating soft sensors whose electrical properties could be adjusted dynamically in fluidic soft robots, in order to suit specific tasks.

Keywords: Soft sensors · Ionic solution · Microfluidic channels

1 Introduction

Soft robots are being increasingly used in the medical field, with applications in surgery, wearables and implants [1–3]. With their inherent compliance and potential biocompatibility, they are ideal for interacting with the human body. Additionally, given the demands of healthcare technologies and the required accuracy, there is a clear need for soft sensors to increase the autonomy of soft robots without compromising their mechanical properties [4]. Extensive work on soft sensors capable of proprioception and/or pressure sensing based on synthesized conductive elastomers has been carried out [5]. There have also been recent developments in the use of ionic solutions and hydrogels, as equivalent and biocompatible conductive liquid for the sensors [6,7], thus getting closer to soft robots being implemented within the human body. The use of ionic solutions for sensing has been previously explored by investigating piezoresistive effect throughout elastomeric models. The effect of varying parameters such as the input AC frequency or concentration has been studied previously [7], but little work has been done on varying the volume within the same sensor. In this work, we present a soft strain sensor that can be embedded into soft actuators, such as shown in Fig. 1 [3]. We characterise its resistance for two different volumes of ionic solution and two different concentrations, demonstrating the potential to tailor the sensor depending on the range of motion to be detected.

© Springer Nature Switzerland AG 2020
A. Mohammad et al. (Eds.): TAROS 2020, LNAI 12228, pp. 49–52, 2020.
https://doi.org/10.1007/978-3-030-63486-5_5

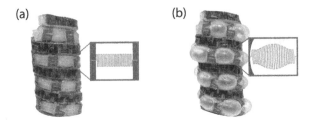

Fig. 1. Conceptual integration of the soft sensor in an implantable soft sensor for tubular tissue regeneration to sense strain/pressure on the tissue [3].

2 Materials and Methods

2.1 Fabrication

3D printed moulds printed on a Form2 3D printer were used to cast the soft sensor layers. These layers were made out of Ecoflex 00–30 (Smooth On Inc.), mixed using an ARE-250 Mixer (Thinky), degassed and then poured into the moulds curing at air temperature (Fig. 2). The Ecoflex was then post-cured in the oven for two hours at 80 °C and one hour at 100 °C. Finally, the sensor layers were bonded together using uncured Ecoflex 00–30, after which the ionic solution was injected and sealed using copper leads. The general dimensions of the sensor are $100 \times 30 \times 3$ mm, with a 1mm^2 cross-sectional area serpentine channel with an active area of 700 mm^2.

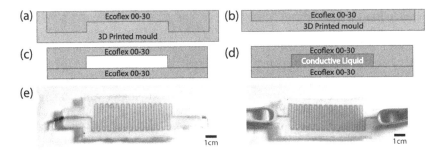

Fig. 2. Schematic of the major fabrication steps. (a) and (b) the layer with the channel and the top layer respectively are moulded and cured separately. (c) The layers are joined using uncured Ecoflex 00–30. (d) The ionic solution is injected. (e) and (f) Photo of the assembled sensor with 1 mL and 3 mL of ionic solution respectively.

2.2 Experimental Procedure

The sensor was tested under tension using a Zwick Roell Z020 tensile test machine at a speed of 20 mm/min. (Fig. 3). For the experiments, two different concentrations - 25% and 33% of NaCl to water by mass - and two different

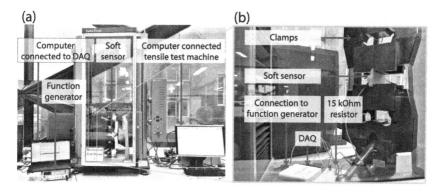

Fig. 3. Experimental Setup (a) Full setup. (b) Enlarged view of the soft sensor attached to the tensile test machine.

volumes - 1 mL and 3 mL - were tested. A 15k Ω resistor was connected in series with the soft sensor, and monitored using a NI USB-6009 DAQ board at a frequency of 2.4 kHz. The circuit was connected to a Gwinstek SFG-1013 function generator and supplied with a 1 V 1 kHz voltage sine wave.

The rectified voltage signals were filtered using a moving average with a window size of 240 points. The sensor resistance was then calculated using the voltage divider equation ($R_{sensor} = R_{15k\Omega} \times \frac{V_{supply} - V_{mes}}{V_{mes}}$).

3 Results

Figure 4 shows the average increase in resistance as the sensor was stretched to 20 mm for the baseline concentration of 33% and volume of 1 mL, as well as the increased volume of 3 mL and the decreased concentration of 25%.

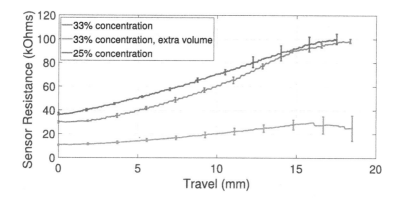

Fig. 4. Sensor resistance vs displacement for the three different testing conditions. The error bars represent one standard deviation across three trials.

The sensor with decreased concentration has a resistance of roughly $10\,k\Omega$ higher than the baseline sensor throughout the travel. The resistance for the sensor with increased volume is around a third of the resistance as the baseline sensor for the same travel.

4   Discussion

A decrease in the sensor resistance with increased volume is observed, as well as an increase in resistance when the concentration decreased. The decrease in resistivity for the increased volume is in accordance with Pouillet's law, which states resistance as inversely proportional to the cross-sectional area, although more work needs to be done to characterise this effect fully.

The large variation of resistance for an increased volume is also promising. With the resistance ideally equal to the series resistor, the sensor with increased volume would be more accurate for larger displacements, while the sensor with less volume would be more accurate for smaller displacements.

5   Conclusion and Future Work

We present and characterise a soft sensor to be integrated as the skin of soft implantable robots. The results in the study are promising and show a potential to tailor not only the concentration, but also the volume of ionic solution for the desired sensing range. As future work, we will investigate techniques to vary the liquid composition of the soft sensors to automatically tune its characteristics. This is desirable when the environment in which the soft robots operate changes.

References

1. Cianchetti, M., Laschi, C., Menciassi, A., Dario, P.: Biomedical applications of soft robotics. Nat. Rev. Mater. **3**(6), 143–153 (2018)
2. Perez-Guagnelli, E.R., et al.: Axially and radially expandable modular helical soft actuator for robotic implantables. In: 2018 IEEE International Conference on Robotics and Automation (ICRA), pp. 1–9. IEEE (2018)
3. Perez-Guagnelli, E., et al.: Characterization, simulation and control of a soft helical pneumatic implantable robot for tissue regeneration. In: IEEE Transactions on Medical Robotics and Bionics (2020)
4. Lai, Y.-C., et al.: Actively perceiving and responsive soft robots enabled by self-powered, highly extensible, and highly sensitive triboelectric proximity-and pressure-sensing skins. Adv. Mater. **30**(28), 1801114 (2018)
5. Wang, H., Totaro, M., Beccai, L.: Toward perceptive soft robots: Progress and challenges. Adv. Sci. **5**(9), 1800541 (2018)
6. Jing, X., et al.: Highly stretchable and biocompatible strain sensors based on mussel-inspired super-adhesive self-healing hydrogels for human motion monitoring. ACS Appl. Mater. Interfaces **10**(24), 20 897–20 909 (2018)
7. Helps, T., Rossiter, J.: Proprioceptive flexible fluidic actuators using conductive working fluids. Soft Robot. **5**(2), 175–189 (2018)

A Low Cost Series Elastic Actuator Test Bench

Oliver Smith[✉] and Swen E. Gaudl[✉] [iD]

School of Engineering, Computing and Mathematics, University of Plymouth,
Drake Circus, Plymouth PL4 8AA, UK
oliver.smith@students.plymouth.ac.uk, swen.gaudl@plymouth.ac.uk

Abstract. The concept of compliance relates to a robot's capability to exert, absorb, and measure forces acting on its joints. The existing research currently available for compliant actuators is promising, but prohibitively expensive, posing a fiscal entry barrier to research.

This paper presents a low cost Series Elastic Actuator test bench, as an initial work towards a modular compliant actuator toolkit (MCAT).

Keywords: Compliance · Variable stiffness · Series elastic actuator · Robotics

1 Introduction

Traditionally, robots are of a rigid body design, where a motor is directly connected to a joint, to control its position. This makes them capable of repeatable precision, ideal for manufacturing applications. Compliant actuators differ in their ability to control both the position and the stiffness of a joint, which unlike rigid body robots, makes them more suitable for operating in a shared human-robot workspace. Different concepts feature different capabilities, including as impact absorption, energy storage, and natural motion generation [11].

To allow for further experimentation and exploration of this domain, we present our work on a series elastic actuator (SEA) test bench. For a wider engagement and to offer an entry point into the research domain, the test bench design will be made available online. Based on this, we then present our first steps towards a novel modular compliant actuator toolkit aimed for the usage in research as well as robotics education, before concluding the paper.

2 Background

In this section, we outline different approaches towards compliant actuators which motivate our work. On the topic of compliance methods in this paper, torque-sensing and virtual stiffness control is the only method to be considered mature and has been since 2008. By using a torque sensor to measure the force acting on a joint, and a sufficiently fast motor and controller, it is possible for

© Springer Nature Switzerland AG 2020
A. Mohammad et al. (Eds.): TAROS 2020, LNAI 12228, pp. 53–57, 2020.
https://doi.org/10.1007/978-3-030-63486-5_6

a joint to respond fast enough to mimic the properties of a joint with a desired "virtual" stiffness [4]. No physical elastic element exists in the system, and thus there is no spring constant to be modified. Regarding control theory, a PID (proportional integral derivative) controller, with a set position and target stiffness suffices, a method also known as equilibrium stiffness control [5].

The technique was pioneered by the German Aerospace Center (DLR) during the 2000s [6,13], has been commercialised by Kuka [2], and features in the leg mechanisms of many quadrupeds, with high bandwidth systems allowing them to respond to impacts and exert force [12]. Virtual stiffness control is comparatively easy to implement, but without a physical element, robots are denied many of the advantages of biological compliance, energy conservation, and explosive motions.

The concept of a series elastic actuator is straightforward. By placing a spring between the driving stiff actuator and the driven output joint, the force exerted on the spring can be measured. Equilibrium stiffness control is limited by the stiffness of the spring, but potential benefits include impact absorption and energy storage, as well as force control [8].

A series elastic actuator with a sufficiently soft spring can be used to absorb impacts in real-time with minimal computation, and to store and release energy. However, softer springs limit the bandwidth of the actuator, mandating faster motor and controller. This limitation spurred research towards torque sensing.

Variable stiffness actuators (VSAs) differ from prior methods in their ability to modulate the stiffness constant of a physical elastic element, such as a spring or tendon. Many methods to control the stiffness constant exist: the spring transmission ratio, structure controlled stiffness, and mechanically controlled stiffness. Further concepts such as agonist-antagonist non-linear spring pairs and artificial muscles also exist [7], but are beyond the scope of this early work [3,11,12].

The existing research in the domain consists almost entirely of one-off manufacturing [1], with compliance concepts designed either as part of the mechanical structure of the robot's arms, legs or other joints [13], or only as a bench test rig [9]. Much of the work from the previously described methods requires custom CNC machined parts, top-quality motors, sensors and computing parts. It follows then, that the existing research is prohibitively expensive to replicate. This problem compounds, in making it harder still to iterate ideas, make direct comparisons or investigate applications on the technology.

3   Series Elastic Actuator Test Bench

To reduce the entry burden into compliance research through lower production costs, a test bench of a series elastic actuator (SEA) is presented, see Fig. 1.

Out of the previously described compliance methods, the SEA was chosen for its design simplicity, which serves as our foundation for future work. This section outlines the SEA design & control and discusses manufacturing observations.

Design: A driving servo motor is connected in series to a compression spring, which in turn is connected to a driven output joint, as illustrated in Fig. 2. An encoder reads the output joint position, and by measuring the difference between

Fig. 1. SEA Test Bench: featuring the output encoder joint, spur and rack gearing, compression spring in series, and driving servo joint.

the two joints, the compression force acting on the spring can be determined using Hooke's Law.

All parts which were not purchased are 3D printed, with design tolerance included in the CAD models. The Fusion360 spur gear generator was used with a rack tooth pitch of 6.28 mm derived from (Eq. 1). The Servo moment $m_t = 0.12$ kg/cm is calculated for a given servo (10.1 kg/cm at 6 V) and gear of radius of 0.012 m using (Eq. 2). Next, the moment is converted from kg/cm to a torque estimate in N/m of $m_t = 0.99$ N/m. Finally, we rearrange for the linear force F = 82.5 N using (Eq. 3).

Based on this max linear force estimate, an optimum spring is chosen. The rs 121–157 datasheet specifies a load of 85.42 N at minimum length, which closely matches the derived linear force estimate. A spring with greater deflection (rs 121–242) was considered, as a greater displacement would best visualise the SEA, but would be liable to buckle under compression unless incorporated into a piston.

$$Pitch_{Rackteeth} = \pi/Diameter_{Pitch} \tag{1}$$

$$m_t = 10.1 \, kg/cm * radius_{gear} \tag{2}$$

$$Force = Moment/distance_{perpendicular} \tag{3}$$

Equilibrium Control: The ams5601 encoder is used for its high counts per revolution (2048), easy to use I^2C interface, and frictionless measurement of rotation from a radial magnet. A Nucleo-F429ZI microcontroller is used to implement PID equilibrium controlled stiffness of the SEA (*with its 180 Mhz CPU it is not capable of real-time virtual stiffness control*).

3.1   SEA Test Bench Observations

The following consists of observations made during the design, manufacture and testing of the SEA test bench. It serves to inform the design of future work.

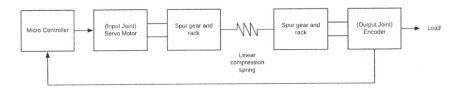

Fig. 2. SEA Test Bench block diagram

Smaller shafts, approximate to that of the motor shaft, should be used. The 8 mm shafts are excessive and add inertia. Smaller shafts would also reduce the overall size, cost, and manufacturing difficulty. Steel shafts of 4 mm can be cut by hand with a junior hacksaw, 8 mm shafts cannot.

3D printing for structural supports and gears is viable. 3D printing for exact tolerances is not viable. So, while the rotational shafts free spin in their bearings the linear slide blocks do not glide without friction, as a result of the two linear shafts being out of alignment, itself caused by manufacturing deviations of the printed linear rail mounts. A linear rail guide rail should also be considered. Typically linear guide rails and carriages are more expensive, but low cost parts are available and should be tested.

The spur gear teeth profile size was too large, resulting in backlash that negated the otherwise reliable precision of the sensor. In the future, helical gears with smaller teeth will remedy this. When accounting for this imprecision, the test bench is able to accurately estimate spring compression forces and can control for a desired stiffness setting.

Non-backdrivability of the input joint is a common requirement for control schemes to measure the force exerted on the spring. In practice, a worm screw is typically used to achieve this non-backdrivability [10]. Sans worm screw, and when a force overcomes the stall torque of the servo, and the force applied becomes two components; spring deflection, and input joint position error. This feature should be included in future as an option for different use cases.

4 Future Work

The series elastic actuator test bench is the first milestone towards the development of a low cost modular compliant actuator toolkit (MCAT). The MCAT concept trades size and material quality in favour of manufacturing cost, and facilitates easy reconfiguration and modification, for the experimentation of a wide variety of variable stiffness concepts. The MCAT is intended for a variety of use cases such as the integration into the knee joint of bipedal humanoid robots, research into the design and application of different variable stiffness actuator (VSA) concepts. To allow for wider dissemination, the project files are to be made freely available for the robotics community. The first MCAT prototype should be designed as an optimisation of the SEA test bench, realising a series elastic actuator in a low cost and easy to use unit.

5   Conclusion

In this paper, the need for a low cost compliant actuator is identified, for use in academic research and education. We present a series elastic actuator test bench that is used to help inform design choices for future work, towards a modular compliant actuator toolkit. This work is offered to the robotics community during these early stages of development to garner feedback that will guide the direction of future work.

References

1. Bicchi, A., Tonietti, A., Bavaro, M., Piccigallo, M.: Variable stiffness actuators for fast and safe motion control. IEEE/ASME Trans. Mechatron. **15**(2), 1 (2005)
2. Gainsford, P.: KUKA.ForceTorqueControl 3.0. KUKA Roboter GmbH, KUKA Roboter GmbH, Zugspitzstraße 140, D-86165 Augsburg, Germany, 2 edn. (2013). an optional note
3. Grioli, G.: Variable stiffness actuators: The user's point of view
4. Hemati, N., Thorp, J.S., Leu, M.C.: Robust nonlinear control of brushless dc motors for direct-drive robotic applications. IEEE Trans. Ind. Electron. **37**(6), 460–468 (1990)
5. Hernández-Guzmán, V.M., Santibáñez, V., Campa, R.: PID control of robot manipulators equipped with brushless DC motors. Robotica **27**(2), 225–233 (2009). https://doi.org/10.1017/S026357470800461X
6. Hirzinger, G., Albu-Schaffer, A., Hahnle, M., Schaefer, I., Sporer, N.: On a new generation of torque controlled light-weight robots. In: Proceedings 2001 ICRA. IEEE International Conference on Robotics and Automation (Cat. No.01CH37164), vol. 4, pp. 3356–3363 (2001)
7. Petit, F., Friedl, W., Höppner, H., Grebenstein, M.: Analysis and synthesis of the bidirectional antagonistic variable stiffness mechanism. Robotics Research. The Eleventh International Symposium. Springer Tracts in Advanced Robotics 20(2), 684–695 (2015)
8. Pratt, G.A., Williamson, M.M.: Series elastic actuators. In: Proceedings 1995 IEEE/RSJ International Conference on Intelligent Robots and Systems. Human Robot Interaction and Cooperative Robots, vol. 1, pp. 399–406. IEEE (1995)
9. Savin, S.: Control system design for two link robot arm with MACCEPA 2.0 variable stiffness actuators
10. Sugar, T.G.: A novel selective compliant actuator. Mechatronics **12**(9–10), 1157–1171 (2002)
11. Van Ham, R.: Compliant actuator designs. IEEE Robot. Autom. Mag. **16**(3), 81–94 (2009)
12. Vanderborght, B.: Variable impedance actuators: a review
13. Wolf, S.: Soft robotics with variable stiffness actuators: tough robots for soft human robot interaction. Soft Rob. **12**(9–10), 1157–1171 (2015)

Shape Reconstruction of Soft-Body Manipulator: A Learning-Based Approach

Ivan Vitanov[✉], Ataka Rizqi, and Kaspar Althoefer

ARQ, School of Electronic Engineering and Computer Science,
Queen Mary University of London, London, UK
i.vitanov@qmul.ac.uk

Abstract. This work explores the use of machine learning to model the curvature of a soft-body continuum robot. Because of their compliant structures, such robots are subject to strains and deformations that are uncharacteristic of their rigid-body counterparts, giving rise to infinite degrees of freedom. Traditional modelling approaches as applied to rigid manipulators – based on Euler-Bernoulli beam theory – are therefore not quite adequate to the task of modelling soft continuum manipulators. Equally, most alternative approaches that have been tried are predicated on the constant curvature assumption, which suffers from limiting assumptions. To enhance model flexibility, we apply a Bayesian learning technique, namely the Gaussian process, for interpolating soft-robot shape from sparse data.

Keywords: Soft robots · Shape estimation · Gaussian process

1 Soft Continuum Manipulators

Soft robotic manipulators are steadily gaining in popularity, as they confer greater inbuilt flexibility and adaptability and can mimic the range of motions characteristic of some aquatic and reptilian organisms. They further have the potential to increase safety in human-robot interaction settings. Such robots are typically constructed from compliant materials, such as flexible fabrics and synthetic polymers. This renders them more lightweight – and often quicker and cheaper to produce and maintain; through, for example, 3-D printing of many of their component parts.

The robot testbed used in this study is an inflatable robotic manipulator developed at Queen Mary, University of London. Designated WormBot (Fig. 1), it has built-in inflatable chambers which, when inflated/deflated, allow a degree of control over the robot's articulation, pose and position [1]. The WormBot is not limited to only lateral or vertical movement; it is also capable of eversion, or varying its length by means of extending its structure using pneumatic pressure.

© Springer Nature Switzerland AG 2020
A. Mohammad et al. (Eds.): TAROS 2020, LNAI 12228, pp. 58–61, 2020.
https://doi.org/10.1007/978-3-030-63486-5_7

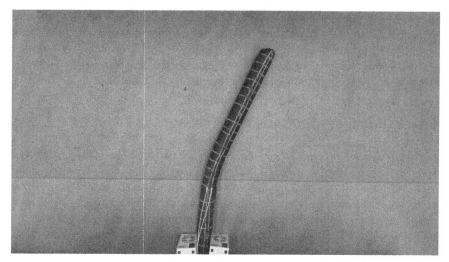

Fig. 1. The WormBot manipulator, showing pressure applied to one of the chambers of a single bending section. Red markers on its visible surface are used for motion capture and acquisition of position information. The length of the manipulator was fixed during the experimental trials carried out, although the WormBot is capable of varying its length by eversion from the tip. (Color figure online)

We wish to perform kinematic modelling of this class of soft manipulators exhibiting continuum behaviour by reconstructing the WormBot's pose using a small set of unevenly spaced sample points. Shape reconstruction from sensory or simulated data, be it noted, is a prerequisite to a full kinematic analysis of a soft robot; we do not, however, attempt the latter within the scope of this study. Put another way, shape modelling provides a lower dimensional parameterisation of the shape of an otherwise infinite dimensional soft continuum robot.

In taking a learning approach to reconstructing the curvature of the WormBot, we first obtain a finite set of discrete observations using visible markers on the robot's body – contained within the field of view of an imaging system. We are interested in fitting a 'backbone' curve that condenses the macroscopic curvature of the WormBot, when constrained to a 2-D plane. The backbone curve can be parameterised in terms of bending angles of the soft robot segments or by a function representation.

The hyper-redundancy of continuum robots, i.e. virtually limitless degrees of freedom, necessitates the adoption of modelling paradigms other than those employed for closed-form kinematic modelling of rigid manipulators. By corollary, there is an increased degree of difficulty in implementing control routines for soft robots as compared to the control of rigid manipulators. Different approaches to shape reconstruction have been reported in the literature: arc-geometric methods under a constant curvature assumption, (deep) neural networks for either modelling or control, various parametric curves such as B-splines and cubic Hermite splines, although the piecewise constant curvature (PCC) model is by far the commonest [2]. The latter, however, is not equipped to handle non-constant curvature deformations, as its name suggests.

Being able to model the shape of the manipulator would subsequently allow for the derivation of an inverse kinematic model; namely, the combinations of actuating pressures needed to be applied to the pneumatic chambers in order to move the structure into desired configurations. For example, we might wish to manoeuvre an effector part of the structure to a specific point in 2-D (or potentially 3-D space).

2   Pose Estimation with Gaussian Processes

We apply Bayesian non-linear regression with Gaussian processes (GP) to interpolating soft-robot shape from sparse data, allowing the modelling of non-constant curvature deformations and potential extensions to state space models. Moreover, the proposed technique can be seen as a generalisation of some existing approaches: splines for example can be treated as a special case of Gaussian processes.

A GP represents a distribution over a space of functions, as opposed to a vector space, and yields a probabilistic model in the Bayesian framework that can be used for regression and interpolation of observed data [3]. GPs have seen wide use in system identification in, e.g., signal estimation, non-linear spatial models, and state–space modelling. The output of a GP gives the full predictive distribution rather than merely a point estimate, permitting confidence bands or intervals to be calculated from pointwise estimates of the variance. GPs represent a compromise between models that are too rigid to describe

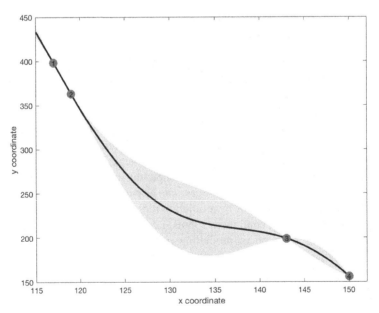

Fig. 2. A WormBot pose modelled with a Gaussian process regression model. The solid red circles represent the markers visible on the surface of the WormBot in Fig. 1. Markers are numbered serially in ascending order from base to tip. The mean pose prediction of the Gaussian process is shown as a solid line; the grey filled-in region represents a confidence interval comprising 2σ error bars computed from the posterior distribution. (Color figure online)

the behaviour of interest, when only a limited data record is on hand, and those that are too flexible and likely to overfit in this scenario.

A GP possesses a systematic way to encode prior knowledge and assumptions; in this way the flexibility of the model can be tuned. It also benefits from built-in regularisation, i.e. there is automatic handling of the bias-variance trade-off [3]. Smoothness and non-constant curvature assumptions are enforced via a Bayesian prior to the Gaussian process and its covariance function.

Figures 2, 3 display results of the GP method being applied to estimate the curvature of WormBot poses. The developed approach enables accurate shape reconstruction from visual data, even for non-constant deformations. Both the shape of the soft actuator and the uncertainty of the function fitted can be approximated in this way.

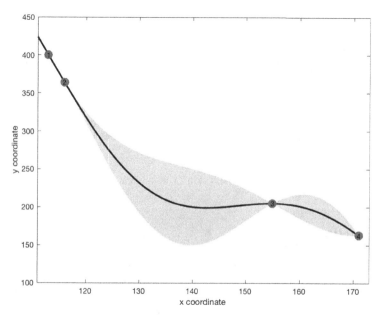

Fig. 3. Another WormBot pose modelled with a Gaussian process. As in Fig. 2, points corresponding to markers on the trunk of the WormBot are indicated by solid circles (with red fill) inscribed with their respective (serial) number. Mean prediction and error bars are shown. (Color figure online)

References

1. Ataka, A., Abrar, A., Putzu, F., Godaba, H., Althoefer, K.: Model-based pose control of inflatable eversion robot with variable stiffness. IEEE Robot. Autom. Letters, **5**(2), 3398–3405 (2020)
2. Wiese, M., Rüstmann, K., Raatzl, A.: Kinematic modeling of a soft pneumatic actuator using cubic hermite splines. In: IEEE/RSJ International Conference on Intelligent Robots and Systems (IROS), pp. 7176–7182. Macau, China (2019)
3. Williams, C.K., Rasmussen, C.E.: Gaussian Processes for Machine Learning. MIT press, Cambridge (2006)

Silicone Based Capacitive E-Skin Sensor for Soft Surgical Robots

Abu Bakar Dawood[1]([✉]), Hareesh Godaba[2], and Kaspar Althoefer[2]

[1] Centre for Advanced Robotics @ Queen Mary, School of Engineering and Materials Science, Queen Mary University of London, London E1 4NS, UK
a.dawood@qmul.ac.uk

[2] Centre for Advanced Robotics @ Queen Mary, School of Electronics Engineering and Computer Science, Queen Mary University of London, London E1 4NS, UK

Abstract. In this extended abstract, we present a soft stretchable multi-modal capacitive skin sensor that can be used for exteroception and proprioception in soft surgical manipulators. A soft skin prototype was made using Ecoflex, embedding three conductive carbon grease terminal layers. This soft skin is capable of measuring stretch and touch simultaneously. The soft skin measures uniaxial stretches from 1 to 1.2475 within an error range of 2.6% and can also quantify as well as localize local indentation. An algorithm is developed that decouples local change, i.e., due to indentation, from global strain, due to stretch. An experimental study was conducted; results are presented.

Keywords: Capacitive sensing · Soft skin · Soft surgical robots

1 Introduction

Soft robots, because of their compliance, have a huge potential to be used in Minimally Invasive Surgery (MIS). Their soft structure and variable stiffness allow them to be used in contact with vital organs, without causing any serious damage [1, 2]. However, the compliance of a soft robot, because of its infinite number of degrees of freedom, becomes a challenge when the pose of the robot is to be determined. Apart from proprioception measuring the robot's pose, the interaction of soft robots with the environment or external stimuli is equally important. A soft robot, having a sense of its own position and capability to detect contact with the environment, is important for better control of the robot.

For exteroception, capacitive [3, 4] and resistive [5, 6] methods have been used extensively. Larson et al. [3] studied the effects of stretch and internal pressure on the capacitance of soft capacitive array. However, the capacitance is dependent upon both the pressure and stretch. This coupling between different stimuli has been overlooked.

To detect more than one stimulus simultaneously, different combinations of sensors have been devised, employing different sensing technologies [7–11]. However, the idea of multi-modality in soft and stretchable sensors has not been fully explored.

We present a multi modal soft capacitive skin, that is stretchable and highly compliant and can be integrated into the periphery of a surgical soft manipulator such as the

© Springer Nature Switzerland AG 2020
A. Mohammad et al. (Eds.): TAROS 2020, LNAI 12228, pp. 62–65, 2020.
https://doi.org/10.1007/978-3-030-63486-5_8

STIFF FLOP manipulator [1, 2] providing feedback on its pose and interaction with the environment for better control during surgery. When the skin is stretched, there is a global change in capacitance, however when a force is applied at a particular point, only a local change would be induced [12]. We propose a decoupling algorithm to distinguish the global sensor stretch from the localised point of force application. Our future work includes quantification of the force applied on a point and application of this skin by wrapping it around a soft robotic actuator.

2   Materials and Methods

The material used for the fabrication of our capacitive sensor is Ecoflex 00-30. Moulds for the curing of the Ecoflex sensor layers were 3D printed on an Ultimaker3 3D printer using PLA. Our sensor consists of 4 silicone layers with a thickness of 0.5 mm each and 3 carbon grease electrode layers, i.e., electrode along X, Y and ground respectively, printed in between these silicone layers.

An experimental setup for stretching was designed using an M8 lead screw driven by a SUNCOR stepper motor. A holder with holes to accommodate for the terminals connecting capacitive skin to the external circuitry, was 3D printed. The capacitance of array sensor was measured using a CAV 424 measurement device by Analog Microelectronics and fed to an Arduino. The X and Y-terminals were connected to the CAV 424 using two 16-1 Multiplexers, which were switched periodically to record the capacitance of the 10 X and 10 Y terminals.

The unstretched length of our soft skin was 101 mm and it was stretched from $\lambda = 1$ to $\lambda = 1.2475$, at increments of 5 mm. A 3D printed spherical indenter of 5 mm diameter was used for the indentation of the sensor to the following depths: 0 mm, 5 mm and 10 mm, respectively. The experimental setup is shown in Fig. 1.

Fig. 1. a) Shows the exploded view of the skin, with x, y terminals and ground encapsulated in Ecoflex layers. b) Shows complete experimental setup showing the clamped skin sensor, the mechanism for stretching and the associated sensor signal acquisition circuitry.

Figure 2 explains the algorithm used for decoupling stretch and indentation. Percentage change in the capacitance values of the 10 horizontal terminals are multiplied by the percentage changes of the 10 vertical terminals to obtain a 10×10 node-matrix. Four heuristic points are defined on the diagonal. The peak value and its coordinates are identified and the distances of peak node from the selected diagonal points are calculated. The two diagonal points having the maximum distance from the peak node are taken into consideration and the corresponding terminals are used to calculate stretch. Average of these two stretches is taken and the data is plotted.

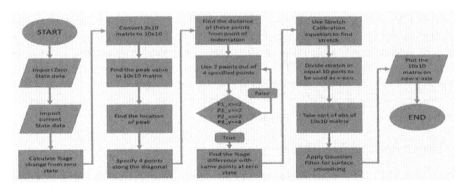

Fig. 2. Flow chart of MATLAB algorithm used for decoupling local indentation and global stretch.

3   Results

The sensor skin was stretched while at the same time indentations of different depths were applied. Each state data set was then processed by the algorithm programmed in MATLAB to compute the global stretch. Figure 3 shows two of the datasets processed by using the algorithm. The Y-axis shows the computed stretch while the peak at the point (6, 6) in Fig. 2a represents the point of indentation. The point of indentation in Fig. 2b is (3, 8) while the calculated stretch is 1.

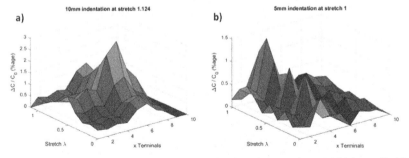

Fig. 3. a) Shows 10 mm indentation at point (6,6) when the stretch = 1.124 is applied by the motor. b) Shows 5 mm indentation at (3,8) when stretch is 1.

4   Conclusion

The algorithm shows promising results in decoupling global stretch and local indentation. For the investigated cases, a maximum of 2.6% error was found between the applied stretch and the calculated stretch. Our capacitive skin sensor has shown promising results and future work will include the measurement of the force applied instead of only the location of the indentation. Further, we plan to apply the skin sensor on a soft robot, such as the STIFF FLOP manipulator [1, 2] for sensing the states of deformation and applied external forces for applications in minimal invasive surgery.

References

1. Fraś, J., Czarnowski, J., Macias, M., Główka, J.: Static modeling of multisection soft continuum manipulator for stiff-flop project. In: Szewczyk, R., Zieliński, C., Kaliczyńska, M. (eds.) Recent Advances in Automation, Robotics and Measuring Techniques. AISC, vol. 267, pp. 365–375. Springer, Cham (2014). https://doi.org/10.1007/978-3-319-05353-0_35

2. Cianchetti, M., et al.: Soft robotics technologies to address shortcomings in today's minimally invasive surgery: the stiff-flop approach. Soft Robot. (2014). https://doi.org/10.1089/soro.2014.0001

3. Larson, C., et al.: Highly stretchable electroluminescent skin for optical signaling and tactile sensing. Science **80** (2016). https://doi.org/10.1126/science.aac5082

4. Kim, S.Y., Park, S., Park, H.W., Park, D.H., Jeong, Y., Kim, D.H.: Highly sensitive and multimodal all-carbon skin sensors capable of simultaneously detecting tactile and biological stimuli. Adv. Mater. (2015). https://doi.org/10.1002/adma.201501408

5. Park, J., et al.: Giant tunneling piezoresistance of composite elastomers with interlocked microdome arrays for ultrasensitive and multimodal electronic skins. ACS Nano (2014). https://doi.org/10.1021/nn500441k

6. Wang, T., et al.: A self-healable, highly stretchable, and solution processable conductive polymer composite for ultrasensitive strain and pressure sensing. Adv. Funct. Mater. (2018). https://doi.org/10.1002/adfm.201705551

7. Ho, D.H., Sun, Q., Kim, S.Y., Han, J.T., Kim, D.H., Cho, J.H.: Stretchable and multimodal all graphene electronic skin. Adv. Mater. (2016). https://doi.org/10.1002/adma.201505739

8. Hua, Q., et al.: Skin-inspired highly stretchable and conformable matrix networks for multifunctional sensing. Nat. Commun. (2018). https://doi.org/10.1038/s41467-017-02685-9

9. Maiolino, P., Maggiali, M., Cannata, G., Metta, G., Natale, L.: A flexible and robust large scale capacitive tactile system for robots. IEEE Sens. J. (2013). https://doi.org/10.1109/JSEN.2013.2258149

10. Wall, V., Zoller, G., Brock, O.: A method for sensorizing soft actuators and its application to the RBO hand 2. In: Proceedings - IEEE International Conference on Robotics and Automation (2017). https://doi.org/10.1109/icra.2017.7989577

11. Totaro, M., Mondini, A., Bellacicca, A., Milani, P., Beccai, L.: Integrated simultaneous detection of tactile and bending cues for soft robotics. Soft Robot. (2017). https://doi.org/10.1089/soro.2016.0049

12. Dawood, A.B., Godaba, H., Althoefer, K.: Modelling of a soft sensor for exteroception and proprioception in a pneumatically actuated soft robot. In: Althoefer, K., Konstantinova, J., Zhang, K. (eds.) TAROS 2019. LNCS (LNAI), vol. 11650, pp. 99–110. Springer, Cham (2019). https://doi.org/10.1007/978-3-030-25332-5_9

Soft Hinge for Magnetically Actuated Millimetre-Size Origami

Quentin Lahondes$^{(\boxtimes)}$ and Shuhei Miyashita

Automatic Control and Systems Engineering Department,
The University of Sheffield, Portobello Ln, Sheffield S1 3JD, UK
{qmplahondes1,shuhei.miyashita}@sheffield.ac.uk

Abstract. Origami-inspired folding techniques are widely applied in the fabrication and actuation of micro- and milli-robots and systems. While soft materials exhibit curved deformation when an external stimulus is applied, implementation of hinges effectively produces sharp edges in the structure. This paper presents the fabrication of millimetre size foldable elastomeric structures, the anisotropic magnetization method of the structure and the remote actuation method using a magnetic field. We specifically focused on the effect of hinges, whose presence resulted in the magnetically induced folding angle of $90 \pm 0.74°$, whereas the absence resulted in the angle of $63.9 \pm 0.93°$.

Keywords: Soft miniature origami · Magnetic folding · Soft lithography

1 Introduction

Sub-centimetre fabrication of soft complex 3D structures has been an engineering challenge due to the infinite degrees-of-freedom and the difficulty of accessing the small space. As a substitute method for the fabrication of soft 3D structures, origami-inspired folding techniques [7] coupled with physical stimuli-sensitive materials show an advantage in attaining an instantaneous deformation through self-folding. The common approach is to use materials that are sensitive to temperature [2,6] and magnetism [1,3–5]. Despite the fact that the fabrication of a soft controllable hinges is desirable, the number of related studies is limited. One solution was proposed by Kim et al. [3] where elastomeric hinges were made passive, but its folding motion was induced by applying opposed torques to the bodies connected via the hinge. Each entity has a unique magnetic isotropy and when an external magnetic field is applied, the connected parts rotate at preprogrammed directions according to their magnetisations and field orientation. Similarly, a magnetically induced folding motion using the magnetic anisotropy was proposed in Hu et al. [1]. Their approaches use constant thickness monolithic film to perform folding motions. They demonstrated movement on and

Supported by Automatic Control and Systems Engineering Department, The University of Sheffield.

© Springer Nature Switzerland AG 2020
A. Mohammad et al. (Eds.): TAROS 2020, LNAI 12228, pp. 66–69, 2020.
https://doi.org/10.1007/978-3-030-63486-5_9

under water, on solid and in constrained environments. The realisation of a sharp angle and the structural rigidity when folded still remain as challenges. Through thickness variations, the origami could enable manipulation by matching the shape of an object. Adding hinges could facilitate the folding of structures into polyhedra, where a uniform deformation could not. Magnetically actuated soft milli-origami could grab millimetric size objects, realise cargo functions or drug delivery applications. In this work, we focused on the effect of varying the thickness of elastomeric film within the same body on their folding angles. We also developed a method of soft lithography where two designs of thick soft magnetic structures were moulded in batches of four. We further implemented a magnetisation method to realize the anisotropy in the body. This way, the different regions of the planar structure become responsive to magnetic field inputs and induce a coordinated folding motion. We demonstrated the self-folding motion with two designs, one with hinges realised through thickness variations of the body, and one without. Finally, we investigated the difference in folding angles of the two structures.

2 Design and Fabrication Process

To obtain the soft magnetic-sensitive material, Ecoflex-0010 was chosen for its flexible properties and Neodymium-Iron-Boron powder was used for its high coercivity. The powder has an initial average-diameter of $500\,\mu m$ and was then ground to $120 \pm 54\,\mu m$ (81 samples), using a smooth marble mortar and pestle. First, the two parts of the Ecoflex-0010 was manually mixed for 30 s. Then, the magnetic powder was added with a 3 : 2 ratio before being mixed again for 30 s as Fig. 1(a) depicts. Second, to eliminate air bubbles, the mixture was put into a desiccator for 3 min. Finally, the composite was deposited onto the moulds, scraped using a razor blade and left to cure for 12 h as seen in Fig. 1(b)). The moulds used are shown in Fig. 1(c) and are made of clear resin in an SLA 3D printer. The moulds produce two different designs in batches of 4. The origami are shaped like crosses made up of 5 panels: 2.5 mm long and wide and 0.3 mm high. Design 1 has hinges of 0.3 mm long and 0.15 mm thick, whereas Design 2 has no hinges. In Hu et al. [1], a laser is used to cut the shape. The local increase of temperature from the laser may induce internal strains in the material and affects

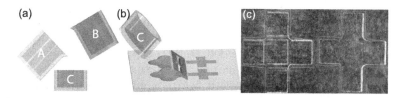

Fig. 1. (a) Mixing of Ecoflex-0010 (A), magnetic particles (B) and the mixing cup (C). (b) Pouring, scraping and curing of the composite. (c) Picture of the two moulds made of Clear Resin in a SLA 3D printer. Scale bar is 2.5 mm.

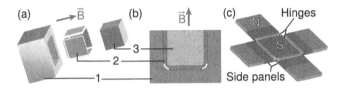

Fig. 2. (a) To give the origami a box shape under a magnetic field, the folded origami (2) was placed inside the holder (1), constrained by the lid (3) and then, magnetized by the field B. (b) The assembly cut view. (c) The resulting magnetization.

the shape of the structure. The moulding has the advantage of not exposing the material to unexpected consequences. However, due to the thin nature of the origami, removing them from the moulds is difficult as there is a high risk of tearing. After being removed from the mould, the structure was placed in a SLA 3D printed cube container to tune the magnetization profile. As seen in Fig. 2(a), the container (1) is a hollow cube that can hold the folded origami (2) so that the inner of the hollow cube is in full contact with the outer of the origami. The lid-cube (3) is placed to constrain the structures prohibiting its random motion. To magnetize the origami, the hollow cube and its contents are placed, for 5 s, between two 1.3 T magnets oriented upward. This causes the structures to be polarized as seen in Fig. 2(b). The developed process exposes the material to repeated manipulation using tweezers which can cause indentation and surface damage.

3   Experiment

The aim of the experiment is to demonstrate how hinges impact the curvature of soft materials. To do so, a 204 mm wide coil was placed horizontally actuating the origami situated 40 mm above with a 5.85 mT magnetic field. The field's intensity is kept constant and actuates the origami in the motion loop seen in Fig. 3. The loop comprises 4 steps of 5 s long. To achieve the movement an upward magnetic field was applied for 5 s, followed by its removal for another 5 s. Then this was repeated with a downwards magnetic field. The Ecoflex adheres strongly to the acrylic sheet used as a workspace. As a result, when laid on the workspace, the origami will not fold and maintain full contact with the acrylic, even with the coil at full power. To give free motion to the side-panels, the origami is balanced at the edge of a tweezer with its side-panels hanging. Due to the mobility given by the hinges, the origami's magnetization brought together the front and back side-panels as seen in Fig. 3(b). The left panel is supported by the tweezer and the right panel is hanging for free motion. The initial deflection of the panel is due to gravity only. When the upward field is applied, the side-panels of the cross-shape origami rise from initial position to fold into a box shape. Once the magnetic field is removed, it returns to its initial position. This is mirrored when the downward field is applied. Figure 3(a) and (d) show the angle obtained between the base of the cross and the end of the curvature when an upward

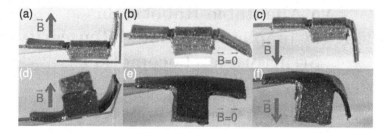

Fig. 3. (a) The upward position of the hinged design achieving 90° of folding. (b) The resting state without magnetic field. (c) Downward position. (d) The upward magnetic field bends the design without hinges at 63.5°. (e) The resting state. (f) Downward position.

magnetic field is applied. The hinge structure achieved an average folding angle of $90 \pm 0.74°$ over three trials, while the structure without hinges presented a curve with an angle of $63.9 \pm 0.93°$.

4   Conclusion

In this study, we developed a magnetically actuated soft self-folding origami. By varying the thickness and magnetization within the structure, we managed to induce folding motions of multiple hinges rotating about different axes. The structure was made using a batch process of soft lithography technique where the variation of thickness was adjusted by the design of 3D printed moulds. The future work includes modeling of the deformation depending on the thickness variation, intensity of the magnetic field and validating the model with various designs and experiments and self-folding of further complex structures.

References

1. Hu, W., Lum, G.Z., Mastrangeli, M., Sitti, M.: Small-scale soft-bodied robot with multimodal locomotion. Nature **554**(7690), 81–85 (2018)
2. Iwata, Y., Miyashita, S., Iwase, E.: Self-rolling up micro 3D structures using temperature-responsive hydrogel sheet. J. Micromech. Microeng. **27**(12), 124003 (2017)
3. Kim, J., Chung, S.E., Choi, S.E., Lee, H., Kim, J., Kwon, S.: Programming magnetic anisotropy in polymeric microactuators. Nat. Mater. **10**(10), 747–752 (2011)
4. Kim, Y., Yuk, H., Zhao, R., Chester, S.A., Zhao, X.: Printing ferromagnetic domains for untethered fast-transforming soft materials. Nature **558**, 274–279 (2018)
5. Li, Y., et al.: Origami NdFeB flexible magnetic membranes with enhanced magnetism and programmable sequences of polarities. Adv. Funct. Mater. **29**(44), 1–10 (2019)
6. Miyashita, S., Guitron, S., Li, S., Rus, D.: Robotic metamorphosis by origami exoskeletons. Sci. Robot. **2**(10), 1–7 (2017)
7. Na, J.H., et al.: Programming reversibly self-folding origami with micropatterned photo-crosslinkable polymer trilayers. Adv. Mater. **27**(1), 79–85 (2015)

An Adaptable Robotic Snake
Using a Compliant Actuated Tensegrity
Structure for Locomotion

Qi He$^{(\boxtimes)}$ (ID) and Mark A. Post (ID)

University of York, York YO10 5DD, UK
qh764@york.ac.uk

Abstract. Compared with traditional rigid robots, tensegrity robots
are closer to imitating biological characteristics that give them unique
advantages in adapting to their environment and saving energy. Robots
for exploring harsh environments must often be compliant with many
modes of motion. This paper proposes a snake-shaped modular robot
design based on tensegrity structural principles. Tension springs and
motorized cables control the relative movement between modules so that
a minimum number of actuated degrees of freedom can produce locomotion while retaining flexibility. The structure is simple but can locomote
by cyclical application of tension to cables. Prototype modules are used
to demonstrate the feasibility of basic snake-like locomotion in physical
experiments and establish a basis for kinematic control.

Keywords: Snake · Tensegrity · Robot · Mobility

1 Introduction

Since 1972, snake robots have been researched with the goal of achieving mobility
on a variety of challenging terrains [1]. Most designs are based on rigid links and
can be easily operated and emulate snake-like movement but lose the compliance
of biological muscle and cannot absorb impacts from the environment. This
causes energy to be wasted [2] due to rigid collisions during movement. A pre-
stressed tensegrity structure allows control to be more robust [3] and efficient.

Tensegrity, a portmanteau of 'tensional integrity' describes rigid compression
elements held in place entirely by the tension of flexible members. A tensegrity structure distributes tension to create rigidity [4] in the manner of biological muscles and bone-tendon skeletal joints. It is a challenge to control [3]
but has many advantages including compliance, low mass, modular construction
from repeated elements, and many more degrees of freedom than a conventional
robot [5] while requiring only simple tension actuators with low torques [6].
These advantages are exactly what the snake-like robot needs. Bionic snakes
have multiple motion modes to adapt to different terrains, so simple and compact structures are required to achieve multi-degree-of-freedom movements, and

© Springer Nature Switzerland AG 2020
A. Mohammad et al. (Eds.): TAROS 2020, LNAI 12228, pp. 70–74, 2020.
https://doi.org/10.1007/978-3-030-63486-5_10

snake-shaped robots are often used in complex and harsh terrains such as alien exploration and post-disaster rescue, requiring robots to resist impact and maintain high endurance, and the tensegrity structure is also good at easing impact and reducing energy consumption of mechanical collisions.

Previous research into creating robot snakes using a tensegrity structure have relied on ideal geometric designs, resulting in a large number of minimalist elements that are difficult to build as a physical robot as there is little space for the number of actuators and other components required [7]. The proposed tensegrity snake robot simplifies practical implementation and provides space for payloads while retaining the minimal required number of actuators for snake-like movement by using springs to replace combinations of cables and actuators. The top and left views of the basic module of the design are shown in Fig. 1.

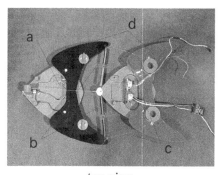 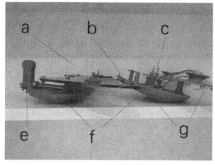

top view   side view

Fig. 1. Module construction. (a – distance control cable, b – spring, c – rotation control cables, d – main module body, e – hanging pulley, f – friction surface, g – rear wing)

2 Dynamics of the Proposed Robot

2.1 Force Analysis of Module Motion

The basic motion patterns of the robot have been demonstrated with two identical modules, while a complete snake robot is scalable and will link many modules in a chain. As shown in Fig. 1, each pair of modules achieve rigidity through the tension of two springs and relative movement through the actuation of three cables. Each segment of the prototype has three motors, one is in the front of the body, and the other two are in the middle of the body, keeping the center of gravity of the joint easy to swing. They separately apply force $f1$, $fl3, fr3$ through the pulley. Motion is divided into relative rotation between modules and linear distance change between modules, allowing combined serpentine and caterpillar motion.

A force analysis is shown in Fig. 2. Relative rotation of the module depends on cable forces $fl3$ and $fr3$. During straight movement, actuated cables will maintain tension, keeping the angle of the two modules unchanged. To turn or achieve serpentine motion with many modules, one cable is tensioned while the other is loosened by motor control, causing the relative module angle to change while maintaining body equilibrium through spring forces $fl2$ and $fr2$.

Linear distance between modules is changed in two ways: through cable force $f1$ by equal change of cable forces $fl3$ and $fr3$, while spring forces $fl2$ and $fr2$ maintain rigidity of the structure. Forward caterpillar motion is facilitated by force $f1$ in two "push-pull" stages. In the "pull" stage, $f1$ is nearly zero, and the two modules are separated due to spring forces. The cable is then tensioned along $f1$ in the leading module, tilting the leading module upward and the trailing module downward due to $f1$ being above the center of mass, then pulling the modules together. The force $f1$ will increase the rear ground pressure of the first module and reduce that of the second module. As the module undersides are angled, this makes the friction of the leading module larger than that of the trailing module, dragging the trailing module forward. In the "push" stage, the cable at $f1$ is loosened, allowing $fl2$ and $fr2$ to tilt the modules parallel to the ground and decreasing the friction of the leading module, pushing it forward.

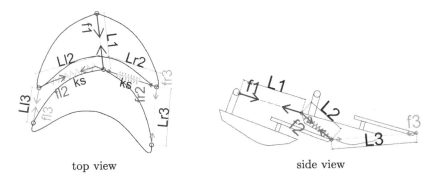

top view   side view

Fig. 2. Force analysis during module movement.

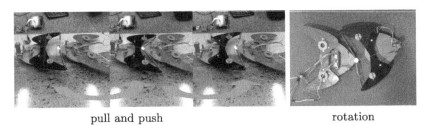

pull and push   rotation

Fig. 3. Physical caterpillar motion experiment

2.2 Body Locomotion Patterns

Using three degrees of freedom per module, a variety of full-body mixed cater-pillar and serpentine movements are possible, two of the most commonly used snake-like movements. Each pair of modules is capable of caterpillar motion, which is slow but precisely controllable and valuable for positioning. Serpentine movement [8], which can produce faster and more efficient movement, requires high side muscle strength and lateral movement of part of a snake's long body to increase friction. This is possible on the robot, since the modules have the abil-ity to rotate and move side to side through cable forces $fl3$ and $fr3$. Serpentine motion can be achieved on this robot with a minimum of five modules.

3 Experiments to Date and Results

While the demonstration of the full snake robot will comprise coordinated cater-pillar and serpentine motion of several modules, at the time of this writing only two modules are available. The use of caterpillar motion has been tested as shown in Fig. 3 using a single pair of segments with 298:1 gear ratio micro-motors that winch the tension elements. A video of testing can be viewed online [9]. By indi-vidually controlling the degrees of freedom of the robot, the current prototype achieves caterpillar movement at approximately 2 cm/s, with a module rotation limit of 30°. To improve the efficiency of this process on a wider range of sur-faces, materials will be added to the undersides of the modules with different friction coefficients and tested in different scenarios before demonstration.

It has also been found that the height of the fixed pulley at the front end of the module limits the ratio of the front-to-back tension and the pressure difference to the ground, and may not be able to adapt to ground surface changes. Other pulley mechanisms will be evaluated to enable better control of changes in back-and-forth pressure and ground pressure difference respectively, so that the ratio between the two can be adjusted, which will minimize the current problem of back-slipping. At present, the prototype performs better on smooth surfaces as rough surface friction can overcome spring forces during the "push" motion stage. Therefore the forward surface of the modules requires very smooth material.

4 Conclusion

A snake-shaped robot based on a tensegrity structure has been designed, and its basic modes of motion defined and verified on a physical prototype with some potential improvements identified. The full demonstration will include a com-plete snake robot prototype of several coordinated modules. Subsequent research work will design and analyze the optimization of movement between modules to accomplish efficient and controllable caterpillar and serpentine movements.

References

1. Hirose, S., Mori, M.: Biologically inspired snake-like robots. In: Proceedings of the IEEE International Conference on Robotics and Biomimetics, pp. 1–7 (2004)
2. Kakogawa, A., Jeon, S., Ma, S.: Stiffness design of a resonance-based planar snake robot with parallel elastic actuators. IEEE Robot. Autom. Lett. **3**(2), 1284–1291 (2018)
3. Aldrich, J.B., Skelton, R.E.: Backlash-free motion control of robotic manipulators driven by tensegrity motor networks. In: Proceedings of the IEEE Conference on Decision and Control, pp. 2300–2306 (2006)
4. Tur, J.M.M., Juan, S., Rovira, A.: Dynamic equations of motion for a 3-bar tensegrity based mobile robot. Technical report (2007)
5. Fest, E., Shea, K., Smith, I.F.C.: Active tensegrity structure. J. Struct. Eng. **130**(10), 1454–1465 (2004)
6. Aldrich, J.B., Skelton, R.E., Kreutz-Delgado, K.: Control synthesis for a class of light and agile robotic tensegrity structures. In: Proceedings of the American Control Conference, vol. 6, pp. 5245–5251 (2003)
7. Tietz, B.R., Carnahan, R.W., Bachmann, R.J., Quinn, R.D., SunSpiral, V.: Tetraspine: robust terrain handling on a tensegrity robot using central pattern generators. In: Proceedings of the IEEE/ASME International Conference on Advanced Intelligent Mechatronics (2013)
8. Ma, S.: Analysis of snake movement forms for realization of snake-like robots. In: Proceedings of the IEEE ICRA, vol. 4, pp. 3007–3013 (1999)
9. He, Q.: Test video. Youtube (2020). https://youtu.be/9cFxdgmn-68

Mobile Robots

Topological Robot Localization in a Large-Scale Water Pipe Network

Rob Worley$^{(\boxtimes)}$ (ID) and Sean Anderson

Department of Automatic Control and Systems Engineering, University of Sheffield,
Sheffield, UK
rfworley1@sheffield.ac.uk

Abstract. Topological localization is well suited to robots operating in water pipe networks because the environment is well defined as a set of discrete connected places like junctions, customer connections, and access points. Topological methods are more computationally efficient than metric methods, which is important for robots operating in pipes as they will be small with limited computational power. A Hidden Markov Model (HMM) based localization method is presented here, with novel incorporation of measured distance travelled. Improvements to the method are presented which use a reduced definition of the robot state to improve computational efficiency and an alternative motion model where the probability of transitioning to each other state is uniform. Simulation in a large realistic map shows that the use of measured distance travelled improves the localization accuracy by around 70%, that the reduction of the state definition gives an reduction in computational requirement by 75% with only a small loss to accuracy dependant on the robot parameters, and that the alternative motion model gives a further improvement to accuracy.

Keywords: Topological localization · Pipe inspection robots

1 Introduction

Buried water pipe infrastructure is in regular need of maintenance, the cost of which may be reduced by more precisely locating faults. Robots could be used for autonomous, persistent monitoring of a pipe network. A principal challenge for this robotic system is to localize itself and faults in the network, and previous work on robot localization in pipes has used metric information from vision [1], inertial sensing [2] and acoustic sensing [3,4]. However, while metric information is required for precise localization of a fault, localization to a single discrete pipe or junction would be sufficient for navigation and for isolating a fault to a part of the network.

S. Anderson—This work is supported by an EPSRC Doctoral Training Partnership Scholarship. S. Anderson acknowledges the support of EPSRC grant EP/S016813/1 (Pipebots).

© Springer Nature Switzerland AG 2020
A. Mohammad et al. (Eds.): TAROS 2020, LNAI 12228, pp. 77–89, 2020.
https://doi.org/10.1007/978-3-030-63486-5_11

A *topological* localization method for a single robot in a network of pipes is presented in this paper, where the robot is localized in a discrete set of places, the connection between which is described by a topological map. This is in contrast with *metric* localization methods, where a robot's location is described in a continuous space. The pipe environment is well defined by topological relations alone, as discrete places like junctions between pipes, customer connections, and above ground access points are connected together by pipes. Therefore, a topological method can be used in this application without the loss in precision that might be found when discretizing other environments into a topological map. In the pipe environment, typical metric methods have drawbacks. Methods that parameterise the robot state probability distribution, such as Kalman filtering and pose-graph optimization, poorly describe the multimodal probability distribution expected in a discrete network. Non-parameteric methods such as particle filtering have a higher computational cost, while a topological method would reduce the computation required for localization compared to metric methods, which is an advantage for robots with limited power and size which must operate in a typical pipe of 150 mm diameter.

Early work in robot localization uses a topological map defined by distinctive places in a structured indoor environment [5] or segments between distinctive places [6]. Grid based maps can be divided into regions separated by narrow passages [7] or from a one-dimensional paths through the environment [8]. In much of this existing work, the focus is on obtaining a topological map from metric sensor data, which is less challenging in a pipe environment which is well described by only a topological map. However, the methods used in localization in the topological map are a useful foundation for this work.

A topological map representation has been shown to be useful in navigation where a Hidden Markov Model (HMM) localization method is extended to a Partially Observable Markov Decision Process (POMDP) [9]. Early work on localization in a pipe network [10] also uses a POMDP for localization and navigation, where the transition model between states is described, as is the observation model which finds the likelihood of an observation of the robot's surroundings at a junction corresponding to a known discrete type of junction.

Recent work on topological localization adds the challenges of erroneous repeated observations of the environment at a topological map node, inclusion of information assigned to nearby nodes, and failing to make an observation at a node [11], the last of which is especially applicable where a robot has limited sensing ability as is the case in a pipe environment. Use of geometric information on the robot's orientation has been applied using prior knowledge of the orientation between two topological map nodes [12]. Recent work on localization in pipe networks also incorporates both metric and topological information [13], and similar methods have been applied to autonomous road vehicles [14–17].

The work presented in this paper presents an incorporation of measurement of distance into the localization method, and improvements to the accuracy and efficiency of the method from previous work [18]. Simulation on a large realistic network of pipes has been used to compare the proposed methods with a typical topological localization method. The effect of four uncertainty parameters on the localization accuracy is measured, and the accuracy and efficiency is measured for the proposed methods.

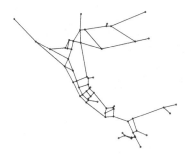

Fig. 1. The example simulated network of pipes used in this work, consisting of 63 nodes, which represent junctions, each connected to 1, 3, or 4 other nodes.

2   Methods

2.1   State Definition

The robot moves in a network of pipes, shown in Fig. 1. The full robot state is defined as $s_{x_t x_{t-1} \theta_t} = [x_t, x_{t-1}, \theta_t]$ and is composed of three components, facilitating localization of the robot [18]. The first component is the robot's discrete position, which is the junction index x at time index t. The second is the robot's discrete direction θ_t which is the index of the pipe which is has arrived from, allowing information about the robot's choice of action to be used in localization. The third is the robot's previous position x_{t-1}, allowing information about the length of the journey between junctions to be used in localization. The robot state is only updated at junctions or at ends of pipes, and the robot's position and orientation are not considered in transitions between these states.

The robot's belief in the state is represented as a vector $\boldsymbol{b}(\boldsymbol{s}_{x_t x_{t-1} \theta_t})$ over all possible values of the state, where each value is the estimated likelihood of being in that particular state. For the full state definition, there are $X^2 D$ possible states, where X is the number of nodes in the network and D is the maximum number of connections between nodes. The size of this vector is not a problem for small networks, however for the network in Fig. 1 there are 63 nodes and a maximum of 4 connection giving 15876 possible values of the state. The computational requirement for a vector this size is expected to be infeasible for the small robot required in this application, therefore alternatives to this state definition are proposed here.

The first improvement proposed is partial robot state definitions which reduce the size of the belief vector. The state definition $s_{x_t \theta_t}$ includes only the current position and direction of the robot. Measurements of the length of the journey between junctions can therefore not be incorporated exactly, however an approximation can be made which is described in Sect. 2.4. The state definition s_{x_t} includes only the current position of the robot. The choice of action can not be incorporated exactly, and an approximate means of doing this is not presented in this work.

The second improvement proposed is to truncate the belief vector at each step, and compute the updated belief only for states that have a predicted likelihood over a threshold, using only information relating to states that have a likelihood over another threshold. The belief in other states is set to a small default value. This is similar to previous implementations [10].

2.2   Robot Model

At a junction, the robot chooses a direction at random, relative to its own unknown orientation. In practice, this action would be chosen to best inspect the network, however this would not affect the localization result so is neglected here. There are four sources of uncertainty in the robot motion. Three of these are discrete uncertainties: There is a chance that the robot incorrectly executes the action and moves in a different direction [10]. Between junctions there is a chance that the robot is turned around and returns to the previous junction. When arriving at a junction there is a chance that the robot does not detect it, and continues moving in a random unknown direction, without updating the state estimate [11]. This model is illustrated as a discrete probability distribution shown in Fig. 2(a). The robot is modelled as moving at a constant velocity with multiplicative Gaussian noise, which is the fourth source of uncertainty.

It is assumed that the robot can make two kinds of observation. Firstly, it can detect the number of exits from a junction, which could be done using a camera, sonar, or a number of other sensing modes. For a robot which is able to control its motion, this measurement is assumed to be accurate as it would be able to hold position to confirm the observation. However in the case where a robot is moved with the flow in the pipe this assumption may be violated. Secondly, it can estimate the distance travelled since its last state update. This could be done using odometry or dead reckoning. To model the distance travelled in the case where a robot is turned around in a pipe and returns to the previous junction, a uniform probability distribution over twice the length of the pipe is used. These observations could be removed, changed, or added to without affecting the localization method. For example, use of an inertial measurement unit (IMU) might be useful for estimating the direction.

2.3   Localization Model

For the transition model between states, written as T, the localization model parameters used are set approximately to the values in the robot model described previously, as shown in Fig. 2(a), so that the robot does not have exact knowledge of the true motion model. An alternative model is also proposed, referred to as

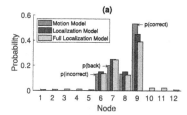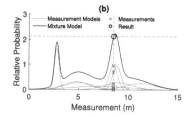

Fig. 2. (a) An example of the probability distribution for robot motion, in this case from node 2 in a 12 node network, showing the motion model used to simulate the robot motion, the estimate of this distribution used for localization, and the full localization model considering the probability of missing a node. (b) An example continuous probability distribution over possible measurements of distance between a pair of nodes.

$\bar{T}$, where the transition probabilities are distributed more evenly. In this work the extreme case of a uniform distribution is used.

For the measurement model, written as M, the probability of making a given continuous measurement must be found. For a given state transition with a number of possible transition lengths, the probability distribution over possible measurements is given by a sum of Gaussian distributions, illustrated in Fig. 2(b). A probability estimate is found as in Eq. 1 where $\tilde{p}$ is the relative probability estimate for measurement m given the possible state s', $K_{s'}$ is the number of Gaussian components, and $\sigma_{i,s'}$ and $\mu_{i,s'}$ are the standard deviation and mean for component i. The Gaussian model is relative and does not sum to one, as this would reduce the probabilities found for junction pairs with multiple short paths between them compared to junction pairs with single short paths where all the probability is concentrated around a single measurement.

$$\tilde{p}(m|s') = \sum_{i=1}^{K_{s'}} \frac{1}{\sigma_{i,s'}\sqrt{2\pi}} e^{-\frac{1}{2}\left(\frac{x-\mu_{i,s'}}{\sigma_{i,s'}}\right)} \tag{1}$$

As with the transition model, the parameters of the distribution used for localization are set to be different to those used to model the motion. In Fig. 2(b) the narrow Gaussian components represent simple transitions where the robot moves to a different junction. The wider Gaussian components model the added uniform distribution used to model the distance travelled when the robot returns to the junction it just left. For a single return incident this is not very accurate as the Gaussian distribution is a poor representation of the uniform distribution. However for multiple return incidents this is more accurate as the sum of multiple uniformly distributed variables is closer to the Gaussian distribution. This broad distribution should challenge the localization method, as a measurement is more likely to be seen as a good match for any given transition.

2.4 State Estimation

The forward algorithm is used to compute the discrete probability distribution, or belief, over the possible robot states in the Hidden Markov Model (HMM). With the state $s = s_{x_t x_{t-1} \theta_t}$, the typical form in Eq. 2 is used to compute the updated belief b' over a vector of all possible new states s', based on the belief b over a vector of possible states s, the observation at the new position o, observation between positions m, action a, and transition and observation models T and P, decomposed into O and M. As the robot's previous position is used, this is similar to a second order HMM.

$$b'(s') = P(m, o|s')T(s'|s, a)b(s) = M(m|s')O(o|s')T(s'|s, a)b(s) \qquad (2)$$

When the state is $s = s_{x_t \theta_t}$, a modified form shown in Eq. 3 is used to approximately incorporate information when measurements of distance between positions do not fit the typical form. A further modified form is used where the state is $s = s_{x_t}$, shown in Eq. 4.

$$b'(s') = H(m|s', b(s))O(o|s')T(s'|s, a)b(s) \qquad (3)$$

$$b'(s') = H(m|s', b(s))O(o|s')T(s'|s)b(s) \qquad (4)$$

where H is a diagonal matrix with each element given by Eq. 5.

$$H(m|s', b(s))_{s'} = g(m|s')b(s) \qquad (5)$$

In these equations M is a diagonal matrix where each element is computed as in Eq. 1, and the vector g is the probability of measuring m for a transition to state s' from each state s and is computed similarly. The observation model O is similarly a diagonal matrix where each element is equal to one where the observation of number of exits from the junction matches the expected observation for the corresponding state. The transition model T is computed as described in Sect. 2.3.

Where the robot's position is to be estimated, and the belief in each discrete position is distributed over a number of states corresponding to different directions and previous positions, some inference must be made. Summing the probabilities for all states for each discrete position and finding the largest value over positions does not necessarily give the same result as finding the largest probability over all states and finding the corresponding position. In this work the former method is used as it was observed to give a slightly better result.

Alternative algorithms such as the forward-backward algorithm or the Viterbi algorithm could be used instead of the forward algorithm. These would give better estimates of the full robot trajectory, at the cost of increased computation, which may be useful for path planning. The sensitivity to parameters and efficiency over each state and motion model definition are expected to be similar using these other algorithms, however this is not investigated in this work.

2.5   Practical Considerations

As the problem is considering only localization in a known environment, rather than mapping, the possible transition and measurement models can be pre-computed for a given network [11].

For each junction for each direction, the transition model can be computed for each possible action, assuming that the connectivity between junctions is known. When junctions can be missed, the state transition model is difficult to compute exactly. For a given network a Monte Carlo method is used to approximate the probability of transition between each state. The measurement model for distance travelled between junctions is also computed using the Monte Carlo method as all junction pairs have multiple possible paths between them. This is done assuming that the path length between junctions is known accurately. In this work using an idealised model network this is the case as all of the pipes are straight lines and the junction positions are known precisely. In practice there may be some uncertainty in these metric values, so a simultaneous localization and mapping approach may be required which uses the robot's measurements of distance travelled as well as prior information to find an accurate model.

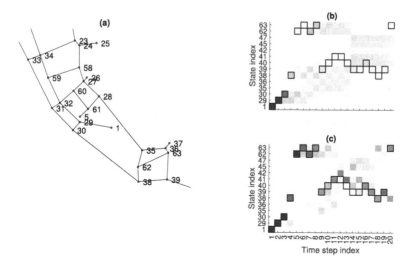

Fig. 3. An example of the localization method. (a) A subset of Fig. 1 showing the nodes labelled as state indices. (b, c) Part of the belief vector over each time step. The darkness corresponds to the belief for each state. The maximum belief at each step is labelled in blue if it is correct and red if it is incorrect. The true robot path through the states is shown by the bordered cells. (b) shows the result found without using the measured distance travelled, (c) shows the result using this measured distance. (Color figure online)

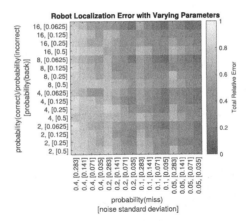

Fig. 4. Variation in localization error in a network with each combination of 4 values for each of the 4 uncertainty parameters: $p(correct)/p(incorrect)$, the relative probability of correctly executing an action, $p(back)$, the probability of returning to the previous node, $p(miss)$, the probability of missing a node, and the measurement noise amplitude. The total relative error is the proportion of the steps for which the localization is incorrect. The axes are labelled directly for each cell as the two quantities on each axis are varied to best visualise the four dimensional data.

3   Results

Experiments are done in simulation to compare the performance and computational requirements of localization using each of the proposed robot state definitions and improvements to efficiency. Aspects of the performance of the method in general can also be observed. An example of the result of the localization in the discrete space is shown in Fig. 3, where it is seen that the use of measured distance travelled improves the localization accuracy considerably.

3.1   Evaluation of Sensitivity to Model Parameters

The accuracy of the localization method is evaluated for different values for the uncertainty parameters described in Sect. 2.2. The robot is simulated moving for 100 steps through the network shown in Fig. 1, and localization is done at each step. This is done ten times, starting from different points, and this is done for four different values for each of the four parameters.

For localization using the state definition $s_{x_t x_{t-1} \theta_t}$ the total relative error, the proportion of steps for which the localization estimate is incorrect, is shown for each of the 256 parameters sets in Fig. 4. Parameter sets which give low estimation error have low measurement noise, low probability of missing a junction and low probability of incorrectly returning to a junction. The relative probability of correctly executing an action is seen not to have much of an effect. It is expected that for a system with no uncertainty, the estimation error will be equal to zero, and that for a desired maximum error lower than that shown here,

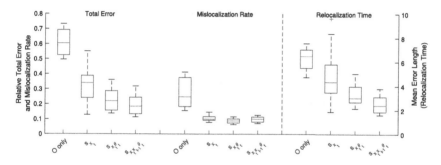

Fig. 5. A comparison of the results using each of the three state definitions (s_{x_t}, $s_{x_t\theta_t}$, $s_{x_t x_{t-1}\theta_t}$), and without using the measured distance m (O only). This is done for each of the three error metrics: *Total Error*, the proportion of steps for which the localization is incorrect, *Error Starts*, the proportion of steps where an initial mislocalization occurs, and the mean *Error Length*, the mean number of steps before relocalizing. The box plots show the quartiles for each value over a range of parameter sets determining the uncertainty in robot motion. The parameter values used are a subset of those shown in Fig. 4, using only the two values for each corresponding to the lower uncertainty.

the required parameter values could be found by following the relationship to accuracy shown here.

These results are as expected. The probability of correctly executing an action affects only the discrete part of the model shown in Fig. 2(a), which is always quite accurate as the localization model in each case uses estimates of the parameter set. The other parameters have an effect on the measurement model shown in Fig. 2(b). The measurement noise directly affects the variance of the Gaussian components, so a larger magnitude of noise will increase the likelihood of an incorrect state appearing to be a good match for the measurement made. The probability of moving back to the previous node increases the impact of the uniformly distributed measurements which are not modelled accurately in the localization model. The probability of missing a node increases the impact of the Gaussian components with higher mean values, which tend to be close together due to many longer paths existing with similar lengths. Therefore it is unsurprising that these parameters have an effect on the localization accuracy.

3.2   Comparison of Methods

Figure 5 compares the results found using each state definition, over the subset of the parameter sets which correspond to the lower uncertainty, indicative of a good performance. The total error in localization is decomposed into two components: the number of steps at which an initial mislocalization occurs, and the mean number of steps before relocalization.

The median total error increases for the more reduced state definitions, largely due to the increase in mean number of steps before relocalizing after an error. Compared to only using observations at junctions, the use of measured

Table 1. Median computation time τ with each state definition.

Network	Time s_{x_t} (s)		Time $s_{x_t \theta_t}$ (s)		Time $s_{x_t x_{t-1} \theta_t}$ (s)	
	Exact[a]	Truncated[b]	Exact	Truncated	Exact	Truncated
Map 1	0.003	0.002	0.007	0.003	0.016	0.007
Map 2	0.062	0.005	0.145	0.010	0.838	0.022

[a] Belief is computed for all possible states.
[b] Belief is computed for likely new states using likely states.

distance travelled is seen to reduce the median localization error over the parameter sets by 66%, 62%, and 43% for each of the state definitions respectively, from least to most reduced. However, the results with the best set of parameters for each state definition are similar, giving around a 70% reduction in error.

Table 1 compares the median computation time per step for each of the state definitions in the exact and truncated methods, for two maps, one with 12 nodes and one with 63 nodes. Note that the exact values are expected to be different in practice on different hardware. The truncated method is shown to reduce the computation time significantly, especially for the larger map. Reducing the state definition is also shown to reduce the computation time substantially.

With a measure of computation time for each set of parameters, a measure of localization efficiency can be found for each method, given by

$$\eta = (1 - \epsilon)/\tau \tag{6}$$

where ϵ is the total relative localization error (the proportion of steps at which the estimate is incorrect), $1 - \epsilon$ is the relative localization accuracy, and τ is the computation time. This is shown for four sets of parameters in Table 2. For each method it can be seen that the ratio of accuracy to computation time is higher for parameters that give higher accuracy, suggesting that a robot able to give low uncertainty would give an improved accuracy and a lower computational power requirement. It is also seen here that this efficiency ratio is better for the more reduced state methods, especially for higher accuracy parameters.

Finally, Fig. 6 compares the localization estimate when using the motion models T and $\bar{T}$ (described in Sect. 2.3), done here for the state definition s_{x_t} over the range of parameter sets. It is seen that the localization error is generally

Table 2. Ratio (η) of accuracy ($1 - \epsilon$) to time taken (τ) for four sets of parameters.

Parameters[a]	s_{x_t}		$s_{x_t \theta_t}$		$s_{x_t x_{t-1} \theta_t}$	
	Accuracy	Ratio	Accuracy	Ratio	Accuracy	Ratio
[8,0.5,0.4,0.005]	0.2	10	0.19	15	0.23	4.7
[8,0.125,0.2,0.005]	0.37	40	0.58	51	0.62	18
[16,0.25,0.1,0.0013]	0.65	170	0.63	64	0.67	23
[16,0.0625,0.05,0.0013]	0.87	310	0.85	100	0.86	45

[a] The parameters are: probability(correct)/probability(incorrect), probability(back), probability(miss), measurement noise.

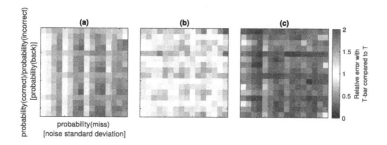

Fig. 6. A comparison between the results found using the models T and $\bar{T}$ with the state definition s_{x_t}, over the range of parameter sets. (a) shows the relative total error, (b) shows the relative mislocalization error, which is the proportion of initial incorrect estimates, and (c) shows the relative relocalization time, which is the mean number of steps before the estimate becomes correct. The value in each cell is equal to the result found using the $\bar{T}$ model divided by that using the T model. The axes are not labelled for conciseness, however they are identical to those found in Fig. 4.

lower when using $\bar{T}$, especially at lower probabilities of missing a junction and lower noise. This is seen to be due to a decrease in the relocalization time, which compensates for a generally increased rate of mislocalization.

Over all of these comparisons between state definitions, the results found using the reduced state definition s_{x_t} are more efficient than those found with more full state definitions. This result is improved by using an alternative motion model $\bar{T}$, which is initially a surprising result, as this method is unable to incorporate information about the choice of action into the estimation. From this, it is suggested that the use of measured distance and observed number of exits at a junction are more important for successful localization than the motion model. It is speculated that the $\bar{T}$ model localization has an improved result as it keeps a more diverse belief across the possible states, so mislocalization is more likely but it is able to recover from error more quickly when a good measurement is made. This will be investigated in future work.

4 Conclusions and Further Work

Simulated results for topological robot localization in a network of pipes have been presented. The effect of four uncertainty parameters on the accuracy has been investigated and results are as would be expected. Parameter values required for good performance in this model are identified.

To improve on identified problems with complexity, two alternative state definitions have been developed and compared to the typical HMM-based method. It is seen more efficient performance is found using a reduced definition of robot state and an augmented HMM. An alternative motion model is also proposed which shows an improvement in accuracy. Future work will investigate this alternate method in more detail, and compare the methods in other network topologies. Further work could extend this method to a multi-robot case.

References

1. Hansen, P., Alismail, H., Rander, P., Browning, B.: Pipe mapping with monocular fisheye imagery. In: IEEE International Conference on Intelligent Robots and Systems, pp. 5180–5185 (2013)
2. Murtra, A.C., Mirats Tur, J.M.: IMU and cable encoder data fusion for in-pipe mobile robot localization. IEEE Conference on Technologies for Practical Robot Applications, TePRA, pp. 1–6 (2013)
3. Bando, Y., Suhara, H., Tanaka, M., Kamegawa, T., Itoyama, K., Yoshii, K., Matsuno, F., Okuno, H.G.: Sound-based online localization for an in-pipe snake robot. In: SSRR 2016 - International Symposium on Safety, Security and Rescue Robotics, pp. 207–213 (2016)
4. Ma, K., et al.: Robot mapping and localisation in metal water pipes using hydrophone induced vibration and map alignment by dynamic time warping. In: Proceedings - IEEE International Conference on Robotics and Automation, pp. 2548–2553 (2017)
5. Kuipers, B., Byun, Y.T.: A robot exploration and mapping strategy based on a semantic hierarchy of spatial representations. Rob. Auton. Syst. **8**(1–2), 47–63 (1991)
6. Kortenkamp, D., Weymouth, T.: Topological mapping for mobile robots using a combination of sonar and vision sensing. Proc. Nat. Conf. Artif. Intell. **2**, 979–984 (1994)
7. Thrun, S.: Learning metric-topological maps for indoor mobile robot navigation. Artif. Intell. **99**(1), 21–71 (1998)
8. Choset, H., Nagatani, K.: Topological simultaneous localization and mapping (SLAM): towardexact localization without explicit localization. IEEE Trans. Robot. Autom. **17**(2), 125–137 (2001)
9. Cassandra, A.R., Kaelbling, L.P., Kurien, J.A.: Acting under uncertainty: discrete Bayesian models for mobile-robot navigation. IEEE Int. Conf. Intell. Rob. Syst. **2**(May), 963–972 (1996)
10. Hertzberg, J., Kirchner, F.: Landmark-based autonomous navigation in sewerage pipes. In: Proceedings of the 1st Euromicro Workshop on Advanced Mobile Robots, EUROBOT 1996, pp. 68–73 (1996)
11. Gomez, C., Hernandez, A.C., Crespo, J., Barber, R.: Uncertainty-based localization in a topological robot navigation system. In: 2017 IEEE International Conference on Autonomous Robot Systems and Competitions, ICARSC 2017, pp. 67–72 (2017)
12. Gomez, C., Hernandez, A.C., Moreno, L., Barber, R.: Qualitative geometrical uncertainty in a topological robot localization system. In: Proceedings - 2018 International Conference on Control, Artificial Intelligence, Robotics and Optimization, ICCAIRO 2018, pp. 183–188 (2018)
13. Alejo, D., Caballero, F., Merino, L.: A robust localization system for inspection robots in sewer networks. Sensors (Switzerland) **19**(22), 1–28 (2019)
14. El Najjar, M.E., Bonnifait, P.: A road-matching method for precise vehicle localization using belief theory and Kalman filtering. Auton. Rob. **19**, 173–191 (2005)
15. Brubaker, M.A., Geiger, A., Urtasun, R.: Map-based probabilistic visual self-localization. IEEE Trans. Pattern Anal. Mach. Intell. **38**(4), 652–665 (2016)
16. Bernuy, F., Ruiz-del Solar, J.: Topological semantic mapping and localization in urban road scenarios. J. Intell. Rob. Syst. Theor. Appl. **92**(1), 19–32 (2018)

17. Fouque, C., Bonnifait, P., Bétaille, D.: Enhancement of global vehicle localization using navigable road maps and dead-reckoning. In: 2008 IEEE/ION Position, Location and Navigation Symposium, pp. 1286–1291 (2008)
18. Worley, R., Anderson, S.: Topological robot localization in a pipe network. In: UKRAS20 Conference: "Robots into the real world" Proceedings, pp. 59–60 (2020)

Visual Topological Mapping Using an Appearance-Based Location Selection Method

Mohammad Asif Khan[1,2]([✉]) [iD] and Frédéric Labrosse[1]([✉]) [iD]

[1] Department of Computer Science, Aberystwyth University,
Aberystwyth SY23 3DB, UK
`{ask2,ffl}@aber.ac.uk`
[2] Sukkur IBA University, Airport Road, Sukkur 65200, Pakistan

Abstract. Visual representation of an environment in topological maps is a challenging task since different factors such as variable lighting conditions, viewpoints, mobility of robots, dynamic and featureless appearance, etc., can affect the representation. This paper presents a novel method for appearance-based visual topological mapping using low resolution omni-directional images. The proposed method employs a pixel-by-pixel comparison strategy. Successive images captured as a mobile robot traverses its environment are compared to estimate their dissimilarity from a reference image. Specific locations (nodes in the topological map) are then selected using a variable sampling rate based on changes in the appearance of the environment. Loop-closures are created using a dynamic threshold based on variability of the environment appearance. The method therefore proposes a full SLAM solution to create topological maps. The method was tested on multiple datasets, which were captured under different weather conditions along various trajectories. GPS coordinates were used to stamp each image as ground truth for evaluation and visualisation only. We also compared our method with state of the art feature-based methods.

Keywords: Topological mapping · Appearance-based · Visual SLAM · Loop closure

1 Introduction

Creating and maintaining a map of the environment of a mobile robot is an important aspect of autonomous navigation. Mapping for robots can be done using various sensors such as GPS, magnetic compass, laser scanner, wheel odometry and cameras [5,9,12]. We present a novel pixel-based technique for creating a visual topological map where specific places are represented as the nodes of a graph and navigation links between them as the edges. The selection of places is based on a purely pixel-based image comparison by contrast to more traditional methods that first extract features from the images and then compare them.

© Springer Nature Switzerland AG 2020
A. Mohammad et al. (Eds.): TAROS 2020, LNAI 12228, pp. 90–102, 2020.
https://doi.org/10.1007/978-3-030-63486-5_12

As the robot moves away from a reference location, the dissimilarity between the reference image (captured at the reference location) and the current image increases, creating a catchment area in which the robot can go back to the reference location [7]. We use this property to select a succession of reference locations (nodes) as the robot traverses its environment. Localisation is performed and loop-closures are created as the map is being built using similarity between nodes and thresholds based on local conditions. The paper therefore proposes a full topological SLAM solution.

The paper is arranged as follows. Section 2 discusses related work. Section 3 presents the proposed method in detail while Sect. 4 gives results and compares the proposed method to the state of the art. Finally, Sect. 5 concludes and discusses future work.

2   Related Work

The mapping of large environments can be done using appearance based visual topological maps. Such method has the advantage of being easily scalable compared to occupancy grids and less sensitive to noise than metric maps. Various methods have been proposed in the literature to visually represent the environment of a robot [4]. We review a few of these here.

The concept of probabilistic topological mapping was introduced in [11], where Bayesian inference is used to explore all possible topologies of the map. Measurements (odometry or appearance of the environment) are used in a Markov chain Monte Carlo algorithm to estimate the posterior probability of solutions in the space of all topologies. The appearance used is a Fourier signature of panoramic images. In [14] another Bayesian approach is used that does not require any motion model or metric information but uses the appearance of previously visited places as colour histograms (histograms are often used to reduce the amount of data to be processed, such as in [13]). Both Fourier signatures and colour histograms are poor representations of an environment and location aliasing therefore needs to be explicitly tackled by the methods.

In general, methods using global image descriptors tend to be faster compared to methods that use local descriptors. However, they suffer from problems such as occlusions, illumination effects and aliasing [4].

Local descriptors such as SIFT (Scale Invariant Features Transform, [8]) and variations over them are often used in topological mapping and localisation. These are particularly appropriate to dynamic environments, variable illumination from and varied view points as these descriptor tend to be scale, rotation and illumination independent. The matching of such features for localisation is often used in a Bag of Words (BoW, [1–3]) or Bag of Raw Features (BoRF, [16]) to improve the matching efficiency.

The concept of BoW (Bag of Words) for features matching has been widely used. These require a visual vocabulary of features that can be built online or offline. Most methods build the visual vocabularies offline during a training period, but some methods have been developed for online incremental building.

In particular, in [3] a method called BIN Map has been presented that uses binary features and creates online binary bags of (binary) words. The method is evaluated on different indoor and outdoor environments with good results.

In [1] the Fast Appearance-based Mapping (FAB-MAP 1.0) was proposed; it uses a probabilistic model for recognising places. The probabilities of visual words occurrences are approximated using a Chow Liu tree, offering efficient observation likelihood computation. The observation likelihood was used in a Bayes filter to predict loop closures. The downside of FAB-MAP 1.0 was that with every observation there was a need to compute the likelihood for existing nodes on the map. FAB-MAP 2.0 overcomes this issue [2], making the method scalable to kilometers long trajectories.

Biologically inspired methods have also been proposed to solve the visual mapping problem. A method was proposed which uses an artificial immune system to automatically select images that are representative of a stream of images, ignoring seldom seen images and preserving a regular sampling of the images in image space [10]. Using the concept of ARB (Artificial Recognition Ball) and a NAT (Network Affinity Threshold) similar images were linked while dissimilar images were not. However, the method can produce incomplete topologies when insignificant images are being removed from the map.

3 Appearance Based Visual Topological Mapping

In the visual topological map, different places are represented by nodes of a graph quantified by the panoramic image of the corresponding place. Connection/edges between the nodes correspond to navigable pathways between the places. We describe below how places are selected to be added as nodes of the graph.

3.1 Image Comparison and Alignment for Mapping

The proposed method uses an omni-directional camera (Fig. 1a). This camera captures omni-directional (360° field of view) images (Fig. 1b), which are then unwrapped into panoramic images (Fig. 1c).

The images are captured at regular time (space) intervals by a mobile robot and each image is stamped with its GPS coordinates obtained using a RTK differential GPS unit.

Image comparison is done using a pixel-wise metric rather than the more usual feature-based method as the holistic metric is more robust to noise and featureless environments [6]. As in other works (e.g. [7]), the comparison between two images I_i and I_j is done using the Euclidean distance where the images are considered as points in a $h \times w \times c$ space, where h and w are the height and width of the images and c is the number of colour components:

$$d\left(I_i, I_j\right) = \sqrt{\sum_{k=1}^{h \times w} \sum_{l=1}^{c} \left(I_i\left(k, l\right) - I_j\left(k, l\right)\right)^2}. \tag{1}$$

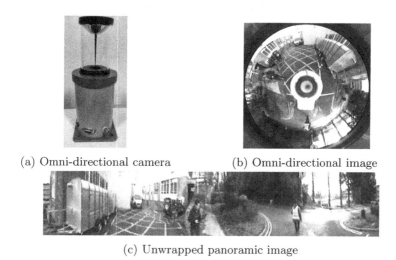

(a) Omni-directional camera   (b) Omni-directional image

(c) Unwrapped panoramic image

Fig. 1. Camera and images used for capturing the appearance of the environment

The literature suggests that it is not a good idea to use the RGB colour space from which luminance cannot be removed. Therefore, the CIE L*a*b colour space was used. Luminance was discarded to make the method less sensitive to changes in brightness [15], resulting in using images in the ab colour space.

Images are aligned to a common heading so that they can be meaningfully compared. This is done using the Visual Compass presented in [6]. In this method two successive panoramic images are aligned by doing a local optimisation of their similarity as a function of the rotation of the second image. To limit drift the comparison is done relative to a moving reference image selected automatically in the stream of images based on the matching quality of the successive images to that reference image. This is done using the amplitude threshold $\phi = 0.41$ [6].

3.2   Creation of the Topological Map with Adaptive Spatial Sampling

The proposed method automatically selects images from a stream to be nodes of the topological map, the edges corresponding to the traveled path of the robot. Additionally, loops are automatically closed when specific conditions happen.

Contrary to many other methods in the literature (e.g. [2,3]), the spatial sampling is automatically adapted to the environment. This offers variable sampling that ensures that the important events of the environment are being recorded.

Figure 2 shows the Euclidean distance (Eq. (1)) between all the images of a sequence and a reference image at the centre of the sequence (image index 213). This sequence was captured by a robot travelling from a grassy patch to another one separated by a road. It can be seen that the Euclidean distance increases as the robot moves away from the reference location (corresponding to the centre image), creating a catchment area. It has been shown that the

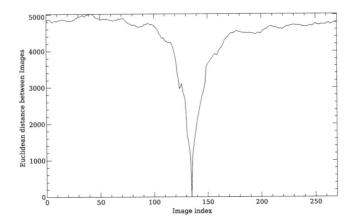

Fig. 2. Dissimilarity between center image and others images captured while the robot translated away from the center/reference image

catchment area can be exploited to make the robot navigate back to its centre [7] using a gradient descent method. This property is used to select nodes from the stream of images.

Nodes Creation/Spatial Sampling: The size of the catchment area is captured using the gradient of the Euclidean distance, a gradient of 0 indicating its maximum size. To ensure that nodes remain within the actual catchment area, a threshold m on the Euclidean distance gradient is used to select the next node from the previous node. A threshold of 0 retains the fewest nodes while a higher threshold increases the number of nodes in the map, controlling the map density. As can be seen in Fig. 2, there is noise in the Euclidean distance. This is due to noisy images but also the attitude of the robot changing on uneven terrain. A running average of the last four gradients is therefore used to filter the noise, as a compromise over efficiency and accuracy of the catchment area detection.

As mentioned above, the images are aligned using the Visual Compass [6]. It can happen that this method produces a suddenly drifting alignment. This is corrected by performing a local alignment (from the one calculated by the Visual Compass) between the previous node and the current image. Finally, to reduce the importance of the luminance information in the *Lab* colour space used by the Visual Compass over colour information, the L component was re-scaled so that its variance matches that of the colour information (components a and b).

The process is as follows. The first image is kept as a node. Subsequent images are compared to the previous node using the Euclidean distance and calculating the gradient of the distance. As the gradient falls below the threshold m, the corresponding image is used to create a new node. The process continues from that node and is repeated until all the images are processed. Figure 3 shows the Euclidean distance between images and the previous node, visible as a 0 distance.

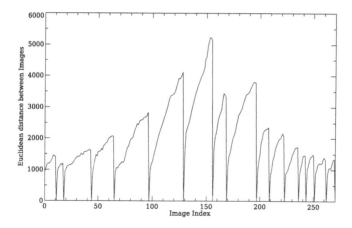

Fig. 3. Creation of nodes as the Euclidean distance to the previous node

In the sequence used for Fig. 3, the first part of the dataset corresponds to a grassy area, the middle part a road crossed by the robot and the final part another grassy area, shown by the differences in Euclidean distances.

Loop Closures: While adding nodes to the map, loop closures are sought for. To this effect, localisation is first performed (is the new node/location already in the map?), potentially followed by the creation of new links. The process involves comparing each newly added node to all existing nodes of that map and link them if the Euclidean distance between them is *low enough*. This is done using a threshold determined for each node based on local appearance. When a node j is created, its Euclidean distance to the previous node i is a measure of the catchment area for nodes i and j. A conservative threshold τ_j for loop closure detection with node j is therefore the minimum of all distances between node j and its neighbours in the stream of nodes:

$$\tau_j = \min\left(d(I_{j-1}, I_j), d(I_j, I_{j+1})\right). \tag{2}$$

At the time node j is created, node $j+1$ does not yet exist. Therefore initially $\tau_j = d(I_{j-1}, I_j)$ and is then updated when node $j+1$ is created using Eq. (2).

A loop between nodes i and j is closed if the distance between the corresponding images is lower than both thresholds:

$$d(I_i, I_j) < \begin{cases} \tau_i \\ \tau_j \end{cases}. \tag{3}$$

When a loop is closed, the corresponding edge is added to the map.

Loop closures are detected and created during the construction of the map. This implies that Eq. (3) can only be met in a two step process, before and after node $j+1$ is created, as described above. When node j is created, a list

---

Algorithm 1. Algorithm for Loop Closure Detection

1: **procedure** LOOPCLOSUREDETECTION(I_j, I_{j-1}, H_{j-1})
2:     ▷ I_j: new node, I_{j-1}: previous node, H_{j-1}: list of hypotheses about node $j-1$
3:     ▷ Check hypotheses for node $j-1$
4:     **while** H_{j-1} no empty **do**
5:         I_i = first image of H_{j-1}
6:         **if** $d(I_{j-1}, I_i) < \min(\tau_i, \tau_{j-1})$ **then**   ▷ Eq. 3 with updated τ_{j-1}
7:             LoopClose(I_i, I_{j-1})
8:         **end if**
9:         remove I_i from H_{j-1}
10:     **end while**
11:     ▷ Create hypotheses for node j
12:     $i = 0$ ▷ Starting from first node
13:     $H_j = \emptyset$ ▷ With an empty list of hypotheses
14:     **while** $(i < j-1)$ **do**   ▷ Checking all nodes up to the previous one
15:         **if** $d(I_i, I_j) < \min(\tau_i, \tau_j)$ **then**   ▷ Eq. 3 with incomplete τ_j
16:             $H_j = \{H_j, I_i\}$ ▷ Add I_i to the set of hypotheses
17:         **end if**
18:         $i = i + 1$
19:     **end while**
20: **end procedure**

---

of hypotheses is created using the partial information about node j. This list contains the images that satisfy the (as yet incomplete) test in Eq. (3):

$$H_j = \{I_i : I_i \in M, d(I_j, I_i) < \min(\tau_i, \tau_j)\}, \qquad (4)$$

where M is the current map. When node $j+1$ is created, the threshold τ_j is updated and the hypotheses in the list H_j confirmed of not based on the new threshold. Algorithm 1 describes the process.

When a loop is closed, the corresponding loop closure thresholds are not updated to take into account the new edges added to the map. Indeed, doing so would result in reducing further and further the threshold (using the Eq. (2)), eventually stopping any new loop closures from being created.

The loop closure threshold in Eq. (2) corresponds to the smallest catchment the node. In some cases this could prevent a navigation strategy from reaching the node should the robot start from the edge of the catchment area. We therefore multiply the threshold τ with a constant $\gamma \leq 1$ that allows the specification of a smaller catchment area for loop closure. This also allows control of the trade-off between high false positives rates and low false negative rates.

3.3 Creating Nodes in Sequence Using Other Strategies

In Sect. 3 we described a method to adaptively select nodes from a stream of images. Other methods are possible, which we describe here and against which we compare our method.

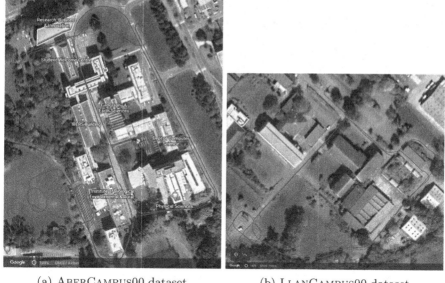

(a) ABERCAMPUS00 dataset   (b) LLANCAMPUS00 dataset

Fig. 4. Aerial view of the datasets

The simplest method is to use regular spatial sampling s. This is what is used in some state of the art work (e.g. [2]). The drawback with such method is that some areas could end up being over-sampled (such as long traverses of homogeneous terrain) or some important events might be missed (such as sudden transitions between two areas).

The second method is to use the reference images created by the Visual Compass [6] as the nodes of the map. The method automatically selects some of the images from the stream of images as reference images against which changes in orientation are calculated. This selection is based upon the quality of match between the reference image and successive images. That quality is the normalised amplitude of the Euclidean distance function expressed as the difference between best and worst match between two images. When that quality falls below a threshold β, the reference image is changed to the current image. See [6] for more detail. In this sampling method, high values of the threshold create a densely populated map while low values create fewer nodes.

4 Experimental Results

Multiple datasets were captured ranging over different lengths using one of our outdoors platforms (the Idris robot, a four wheel drive robot equipped with various sensors). The panoramic images have a resolution of 720×138. In other words, the angular resolution is 2 pixels per degree of rotation. We present here results on two datasets captured over paths 1000 m for LLANCAMPUS00 2400 m for ABERCAMPUS00. These are shown in Fig. 4.

While mapping an environment, each node is stamped with its GPS coordinates. The GPS coordinates are only used to estimate the size of the catchment area in Cartesian space in order to evaluate the method as well as to visualise maps. This is computed using the physical distance traveled up to the point where the filtered gradient of Euclidean distance reaches zero (Fig. 2). Each node therefore has its own catchment area and any other node falling within it is considered as a TP (True Positive) loop closure. The loop closures with nodes outside the catchment area are considered FP (False Positives). Similarly, TN (True Negatives) are those tested connections that are not retained as loop closures and are outside of the catchment area the node. Finally, FN (False Negatives) are connections that are inside the catchment area but not detected as loop closures by the method.

The performance of loop closure detection is evaluated by the precision (P_r) and recall (R_e) of loop closures:

$$P_r = \frac{TP}{TP + FP} \tag{5}$$

$$R_e = \frac{TP}{TP + FN} \tag{6}$$

Precision gives the proportion of the detected connections that are correct. The recall gives the proportion of correctly identified loop closures out of the total number of actual loop closures. A precision of 1 indicates that there are no falsely detected connections. A recall of 1 indicates that no actual connections are missed. A value of 0 for precision and recall indicates that no connections were detected. The trend in the literature is to increase recall while maintaining a precision of 1 [2,4].

Our method is compared with two well-known methods [2,4], which are discussed in Sect. 2. This comparison is based on the correctness of the loop closure detection. Since neither of these methods provides an automatic way of sampling the stream of images, we use our sampling method (gradient-based) to provide images to these two methods. Figure 5 is the plot of precision-recall for loop closures the datasets. The topological maps created using the gradient-based sampling method are shown in Fig. 6.

For the gradient-based sampling method we used values of the threshold m from 0 to 30 with increment of 1. For all results presented here, the multiplier γ was kept at 0.8. The threshold β for the Visual Compass sampling method was set from 0.1 to 0.65 with increments of 0.05. The fixed spatial sampling s was set 1 m 30 m with increments of 1m, but limited 18 m for LLANCAMPUS00 because no loop closures were detected beyond that sampling, the dataset being smaller. For both FAB-MAP 2.0 and BIN Map, loop closures were selected if their probability was higher than 0.99.

The results in Fig. 5 show that precision and recall of the gradient-based sampling method performs better for all threshold values compared to the other methods (maximum precision, high recall). That is why gradient-based sampled data (same range of the m) was used with the other methods [2,4] for comparison.

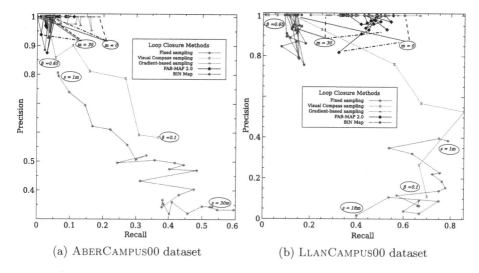

(a) ABERCAMPUS00 dataset   (b) LLANCAMPUS00 dataset

Fig. 5. Loop closure precision and recall for various methods. The extreme values of the control parameters (m, β and s) are indicated in ovals with lines pointing to the corresponding ends of the plots, with dashes for the gradient-based sampling method, dot-dash for FAB-MAP 2.0 and solid for BIN Map.

For the ABERCAMPUS00 dataset, both methods in [2,4] have high precision but low recall compared to the gradient-based sampling method, which has high recall when the map is sparsely (lower m value) populated and low recall when densely (higher m value) populated. In densely populated maps, the Cartesian space distance between nodes is shorter, resulting in a lower threshold τ (the Euclidean distance at the point of creation of the node. This in turn reduces the effective catchment area of nodes for loop closure detection. Coupled with the increased number of actual loop closures (denser nodes imply more loop closures), the detection rate (TP) decreases, resulting in a lower recall.

The results for the LLANCAMPUS00 dataset show a higher recall than for ABERCAMPUS00, for all methods. This is due to most of the parallel paths being detected as loop closures for the former. In particular a long stretch of parallel paths in the ABERCAMPUS00 dataset has not been detected as loop closures. This is due to large image differences between the two paths because of close proximity to grass on one side and bushed/buildings on the other, both sides being different in colour. This is visible in Figs. 4 and 6.

The results using the FAB-MAP 2.0 and BIN Map methods are not consistent when varying m; this is likely due to the fact that the sampling used was not based on the features used by the methods. FAB-MAP 2.0 performs better than BIN Map on both datasets.

The loop closure (localisation) time complexity is linear in the number of nodes in the map since a comparison is made with all existing nodes for each

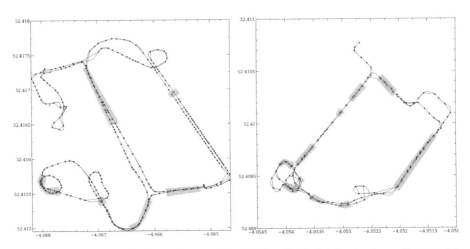

(a) Topological map for ABERCAMPUS00   (b) Topological Map for LLANCAMPUS00

Fig. 6. Topological maps for ABERCAMPUS00 and LLANCAMPUS00. The green connections (highlighted in yellow) are loop closures while the red connections correspond to the creation sequence. These were produced with $m = 10$.(Color figure online)

newly added node. For a map of 175 nodes, the loop closure computation time on an Intel core $i7$ (6th generation) is 400 ms.

Both fixed and Visual Compass sampling methods can produce higher recalls at the expanse of lower precision. This is due to these methods producing sparser maps at settings of lower sampling rates of their parameters ($s = 30$ and $\beta = 0.1$). This behaviour is similar to that of the gradient-based sampling method at low values of the gradient threshold (large distance between nodes). These two methods however never reach a precision of 1. This may be due to a spatial sampling not adequate at the other end of the parameter range. In any case, the sampling not being adapted to the information used in the loop closures, it is unlikely that such method will perform well. Note that the behaviour of the fixed sampling method on the LLANCAMPUS00 dataset is erratic, probably due to the relative small size of the environment/dataset and that fixed sampling can randomly select nodes that are nearby or not at key locations.

As can be seen on the top right corner of the map in Fig. 6b, some loop closures at junctions of paths are missed. This is due to nodes not being created in synchronisation between the multiple branches of the junction.

5   Conclusion and Future Work

In this paper, we have presented a novel appearance-based visual topological mapping method, which uses an adaptive sampling method to select relevant images and creates loop closures that are based on local properties of the map (changes of the local appearance). The method uses panoramic images captured at regular intervals while traversing the environment of the robot. The method was evaluated here using precision and recall. Other metric need to be devised to measure the quality of the produced topologies.

The purely gradient-based sampling method adapts to rapidity of change of the environment but sometimes creates nodes that prevent some loop closures from being created.

One major drawback of our approach is the time complexity associated to loop closures and localisation. Work is in progress to build hierarchies onto the map to reduce the time complexity allowing larger environments to be covered.

References

1. Cummins, M., Newman, P.: FAB-MAP: Probabilistic localization and mapping in the space of appearance. Int. J. Robot. Res. **27**(6), 647–665 (2008)
2. Cummins, M., Newman, P.: Appearance-only SLAM at large scale with FAB-MAP 20. Int. J. Robot. Res. **30**(9), 1100–1123 (2011)
3. Garcia-Fidalgo, E., Ortiz, A.: iBoW-LCD: an appearance-based loop-closure detection approach using incremental bags of binary words. IEEE Robot. Autom. Lett. **3**(4), 3051–3057 (2018)
4. Garcia-Fidalgo, E., Ortiz, A.: Vision-based topological mapping and localization methods: a survey. Robot. Auton. Syst. **64**, 1–20 (2015)
5. Ismail, K., Liu, R., Zheng, J., Yuen, C., Guan, Y.L., Tan, U.: Mobile robot localization based on low-cost LTE and odometry in GPS-denied outdoor environment. In: 2019 IEEE International Conference on Robotics and Biomimetics (ROBIO), pp. 2338–2343 (2019)
6. Labrosse, F.: The visual compass: performance and limitations of an appearance-based method. J. Field Robot. **23**(10), 913–941 (2006)
7. Labrosse, F.: Short and long-range visual navigation using warped panoramic images. Robot. Auton. Syst. **55**(9), 675–684 (2007)
8. Lowe, D.G.: Distinctive image features from scale-invariant keypoints. Int. J. Comput. Vis. **60**(2), 91–110 (2004)
9. Lowry, S., et al.: Visual place recognition: a survey. IEEE Trans. Robot. **32**(1), 1–19 (2015)
10. Neal, M., Labrosse, F.: Rotation-invariant appearance based maps for robot navigation using an artificial immune network algorithm. In: Proceedings of the 2004 Congress on Evolutionary Computation, vol. 1, pp. 863–870 (2004)
11. Ranganathan, A., Menegatti, E., Dellaert, F.: Bayesian inference in the space of topological maps. IEEE Trans. Robot. **22**(1), 92–107 (2006)
12. Ray, A.K., Behera, L., Jamshidi, M.: GPS and sonar based area mapping and navigation by mobile robots. In: 2009 7th IEEE International Conference on Industrial Informatics, pp. 801–806 (2009)
13. Ulrich, I., Nourbakhsh, I.: Appearance-based place recognition for topological localization. In: Proceedings of the IEEE International Conference on Robotics and Automation, vol. 2, pp. 1023–1029 (2000)
14. Werner, F., Maire, F., Sitte, J.: Topological SLAM using fast vision techniques. In: Kim, J.-H., et al. (eds.) FIRA 2009. LNCS, vol. 5744, pp. 187–196. Springer, Heidelberg (2009). https://doi.org/10.1007/978-3-642-03983-6_23

15. Woodland, A., Labrosse, F.: On the separation of luminance from colour in images. In: Proceedings of the International Conference on Vision, Video, and Graphics, pp. 29–36. University of Edinburgh (2005)
16. Zhang, H.: BoRF: Loop-closure detection with scale invariant visual features. In: Proceedings of the IEEE International Conference on Robotics and Automation, pp. 3125–3130 (2011)

Building a Navigation System for a Shopping Assistant Robot from Off-the-Shelf Components

Kenny Schlegel$^{(\boxtimes)}$ ⓘ, Peer Neubert ⓘ, and Peter Protzel ⓘ

Chemnitz University of Technology, Chemnitz, Germany
`kenny.schlegel@etit.tu-chemnitz.de`

Abstract. A primary goal of developing robots is to relieve people from hard work or help them in difficult situations. An example for such a situation is a shopping assistant robot that supports people who need help in their daily life. Such a mobile robot has to be able to deal with dynamic environments (moving people) and navigate safely and efficiently. In the present paper, we provide a system description of our navigation strategy for an assistant robot that is developed for autonomous operation in a supermarket. Creating an appropriate experimental environment can be quite challenging, and access to the application place can be limited (e.g., a real supermarket). Therefore we complement our real robot with a digital twin and describe our approach to create a suitable simulation of a real-world supermarket. Further, we discuss how off-the-shelf software can be used to implement a three-stage navigation strategy (planing a route with a TSP solver, global path planning, and incorporating dynamic obstacles in an optimization-based TEB approach) that is suitable for environments with dynamic obstacles. The paper presents our approaches to create a 3D map from 2D floor plans, as well as the preprocessing of the sensor data for usage in the TEB planner. Finally, we provide our hands-on experience with implementing a complex state-machine using the graphical RAFCON framework.

Keywords: Mobile robots · Dynamic environments · Navigation

1 Introduction

As a result of the technical progress, robots are going to be more widely used not only in industrial fields but also in people's daily life. They can be designed as mobile platforms to make people's lives easier. One application scenario is a shopping assistant for supermarkets. In the context of ambient assisted living, such robots can be helpful for older or disabled people, but also for other consumers shopping can become more convenient. For example, the robot provides product information or their position in the market, works as a guide, or as a

Supported by the Federal Ministry of Education and Research, Germany.

ⓒ Springer Nature Switzerland AG 2020

A. Mohammad et al. (Eds.): TAROS 2020, LNAI 12228, pp. 103–115, 2020.
https://doi.org/10.1007/978-3-030-63486-5_13

shopping cart, which follows a customer. However, a major goal of this development is autonomous shopping: with a list of items, the robot collects them efficiently and bring them to the customer or checkout.

Moving people, shopping carts, and narrow shelves make autonomous navigation within a supermarket quite challenging. The requirements for the robot are high: it should be fast, efficient, and safe. Compared to applications in autonomous logistic centers, a supermarket is less constraint and especially navigation in the vicinity of moving people in an efficient way is difficult. It requires an extensive perception of the environment and sophisticated planning algorithms. But such an unconstrained system offers the opportunity to work in unprepared environments and has a wider applicability. Beside robot application like Home-care, a shopping assistant robot must be fast while ensuring safety, since costumers usually have limited time. This leads to a difficult trade-off between speed and safety. Furthermore, in order to fulfill complex tasks, a shopping assistant robot has to have a large set of skills (autonomous shopping, leading, following, etc.) - the coordination and ordered execution of these skills, as well as monitoring and coordinating the various hardware and software modules are essential. In particular, the exception handling requires a robust robot control architecture.

Although robots designed for such complex tasks are typically customized and vary in a lot of details, the design decisions and challenges when building and programming such a robot are quite similar. In this paper, we present our experiences in building the navigation module for such a shopping assistant robot in order to facilitate the development of other robots for similar tasks. This work is part of an ongoing larger project to create a fully functional shopping assistant robot that is capable of navigating in crowded environments and autonomously collect a list of shopping items. This paper presents the following aspects of our shopping robot[1]:

- Section 2.1 provides a short presentation of the custom made robot and its sensor layout designed for the complete autonomous shopping task.
- Since navigating a larger robot in the vicinity of humans is dangerous, extensive testing and evaluation of the navigation algorithms is mandatory. Section 2.2 describes how we complement the real robot with a digital twin in a simulated supermarket environment. This simulation can later also be used for visualization purposes for customers.
- To circumvent the (still existing) challenges of SLAM, we present a semi-automatic procedure to create 3D maps from a priori known 2D floor plans in Sect. 3.1. These maps are used to create the simulation, as well as for navigation of the real robot.
- The core navigation capabilities result from a combination of three off-the-shelve components: we use a state-of-the-art optimization-based time elastic band planer in combination with a TSP solver and a global A* planner to approach navigation tasks in supermarket environments (see Sect. 3.1).

---

[1] Videos and other supplementary material can be found on our website https://www.tu-chemnitz.de/etit/proaut/shopping-robot.

– Section 3.2 presents hands-on experiences with the recently published RAF-CON [2] framework to create, run, and monitor state-machines (in particular, hardware-sensor monitoring).

The purpose of the paper is to provide an example of a navigation system to support researchers and developers who want to design a robot for navigation in dynamic environments, especially those with humans. The list of similar examples of robots is not very long. A historical milestone and the first mobile robot that could navigate autonomously was Shakey the robot [14]. Although we still use a variant of Shakey's A* planner in our system, since then, technology and software have been improved, and further applications became possible. There were mobile robots in the field of human interactions, like the RHINO robot [3], which works as an interactive tour guide in a museum or the LINO robot [10] as an example of a domestic user interface robot. Based on these early-stage systems and more recent developments, applications of service robots in more complex environments became possible. For instance, the SPENCER robot [21] can support people at a large airport. Such a system is similar to our shopping assistant robot since both operate in dynamic environments with moving people. SPENCER uses multimodal people tracking with a laser scanner and RGB-D cameras to estimate people's motion and accordingly adapt the planned paths based on an RRT* planner. Also related is the STRANDS [9] project that deals with long-term autonomy in dynamic environments. Cheng [4] describes another system in a supermarket environment that can grasp items and put them into the bag. They used an A* algorithm to compute waypoints to navigate the robot. However, since the main task is focused on grasping, the navigation strategy does not provide specific dealing with dynamic obstacles.

All these presented references have individual requirements and different implementations. Although our system shares some properties with the existing approaches, there are significant differences that are supposed to provide additional insights and guidance for developers of new systems. In particular, we see value in the parallel usage of 3D maps created from floor plans in simulation and real-world navigation, as well as the integration and experiences with the recently presented TEB planner as well as the RAFCON framework. Although we build on off-the-shelve components, they require modifications and extensions to work in combination to approach the challenging task of navigation in supermarket environments.

2   System Components

In the following two sections, we will describe the system components, starting with the hardware platform, followed by our simulation environment.

2.1   Robot Platform

The complete robot system prototype is visualized in Fig. 1. It shows the real system on the left and its digital twin for our simulation on the right (described in Sect. 2.2). The robot is based on an omnidirectional wheel drive. This is an important design decision since it significantly simplifies acting in a narrow and crowded environment like a supermarket, in particular since picking items from shelves requires small motions parallel to the shelf. The omnidirectional wheel drive allows us to perform them without additional rotations of the platform. The size of the platform is limited to the dimensions of a regular shopping cart. For perception, we use the following sensors:

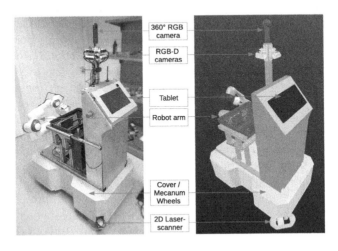

Fig. 1. Left: the real robot system, right: the digital twin in simulation environment.

- Two 2D laser-scanners (Hokuyo UTM-30LX-EW), which are located on diagonal corners of the case to get a 360° field of view. They are used for localization and collision avoidance. They are mounted very low (6 cm over the ground) in order to perceive the bottom panel of the supermarket shelves.
- One inertial measurement unit (IMU MTI-3-8A7G6-DK) located in the center of the robot to improve the wheel odometry based on wheel encoders.
- In total, there are eight RGB-D cameras (Realsense D435), arranged in two horizontal rings of four cameras to allow 360° perception and a large vertical field of view.

The main exteroceptive sensors for navigation and collision avoidance are the laser scanner and the lower ring of RGB-D cameras. The second RGB-D camera ring is primarily used for interaction with potential customers by recognizing intentions with an eye gaze tracking system described in [13]. Although it is part of this shopping robot, this interaction system is beyond the scope of this paper. Eight RGB-D cameras produce high data traffic on the hardware. Grunnet-Jepsen et al. [8] provide a system description with up to four cameras. However, our experience shows that it is possible to use simultaneously eight D435 cameras with a PCIe extension for USB3.0 (DELOCK 89297 PCIe card mounted in an

Aprotech GOLUB 5000 i7 industry PC) if the resolution and frequency are set to a mid-level (480 × 270 pixel depth resolution and 15 fps).

Furthermore, on top of the RGB-D camera rings, there is a 360° RGB camera to detect people and their skeleton in images. In addition, the robot system also has a tablet to interact with users, which is located in an ergonomic position, and a 'Panda' robot arm from the company 'Franka Emika' to grasp objects and put them into the basket. However, the components that are not related to navigation are not further discussed in the present paper.

2.2   Simulation Environment

Since it provides a more accessible test environment in contrast to a real super-market, we use a simulation environment to develop and evaluate the algorithms parallel to the real robot platform. We decided to use V-Rep [17] as simulation software[2] based on the publication [15] that compares three different simulation frameworks - V-Rep has the overall best evaluation. V-Rep has the advantages of a large object library, for example people who can be static or dynamic (well suited for supermarket environments) and the simple ROS compatibility with an appropriate plug-in. To create the 3D model of the simulated supermarket, we evaluated two approaches:

1. Using 3D point cloud SLAM. We did a 3D measurement of a real super-market with another robot [11] that is equipped with the 360° laser scanner from [20] to produce a real representation of the market. After getting several 3D scans of different places in the supermarket, we fused these to one map with the ICP registration algorithm and aligned RGB images with the 3D point cloud to obtain a colored point cloud representation of the market. Afterward, we cre-ated a mesh from the points to use it in the simulation. Figure 2 shows the result of the point cloud and the constructed mesh (for visualization, the image con-tains both - from left to right is going from the point cloud to the mesh (shown in gray tones)).

2. Creating 3D maps from available 2D floor plans. The target shopping assistant robot is developed in cooperation with a supermarket company. Thus, we are in the comfortable position to have floor plans available that also include a layout of the larger furniture (e.g., the shelves). If such robots are deployed in real supermarkets or other public places for practical usage, this will presumably also be based on corporations with the owners of these places; thus, the availability of floor plans is a reasonable assumption.

To create a 3D model with primitive geometric objects from the 2D floor plan, we conduct the following steps:

1. We use standard image processing tools to transform the floor plan to pre-defined color code for the different semantic objects and categories (e.g., the floor has the color white, all shelves of a particular type have another color value, and so on). This requires some manual configuration and supervision.

---

[2] Version 3.5; latest version (CoppeliaSim) does not work with the used V-Rep plug-in.

2. Based on our previous work [16] we can create a 3D model automatically from the 2D color-coded image (basically, each area in the 2D image with a specific color becomes a 3D object with the corresponding predefined height).
3. Finally, texturing all these primitive geometric objects with supermarket images creates the environment visualized in Fig. 3.

When creating the simulation environment based on the mesh obtained from 3D SLAM in the real supermarket, we faced three challenges: First, error correction and loop closure detection in our point-cloud SLAM required some careful human intervention. Second, the created mesh needs a high effort to smooth some irregularities and reducing the complexity of the surface. The third was the high resolution of the created mesh, which made the simulation very slow and increased the computation time for rendering and sensing. Although all three challenges can be addressed with more sophisticated algorithms and more manual intervention, we found the alternative approach based on the 2D floor plans to be preferable: The 3D representation based on simple geometric objects allows a sufficiently detailed representation of the static structure of the market while it is still possible to simulate with low computational effort. The high-resolution 3D model provides a very detailed and realistic appearance of the real world but is not suitable for a simulation with V-Rep. For instance, the simple 3D map has with 2500 vertices only 0.02% of the size compared to the high-resolution mesh visualized in Fig. 2. Even if the detailed mesh is reduced in size, the simulation with the simple 3D model is still resource-hungry. For instance, simulating with a frequency 10 Hz on an i7-8550U CPU is possible in real-time but requires a complete CPU kernel. The scripts of the sensors (laser and camera data-processing) need the most CPU power.

Fig. 2. The result of the supermarket pointcloud and its resulting mesh (left to right is going from points to surface).

Fig. 3. The simulation environment of the supermarket with V-REP.

3 Software Components

The presentation of the software architecture is again divided into two sections: 3.1 provides information about the navigation software and 3.2 the concept of our state control (state machine). The implementation uses ROS in version Kinetic.

3.1   Navigation

Where I am? (Localization). As described in Sect. 2.2, we create a map from available floor plans for simulation. We use the same map to create an occupancy grid map for the localization of the robot in the supermarket. In combination with the well known Monte Carlo localization from [7] and the available ROS implementation[3] we are able to localize the robot using the 360° 2D laser scans. The repetitive structure of supermarkets makes the initial global localization particularly challenging. The traversal of a relatively long route might be required to solve localization ambiguities due to visual aliasing. We circumvent this problem by assuming a known start position of the robot. In practice, this could be, e.g., the power charger station. Additionally, we improve the motion estimation of the wheel odometry by combination with IMU measurements in a Kalman filter based on an available ROS-implementation[4]. We did experiments in a real supermarket (with the robot from [11]), which showed that it is possible to hold the localization even if the initial floor map is sometimes unrelated to the real measurements (in particular, there were unknown and temporary shelves in the market).

Where do I need to go? (Planning the route). In the autonomous shopping use-case, the user selects several items on the tablet and it sends a list of articles and their positions to the robot. Then, the robot has to find the shortest route to collect all items as quickly as possible. This optimization problem is called 'Traveling Salesman Problem' (TSP) and is intensively studied in particular in the field of operations research. An approximate solution can be achieved with the nearest neighbor method described in [5]. It is a deterministic heuristic procedure that starts at one point and selects the next item based on the smallest distance to all other open items. This greedy algorithm produces only an approximated solution and not necessarily an optimal order of all items. Besides the nearest neighbor method, there are also other solvers of the TSP. For instance, an optimal TSP solver called CONCORDE[5], which outputs the item order with the shortest entire path. We use this solver in combination with a ROS package[6] for our supermarket robot system. Since the computing time for exactly solving the TSP can increase exponentially, it is important to know when it gets too time-consuming and how are the difference of the lengths of the entire paths compared to the approximate solver. Experiments in our supermarket environment with 20 items show that the exact Concorde TSP solver needs roughly 500 ms more than the approximate TSP solver (nearest neighbor) with less than 1 ms. A significant growth of computing time with the Concorde solver starts at round about 60 to 80 items. Additionally, it has to be noticed that the most time-consuming step is constructing the distance matrix. An A* planner calculates

---

[3] Brian P. Gerkey, AMCL, ROS Wiki, http://wiki.ros.org/amcl.

[4] Tom Moore, robot_localization, ROS Wiki, http://wiki.ros.org/robot_localization.

[5] Applegate, D. et al., "Concorde tsp solver". http://math.uwaterloo.ca/tsp/concorde.

[6] Richard Bormann, ipa_building_navigation, http://wiki.ros.org/ipa_building_navigation.

distances between all possible points and saves these in a matrix. This matrix can be precomputed concerning all item positions in the market and is given while solving the TSP problem to save computing time. However, with a view on the average number of items that are bought in the supermarket per stay, we recognize that the computing time of the solver is negligible - only an average of 10 items are purchased per visit[7]. Finally, a comparison of the entire path lengths indicates that between 10 and 60 items, the Concorde solver calculates a path that is 15% shorter than the path from the nearest neighbor approach. Based on these significant differences and the relatively short computing time of the exact solver within the range of typical human behaviors, the exact TSP solver can be used for creating a global order in the market. One example of the route planning with 16 items can be seen in Fig. 4 on the left image - it is the first step of navigation planning.

What is the fastest way to the next item? (Path and motion planning). If we have the correct order of all items, we have to navigate between the subgoals. The whole path and motion planning of our system is based on the ROS navigation stack[8]. We use an A* planner on the grid map from the given floorplan of the supermarket (enhanced with current sensor data) to get the global path from the current position to the next item according to the results of the TSP (visualized in the middle image in Fig. 4 with a blue line as global path). After having our global path from the current position to the next item, we need a planner that reacts to unknown obstacles (static objects which are not in floor plan) and dynamic objects like people. A local planner can realize such behavior - it uses the global plan and adopts it regarding currently seen obstacles. In the literature are existing ready-to-use algorithms; for example, the dynamic windows approach (DWA) planner [6]. It is also part of the ROS navigation stack. The DWA planner is a sample-based trajectory generation algorithm that samples a set of velocities for translation and rotation (concerning the dynamic constraints of the robot). These hypotheses are evaluated with the so-called 'trajectory rollout' that simulates a path for all possible velocities and compares them with the current environment for potential

Fig. 4. Visualization of the three steps of navigation - left: calculate the route with TSP solver to collect all items; middle: result the global plan to the next item with A*; right: motion planning with TEB. Pillars are recognized people. (Color figure online)

---

[7] Statistic from our cooperation partner of the supermarket.

[8] Michael Ferguson, navigation, ROS Wiki, http://wiki.ros.org/navigation.

collisions. It results in a score, and the best trajectory for the next time step can be chosen. A disadvantage of this planner is that it cannot predict a more complex path to avoid collisions of dynamic obstacles in the future - it is rather a reactive planner with a constant velocity model.

A more suitable planner to incorporate dynamic obstacles is the more recent *TEB (time elastic band)* planner from [19] and [18] with its ROS implementation[9]. It is an online optimization algorithm based on a hypergraph (factor graph) and optimizes towards a minimum execution time. All nodes within the graph are waypoints (sampled from the solution of the global A* planner), and all edges represent the penalization functions (e.g., close to an obstacle). The current implementation provides an extension to incorporate dynamic obstacles and adapt the trajectory with the optimization of the factor graph. It enables long term planning and creates a path that avoids any collisions (static or dynamic) efficiently. In addition, the implementation of the TEB planner also includes the calculation of the velocities (path execution). Therefore, we chose the TEB planner for our local navigation within the supermarket.

However, it is essential to preprocess and provide the map and sensor data in a suitable way. The TEB planner uses two inputs of obstacles: one *static* and one *dynamic*. A local costmap, which is a gridmap with occupancy probabilities, represents the environment for static navigation. In contrast, a list of object descriptions contains all dynamic obstacles with properties like position, velocity, and appearance (shape). We developed a pipeline to separate our environment perceptions, which is based on the laser scanner and the RGB-D cameras. The first step is to detect and locate humans in our environment. As described in Sect. 2.1, we are planning to use a 360° RGB camera to detect people around the robot. Since it is work in progress, we use a simple laser scanner detector from [12] that can locate people in a 2D laser scanner (similar to the approach of [21] and [9]). In combination with a Kalman filter, we can use it as a basic human tracker. Another way is to use the ground truth positions from the simulation environment - it provides an error-free evaluating of the navigation algorithms. Once we have all the positions of the people in the environment, we can go to the next step: create the **dynamic obstacle** description. Based on the information

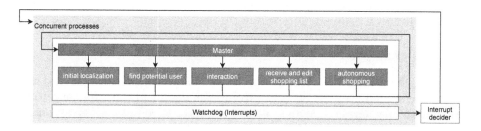

Fig. 5. High-level concept of state control within the statemachine.

---

[9] Christoph Roesmann, teb_local_planner, http://wiki.ros.org/teb_local_planner.

about the position and velocity of the laser tracker, we used these to create the description for the TEB planner.

The third step of our preprocessing pipeline is constructing the appropriate **static costmap**. It should contain no obstacles, which were already described in the obstacle message (including the people). To do so, we have to remove the points assigned to humans from the laser scan and RGB-D point cloud (we denote the input point cloud as P). We did this by grouping the point cloud P with an euclidean clustering. Afterward, we calculated for all clusters the centers and compared them to the given people positions. If one center is closer than a predefined threshold, it is marked as assigned and removed from the point cloud P - the result is a non-person point cloud P_{nP}. Notice, such a threshold-based method can be sensitive to the selected value (hyperparameter) and can remove clusters that are not related to a person (e.g., a person is standing close to a wall). To prevent such behavior with the point-cloud clustering, we set a maximum number of points per cluster - thus, merging of people and non-people objects becomes less likely, and more importantly, less harmful (since only small additional set of points is removed).

Now, the last step is to create a costmap from point cloud P_{nP}. For that, we use a so-called 'Nearfieldmap' from [22], which accumulates the input (our P_{nP}) over a specific time interval in a discretized 3D representation (voxel) - it prevents outliers from camera noise. We recognized that it would be more suitable to apply the clustering separately to the laser and the cameras, and fuse these two data into the nearfieldmap. It ensures a better parameterization of the sensor data probability (the laser is more reliably than the cameras). After a projection to the 2D plane, we obtain a 2D costmap with all non-person obstacles and can use it as the input of the TEB planner. Besides, methods to directly remove the people from the 2D costmap did not work because regions of the people are sometimes connected with other non-people objects (through projection from 3D to 2D). It leads to removing objects like walls or other obstacles if the person is to close to it.

With such a preprocessing pipeline, it is possible to use the TEB planner for navigation in a dynamic environment with people. Figure 4 visualize this third step on the right sight with a local path shown in green (robot avoids the person). Further results and visualizations can be found on our web-page (see footnote 1).

3.2   State Control

After describing the robot and its appropriate simulation environment and creating a navigation strategy, we want to provide our hands-on experience concerning state machine design. Such a task control software is necessary to control the order of all tasks and subtasks (e.g., localization, global planning, or reaction on inputs by the customer). One well-known framework to create a state machine within ROS is SMACH [1]. It is based on python scripts that execute specific tasks and return values indicating success or failure. One disadvantage of SMACH is the lack of tools to reduce the complexity of the state machine.

Debugging in case of errors is hard and strongly benefits from a visualization of the states. Even though SMACH provides a graph visualization of all states and their connections, it cannot be used to intervene when the machine is running, and editing of the code is only possible in the concerning python script, not in the visual graph.

Another recently published framework for efficient and transparent programming of a state machine is RAFCON [2]. It is a graphical tool to construct hierarchical tasks and allows real-time intervention and monitoring. All states contain a Python script that represents the executed code if the state is active. Based on the simple and clear designing as well as the monitoring while execution, we decide to use RAFCON to create our state machine.

Figure 5 visualizes the high-level concept of the entire system and how it is divided into several parts. The head of all tasks is the Master state that decides the order of given subtasks which are:

1. initial localization (robot moves to localize with MCL, see 3.1)
2. find potential user (work in progress; currently the nearest person will be selected as a potential user - the robot rotate to it)
3. interaction (the robot starts an interaction with a selected person by the tablet)
4. receive and edit shopping list (the user enters a shopping list for autonomous shopping, and the robot saves it for navigation)
5. autonomous shopping (the robot plans the route and executes it)

Since the project of the shopping assistant robot is not finished yet, the number of possible states will be increased (e.g., following a person) and adopted (interaction state gets more modalities like verbal communication). We want to emphasize that each state, like the autonomous shopping, consists of multiple subtasks summarized into on hierarchical state. Beside the Master and its tasks, the state machine has a concurrent "Watchdog" state that monitors all processes and reacts to interrupts or errors in the system. Additionally, user interaction on the robot mounted tablet could trigger interrupts (e.g., a customer press the stop button) and the state machine has to react on it. If such an interrupt arises, the following state 'Interrupt decider' creates a specific code and sends it to the Master that can react (for instance, repeat a state, go to a specific state, etc.). Another important class of interrupts comes from our sensor monitoring software. Basically, this is implemented as a ROS node that regularly checks the sensors concerning their connection, driver and data. If something goes wrong, the node sends an interrupt, and the state machine decides an appropriate reaction; for example restart the driver of the sensor. This monitoring node turned out to be of very high value in a complex robotic system with many sensors and a large number of different soft- and hardware components.

The combination of the presented high-level concept and the RAFCON framework allowed to create a complex state machine with monitoring of the hardware and reacting on signals from the tablet interaction. Based on our experience with both, SMACH and RAFCON, we find that RAFCON provides a better solution for complex task control then SMACH, in particular since RAFCON provides a user-friendly GUI with several options for better debugging (step by step execution, go backwards, set breakpoints, etc.).

4 Conclusion and Discussion

The paper provided an overview of the navigation strategy of our shopping assistant robot. We started with describing the system in both the real hardware platform and the simulation environment. We discussed how an available floor plan can be used to create a suitable simulation environment and discussed why we preferred this over a SLAM based approach. Such a simulation benefits from easier access to the test environment and ensures repeatable test scenarios (e.g., people are always moving on the same path and react consistently). After describing the hardware components and the simulation, we presented the software components, particularly the three-stage navigation process that consists of planning the most efficient route with a TSP solver, generate a global path to the next subgoal and plan the motion with the local TEB planner afterward. Using the TEB planner in an environment with people as dynamic obstacles was not described in the literature yet and required a specific preprocessing of the obstacle perception. With our presented concept, we can use the TEB planner in the presence of humans. However, future work includes an extension to the 'freezing robot' problem in dense human crowds. The current system is a promising basis for addressing this problem in the ongoing research project. For example, the factor graph representation in the TEB planer provides a general framework to include additional information about predicted human motions and their uncertainty in the planning process.

Finally, we presented why and how we use RAFCON to implement the high-level concept of handling multiple states (tasks) and monitoring of our sensor hardware as well as the interrupts, e.g., triggered by user interaction on the tablet. The implementation with RAFCON showed beneficial properties like user-friendly GUI, intuitive debugging and rapid development.

References

1. Bohren, J., Cousins, S.: The SMACH high-level executive [ROS News]. IEEE Robot. Autom. Mag. **17**(4), 18–20 (2010)
2. Brunner, S.G., et al.: RAFCON: a graphical tool for engineering complex, robotic tasks. In: IEEE International Conference on Intelligent Robots and Systems (2016)
3. Burgard, W., et al.: Experiences with an interactive museum tour-guide robot. Artif. Intell. **114**, 3–55 (1999)
4. Cheng, C.H., et al.: Design and implementation of prototype service robot for shopping in a supermarket. In: ARIS (2018)
5. Domschke, W., Drexl, A., Klein, R., Scholl, A.: Einführung in Operations Research, 9th edn. Springer, Heidelberg (2015). https://doi.org/10.1007/978-3-662-48216-2
6. Fox, D., Burgard, W., Thrun, S.: The dynamic window approach to collision avoidance. IEEE Robot. Autom. Mag. **4**(1), 23–33 (1997)

7. Fox, D., et al.: Monte carlo localization: efficient position estimation for mobile robots. In: National Conference on Artificial Intelligence (1999)
8. Grunnet-Jepsen, A., et al.: Using the Intel ® RealSense TM Depth cameras D4xx in Multi-Camera Configurations. Technical report (2018)
9. Hawes, N., et al.: The STRANDS project: long-term autonomy in everyday environments. IEEE Robot. Autom. Mag. 24(3), 146–156 (2017)
10. Kröse, B.J.A., Porta, J.M., van Breemen, A.J.N., Crucq, K., Nuttin, M., Demeester, E.: Lino, the user-interface robot. In: Aarts, E., Collier, R.W., van Loenen, E., de Ruyter, B. (eds.) EUSAI 2003. LNCS, vol. 2875, pp. 264–274. Springer, Heidelberg (2003). https://doi.org/10.1007/978-3-540-39863-9_20
11. Lange, S., et al.: Two autonomous robots for the DLR spacebot cup -lessons learned from 60 minutes on the moon. In: International Symposium on Robotics, ISR (2016)
12. Leigh, A., et al.: Person tracking and following with 2D laser scanners. In: Proceedings of IEEE International Conference on Robotics and Automation (2015)
13. Lorenz, O., Thomas, U.: Real time eye gaze tracking system using CNN-based facial features for human attention measurement. In: VISIGRAPP (2019)
14. Nilsson, N.J.: Shakey the Robot. SRI INTERNATIONAL MENLO PARK CA (1984). https://www.sri.com/work/publications/shakey-robot
15. Pitonakova, L., Giuliani, M., Pipe, A., Winfield, A.: Feature and performance comparison of the V-REP, Gazebo and ARGoS robot simulators. In: Giuliani, M., Assaf, T., Giannaccini, M.E. (eds.) TAROS 2018. LNCS (LNAI), vol. 10965, pp. 357–368. Springer, Cham (2018). https://doi.org/10.1007/978-3-319-96728-8_30
16. Poschmann, J., et al.: Synthesized semantic views for mobile robot localization. In: European Conference on Mobile Robots, ECMR (2017)
17. Rohmer, E., et al.: CoppeliaSim (formerly v-REP): a versatile and scalable robot simulation framework. In: International Conference on Intelligent Robots and Systems (IROS) (2013)
18. Rösmann, C., et al.: Trajectory modification considering dynamic constraints of autonomous robots. In: Robotik 2012, pp. 74–79 (2012)
19. Rösmann, C., et al.: Efficient trajectory optimization using a sparse model. In: 2013 European Conference on Mobile Robots, pp. 138–143 (2013)
20. Schubert, S., Neubert, P., Protzel, P.: How to build and customize a high-resolution 3D laserscanner using off-the-shelf components. In: Alboul, L., Damian, D., Aitken, J.M.M. (eds.) TAROS 2016. LNCS (LNAI), vol. 9716, pp. 314–326. Springer, Cham (2016). https://doi.org/10.1007/978-3-319-40379-3_33
21. Triebel, R., et al.: SPENCER: a socially aware service robot for passenger guidance and help in busy airports. In: Wettergreen, D.S., Barfoot, T.D. (eds.) Field and Service Robotics. STAR, vol. 113, pp. 607–622. Springer, Cham (2016). https://doi.org/10.1007/978-3-319-27702-8_40
22. Weissig, P., Protzel, P.: Properties of timebased local OctoMaps. In: Workshop on State Estimation and Terrain Perception for All Terrain Mobile Robots held in conjunction with IROS (2016)

Testing an Underwater Robot Executing Transect Missions in Mayotte

Adrien Hereau[1]([✉]), Karen Godary-Dejean[1], Jérémie Guiochet[2],
Clément Robert[2], Thomas Claverie[3], and Didier Crestani[1]

[1] LIRMM, UMR 5506, Univ of Montpellier, CNRS, Montpellier, France
{adrien.hereau,karen.godary-dejean,didier.crestani}@lirmm.fr
[2] LAAS-CNRS, Univ of Toulouse, CNRS, UPS, Toulouse, France
{jeremie.guiochet,clement.robert,}@laas.fr
[3] CUFR de Mayotte and MARBEC, Univ of Montpellier, CNRS, Ifremer, IRD,
Montpellier, France
thomas.claverie@univ-mayotte.fr

Abstract. In this paper, we present an approach to test underwater robots with a mission perspective. We propose five classes of oracle mission properties, used to perform test verification and evaluation: mission phases, time, energy, safety and localization. We study how these properties can be used, using data from the generated logs and analyzing the set of measurements. We apply this methodology on our semi-AUV prototype which executes autonomously biologic observation protocols in the Mayotte lagoon. For that we use an offline oracle property checker, and we focus on the issues of test acceptance criteria and ground truth despite low cost localization sensors. Results and lessons learned from this experiment are presented.

Keywords: Mobile robotics · Semi-AUV (Semi-Autonomous Underwater Vehicle) · Field testing · Oracle properties

1 Introduction

The emergence of new technologies in the fields of underwater robotics and image processing have made it possible for roboticists and marine biologists to collaborate and define complex automatized protocols for marine environment assessment. For instance, monitoring fish assemblages is a challenging task [3] as it requires deep and large area surveys at a high monitoring frequency which could not be done with traditional diver-based observation methods.

Underwater robots turn out to be an efficient mean to intervene in the fragile or hazardous environment that is marine ecosystem. For example, [13] and

This work is part of the BUBOT project (http://www.lirmm.fr/bubot/) funded through the national research agency ANR under the PIA ANR-16-IDEX-0006. It has also partially been funded by the CUFR of Mayotte, the Occitanie region and the CNRS/IRD natural hazard challenge.

© Springer Nature Switzerland AG 2020
A. Mohammad et al. (Eds.): TAROS 2020, LNAI 12228, pp. 116–127, 2020.
https://doi.org/10.1007/978-3-030-63486-5_14

[4] respectively use two different AUVs (Autonomous Underwater Vehicles) to observe coral reef or to regulate population of invasive starfishes in Australia. In this context, we develop an underwater robot executing autonomously a mission, called "transect", that consists in traveling along a virtual line for 50 m while embedding stereo cameras to record videos. Performing this protocol with a robot would lead to a more objective and efficient observation than with humans.

Nevertheless, the harsh constraints of operation in marine environment lead to several issues. Among them, localization for AUVs is of paramount importance, mainly due to the lack of GPS signal underwater. An alternative is the use of acoustic sensors, which are however often expensive, imprecise and not robust to the environmental conditions.

We also have to deal with obstacles that could be static such as coral head, or dynamic like marine wildlife or drift fishing nets. Underwater robots are also facing ocean currents making non-desirable (and often unpredictable) displacements. All other issues regarding traditional embedded systems failures should also be considered (e.g., software bugs, hardware or mechanical failures).

Validation of such systems is usually based on field testing. Embedded technologies on underwater robots need to be assessed not only in simulation or in swimming-pools, but also in real uncertain environment to verify their robustness. However, most of current experiments in the sea are focusing on function validation (e.g., sensing functions, or control), and rarely on full mission testing. We propose to address the issue of the validation in field testing at a mission level, of an underwater robot in a highly uncertain and adverse environment.

Our approach is based on the use of the oracle concept mainly deployed in the testing community. We define a method to consider and classify different types of properties including at the mission level, we illustrate this method proposing properties that could be used for the validation of our robot in an marine-life observation mission. To do so, the testing protocol basically relies on the definition of the test inputs that are the mission and the environment, a run of the mission, and the final off-line analysis of the properties.

The structure of the paper is as follows. We present some background and related works in Sect. 2, then we describe the system under test in Sect. 3. The test case and oracle properties are presented in Sect. 4. In Sect. 5, we analyze the results of the underwater robotic field mission and we draw some lessons. Finally we conclude in Sect. 6.

2   Baseline and Related Works

Testing is part of dynamic verification techniques in dependability [1]. It is the most intuitive way to reveal faults or assess robustness: a test case is provided to the system, then its outputs are analyzed to determine if they are correct, which constitutes what is called the oracle. In our context, the oracle can be defined as a list of properties that needs to be checked. Mainly two issues are studied in testing: the completeness of test inputs (e.g. missions and environmental conditions), and the definition of the oracle. In this paper we mainly focus on the latter element, because in long-term missions we believe that a poor or erroneous description of the oracle may lead to miss some faults in the design. This is especially important in underwater robotics as in the field validation is challenging because of the heavy logistics and the complexity to obtain the ground truth under the sea.

In the area of testing underwater robots, papers often bring out the performance of one specific function of their system (e.g., localization). For example, in [5], the authors performed tests in a river with several marine robots and only compared the localization performance of an Extended Kalman Filter (EKF) with other filters. In [10], the authors measured the precision of the navigation of their AUV by evaluating the position of the robot after resurfacing. In [6], the authors also performed sea trial tests comparing the speed measurement of their DVL sensor with the data of an accurate GNSS-USBL used as ground truth. In [9], the authors tested the AUV station keeping and waypoint following functions, estimating the position errors in presence of waves.

Moreover, few works deal with testing and validating functionalities with a complete specification comparisons. From the authors cited previously, in [10], the authors validate that the final error is below a desired threshold (5%). In [6], the authors validate that the DVL used meets the indicated developer specification (0.2% maximum error). An attempt to standardize test methods for measuring the functionality performances of underwater robots has been done in [7], which developed a set of test benches for ROVs and AUVs. The evaluation relies on varied criteria, from the robot capacity (maximal thrust, sensor resolution...) to the robotic task itself (station keeping, object grasping...). Nevertheless, it did not fix a methodological frame for testing.

Finally, to our knowledge, there is no real in-depth study of test approaches related to complex missions of underwater robots. Considering that the mission level would necessitate more complex system validation process than the traditional test methods, an important work has been done with mobile ground robots which may have complex missions. However, according to [11,12], few works are also focusing on the mission testing (which are usually ad-hoc). We try here to answer to all these issues in the context of underwater robotics.

3   The System Under Test

In this section, we describe our robotic system (Fig. 1) and its software architecture (Fig. 2). The system under test includes two main parts: the surface devices, embedded on a boat, and the underwater robot[1]. The communication between both parts is provided through a 200 m ethernet cable with neutral buoyancy. Modbus protocol is used for sending command to the robot and receiving mission status.

With 4 vertical and 4 horizontal thrusters, the robot is a 6 degrees of freedom (DoF) semi-AUV which executes autonomously the classical transect mission

---

[1] Designed and supplied by Syera (http://syera.fr) and REEDS companies.

Dimensions	80cm x 40cm x 20cm
Weight	29kg with batteries
Controller	Dropix controller
Actuators	T200 thrusters (x8)
Navigation sensors	IMU (on Dropix) MS5837 depth sensor Ping BR echosounder Seatrac X010 USBL
Batteries	NiMH batteries (x4)

Fig. 1. Our 6DoF semi-AUV

under the supervision of an operator. As in most of hybrid-ROV or semi-AUV [2], the operator can launch, interrupt the current mission and take control of the robot in remote control mode. Our underwater robot named REMI embeds an IMU, an echosounder for altitude (i.e. distance between robot and seabed) and a pressure sensor for depth. Some sensors dedicated to safety help to supervise the robot such as water leak detector or intensity and voltage sensors in the powerswitchs. The main front camera sends real time video to the operator. Not considered in the system under test, two pairs of stereo cameras fixed afterward on the robot give the 3D visual information used by the biologists. One pair is oriented towards the front filming marine wildlife, the other facing down provides information about the seabed and fish habitats.

The surface devices include a user PC which displays the user interface to monitor the mission (*GUI module*) and allows to remotely control the robot. The user PC also processes the sensors connected to its serial ports: the GPS beacon receives its own georeferenced position and the USBL transducer calculates the 3D relative position of the robot thanks to an acoustic signal emitted by the transponder on the robot. By combining the GPS and USBL measurements

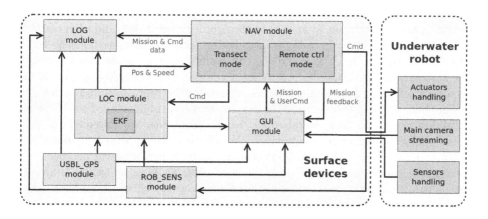

Fig. 2. The navigation module in the software architecture

in the *USBL_GPS module*, the georeferenced position of the robot along the 3 dimensions of the NED frame (North-East-Down local frame) is calculated.

In this first prototype, we chose to implement the navigation and localization modules in the user PC for debugging ease. The *ROB_SENS module* gets the sensors data provided by the embedded controller on the robot. *LOG module* records continually every mission, sensors, command or state time-stamped data in an output file. To minimize the process calculation time in the *LOC module* (localization module), we choose a simple EKF to get the robot estimated state $\hat{X} = [\nu, \eta]$ with ν the robot velocity along the 6 DoF in the body-frame and η the robot position and quaternion attitude in the local NED frame. The EKF relies on the robot's dynamic equations in the prediction part and merges the sensors data and the predicted state in the innovation part.

Our robot has two functioning modes: the remote control mode and the transect mode. Knowing the estimated state and the mission data in transect mode, the *NAV module* calculates the desired actuator propulsion in the body frame using a classic PID and sends it to the robot embedded controller which redistributes the command towards each thruster using the Moore–Penrose inverse of the thruster configuration matrix. In remote control mode, the *NAV module* only transfers the command generated by the operator on the boat to the robot.

Having defined our system under test, we describe the test characteristics in the following section.

4   Test Design

The main objective of the tests is to validate that our robot can perform the transect mission. In this section, we present our methodology, we introduce our tests inputs and properties applied to the in-the-field test campaign of our robot prototype.

4.1   Our Methodology

As said in Sect. 2, we want to answer to the problematic of the validation testing in the field for underwater robots, introducing into the test method the consideration of the whole system and the constraints related to complex missions. The system must be validated verifying a complete specification, i.e. a set of properties reflecting all the different constraints of the robot and its mission.

For that, we adapt and extend the oracle test protocol developed in [11] used to validate a mobile agricultural robot, where properties are classified according to safety and mission perspectives. We also use the approach proposed in [8] to define several performance classes driven by a performance perspective: *localization, energy, safety* and *time*. We keep these 4 classes as well as the mission phases breakdown of [11] to constitute our property classes. The *time* class imposes constraints over the duration of the mission phases. The *safety* class imposes constraints to preserve the robot integrity whereas the *energy* class imposes constraints to make sure there is enough energy left. The *localization* class imposes constraints on the precision of the localization. Finally, the *mission phases* class deals with the specifications of the user-oriented constraints over the whole mission.

During the oracle test, logged data are analyzed to verify if the properties are violated or not. In our case, the consideration of different mission phases (MPi) introduce a temporal constraint on the period of properties verification. We consider that there are 2 types of timing for a property verification: *During one (or several) mission phases* means that the property must be verified all along the concerned MPi; and *At the end of a mission phase* means that the property must only be verified at the end of the concerned phase. For a set of *mission runs*, we consider that the violation rate of a property is the number of times this property is violated out of the number of times the property is actually evaluated.

4.2 Test Case

We choose to focus on the transect mission in autonomous mode. A transect is basically defined (Fig. 3a) by its Start Point (SP) and End Point (EP). We draw a virtual line between SP and EP called Transect Line (TL). A transect can be executed either at constant depth or constant altitude according to operator wishes. Thus in the latter case, TL becomes relative to altitude. The surge velocity fixed by the operator should not be too high to minimize the impact of the robot presence on submarine species.

We count 3 mission phases during the mission. As the USBL signal is not received when the robot is at surface, in the first mission phase 0 (MP0) the robot dives vertically until a certain depth to capture USBL signal from surface in order to be georeferenced. As soon as the robot receives the USBL signal, it switches to mission phase 1 (MP1) in which it navigates toward SP. Once SP is reached, mission phase 2 (MP2) consists in the core process of the transect: navigating horizontally toward EP along TL.

(a) Transect mission   (b) Test areas

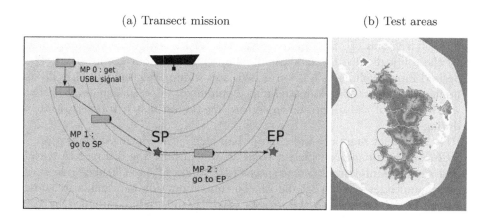

Fig. 3. Test inputs: mission description and test areas

We decided to execute transect in different GPS localization around Mayotte to have different environment contexts (Fig. 3b). Swell was mainly present at the limit of coral reef sites (the 2 left zones on the map) and did not exceed 1 m high. The distance between the surface and the seabed varied from 5 m to 80 m, the target transect depth varied between 2 m and 40 m and the target transect altitude between 1 m and 5 m. We varied the surge velocity from 0.5 m/s to 1.0 m/s for phase 1 and 0.1 m/s to 0.4 m/s for phase 2. We did not estimate more than 0.5 m/s of sea current at surface. We performed test only during day-light in order to maximize the visibility of the front camera, even if water turbidity sometimes prevented it. The user boat was either anchored or could follow the underwater robot, especially in coral reef areas.

4.3   Oracle Properties

Table 1 shows the 20 properties we have defined following our classification method. Figure 4 represents the property verification period.

- Property P1 means that the georeferenced position of the robot must be known, i.e. the USBL and GPS signals must be received by the user PC. P1 must be verified at the end of MP0, and is a precondition to start MP1 (represented on Fig. 4 by the arrow on the right of the verification period).
- P2 & P3: MP1 is finished if the position and attitude of the robot are close enough to SP with δpos^{SP} the distance between current position and SP; δang^{SP} the absolute value of the angle between the desired attitude at SP and the current attitude.
- P8 & P9: Likewise, MP2 is finished when the robot has reached EP.
- P4 & P5: These properties check the distance to TL with δpos^{TL} the distance between current position and its projection on TL and δang^{TL} the difference between the actual and desired angular positions of the robot. As shown on Fig. 4, these properties must be verified all along MP2.
- P6 & P7: During MP2, we check the robot speeds with $U^{TL} = \sqrt{u^2 + v^2 + w^2}$ and $\omega^{TL} = \sqrt{p^2 + q^2 + r^2}$ where (u, v, w, p, q, r) are respectively the surge, sway, heave, roll, pitch, and yaw velocities of the robot.
- P10: At the end of MP2, the coverage rate of the estimated volume filmed by the robot divided by the desired volume must be above a threshold. The desired filmed volume is a 6×6 m high and wide parallelepiped with TL as its main segment. The estimated filmed volume is a 6×6 m square projected 4 m in front of the robot and integrated on the estimated robot trajectory during MP2.
- P11: The robot must not takes more than δt_{init}^{max} time during initialization.
- P12 & P13: For mission phases 1 and 2, we consider the distance to travel and we define minimum average speeds (v_{min}^{SP} and v_{min}^{EP}) to calculate reference maximum times to reach SP and EP. The maximum time thresholds are equal to the initial distance to the targets ($dist_{init}^{SP}$ and $dist_{init}^{EP}$) divided by the minimum average speeds to perform that motion.
- P14: We check the absence of water in the robot.

Table 1. Properties to verify

Class	Objective	Property	ID
Mission phases	MP0: get localized	$loc_{signal} = true$	P1
	MP1: reach start point	$\delta pos^{SP} < \delta pos_{max}^{SP}$	P2
		$\delta ang^{SP} < \delta ang_{max}^{SP}$	P3
	MP2: reach end point through transect line	$\delta pos^{TL} < \delta pos_{max}^{TL}$	P4
		$\delta ang^{TL} < \delta ang_{max}^{TL}$	P5
		$U^{TL} < U_{max}^{TL}$	P6
		$\omega^{TL} < \omega_{max}^{TL}$	P7
		$\delta pos^{EP} < \delta pos_{max}^{EP}$	P8
		$\delta ang^{EP} < \delta ang_{max}^{EP}$	P9
		$cov > cov_{min}$	P10
Time	Time taken for mission phases not too long	$\delta t_{init} < \delta t_{init}^{max}$	P11
		$\delta t^{SP} < \dfrac{dist_{init}^{SP}}{v_{min}^{SP}}$	P12
		$\delta t^{EP} < \dfrac{dist_{init}^{EP}}{v_{min}^{EP}}$	P13
Safety	No water leak	$W_{detect} = false$	P14
	No high intern temperature	$T < T_{max}$	P15
	No low altitude	$alti > alti_{min}$	P16
	No high pressure	$press < press_{max}$	P17
	No communication loss	$\delta t_{com} < \delta t_{com}^{max}$	P18
Energy	No low battery voltage	$volt > volt_{min}$	P19
Loc	Precision estimated good enough	$var < var_{max}$	P20

- P15: We check that the intern temperature is not too high since it could indicate abnormal component behavior or fire start.
- P16: The altitude of the robot must remain above a threshold to prevent any collision with seabed.
- P17: The water pressure that must remain below a threshold to prevent any leaks of damage on components.
- P18: Communication between the user PC and the robot must not be interrupted too much time, especially with our deported control loop.
- P19: Energy axis is currently under study in LIRMM. For now, we only express one property as "having enough battery voltage".
- P20: Localization property class guarantees that the robot can localize itself in its environment. We check that each diagonal term of the estimated state covariance provided by the EKF is below a threshold.

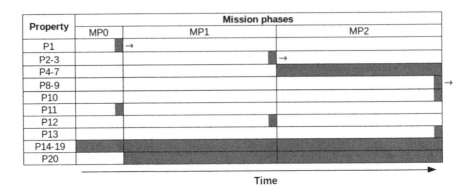

Fig. 4. The verification period for each property (in blue) (Color figure online)

Defining all these properties leads to a more systematic analysis of the test in order to find weaknesses in our design.

5   Experimental Results and Lesson Learned

In this section, we present and analyzed the results of the validation test campaign we performed in Mayotte early 2019. We logged 108 transects over 8 days on the field, at different localization around Mayotte as presented before. The log files generated contain the data to evaluate oracle properties: the estimated state, the sensor measurements and the different events that occurred over time. The properties P14, P15, P19 and P20 are not evaluated since we lack log data to do so. This campaign was done to confront our first robot's prototype with real in-the-field environment conditions. Table 2 shows the values of the property thresholds we fixed and the associated violation rate for all the transects. An important issue is the choice of the property threshold values, chosen accordingly to the biologist specifications and the physical constraints.

The first conclusion we made after this test campaign is that **the current performances of our low cost sensors are not sufficient for the transect mission**. The sensor uncertainties were prejudicial for the mission fulfillment as most of the properties were not respected. Indeed, the properties P4 & P10 involving the estimated position of the robot were often violated (resp. 72.9% and 44.4%). Some trajectory errors may come from the imperfection of the imperfect servoing and the latency of the echosounder, but the main reason is the imprecision of the USBL sensor. To illustrate this issue, Fig. 5b represents the robot trajectory during MP2 of a transect. The real-time estimated trajectory (EKF) appears in orange, the USBL data in purple, and the transect line TL is plotted in blue between SP and EP. The USBL gave erratic values in these experiment conditions since it measured up to 19 m difference between two consecutive measurements that were taken 10 s apart with an estimated robot velocity of only 0.3 m/s (Fig. 5c). In addition, we also noticed that the time to

Table 2. Property violation rates over all runs

Property	Threshold	Property violation rate
P1	$USBL_{sig} = true$	8.3%
P2	$\delta pos^{SP}_{max} = 3\,\text{m}$	51.5%
P3	$\delta ang^{SP}_{max} = 22.5°$	51.5%
P4	$\delta pos^{TL}_{max} = 3\,\text{m}$	72.9%
P5	$\delta ang^{TL}_{max} = 22.5°$	37.5%
P6	$U^{TL}_{max} = 0.75\,\text{m/s}$	27.1%
P7	$\omega^{TL}_{max} = 22.5°/s$	81.2%
P8	$\delta pos^{EP}_{max} = 3\,\text{m}$	25.0%
P9	$\delta ang^{EP}_{max} = 22.5°$	25.0%
P10	$cov_{min} = 70\%$	44.4%
P11	$\delta t^{max}_{init} = 12\,\text{s}$	0.0%
P12	$v^{SP}_{min} = 0.2\,\text{m/s}$	14.6%
P13	$v^{EP}_{min} = 0.1\,\text{m/s}$	13.9%
P16	$alti_{min} = 0.75\,\text{m}$	3.7%
P17	$press_{max} = 9bars$	0.0%
P18	$\delta t^{max}_{com} = 3\,\text{s}$	37.0%

update measurement value varied between 2 s and 25 s for that transect. For performing precise underwater robotic missions, efficient and often costly sensors are needed. However, a trend is also to deploy smaller and cheaper robots. A compromise is thus required and our approach using oracle properties may be useful to establish this compromise.

Getting the Ground Truth is Complex for Underwater Experiments. As the properties are based on the robot state estimation, the problem is how to guarantee that this estimation is sufficiently closed to the reality, and this despite all the uncertainties? In order to verify the consistency of the localization data in our validation campaign, we materialized TL with a rope placed on the seabed (Fig. 5a). Looking at external videos, we checked the robot relative position on the rope and we compared it to the EKF estimation data. Even if this method is largely imprecise as it is based on a human evaluation, it was sufficient to detect some anomalies. This issue of ground truth is still an open issue [5], especially in underwater robotics where the logistics implementation of traditional solutions to obtain the ground truth (often environment instrumentation or used of accurate sensors) is difficult and very expensive.

The Difficulty of Building the Oracle Properties Database is Underestimated. Defining an exhaustive and sufficient set of properties requires a high level of expertise particularly to determine the thresholds. Before the tests in Mayotte, we first defined an initial set of properties which is a subset of the one

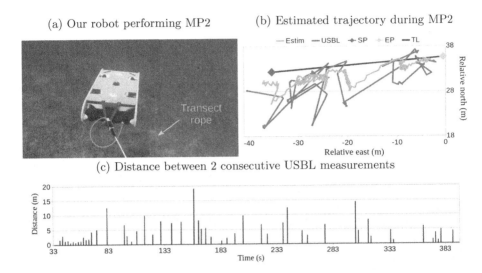

(a) Our robot performing MP2   (b) Estimated trajectory during MP2

(c) Distance between 2 consecutive USBL measurements

Fig. 5. Localization error with USB (Color figure online)

presented Sect. 4.3. For example we initially did not consider the P7 property, and the system was not designed to stabilize precisely the angular velocity of the robot. But P7 shows a significant percentage of violations (81.2%), which proves that we must enhance our controller on that point. Another example is P18, with a violation rate of 37.0%. When violated, the robot is unable to reach SP and thus it prevents to respect all the properties related to MP1 and MP2. This fault was due to the presence of resettable fuse protecting the battery. The power cutting triggered a software failure of the communication protocol that remained persistent even after energy recovering. We did not planned this problem before as this fault was difficult to diagnose. Thus, experience in field experiments also played a key role to define a efficient set of properties to validate. The simple question "is the mission a success?" is not so simple to define. From the robot user's point of view, achieving MP2 is the main objective. If we consider only the completion of MP2 (P8 & P9), and considering all the transects (including the ones where the MP0 and MP1 phases did not finished), the rate of mission success is 33.3% (failure rate of 66.7%). If we consider only the biologist initial specification defined by P10 for the video area verification, the rate of mission success is 18.5%. As this experiment was a first step in our development process, we did not investigate the formalization of such a mission success function. However, this would be an important tool, particularly to communicate with the biologists or even with certification bodies.

6   Conclusion

In this paper, we proposed a generic methodology to characterize tests with a mission point of view for the complete system. We identified several properties belonging to different property classes. Properties were associated with a period of verification: they could be check during or at the end of mission phases.

We applied this methodology on our semi-AUV prototype during a test campaign in the Mayotte lagoon. The analysis of these results first shows that our prototype must be improved since most of the oracle properties were not respected. This is globally not surprising as our robot is a first prototype and we use low-cost sensors. We plan to enhance both the hardware (with additional sensors) and software (with more efficient algorithm for example for data fusion) sides, and to carry out others test campaigns, enhancing again the oracle properties database and the test methodology.

We also plan to link our methodology of test with other dependability approaches such as fault identification and diagnosis methods and fault trees to identify the different faults in real time. A real time property violation would then be the same as a fault detection in a fault tolerance approach, leading to basic recovery actions (stop of the mission, reboot) or more sophisticated ones at the decisional level.

References

1. Avizienis, A., et al.: Basic concepts and taxonomy of dependable and secure computing. IEEE Trans. Dependable Secure Comput. **1**, 11–33 (2004)
2. Bowen, A., et al.: The Nereus hybrid underwater robotic vehicle. Underwater Technol. **28**, 79–89 (2009)
3. Cinner, J.E., et al.: Bright spots among the world's coral reefs. Nature **535**, 416–419 (2016)
4. Dunbabin, M., et al.: Real-time Vision-only Perception for Robotic Coral Reef Monitoring and Management (2019)
5. Fallon, M.F., et al.: Cooperative AUV navigation using a single maneuvering surface craft. Int. J. Robot. Res. **29**, 1461–1474 (2010)
6. Hegrenaes, O., et al.: Validation of a new generation DVL for underwater vehicle navigation. In: Autonomous Underwater Vehicles (AUV), Tokyo, Japan, pp. 342–348. IEEE (2016)
7. Jacoff, A., et al.: Development of standard test methods for evaluation of ROV/AUV performance for emergency response applications. In: OCEANS 2015, Washington, DC, pp. 1–10. MTS/IEEE (2015)
8. Lambert, P., et al.: An approach for fault tolerant and performance guarantee autonomous robotic mission. In: 2019 NASA/ESA Conference on Adaptive Hardware and Systems (AHS), Colchester, UK, pp. 87–94. IEEE (2019)
9. Lawrance, N.R., et al.: Ocean deployment and testing of a semi-autonomous underwater vehicle. In: OCEANS, Monterey, CA, USA, pp. 1–6. IEEE (2016)
10. Ramesh, R., et al.: Development and performance validation of a navigation system for an underwater vehicle. J. Navig. **69**, 1097–1113 (2016)
11. Robert, C., et al.: The virtual lands of Oz: testing an agribot in simulation. Empirical Softw. Eng. J. (2020)
12. Sotiropoulos, T., et al.: Can robot navigation bugs be found in simulation? An exploratory study. In: International Conference on Software Quality, Reliability and Security (QRS), Prague, Czech Republic. IEEE (2017)
13. Williams, S., et al.: Monitoring of benthic reference sites: using an autonomous underwater vehicle. IEEE Robot. Autom. Mag. **19**, 73–84 (2012)

Modelling and Control of an End-Over-End Walking Robot

Manu H. Nair$^{(\boxtimes)}$, Chakravarthini M. Saaj, and Amir G. Esfahani

Lincoln Centre for Autonomous Systems, University of Lincoln, Lincoln LN6 7TS, UK
18710796@students.lincoln.ac.uk,
{MSaaj,AGhalamzanEsfahani}@lincoln.ac.uk

Abstract. Over the last few decades, Space robots have found their applications in various in-orbit operations. The Canadarm2 and the European Robotic Arm (ERA), onboard the International Space Station (ISS), are exceptional examples of supervised robotic manipulators (RMs) used for station assembly and maintenance. However, in the case of in-space assembly of structures, like Large-Aperture Space Telescope (LAT) with an aperture larger than the Hubble Space Telescope (HST) and James Webb Space Telescope (JWST), missions are still in its infancy; this is heavily attributed to the limitations of current state-of-the-art Robotics, Automation and Autonomous Systems (RAAS) for the extreme space environment. To address this challenge, this paper introduces the modelling and control of a candidate robotic architecture, inspired by Canadarm2 and ERA, for in-situ assembly of LAT. The kinematic and dynamic models of a five degrees-of-freedom (DoF) End-Over-End Walking robot's (E-Walker's) first phase of motion is presented. A closed-loop feedback system validates the system's accurate gait pattern. The simulation results presented show that a Proportional-Integral-Derivative (PID) controller is able to track the desired joint angles without exceeding the joint torque limits; this ensures precise motion along the desired trajectory for one full cycle comprising of Phase-1 and Phase-2 respectively. The gait pattern of the E-Walker for the next phases is also briefly discussed.

Keywords: End-Over-End Walking robot · Kinematics · Dynamics · Control · Trajectory generation · Large-Aperture space telescopes

1 Introduction

The use of space telescopes can enable unprecedented astronomical missions in the years to come. The HST and the soon-to-be-launched JWST are notable examples. However, in-orbit assembly of LAT using teleoperation or autonomous space robots is highly challenging. The Primary Mirrors (PMs) of the LAT cannot be monolithically manufactured, leading to the adoption of a segmented design. Even if the PMs were monolithically manufactured, the problems arise in stowing the huge mirror modules into the current and planned launch vehicles. To overcome these limitations, there is now a move towards assembling the PMs, in-orbit, using a space robot. Based on an

© Springer Nature Switzerland AG 2020
A. Mohammad et al. (Eds.): TAROS 2020, LNAI 12228, pp. 128–133, 2020.
https://doi.org/10.1007/978-3-030-63486-5_15

extensive review presented in [1] and [2], alongside the proposed architecture in [3], the concept of an E-Walker looks promising for in-space assembly missions. As shown in Fig. 1, the E-Walker, is a 5 DoF limbed-robotic system, that can latch itself onto different connector points around the spacecraft; thereby, it offers larger workspace compared to manipulators with a fixed base. As the E-Walker can move along the spacecraft, the prime design requirement is to have adequate range to assemble the inner and outer rings of the telescope. The gait pattern of the E-Walker is comprised of two phases, which makes a full cycle. In Phase-1, shown in Fig. 2, joint 5's motion is tracked with joint 1 fixed to the base, for the robot to attain its first walking position. For Phase-2, joint 5 is fixed to the base and joint 1's motion is tracked. The kinematic and dynamic equations of the E-Walker's first phase of motion is presented here with simulation results that show controlling it to follow a straight-line trajectory using a PID Controller. An insight into the successive gait pattern is also provided.

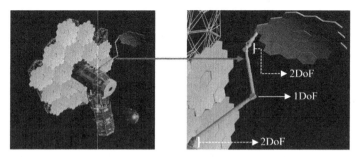

Fig. 1. Assembly of a 25 m space telescope by a robotic manipulator [1]

2   E-Walker Kinematic Modelling for Phase-1

For the kinematic analysis of the 5 DoF E-Walker, the Denavit Hartenberg (DH) convention was used to select the reference frames. Inverse kinematics was used to calculate the joint angles $(\theta_1 - \theta_5)$ with the known end-effector position and orientation.

Using kinematic formulations, joint angles for Phase-1 were calculated from Fig. 2 as:

$$r = [(b)^2 + (z_e - d(1 - \cos\alpha))^2]^{1/2} \tag{1}$$

$$b = (c^2 - d\sin\alpha)^{1/2} \tag{2}$$

$$c = (x_e^2 + y_e^2)^{1/2} \tag{3}$$

$$\theta_3 = \cos^{-1}((r^2 - 2l_2^2)/2l_2^2) \tag{4}$$

$$\theta_1 = \tan^{-1}(-x_e/y_e) \tag{5}$$

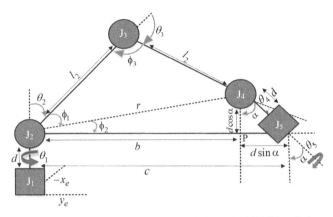

Fig. 2. Kinematic model of 5 DoF End-Over-End Walking Robot

$$\theta_2 = \pi/2 - cos^{-1}(r/2l_2) - cos^{-1}(((x_e^2 + y_e^2)^{1/2} - dsin\alpha)/r) \qquad (6)$$

where, l - link lengths, d - offset distance, (x_e, y_e) - end-effector (EE) coordinates. It is known that rotation matrix $\mathbf{R}_{05} = [\mathbf{R}_{03}\mathbf{R}_{35}]$ provides EE orientation. The angles θ_4 and θ_5 were calculated from $\mathbf{R}_{35} = [(\mathbf{R}_{03})^{-1}\mathbf{R}_{05}]$, where $\mathbf{R}_{35} \in \mathbb{R}^{3\times3}$, $\mathbf{R}_{03} \in \mathbb{R}^{3\times3}$ and $\mathbf{R}_{05} \in \mathbb{R}^{3\times3}$. $\mathbf{R}_{03}$ and $\mathbf{R}_{05}$ denotes the transformations from joints 1–3 and joints 1–5.

3   E-Walker Dynamic Modelling for Phase -1 and Gait Pattern

For an n-DoF manipulator with joint angle θ, the velocity of each link is represented by the Jacobian matrix and the joint velocity $\dot{\theta}$. $\theta \in \mathbb{R}^5$ is the vector comprising of the joint angles and $\dot{\theta} \in \mathbb{R}^5$ is the joint velocity vector. From [4], linear and angular velocities for the ith joint is expressed as $v_i = \mathbf{J_{vmi}}\dot{\theta}$, $\omega_i = \mathbf{J_{\omega mi}}\dot{\theta}$, where $\mathbf{J_{vmi}} \in \mathbb{R}^{3\times n}$ and $\mathbf{J_{\omega mi}} \in \mathbb{R}^{3\times n}$ are the linear and angular terms of the $6 \times n$ Jacobian matrix. The Kinetic Energy of the ith link with a mass m_i and an inertia matrix calculated about its centre of mass (CoM), is given by:

$$K = (1/2)\dot{\theta}^T \sum_{i=1}^{n} [m_i\mathbf{J_{vmi}}(\theta)^T\mathbf{J_{vmi}}(\theta) + \mathbf{J_{\omega mi}}(\theta)^T\mathbf{R_i}(\theta)\mathbf{I_i}\mathbf{R_i}(\theta)^T\mathbf{J_{\omega mi}}(\theta)]\dot{\theta} \qquad (7)$$

and, $K = (1/2)\dot{\theta}^T\mathbf{D}(\theta)\dot{\theta}$, where $\mathbf{D}(\theta) \in \mathbb{R}^{5\times5}$ is the mass matrix and is useful to calculate $\mathbf{C}(\theta, \dot{\theta}) \in \mathbb{R}^{5\times5}$ which comprises of the Coriolis and centrifugal terms,

$$c_{ij} = \sum_{i=1}^{n} c_{ijk}(\theta)\dot{\theta}_k = \sum_{i=1}^{n} (1/2)\{(\partial d_{ij}/\partial\theta_k) + (\partial d_{ik}/\partial\theta_j) - (\partial d_{kj}/\partial\theta_i)\}\dot{\theta}_k \qquad (8)$$

The effect of potential energy will be negligible during a space operation. In this paper, for the initial verification in an Earth-analog condition, potential energy is taken into consideration which is $P = \sum\limits_{i=1}^{n} P_i = \sum\limits_{i=1}^{n} g^T r_{ci} m_i$. Now, using the Euler-Lagrange equations, the Torque vector is given by:

$$\tau_i = \Delta\{(\partial/\partial\dot{\theta}_i)(K - P)\} - ((\partial/\partial\theta_i)(K - P)) = \Delta\{(\partial/\partial\dot{\theta}_i)(L)\} - ((\partial/\partial\theta_i)(L)) \quad (9)$$

where $\Delta = \partial/\partial t$ and L is the Lagrangian. Using Eq. (6) for the $\mathbf{C}(\theta, \dot{\theta})$ matrix and the gravity matrix $\mathbf{G}(\theta)$, The dynamic equation is simplified as:

$$\mathbf{D}(\theta)\ddot{\theta} + \mathbf{C}(\theta, \dot{\theta})\dot{\theta} + \mathbf{G}(\theta) = \tau \quad (10)$$

From Fig. 3, starting at the initial position, the E-Walker's motion is followed by Phase-1 and Phase-2. The motion in the individual phases can be considered to be that of a fixed-to-base RM. Thereafter, the motion of Phase-1 and Phase-2 is switched, in a cyclic manner, to generate the desired gait pattern for traversing along a straight line.

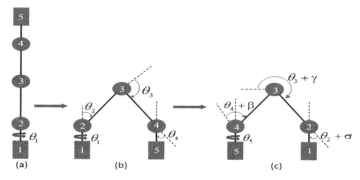

Fig. 3. Cycle-1 walking pattern of an E-Walker (a) initial position, (b) phase-1, (c) phase-2

4 Trajectory Generation and Control for Cycle - 1

The trajectory of the E-Walker is defined by a 5th order polynomial function $P(T')$ that satisfies all initial and final conditions for the joint's displacement, velocity and acceleration [5]. It helps to avoid any discontinuities in acceleration and impulsive jerks, thereby improves the tracking accuracy [4]. Time T was set as the period of execution of the trajectory from $t = 0$ to $t = t_f$. The normalized time was then $T' = (t/T)$ where $T' \in [0, 1]$. The desired joint angle for the ith joint is $\theta_i^d = \theta_{i_0} + (\theta_{i_f} - \theta_{i_0})P(T')$.

The gains of the PID controller were tuned to track the straight-line trajectory. The PID control equation becomes:

$$\tau' = \ddot{\theta}^d + K_p(\theta^d - \theta) + K_i \int (\theta^d - \theta)dt + K_d(\dot{\theta}^d - \dot{\theta}), \quad (11)$$

where, $\ddot{\theta}^d$ is the desired joint acceleration vector, K_p, K_i and K_d are the proportional, integral and derivative gains. θ^d and θ are the desired and real joint angles.

Therefore, the overall control law is obtained as:

$$\boldsymbol{\tau} = \mathbf{D}(\theta)\boldsymbol{\tau}' + \mathbf{C}(\theta, \dot{\theta})\dot{\boldsymbol{\theta}} + \mathbf{G}(\theta) \tag{12}$$

Figure 4 shows plots of the desired and real joint angles, velocities, torques and trajectory.

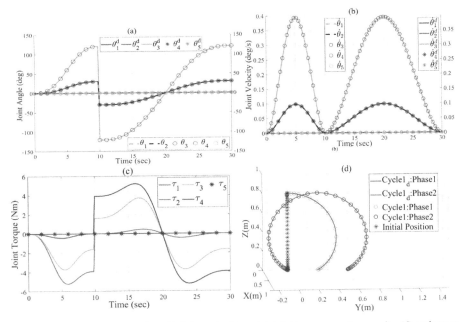

Fig. 4. Outputs: (a) joint angles, (b) joint velocities, (c) joint torques under gravity (d) trajectory

5 Simulation Results

In the above simulations, joint configuration A = [0;0;0;0;0], B = [0;30;120;30;0], C = [0; −30; −120; −30; 0]. In Fig. 4, Phase-1 (A–B) is run from t = 0:10, while Phase-2 (C–B) is run from t = 10:30. Post completion of Phase-1, the joint configuration attained by the E-Walker (here, B) is made equal to the required starting configuration for Phase-2 (C). Figure 4(a) shows that the desired and real joint angle configurations match at every time step. In Fig. 4(b), it is seen that in each phase, the initial and the final velocity is zero, with the peak velocity of each joint achieved halfway through the phase. Figure 4(c) shows that during Phase-1, the E-Walker lands back on the ground, thus producing a negative torque. On the other hand, during Phase-2, a positive torque is generated as the E-Walker lifts itself initially, whereas in the other-half produces a negative torque similar to Phase-1. The peak torque attained is ~5Nm, under Earth's gravity. Without gravity, the peak torque was found to be ~0.045Nm. These results matched the design requirements. Figure 4(d) showcases the trajectory followed by the E-Walker. During Phase-1, with joint 1 fixed to the base, the E-walker traverses 0.3 m along the Y-axis. In Phase-2, with joint 5 fixed to the base, the E-walker completes a full motion, traversing 0.6 m along the Y-axis. These initial results help to validate the model and the gait controller for walking along a straight line.

6   Conclusion and Future Work

In this paper, an End-Over-End Walking Robot is introduced and its motion control and gait analysis are briefly discussed. The kinematic and dynamic equations of Phase-1 is presented with simulation results of a complete cycle showing the desired performance. It is inferred that the model of the E-Walker presented in this paper is accurate and the PID controller can track the desired path, without exceeding the joint torque limits. Current research involves extensive gait analysis for accomplishing complex trajectories encountered in space missions.

References

1. Nanjangud, A., Underwood, C.I. , Bridges, C.P., Saaj, C.M., Eckersley, S., Sweeting, M., Bianco, P.: Towards robotic on-orbit assembly of large space telescopes: Mission architectures, concepts, and analysis. In: Proceedings of 70th International Astronautical Congress (IAC), Washington DC, USA, October 21–25, 2019
2. Nanjangud, A., et al.: Robotic architectures for the on-orbit assembly of large space telescopes. In: Proceedings of the ASTRA 2019 Symposium, Noordwijk, Netherlands, 27–28 May 2019
3. Deremetz, M., et al.: MOSAR: Modular Spacecraft Assembly and Reconfiguration Demonstrator. In: Proceedings of the ASTRA 2019 Symposium, Noordwijk, Netherlands, 27–28 May 2019
4. Spong, M., Hutchinson, S., Vidyasagar, M.: Robot Dynamics and Control, 2nd edn. John Wiley & Sons, (2005). ISBN – 0471649902
5. Ata, A.A.: Optimal trajectory planning of manipulators: a review. J. Eng. Sci. Technol. 2(1), 32–54 (2007)

Deep Learning-Based Decision Making for Autonomous Vehicle at Roundabout

Weichao Wang$^{(\boxtimes)}$, Lei Jiang, Shiran Lin, Hui Fang, and Qinggang Meng

Computer Science Department, Loughborough University, Loughborough, UK
w.wang3@lboro.ac.uk
https://www.lboro.ac.uk/departments/compsci/

Abstract. This study looks at the facilitation of computer vision and machine learning, which helps Autonomous vehicles (AVs) make pertinent decisions before entering a roundabout. A deep learning-based decision-making system (DBDM) is proposed in order to make a correct "Enter" or "Wait" decision when an AV enters a roundabout. In this regard, videos of human drivers negotiating different normal roundabouts, differing in terms of size, are employed alongside a range of different learning algorithms (e.g. VGG-16, Resnet-50 and Xception). In total, 130 videos captured at normal roundabouts were used to test the models, and VGG-16 performed best with an accuracy rate of 92.57% comparing with pervious work (GBIPA-SC-NR), thus suggesting that the proposed DBDM method can be applied effectively for AVs.

Keywords: Autonomous Vehicle · Deep learning · Roundabout

1 Introduction

Autonomous vehicles (AVs) are designed in such a way that they map out and sense their environment autonomously and then navigate through this environment without any form of human intervention [1]. [7] consider that AVs have the ability to drive in different situations based on decisions made via artificial intelligence. However, complex environments are still significant obstacles for AV decision-making. [4,6,8,9] consider that roundabouts not controlled by traffic signals, which represent the majority of such junctions, result in many accidents – caused mainly by human error, especially when they enter a roundabout. Therefore, it is important for an AV to learn how to safely and quickly enter a roundabout. In this work, we propose a deep learning-based decision-making (DBDM) system to helps AVs make a correct "Enter" or "Wait" decision when an AV enters a roundabout.

Supported by Loughborough University.

© Springer Nature Switzerland AG 2020
A. Mohammad et al. (Eds.): TAROS 2020, LNAI 12228, pp. 134–137, 2020.
https://doi.org/10.1007/978-3-030-63486-5_16

2   Proposed Deep-Learning Based Decision-Making System

This work proposes a fast and reliable DBDM system to help AVs make a correct "Enter" or "Wait" decision before entering a roundabout. Figure 1 shows the proposed DBDM framework, comprising three elements. The first section, namely "pre-processing," involves vehicle detection, whereby an approaching car's position can be detected based on the Faster R-CNN network. The second section then acquires the approaching car's speed, based on the optical flow algorithm, the optical flow algorithm in [5] is deployed to extract features for representing the vehicle movements. The third section includes the "AV decision-making" stage based on two learning inputs (Approaching vehicle's movement and position), whereby different learning networks (VGG-16, ResNet-50 and Xception) label captured frames either "Wait" or "Enter".

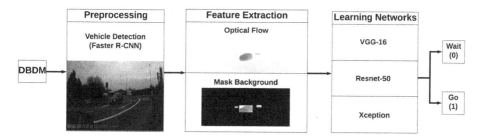

Fig. 1. The main architecture of the DBDM system

3   Experiment Results

This section provides the experiment setting, decision-making results and a discussion.

3.1   Experiment Setting

130 videos used for this study are taken from real-life driving situations and recorded with a Nextbase 312GW camera [9] fixed to the right-hand side of an ego vehicle, in order to represent true driving and road conditions for the UK. Nearly 50 different normal roundabouts across the Leicestershire, UK were filmed in 18 months, from October 2016 to April 2018. The time frames were 9 am to 11 am and 3 pm to 6 pm in rainless days. The morning time normally provides satisfactory quality video in a natural daylight condition. The afternoon time provides busy traffic in the peak hours that maximized the intricacy in the roundabouts.

3.2   Decision-Making Results

Each of the 130 videos was filmed at 30 frames per second in proposed DBDM system, following which each frame was assigned either a positive (1) or a negative (0) sample based on the ego vehicle's "Wait" or "Enter" status. This resulted in 18,180 samples in total, and these were divided further into 16,380 training samples, and 1,800 test samples. The training set included 5,965 positive frame samples ("Enter") and 10,415 negatives ("Wait"), whilst 800 positive samples and 1,000 negative samples were produced for the test dataset. Based on Table 1, the AV performs best at roundabouts when employing the deep learning approach (DBDM). The VGG-16, ResNet-50 and Xception produce different results, with VGG-16 the best at 92.57%. Besides, we also test the same data with our previous work named GBIPA-SC-NR in [8]. The GBIPA-SC-NR is a grid-based decision-making algorithm. After extracting measurements from grids divided evenly on an image, three conventional classifiers, including SVM, kNN and artificial neural netowork (ANN) are used to classify the data into decisions. The accuracy demonstrates that the overall performance of the proposed system DBDM is significantly better comparing to the GBIPA-SC-NR methods.

Table 1. Decision-making results (TP: True Positives. TN: True negatives, FP: False positives, FN: False negatives, R.rate: Recall rate, P: Precision, Acc: accuracy, GB: GBIPA-SC-NR)

Methods	TP	TN	FP	FN	R.rate(%)	P (%)	Acc
Xception	504	978	107	211	70.49	82.49	82.36
VGG-16	670	996	50	84	88.86	93.06	92.57
Resnet-50	519	1012	116	153	77.23	81.73	85.08
GB-SVM	526	1051	86	137	79.34	85.95	87.63
GB-ANN	496	971	100	233	68.04	83.22	81.49
GB-kNN	407	990	154	249	62.04	72.55	77.62

3.3   Discussion

The proposed DBDM contributes to the literature as follows. First, it makes decisions in an effective and safe way, and it is therefore suitable for application in real-life scenarios, and it is based on real-world experiments, unlike many studies, for example [3]. Second, proposed DBDM system improvs our previous work of the grid based method, GBIPA-SC-NR in [8], both of the accuracy and inference timing are improved significantly. Furthermore, the accuracy rate of nearly 93% means the system is robust and reliable, especially in terms of different approaching car speeds, and it achieves this by providing the car detection and optical flow methods to track, measure and calculate distance and speed. Again, current studies do not identify these factors [2,10].

4   Conclusion

This paper introduces a deep learning system (DBDM) for AVs that enables them to make correct decisions, quickly and safely, when approaching a roundabout. The DBDM system introduces the car detection method based on Faster R-CNN, a feature extracted from optical flow and decision-making learning via VGG-16, ResNet-50 and Xception, each of which was evaluated against 130 test videos. The best performing network was VGG-16 at nearly 93% learning accuracy. This study contributes in the following ways. In relation to data collection, a significant amount of real-world, high-quality data was produced by filming at almost 50 normal roundabouts over a few days, resulting in real-life scenarios and how they are handled by human drivers. Moreover, the DBDM system provides better learning performance comparing with pervious study GBIPA-SC-NR when an AV enters a roundabout.

References

1. Adler, B., Xiao, J., Zhang, J.: Autonomous exploration of urban environments using unmanned aerial vehicles. J. Field Robot. **31**(6), 912–939 (2014)
2. Gonzalez, D., Pérez, J., Milanés, V.: Parametric-based path generation for automated vehicles at roundabouts. Expert Syst. Appl. **71**, 332–341 (2017)
3. Gritschneder, F., Hatzelmann, P., Thom, M., Kunz, F., Dietmayer, K.: Adaptive learning based on guided exploration for decision making at roundabouts. In 2016 IEEE Intelligent Vehicles Symposium (IV), pp. 433–440. IEEE (2016)
4. Hassannejad, H., Medici, P., Cardarelli, E., Cerri, P.: Detection of moving objects in roundabouts based on a monocular system. Expert Syst. Appl. **42**(9), 4167–4176 (2015)
5. Liu, C., et al.: Beyond pixels: exploring new representations and applications for motion analysis. PhD Thesis, Massachusetts Institute of Technology (2009)
6. Okumura, B., et al.: Challenges in perception and decision making for intelligent automotive vehicles: a case study. IEEE Trans. Intell. Veh. **1**(1), 20–32 (2016)
7. Rodrigues, M., McGordon, A., Gest, G., Marco, J.: Autonomous navigation in interaction-based environments—a case of non-signalized roundabouts. IEEE Trans. Intell. Veh. **3**(4), 425–438 (2018)
8. Wang, W., Meng, Q., Chung, P.W.H.: Camera based decision making at roundabouts for autonomous vehicles. In 2018 15th International Conference on Control, Automation, Robotics and Vision (ICARCV), pp. 1460–1465. IEEE (2018)
9. Wang, W., Nguyen, Q.A., Ma, W., Wei, J., Chung, P.W.H., Meng, Q.: Multi-grid based decision making at roundabout for autonomous vehicles. In: 2019 IEEE International Conference of Vehicular Electronics and Safety (ICVES), pp. 1–6. IEEE (2019)
10. Ziegler, J., et al.: Making bertha drive—an autonomous journey on a historic route. IEEE Intell. Transp. Syst. Mag. **6**(2), 8–20 (2014)

A Study Assessing the Impact of Task Duration on Performance Metrics for Multi-robot Teams

Genki Miyauchi[1]([✉]) and Elizabeth I. Sklar[2]

[1] Department of Automatic Control and Systems Engineering,
The University of Sheffield, Sheffield, UK
`g.miyauchi@sheffield.ac.uk`
[2] Lincoln Institute for Agri-food Technology, University of Lincoln, Lincoln, UK
`esklar@lincoln.ac.uk`

Abstract. The allocation of tasks to members of a team is a well-studied problem in robotics. Applying market-based mechanisms, particularly auctions, is a popular solution. We focus on evaluating the performance of the team when executing the tasks that have been allocated. The work presented here examines the impact of one such factor, namely task duration. Building on prior work, a new bidding strategy and performance metric are introduced. Experimental results are presented showing that there are statistically significant differences in both time and distance-based performance metrics when tasks have zero vs greater-than-zero duration.

Keywords: Multi-robot team · Auction mechanism · Task allocation

1 Introduction

Assigning a set of tasks within a team of robots is known as the *multi-robot task allocation (MRTA)* problem. As the number of tasks and size of the robot team increases, the number of possible allocations rises at an exponential rate. The complexity further increases when factors are added, such as a dynamic environment that changes over time, a heterogeneous team of robots with various capabilities or tasks that have prerequisites which must be satisfied before they can be executed. Finding the optimal solution to an MRTA problem is known to be NP-hard [2,4], so a popular family of strategies takes a *market-* or *auction*-based approach. Auctions are useful because they can distribute workload amongst team members whilst reflecting preferences of individuals [4,7,9]. A local optimum is determined by each robot (labelled *bidder*) and these optima are collectively reconciled by an *auctioneer*. The team can operate in real-time and respond dynamically to changes in the task landscape, such as the arrival of new tasks to be addressed while already executing tasks previously allocated.

The work presented here extends our prior work in which we demonstrated the importance of mission execution and weighing various performance metrics

© Springer Nature Switzerland AG 2020
A. Mohammad et al. (Eds.): TAROS 2020, LNAI 12228, pp. 138–143, 2020.
https://doi.org/10.1007/978-3-030-63486-5_17

when comparing task allocation mechanisms [9,10]. Here we assess the impact of *task duration*. Our contributions include: (a) a new methodology for robots to bid on tasks with varying durations; (b) a new metric that attempts to capture aspects of task duration; (c) results of experiments conducted both in simulation and on physical robots across a landscape of mission parameters; and (d) statistical analysis of results to highlight the impact on performance metrics when task duration varies.

2 Background

Koenig et al. [4] proposed *sequential single-item (SSI)* auctions in which several tasks are announced to team members at once; each robot responds with a bid representing a cost to the robot for executing the task, e.g. the distance the robot must travel to reach the task location. An auctioneer identifies the winner as the robot with the smallest bid. The auction repeats in *rounds* until all tasks have been allocated. SSI combines the strength of *combinatorial* [1] (bidding on bundles of tasks) and *parallel single-item (PSI)* [4] (allocating all tasks in a single round) auctions. SSI has been a popular choice for MRTA and several variants have been studied, for example tasks with temporal constraints [7], tasks with precedence constraints [6,8] and tasks with pickup-and-delivery constraints [3]. Our prior work has focused on empirical analysis of auction mechanisms [10], comparing SSI, PSI and a baseline *Round Robin (RR)* (first come, first served) in experiments conducted on physical and simulated robots. We have defined a comprehensive set of performance metrics [11] and learned a model for selecting an appropriate mechanism given mission parameters [12].

3 Approach

We assess the impact of varying task durations on multi-robot team performance by executing missions on physical robots and in simulation, and then analysing differences in performance metrics. Missions are defined across a landscape of parameters [2,5] which distinguish characteristics of tasks, robots and the environment: *single robot (SR)* vs *multi-robot (MR)*—SR tasks can be completed by one robot, whereas MR tasks require the cooperation of multiple robots; *independent (IT)* vs *constrained (CT)*—IT tasks can be executed in any order, whereas CT tasks are dependent on others due to factors such as precedence order; *static (SA)* vs *dynamic (DA)*—SA tasks are known before a mission starts and can be allocated before any execution, whereas DA tasks arrive dynamically and are allocated during execution of other tasks.

Here, we introduce a *task duration* parameter, i.e. the time it takes to execute a task: *instantaneous (ID)* vs *extended (XD)*—ID tasks take no time to execute (i.e., 0 s), whereas XD task length is >0. We compare four XD variants: *XDC*, where all tasks have the same constant length; *XDG*, where task length is chosen randomly from a Gaussian distribution; *XDP*, where task length is

(a) TurtleBot3 Burger   (b) arena

Fig. 1. Experimental setup.

chosen randomly from a Poisson distribution; and *XDR*, where task length is chosen randomly from a uniform distribution[1].

We also introduce a new bidding strategy that calculates the estimated time for a robot to travel to a task location instead of using travel distance as the basis of a bid. Thus the bid takes into account the estimated travel time as well as predicted task duration. The bid value b of robot r for a new task x is calculated as: $b(r, x) = \sum_{i=1}^{N_r}(T_{i-1,i} + E_i) + T_{N_r,x}$, where N_r is the number of uncompleted tasks robot r is assigned, T is the estimated time to travel between two task locations[2] and E is the predicted duration of task i.

4   Experiments

We conducted a series of experiments with physical and simulated Turtlebot3 robots (Fig. 1a) using the *MRTeAm* [10,11] framework built with Robot Operating System (ROS). Our experimental arena emulates an office-like area divided into rooms and corridors (Fig. 1b).

For our experiments, we employed three different *auction mechanisms* (*RR, PSI, SSI*) two different *starting configurations*: *clustered* together in one portion of the arena or *distributed* around the arena; two different task constraints (*IT, CT*); and five task durations (*ID, XDC, XDG, XDP, XDR*). For each combination of parameters, at least 5 runs were conducted in the physical environment and 15 runs in simulation. In total, 1926 runs were completed.

Three performance metrics are analysed to assess the impact of task duration: the total *distance travelled* collectively by all the members of the robot team; the total *run time* from the start of a mission until all tasks are completed; and *service delay time*, the time from when an auctioneer awards a task until a robot begins executing the task. Service time is a new metric introduced here to reflect the time each task "waits" before a robot arrives at its location. Service time measures how quickly a task's execution can commence or how long the task was

---

[1] The values employed here are: XDC: length $= 15$ s; XDG: $\mu = 15$ and $\sigma = 3$; XDP: $\lambda = 15$; XDR: range $= (5, 35)$.

[2] T is calculated as the predicted travel distance times the average robot velocity, which was determined experimentally to be 0.12 m/s.

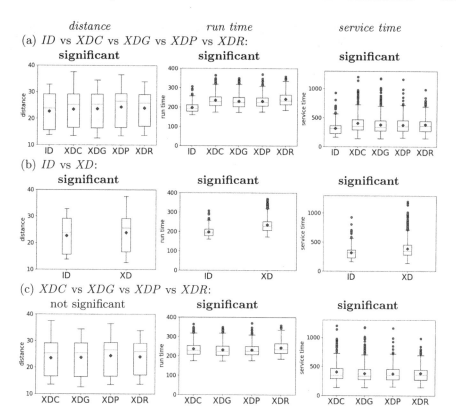

Fig. 2. Statistical differences. Statistical significance is noted where ANOVA produces $p < 0.01$.

delayed, i.e. left unattended. Arriving at a task location quickly is an important factor in many application domains, especially in emergency situations. A shorter service time is preferred because it means the robot team is able to arrive at task locations more promptly.

5   Results

Our analysis assesses the impact of task duration on the three performance metrics. For brevity here, we present aggregated results and make three comparisons: (a) across all five task duration values; (b) instant versus extended time; and (c) across the four extended time values. The number of runs per aggregate are: ID: $N = 330$, XDC: $N = 508$, XDG: $N = 469$, XDP: $N = 379$, and XDR: $N = 240$.

We looked for statistically significant results. After checking that the data within each sample is normally distributed[3], we tested for differences using *anal-*

---

[3] Using the Shapiro-Wilk test [13].

ysis of variance (ANOVA), with $p < 0.01$ as the threshold for statistical significance. The results of statistical testing on individual variables are shown in Fig. 2, which illustrates the distributions for each sample and indicates, for each of the three types of analysis (above), which differences amongst samples are statistically significant.

6 Summary

We have presented a study assessing the impact of task duration on three different performance metrics collected from experiments with multi-robot teams. We have introduced a new bidding strategy which accounts for task duration and a new metric for measuring performance delay due to task duration. Statistical analysis of our results shows that there are significant differences in all performance metrics when tasks have non-zero duration (*ID* vs *XD**) and in time-related metrics when duration varies randomly according to probability distributions defined by similar parameter values.

Acknowledgement. This work was conducted while the first author was a masters student in the Department of Informatics at King's College London, UK. The second author was a professor in the same department and project supervisor.

References

1. Berhault, M., et al.: Robot exploration with combinatorial auctions. In: IEEE/RSJ International Conference on Intelligent Robots and Systems (IROS), vol. 2 (2003)
2. Gerkey, B., Matarić, M.: A formal analysis and taxonomy of task allocation in multi-robot systems. Int. J. Robot. Res. **23**(9), 939–954 (2004)
3. Heap, B., Pagnucco, M.: Repeated sequential single-cluster auctions with dynamic tasks for multi-robot task allocation with pickup and delivery. In: Klusch, M., Thimm, M., Paprzycki, M. (eds.) MATES 2013. LNCS (LNAI), vol. 8076, pp. 87–100. Springer, Heidelberg (2013). https://doi.org/10.1007/978-3-642-40776-5_10
4. Koenig, S., et al.: The power of sequential single-item auctions for agent coordination. In: 21st National Conference on Artificial Intelligence (AAAI), vol. 2 (2006)
5. Landén, D., Heintz, F., Doherty, P.: Complex task allocation in mixed-initiative delegation: a UAV case study. In: Desai, N., Liu, A., Winikoff, M. (eds.) PRIMA 2010. LNCS (LNAI), vol. 7057, pp. 288–303. Springer, Heidelberg (2012). https://doi.org/10.1007/978-3-642-25920-3_20
6. McIntire, M., Nunes, E., Gini, M.: Iterated multi-robot auctions for precedence-constrained task scheduling. In: International Conference on Autonomous Agents and Multiagent Systems (AAMAS) (2016)
7. Nunes, E., Gini, M.: Multi-robot auctions for allocation of tasks with temporal constraints. In: 29th Conference on Artificial Intelligence (AAAI) (2015)
8. Nunes, E., McIntire, M., Gini, M.: Decentralized allocation of tasks with temporal and precedence constraints to a team of robots. In: IEEE International Conference on Simulation, Modeling, and Programming for Autonomous Robots (SIMPAR) (2016)

9. Schneider, E.: Mechanism Selection for Multi-Robot Task Allocation. Ph.D. Thesis, University of Liverpool (2018)
10. Schneider, E., Sklar, E.I., Parsons, S., Özgelen, A.T.: Auction-based task allocation for multi-robot teams in dynamic environments. In: Dixon, C., Tuyls, K. (eds.) TAROS 2015. LNCS (LNAI), vol. 9287, pp. 246–257. Springer, Cham (2015). https://doi.org/10.1007/978-3-319-22416-9_29
11. Schneider, E., Sklar, E.I., Parsons, S.: Evaluating multi-robot teamwork in parameterised environments. In: Alboul, L., Damian, D., Aitken, J.M.M. (eds.) TAROS 2016. LNCS (LNAI), vol. 9716, pp. 301–313. Springer, Cham (2016). https://doi.org/10.1007/978-3-319-40379-3_32
12. Schneider, E., Sklar, E.I., Parsons, S.: Mechanism selection for multi-robot task allocation. In: Gao, Y., Fallah, S., Jin, Y., Lekakou, C. (eds.) TAROS 2017. LNCS (LNAI), vol. 10454, pp. 421–435. Springer, Cham (2017). https://doi.org/10.1007/978-3-319-64107-2_33
13. Shapiro, S.S., Wilk, M.B.: An analysis of variance test for normality (Complete samples). Biometrika 52(3/4), 591–611 (1965)

Learning, Mapping and Planning

A Comparative Study for Obstacle Avoidance Inverse Kinematics: Null-Space Based vs. Optimisation-Based

Neil Harrison$^{(\boxtimes)}$, Wenxing Liu, Inmo Jang, Joaquin Carrasco,
Guido Herrmann, and Nick Sykes

University of Manchester, Manchester M13 9PL, UK
neil.harrison@manchester.ac.uk
https://www.uomrobotics.com/

Abstract. Obstacle avoidance for robotic manipulators has attracted much attention in robotics literature, and many algorithms have been developed. In this paper, two algorithms are explored which perform obstacle avoidance within the inverse kinematics calculation process. The first algorithm applies a velocity to the null-space of the manipulator's Jacobian matrix which directs the manipulator away from obstacles. The second algorithm uses an optimisation-based approach to calculate joint positions which incorporates constraints to prevent the manipulator from violating obstacle boundaries. Applying obstacle avoidance at the inverse kinematics level of the control process is particularly applicable to teleoperation and allows the robotic manipulator to react to obstacles at a faster rate without involving a path planner which operates on a slower cycle time. The two algorithms were implemented for a direct comparison in terms of obstacle avoidance capability and processing times. It was found that the processing time of the null-space method was substantially quicker than the optimisation-based algorithm. However, the null-space method did not guarantee collision avoidance which may not be suitable for safety critical applications without supervision.

Keywords: Obstacle avoidance · Inverse kinematics · Manipulators · Null-space · Optimisation

1 Introduction and Motivation

Robotic manipulators are often used in scenarios where it is paramount for the manipulator to avoid obstacles within the workplace. In the nuclear industry, manipulators are teleoperated in real-time to perform delicate tasks in areas that are unsafe for humans to access. In these applications the consequences of colliding with obstacles can be disastrous. Obstacle avoidance is especially

---

This work was supported by EPSRC RAIN project No. EP/R026084/1 and EUROFusion/Horizon2020.

© Springer Nature Switzerland AG 2020
A. Mohammad et al. (Eds.): TAROS 2020, LNAI 12228, pp. 147–158, 2020.
https://doi.org/10.1007/978-3-030-63486-5_18

necessary for decommissioning tasks, as manipulators must be used in hazardous areas which are largely un-structured and un-documented.

Real-time obstacle avoidance is also important for operation within confined spaces, such as glove box environments which can be complicated, cluttered and often un-mapped areas. A robust, reliable obstacle avoidance algorithm allows an operator to focus on controlling the end-effector and completing the desired task without worrying about the rest of the manipulator.

Obstacle avoidance is commonly approached as a path planning problem, [1–3], which is generally computed off-line, with the obstacle locations given as prior knowledge. Work has been done to present real-time path planning solutions with dynamic obstacle avoidance [4,5].

An alternative to this high level path planning approach is to avoid obstacles during the calculation the inverse kinematics of the manipulator. By avoiding obstacles at this lower level of the control process, real time obstacle avoidance becomes possible for uses in teleoperation and in conjunction with less intensive/intelligent path planning. Khatib [6] designed a method using artificial potential fields to apply obstacle avoidance at a lower control level rather than during the path planning process. By applying an attractive force at the goal position that only affects the end-effector, and creating repulsive forces at obstacles which have an effect throughout the manipulator, the manipulator can navigate through towards the goal while avoiding obstacles.

This work presents two opposing methods of avoiding obstacles within the inverse kinematics process in real-time. The first takes advantage of the null-space of the Jacobian matrix and directs the free degrees of freedom away from potential obstacles. The second, a non linear optimisation algorithm with constraints which prevent the manipulator from colliding with an object. The null-space approach was chosen as it has been widely explored in the literature and provides a good demonstration of current capability of real-time obstacle avoidance. While historically optimisation-based solvers have been too computationally expensive to perform at the inverse kinematic level, recent computational power improvements have allowed for optimisation-based algorithms to run at a rate fast enough for responsive control.

Both algorithms were implemented in MATLAB to allow for a direct comparison in terms of obstacle avoidance and processing time. For implementation, both these algorithms use a single obstacle which is predefined, however they are capable of being extended to multiple, dynamic obstacles which could be provided in the form of a point cloud. The MATLAB implementation in this paper is not expected to provide real-time capable results but aims to serve as a comparison between the two algorithms. As the null-space algorithm is well-documented as a real-time method, it is treated as a baseline for real-time performance.

2   Related Work

Optimisation-based methods have been commonly used in solving robotic path planning and motion planning problems. Optimisation-based methods are algorithms that can eventually be reduced to finding the minimum or maximum value of an objective function. In [7] Ratliff illustrated CHOMP which is a gradient optimisation method for standalone motion planning. The obstacle cost function should be optimised in smoothness analysis. Schulman [8] has introduced a refined optimisation-based algorithm called TrajOpt where the collision cost was considered. Similar to CHOMP, Kalakrishnan [9] describes a new optimisation-based method called STOMP which can escape from the local minimum problem that CHOMP cannot avoid. Park [10] also demonstrates the ITOMP method which does not require the locations of dynamic obstacles in advance. Compared with other methods, ITOMP is the most suitable for real-time motion planning using optimisation.

Optimisation-based methods can be also applied for real-time robot applications. For instance, work by Werner [11] introduces how optimisation-based control can be used in real-time robot walking gaits. Lampariello [12] focuses on how to reduce the computation time for real-time robot catching tasks. Work by Tassa [13] illustrates that trajectory optimisation-based control can be used in real-time in a complex environment with disturbances present.

Instead of motion planning, this work focuses on the use of optimisation algorithms which are capable of avoiding obstacles in real-time within the inverse kinematics solver. By implementing the obstacle avoidance on this lower level of control, the path planning algorithm does not have to react to obstacles directly and only has to perform re-planning if the initial path results in the manipulator becoming trapped in a local minima.

3   Obstacle Avoidance Methods

3.1   Null-Space Method

The use of the null-space of the Jacobian matrix for avoiding obstacles was introduced by Maciejewski & Klein [14]. This method, demonstrated in Fig. 1, identifies a closest obstacle point on the manipulator and creates a obstacle Jacobian, J_o, and a obstacle avoidance velocity, $\dot{\mathbf{x}}_o$, from the closest point to the obstacle, which directs the free degrees of freedom away from the obstacle. The obstacle Jacobian is defined as the Jacobian computed for an arbitrary point on a link, at the closest point on the manipulator to the obstacle. The obstacle

Fig. 1. Null-space method working principle.

avoidance velocity is a normalised vector with a direction that would produce a motion away from the obstacle.

For a redundant manipulator, the null-space of the manipulator Jacobian, J_e, represents the free degrees of freedom on the manipulator. This null-space matrix is multiplied with the obstacle avoidance velocity as follows;

$$\dot{\theta} = \mathbf{J_e^+ \dot{x}_e} + [\mathbf{J_o(I - J_e^+ J_e)}]^+ (\mathbf{\dot{x}_o - J_o J_e^+ \dot{x}_e}), \tag{1}$$

which produces individual joint velocities, $\dot{\theta}$, which direct the end-effector towards the goal while also avoiding the obstacle with the redundant degrees of freedom. The $^+$ operator used here and throughout the paper represents the Moore-Penrose pseudo inverse.

Task Priority. This implementation of the null-space method grants priority to end-effector velocity, meaning that if the end-effector path is directed through an obstacle then the manipulator will prioritise reaching the goal position over colliding with the obstacle, as in Fig. 2.

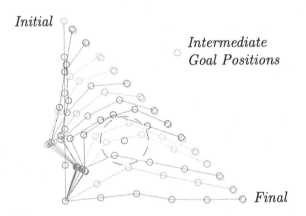

Fig. 2. Null-space method failure scenario.

In some scenarios, following a precise path is necessary but for safety critical applications it is more likely that obstacle avoidance will be the desired priority. Žlajpah and Petrič [15] showed that reversing the priority of these tasks and making the obstacle avoidance the primary task would be a more applicable solution to safety critical tasks.

To allow the smooth handover between the primary obstacle avoidance task and the secondary goal task, a scalar measure, $\lambda(d_o)$, was introduced which determines how 'active' the task should be, based on the distance to the obstacle. In [15], $\lambda(d_o)$ is defined as;

$$\lambda(d_o) = \begin{cases} \left(\dfrac{d_m}{\|d_o\|}\right)^n & , \; n = 1,2,3... \quad \|d_o\| \geq d_m, \\ 1 & \|d_o\| < d_m, \end{cases} \tag{2}$$

where d_m is the boundary distance allowed from an obstacle and d_o is the distance from closest point on the manipulator to the obstacle. The value of the power, n, can be varied to affect how quickly the transition between tasks occurs, for this work a value of 5 was chosen. This results in a value that slides smoothly between 0 and 1 based on proximity to the obstacle.

$$\dot{\theta} = \mathbf{J_o^+}\lambda(\mathbf{d_o})\dot{\mathbf{x}_o} + [\mathbf{I} - \lambda(\mathbf{d_o})\mathbf{J_o^+}\mathbf{J_o}](\mathbf{J_e^+}\dot{\mathbf{x}_e}) \tag{3}$$

The equation above, proposed by Žlajpah and Petrič shows how the tasks are split based on the λ value. When the manipulator is close to the obstacle and $\lambda = 1$, the second component of the equation becomes the null-space of the obstacle avoidance task and the end-effector will only be able to move in directions which do not affect the obstacle avoidance. Similarly, when $\lambda = 0$, the obstacle avoidance task is not active and the second component becomes the standard inverse Jacobian problem which solves for end-effector position. This produces a desired behaviour as shown in Fig. 3, where the manipulator does not enter the boundary area while the end-effector attempts to move as close as it can to the goal positions.

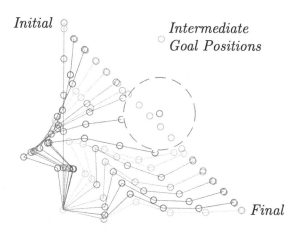

Initial   *Intermediate*
                            Goal Positions

Final

Fig. 3. Obstacle avoidance as primary task.

This method does not guarantee obstacle avoidance in every situation but does make it very unlikely. One potential issue occurs when the manipulator approaches a singularity, this can cause joint velocities to become very large which could cause collisions. The use of the damped least squares method for calculating a pseudo inverse [16] could reduce these singularity issues however this was not explored within this paper.

3.2   Optimisation-Based Method

Bosscher & Hedman [17] described an optimisation algorithm which solves for joint velocities, using constraints to prevent collisions with obstacles. These constraints are calculated using a similar method to [14], described in Sect. 3.1, with an obstacle Jacobian which describes velocity towards the obstacle and maps it to joint velocities.

Rakita [18,19] introduced RelaxedIK which is a generalised IK solver which uses the SLSQP optimisation algorithm to calculate optimal joint positions for the manipulator to match the end-effector position and pose. As well as position and pose, the solver includes objective functions which minimise joint velocities, acceleration and jerk to produce a smooth motion in the manipulator. The various objective functions, $\mathbf{f}_i(\theta)$, are normalised and summed as in the following equation;

$$\theta = \arg\min_{\theta} \sum_{i=1}^{k} w_i \cdot \mathbf{f}_i(\theta) \quad \mathbf{c}_i(\theta) \geq 0, \tag{4}$$

where the weighting, w_i, allows for prioritising certain objective functions like end-effector position matching, and $\mathbf{c}_i(\Theta)$ defines constraints to be met while solving the optimisation problem.

The work in this paper implements an obstacle avoidance strategy using an optimisation-based inverse kinematics solver through the use of a non-linear constraint which prevents the manipulator colliding with obstacles in real-time. The obstacle avoidance constraint, $\mathbf{c}_o(\Theta)$, is defined as;

$$\mathbf{c}_o(\theta) = d_m - d_o(\theta), \tag{5}$$

where d_m is the minimum distance that must be maintained and $d_o(\theta)$ is the minimum distance from the manipulator to the obstacle based on the current joint angles, θ. The MATLAB implementation of this inverse kinematics solver uses the 'fmincon' function which utilises the SQP optimisation algorithm.

This method guarantees that the obstacle avoidance boundary will not be entered, as the optimisation algorithm will not update the position of the manipulator if its solution violates any of the constraints defined. Having hard constraints like this produces a robust obstacle avoidance system but does not guarantee that the manipulator will have a feasible solution, which in turn will prevent the manipulator reaching its goal position. Multiple situations could arise which would prevent the manipulator reaching its goal, for example when the goal position is inside of an obstacle or if the goal position is outside of the operating envelope of the manipulator. In these situations, the operator or a higher level path planning algorithm must re-plan to allow the manipulator to reach its goal.

4   Comparison of Implementation

The two methods presented have been implemented in MATLAB, using a 2D manipulator with five revolute joints. One of the main differences between the two algorithms is that the null-space method calculates joint velocities while the optimisation-based controller solves for joint angles. If these were to be implemented on a real robot, the controllers would have to differ to perform velocity or position based control. For the MATLAB simulation of the null-space method, at each iteration the velocities calculated were discretely integrated with a fixed time-step to determine the position (joint angles). The psuedo-code for both these algorithms is included in the Appendix.

To directly compare the two techniques, an obstacle was located in the centre of the workspace and a random goal position was generated within the operating space of the manipulator. A path was generated with a 1000 evenly distributed points between the initial position of the robot and this goal. The time taken for the manipulator to traverse the path was recorded and also whether or not the manipulator was able to reach the goal. This test was repeated for 1000 random goals for each of the algorithms, the mean processing times of which can be seen in Table 1 in Sect. 4.1, where the standard deviations have been included.

4.1 Algorithm Limitations

The main scenario in which both algorithms fail to reach the final goal position occurs when the path forces the manipulator into a local minima, for example when the manipulator is wrapped around the object as in Fig. 4 making it impossible for it to reach the goal.

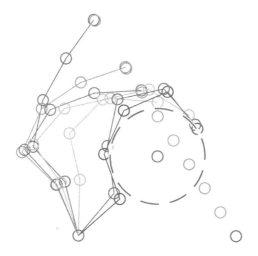

Fig. 4. Both methods can be trapped by obstacles.

Clearly, this is not an issue with the inverse kinematics solver but instead with the planned path for the end-effector. If the algorithms were implemented for teleoperation use, the operator would be able to safely navigate the manipulator out of the local minima without colliding with obstacles. If either of these algorithms were to be used for autonomous applications, they would have to be combined with a higher-level path planning algorithm capable of escaping from local minima.

Table 1 shows that the null-space method failed to complete its required path nearly 10% more than the optimisation-based method. The null-space method has a transition zone in which the lambda value begins to apply obstacle avoidance prior to the manipulator reaching the obstacle boundary. It is likely this is the reason for the additional failures as goal positions that are generated near the obstacle boundary are more likely to be unreachable with the null-space method.

Table 1. Algorithm comparison for a standard task.

	Collisions (%)	Completed Paths (%)	Processing Time (ms)
Null-space	0	83.8	2.42 ± 1.83
Optimisation	0	92.9	9.81 ± 0.77

4.2 Collision Avoidance

To verify the robustness of the collision avoidance algorithms, a similar simulation was set up in which the defined path was likely to encourage the manipulator to collide with the obstacle. The location of the obstacle and the initial position of the manipulator were kept constant but the obstacle area was increased by 900% to fill the majority of the workspace. This randomised goal often caused an impossible task for the manipulator and it was expected that the majority of paths would result in failure. For each algorithm, the randomised path was generated a 1000 times and a flag was raised if the manipulator entered the avoidance zone of the obstacle. The results are shown in Table 2.

Table 2. Algorithm comparison for a task which encourages collisions.

	Collisions (%)	Completed Paths (%)	Processing Time (ms)
Null-space	1.1	27.7	4.83 ± 1.74
Optimisation	0	61.0	9.72 ± 1.83

It should be noted that this test is often deliberately driving the path through an obstacle which represents an extreme worst case scenario. For the majority of normal use in teleoperation, the operator will (hopefully) not be trying to crash the robot.

As expected, the optimisation-based algorithm does guarantee collision avoidance, as the algorithm will not update the joint positions if its obstacle constraints are not met. This behaviour is as desired, if the operator commands the manipulator into an obstacle, it will travel as close as it can without entering the obstacle boundary; and it will come to a stop while the goal is unreachable.

The null-space method does not guarantee the manipulator will not enter the obstacle boundary. Only the closest single point on the manipulator is being directed away from the obstacle per iteration. If the manipulator is wrapped around the obstacle as in Fig. 4, the avoidance velocity could direct other links into the obstacle boundary. On the following iteration, this point would become the closest point and would be moved away from the obstacle, but if the speed of the manipulator is high enough, the link might enter the boundary until the next iteration begins. Maciejewski & Klein [14] suggested that considering the two closest points and blending the solutions based on the distance to the obstacle may reduce oscillations such as these.

Despite the null-space method not guaranteeing obstacle avoidance it does perform well, with only a 1.1% collision rate when tasked with a path which encourages collisions. In real use case scenarios, the number of collisions would be much lower as found in the first simulation with a smaller obstacle (Table 1). As this algorithm is likely to be used in teleoperation, a competent operator is unlikely to put the manipulator in situations similar to this test, therefore the low chance of collision may be acceptable depending on the consequences of collision.

4.3   Processing Time

For comparison, these algorithms were implemented in MATLAB 2019b on 3 GHz dual-core CPU. The processing time of the null-space method proves consistently faster than the optimisation-based method. This result was expected, as the null-space method calculates joint velocity updates based on matrix multiplications which can be calculated very quickly. The optimisation-based solution requires multiple objective functions to be evaluated along with a non-linear constraint to determine the manipulators distance to the obstacle.

The null-space method experienced a significant increase in processing time when tasked with the larger obstacle test. This can be attributed to the stopping condition of the algorithm, which iterates until the end-effector position reaches the goal or the number of iterations reaches a timeout value. When the manipulator is stuck in a local minima, it will never reach the goal position, meaning that the iteration runs until timeout. The intended behaviour is that the system moves on to the next goal position if the manipulator cannot reach the goal. The value of this timeout can be optimised to reduce the timeout time, but may sacrifice the positional accuracy of the end-effector.

An early stopping condition could be introduced which detects when the manipulator is no longer making progress towards the goal, this should improve the processing times when dealing with tasks where the manipulator is likely to get stuck around an obstacle.

The processing time of both algorithms in MATLAB prove promising for implementation in a more efficient programming language such as C++ for real-time obstacle avoidance. To be capable of real-time performance, the inverse kinematics solver must provide a solution at least as fast as the control loop sampling frequency. As an example, the sampling rate of the Universal Robots UR5 is 8 ms. Table 1 shows that the MATLAB implementation of the null-space method is already capable of performing at this speed. Other industrial manipulators are capable of faster sampling rates, such as the Kinova Gen3 which has a control sampling rate of 1 ms, but it is expected that the increase in performance through optimisation and implementation in C++ would allow both algorithms to perform at these rates.

The decision between which algorithm to use must be made considering the environment and tasks in which the manipulator will be working. For safety critical tasks where the speed of the manipulator is less of an issue then the optimisation-based method may be more suitable. However for use in teleoperation with a competent operator who is aware of the pitfalls of the null-space method, the improved processing time would provide a more responsive manipulator which may be more desirable.

5   Conclusion

This work explored two methods of implementing obstacle avoidance during the calculation of the inverse kinematics of a serial manipulator. The first creates a Jacobian matrix at the closest point to the obstacle and directs the manipulator away from collision while a secondary task moves the end-effector towards its goal. The second uses an optimisation-based approach which calculates joint positions that minimise the distance from the end-effector to the goal while maintaining a distance to the obstacle through constraints. The two implementations were directly compared in terms of path differences, collision avoidance and processing time. It was found that the null-space method provides a solution consistently faster than the optimisation approach, however it does not guarantee collision avoidance in extreme cases. When deciding between the use of one of these algorithms, one must take into account the environment the manipulator is to be used in, the consequences of a collision, and the higher level control mechanism to be used in conjunction with the inverse kinematics algorithm.

Appendix

Algorithm 1: Null-space Method

Forward kinematics;
Calculate end-effector error;
while *end-effector error > tolerance* **do**
  Calculate distance and direction to obstacle;
  Create obstacle Jacobian;
  Calculate λ;
  Calculate joint velocity from null-space equation;
  Integrate velocity to update joint position;
  Forward kinematics;
  Calculate end-effector error
end

Algorithm 2: Optimisation-based Method

Forward kinematics;
Calculate end-effector error;
while *end-effector error > tolerance* **do**
  Calculate obstacle distance constraint;
  Minimise objective function s.t. obstacle constraint;
  Update joint positions;
  Forward kinematics;
  Calculate end-effector error
end

References

1. Silva, J.S., Costa, P., Lima, J.: Manipulator path planning for pick-and-place operations with obstacles avoidance: an A* algorithm approach. In: Neto, P., Moreira, A.P. (eds.) WRSM 2013. CCIS, vol. 371, pp. 213–224. Springer, Heidelberg (2013). https://doi.org/10.1007/978-3-642-39223-8_20
2. Warren, C.W.: Global path planning using artificial potential fields. In: Proceedings of International Conference on Robotics and Automation, vol. 1, pp. 316–321, May 1989
3. Papadopoulos, E., Poulakakis, I., Papadimitriou, I.: On path planning and obstacle avoidance for nonholonomic platforms with manipulators: a polynomial approach. Int. J. Robot. Res. **21**(4), 367–383 (2002)
4. Chen, G., Liu, D., Wang, Y., Jia, Q., Zhang, X.: Path planning method with obstacle avoidance for manipulators in dynamic environment. Int. J. Adv. Robot. Syst. **15**(6) (2018). 1729881418820223
5. Wei, K., Ren, B.: A method on dynamic path planning for robotic manipulator autonomous obstacle avoidance based on an improved RRT algorithm. Sensors **18**, 571 (2018)
6. Khatib, O.: Real-time obstacle avoidance for manipulators and mobile robots. Int. J. Robot. Res. **5**(1), 90–98 (1986)

7. Ratliff, N., Zucker, M., Bagnell, J. A., Srinivasa, S.: CHOMP: Gradient optimization techniques for efficient motion planning. In: Proceedings of IEEE International Conference on Robotics and Automation (ICRA), May 2009
8. Schulman, J., et al.: Motion planning with sequential convex optimization and convex collision checking. Int. J. Robot. Res. **33**(9), 1251–1270 (2014)
9. Kalakrishnan, M., Chitta, S., Theodorou, E., Pastor, P., Schaal., S.: STOMP: Stochastic trajectory optimization for motion planning. In: 2011 IEEE International Conference on Robotics and Automation, pp. 4569–4574, May 2011
10. Park, C., Pan, J., Manocha, D.: ITOMP: Incremental trajectory optimization for real-time replanning in dynamic environments. In: Proceedings of the Twenty-Second International Conference on International Conference on Automated Planning and Scheduling, ICAPS 2012, pp. 207–215. AAAI Press (2012)
11. Werner, A., Lampariello, R., Ott, C.: Optimization-based generation and experimental validation of optimal walking trajectories for biped robots. In: 2012 IEEE/RSJ International Conference on Intelligent Robots and Systems, pp. 4373–4379, October 2012
12. Lampariello, R., Nguyen-Tuong, D., Castellini, C., Hirzinger, G., Peters, J.: Trajectory planning for optimal robot catching in real-time. In: 2011 IEEE International Conference on Robotics and Automation, pp. 3719–3726, May 2011
13. Tassa, Y., Erez, T., Todorov, E.: Synthesis and stabilization of complex behaviors through online trajectory optimization. In: 2012 IEEE/RSJ International Conference on Intelligent Robots and Systems, pp. 4906–4913, October 2012
14. Maciejewski, A., Klein, C.: Obstacle avoidance for kinematically redundant manipulators in dynamically varying environments. Int. J. Robot. Res. **4**(3), 109–117 (1985)
15. Zlajpah, L., Petric, T.: Obstacle Avoidance for Redundant Manipulators as Control Problem (2012)
16. Buss, S.R.: Introduction to inverse kinematics with Jacobian transpose, pseudoinverse and damped least squares methods. Int. J. Robot. Autom. **17**, 16 (2004)
17. Bosscher, P., Hedman, D.: Real-time collision avoidance algorithm for robotic manipulators, vol. 38, pp. 113–122 (2009)
18. Rakita, D., Mutlu, B., Gleicher., M.: A motion retargeting method for effective mimicry-based teleoperation of robot arms. In: 2017 12th ACM/IEEE International Conference on Human-Robot Interaction, HRI, pp. 361–370, March 2017
19. Rakita, D., Mutlu, B., Gleicher, M.: RelaxedIK: Real-time synthesis of accurate and feasible robot arm motion. In: Proceedings of Robotics: Science and Systems, Pittsburgh, Pennsylvania, June 2018

A Structural Approach to Dealing with High Dimensionality Parameter Search Spaces

Benjamin Hawker$^{(\boxtimes)}$ and Roger K. Moore

Department of Computer Science, University of Sheffield, Sheffield, UK
{ben.hawker,r.k.moore}@sheffield.ac.uk

Abstract. In the field of robotics, searching for effective control parameters is a challenge as controllers become more complex. As the number of parameters increases, the dimensionality of the search problem causes results to become varied because the search cannot effectively traverse the whole search space. In applications such as autonomous robotics, quick training that provides consistent and robust results is key. Hierarchical controllers are often employed to solve multi-input control problems, but multiple controllers increases the number of parameters and thus the dimensionality of the search problem. It is unknown whether hierarchies in controllers allows for effective staged parameter optimisation. Furthermore, it is unknown if a staged optimisation approach would avoid the issues high dimensional spaces cause to searches. Here we compare two hierarchical controllers, where one was trained in a staged manner based on the hierarchy and the other was trained with all parameters being optimised at once. This paper shows that the staged approach is strained less by the dimensionality of the problem. The solutions scoring in the bottom 25% of both approaches were compared, with the staged approach having significantly lower error. This demonstrates that the staged approach is capable of avoiding highly varied results by reducing the computational complexity of the search space. Computational complexity across AI has troubled engineers, resulting in increasingly intense algorithms to handle the high dimensionality. These results will hopefully prompt approaches that use of developmental or staged strategies to tackle high dimensionality spaces.

Keywords: Hierarchical · Control · Developmental · Learning

1 Introduction

Optimising parameters in functions is key to tailoring their competences to a problem. The more parameters to optimise puts strain on the chosen search algorithm. Eventually, a sufficiently challenging search will result in inconsistent results from the search algorithm, or no success at all [18]. In the field of robotics, this has limitations and challenges particularly in robots searching

© Springer Nature Switzerland AG 2020
A. Mohammad et al. (Eds.): TAROS 2020, LNAI 12228, pp. 159–170, 2020.
https://doi.org/10.1007/978-3-030-63486-5_19

for parameters autonomously. Many of the solutions rely heavily on kinematic and mechanical information that is implicitly or explicitly applied to the search algorithm to minimise the complexity of the search. Such information is not always available without an expert in the particular mechanical objective being learned. Furthermore, this information can vary greatly based on subtle properties of the robot or environment. While rewarding, the process of acquiring and implementing a lot of these priors is demanding. Furthermore, there are many domains where this approach isn't feasible due to the required information or expertise being unavailable. Being able to learn a problem without expressed detail of the problem is a valuable skill for autonomous agents to have.

1.1 Alternative Approaches

Model-based approaches solve the issue of complex search spaces through exhaustive search. Models can often be evaluated quicker than the robot can run in real time. This allows rudimentary algorithms to brute-force search with many trials in order to find a suitable solution [19]. However, exact models of a particular robot, environment and task are not always available. To build these have thorough knowledge of the robot and environment. Even then, it is easy to forget key details of the problem resulting in the parameters requiring manual tuning afterwards to optimise. Any time saved by making a simpler model places the engineer in a situation later where extra effort is required to manually tune the parameters to better fit the problem.

Machine Learning has a variety of approaches that generalise the kinematic properties in an environment. The extrapolation employed by the statistically based approaches allows inferences to be drawn about the search space, giving success in parameter selection where the parameters have generalisable or predictable behaviour [9–11]. However, approaches can require many trials in order to be successful. Modifications have been developed to improve the search to allow better generalisation in a limited number of trials. Approaches that succeed with consistent results in a handful of trials exist, but often require heavily informative priors or sensitive selection of key meta-parameters to guide the search algorithm [2]. This can be in the explicit model of the problem, or implicitly via a policy which guides the search to suit a particular demographic of problem. Again, these require an expert on the agent's environment who must select or build an informed policy or model. A "general policy" with which to solve robotic kinematic problems is not available due to the diversity among robots and environments.

1.2 Hierarchical Control

Hierarchical Control as a field has considered developmental approaches to optimisation [1,4,13]. Fields such as Perceptual Control Theory have noted that optimisation of higher levels of a hierarchy requires the lower levels to function [14]. What remains untested is whether the hierarchy is an indicator of which parameters can be optimised independent of the others. Can each level of the hierarchy, starting at the bottom, be optimised independent of what comes above it in the hierarchy? Whether this has been done has not been tested. Furthermore, if this is possible, it is not clear if this approach avoids the downsides that increased dimensionality causes.

1.3   Summary

This requirement of expert knowledge to minimise complexity presents limitations in autonomous robotics. Furthermore, autonomous robots have a restricted number of trials with which to find a new parameter set. New methodological approaches that aid reducing the complexity of searches would benefit autonomous robots.

This paper describes an approach to the problem based on hierarchical control and staged optimisation of parameters. An experiment was conducted in order to show whether the staged approach suffers less from inconsistent results which is a common effect of dimensionality issues.

2   Experimental Setup

2.1   Baxter Robot

The experiment was conducted with the Baxter Robot, a six foot 14-DOF industrial robot. The task concerned the left arm, specifically the joint shown on the left of Fig. 1, named s0. This joint rotates the arm along the X-Z plane. The rest of the arm was held in the position shown in the picture on the left in Fig. 1, so the controller could consistently achieve control.

The task was to control the angular position of the elbow (e1) with respect to the shoulder joint (s0) in the X-Z plane. Applying force in either direction of the s0 joint moves the arm around Baxter, changing the angle between s0 and e1 as indicated in the right panel of Fig. 1.

2.2   PID Cascade Control

A Proportional-Integral-Derivative Controller (also referred to as a PID Controller) is a negative-feedback controller widely used within control systems engineering due to the simplicity and effectiveness of control provided [5].

A negative feedback controller controls a particular external variable by continuously minimising error, where error is defined as the difference between the actual value and the desired value for the controlled variable [20]. If e is the error, then the control process can be defined as:

$$u(t) = K_p e(t) + K_i \int_0^t e(t)dt + K_d \frac{de(t)}{dt} \tag{1}$$

where $u(t)$ is the control output at time t, $e(t)$ is the error at time t and k_p, k_i and k_d are parameters. The original inspiration was from manual control of steering

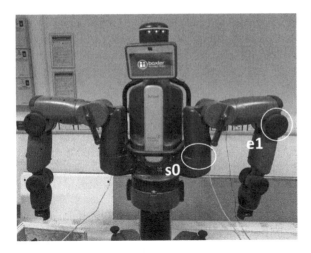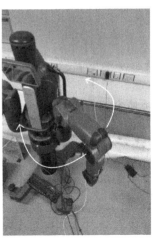

Fig. 1. A pair of images of the Baxter Robot. The left image shows the whole robot, the controlled joint (s0) and the location that was being controlled (e1) through moving s0. The right image shows the effect of applying force to the s0 joint, either positive or negative.

ships, where it was realised that a sailor would not just aim to minimise error proportionally but also aim to account for lingering error and avoid large rates of change [12]. The elegant and simple design affords utility while being Bounded-Input Bounded-Output Stable, making the general responses predictable.

Cascading PID Control (also known as Cascade Control) refers to two (or more) PID controllers where the reference signal for one PID controller is the control output (u) from the higher controller. Cascade control is used for many control applications in recent literature both as is [17] and with modifications [3,16].

2.3 Control System for This Experiment

For this experiment, a cascading PID controller was employed to control Baxter's inner shoulder joint (known as s0) to position the elbow at a particular angular position. The higher order controller controlled the angular position of the elbow, sending signals to the lower controller which controlled the velocity of the s0 joint. The lower controller sent a control signal applying torque to the joint. The controller is shown in Fig. 2.

2.4 Bat Algorithm

Evolutionary Algorithms, inspired by the Genetic Algorithm, benefit from good convergence in a small amount of trials. Evolutionary Algorithms are inspired by patterns noticed in nature, where Bat Algorithm is inspired by the echo-location used by bats to search an area for possible prey [21]. These properties have made

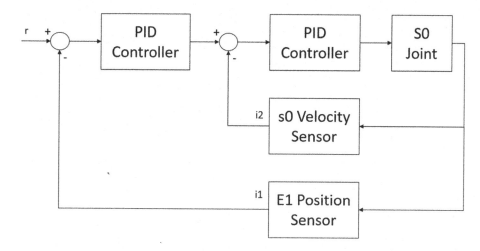

Fig. 2. A diagram showing the cascading PID controller used in this experiment.

the Bat Algorithm useful in control of robots [15] and more generalised AI tasks such as path planning [8].

The variant of the algorithm used in this experiment extends Yang's work. A velocity based approach to updating the candidates [6,7] and a levy-flights based random walk are utilised. The algorithm optimised candidates to minimise error on the staged and all-in-one curriculums, with 30 iterations in total (which were divided equally between the two training stages in the staged approach). See Fig. 3.

2.5 Designing Curricula for Developmental Learning

Two curricula were developed for learning the problem. One expressed the higher level problem of controlling the angular position, which both approaches used. The staged curriculum also trained the lower controller on how to control the velocity of the s0 joint. For each curriculum, the average error over each task is the score. A curriculum could be built based on a particular task where the candidate simply passes or fails. This is realistic to the environment, as often a difference between average error is not important as long as the candidate passes the task. However, pass or fail tasks are usually domain specific. Average error, while not necessarily indicative of passing or failing, implicitly tests important properties of a controller. The rise time, settling time, overshoot and steady state error all impact the average error and are four important properties which one would test in a domain specific environment. Therefore, average error suffices as a good indicator of improving performance. Modifying the curriculum to account for particular properties would be simple to do, if knowledge of the domain is provided to indicate which of the four properties is most important to control.

Algorithm 1 Bat Algorithm

Require: Loudness Parameter (1)
Require: Pulserate Parameter (0.75)
Require: Number of bats, N_b (20)
Require: Number of trials, N_t
  1: $X \leftarrow$ *Establish Bat Populations randomly* X_i *for 1...N_b*
  2: $F \leftarrow$ *Establish* F_i *as runTrial(X_i) for 1...N_b*
  3: $Q \leftarrow$ *Establish* Q_i *between 0.0 and 0.2 for 1...N_b*
  4: **while** *Loop count below N_t* **do**
  5:    **for** X_i *in* X **do**
  6:        $V_i \leftarrow V_i + (X_i - X_{best}) * Q_i$
  7:        $X_{temp} \leftarrow X_i + V_i$
  8:        **if** *rand(0,1)* $>$ *Pulserate)* **then**
  9:            $X_{temp} \leftarrow$ *New Random Solution from Levy Distribution * 0.001*
 10:        **fitness** $\leftarrow$ *runTrial(X_{temp})*
 11:        **if** *fitness* $<$ F_i **and** *rand(0,1)* $<$ *Loudness* **then**
 12:            $X_i \leftarrow X_{temp}$
 13:            $F_i \leftarrow$ **fitness**
 14:            **if** $fitness > F_{best}$ **then**
 15:               $X_{best} \leftarrow X_{temp}$
 16:               $F_{best} \leftarrow$ **fitness**

Fig. 3. The algorithm employed in this experiment, inspired by Fister's velocity adaptations of the Bat Algorithm [6].

Top Level: Position Control. The position curriculum had three trials that the candidates were tested on. Between each of these trials, the controller and position of the robot were reset. The reset point was the middle point of the range of movement, which is approximately 40°. The error over time for all three trials was recorded and averaged.

– Move to 5°, 8 s time limit
– Move to 55°, 8 s time limit
– Move to 95°, 8 s time limit

Bottom Level: Velocity Control. The Velocity Control curriculum was designed as one continuous trial, so changes in behaviours are accounted for in the curriculum. The agent began at the middle point as before, but then each of these tests immediately moved onto the next. Again, the average error over the whole period was the score for those parameters.

– Maintain a velocity of -0.3 m/s until past $-10°$.
– Maintain a velocity of 0 for 3 s.
– Maintain a velocity of 0.6 m/s until past 110°.
– Maintain a velocity of -0.6 m/s until past $-10°$.
– Maintain a velocity of 0.3 m/s until past 110°.
– Maintain a velocity of 0 for 4 s.

2.6   The Full Architecture

An overarching control program assigns which optimisation approach the Bat Algorithm will use, staged or all in one, as well as the number of trials to be run. The Bat Algorithm produces possible parameter combinations (hereafter called candidates) which need to be tested. When one needs testing, it is sent to the curriculum trial controller, which tests the candidate on the curriculum through a series of control tasks. On receiving a candidate to test, the curricula trial controller will set the parameters of the Cascading PID Controller to those of the candidate. Then, it passes reference signals to the Cascading PID Controller for each control task. It will keep doing this until all control tasks that are part of this curriculum have been sent. Once the Cascading PID Controller receives reference signals for a control task, the Cascading PID Controller sends control signals to the robot which returns sensory feedback. From this feedback, the Cascading PID Controller calculates the average error over the period of the control task. This average error is fed back to the curricula trial controller, which then averages the average error across all the control tasks. This is fed back to the Bat Algorithm, which feeds into whether this candidate should be kept or discarded. Eventually, when all the trials are complete, the Bat Algorithm feeds back to the overarching control program the best candidate at minimising average error.

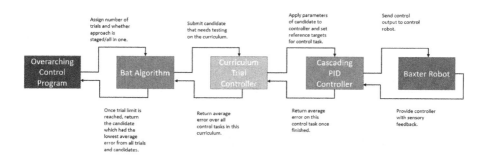

Fig. 4. A Flow Chart showing the program flow of the combined architecture. Each arrow indicates some information or a command being sent from one part of the architecture to another. (Color figure online)

3   Experimental Results and Discussion

3.1   Execution Time

Due to the size of Baxter and the heavy weight of the limbs, each test on the curriculum required 20 to 30 s. With 20 trials and 20 candidates, this results in a running period of several hours, which is not suitable across all robotics solutions. However, in each run of the algorithm, effective candidates were found in the first two to four trials. Each staged approach took only two to four trials to acquire a candidate that was below or equal to 110% of the average error of the eventually found best candidate. For the all-in-one approach, this was between four and eight trials. This presents a quicker time frame than the maximum number of trials used, but is important to test the effectiveness in situations where greater time is allowed. Furthermore, many autonomous robots will be able to act faster than Baxter, whose joints are not built to be quick or responsive. With a robot which enacts trials quicker combined with the low number of trials required, this reduces the time to be effective from hours to minutes.

3.2   Comparison of the Chosen Parameters

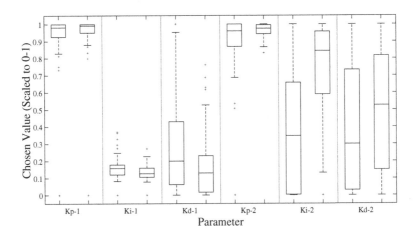

Fig. 5. A graph showing the spread of choices for the six parameters chosen by each approach. For each parameter labelled on the x-axis, there are two boxplots representing the spread of parameter values chosen. The middle line represents the mean, the box's upper and lower bounds represent the 75th and 25th percentile respectively, and the upper and lower whiskers are the upper and lower adjacent values respectively. The left box in each section indicates the chosen values by the all-in-one approach and the right box represents the values chosen by the staged approach. The most notable difference is the choice of K_i in the velocity controller, Ki-2, where the staged approach went for an integral-heavy parameter set.

The Staged Approach had a separate training procedure for the three parameters in the lower controller. However, the values chosen for the lower controller influenced the choices of the second stage of training. Given this, it is notable that both approaches found similar parameters for the higher controller. This can be seen in the first three pairs of boxes and means (labelled kp-1, ki-1 and kd-1) in Fig. 5. For each pair in Fig. 5, the all-in-one approach has chosen parameters similar to the staged approach.

The most notable difference between the two schemes is in the K_i value for the lower controller indicated by the third and fourth columns from the right in Fig. 5. The staged approach on average has a much higher K_i value, whereas the all-in-one approach favours a lower value. The integral typically causes the controller to overcome steady state error which would be expected in a velocity controller. The amount of force required to counter a small error (or apply a small amount of velocity) is more than the proportional term would allow. As such, an integral is expected here to allow error to build and apply more torque to the joints. The slightly higher K_d value is also expected as a result, as the K_d value offsets the overshooting a high K_i value can often cause (Fig. 6).

3.3   Comparison of Error

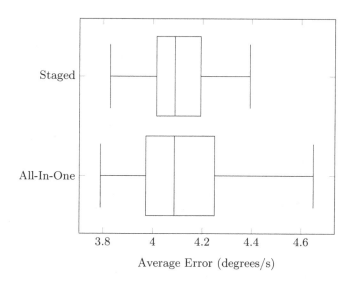

Fig. 6. Box Plots of the average error of the best solutions found by the all-in-one and staged approaches. The middle line represents the mean, the box's upper and lower bounds represent the 75th and 25th percentile respectively, and the upper and lower whiskers are the upper and lower adjacent values respectively.

Both medians are similar with no significant difference, but the spread of results differs. The all-in-one approach has a greater degree of both excellent and poor results further from the median. This is as hypothesised, as the higher dimensionality of the search space allows for all possible combinations to be considered. However, the dimensionality also increases the complexity of the search space. Given the initial candidates are randomly selected, these can be a poor selection from the state space and not allow the algorithm to appropriately minimise error (Fig. 6).

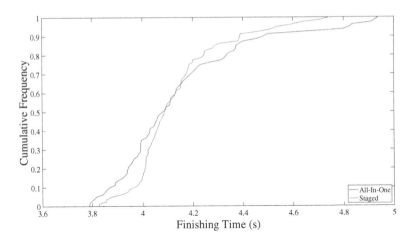

Fig. 7. A graph showing a Cumulative Distribution Function of the average error of the best solutions found by the all-in-one and staged approaches.

When comparing all the solutions and their scores from both approaches, neither has significantly lower error than the other. However, The poorest 25% of solutions from the staged approach perform significantly better than the poorest 25% of solutions from the all-in-one approach. The best 25% of the all-in-one solutions significantly outperform the best 25% of the staged solutions (Fig. 7).

This result is applicable in fields where consistent reoptimisation of parameters is preferred, as poor results can result in catastrophic failure and are not worth the occasionally better performances such as autonomous robotics. Furthermore, it is notable that the solutions do not have distinctly different medians given the staged approach is computationally simpler. Two three-dimensional search spaces are less complex to traverse than one six-dimensional search space, meaning the same results on average are being achieved on a simpler version of the problem. The staged approach is computationally simpler as it does not consider every possible combination of all six parameters, but rather optimising three independent of what values may be selected for the other three. This could theoretically limit the controller by not allowing it to find suitable parameter combinations between the higher and lower controller. However, given the medians are similar, this indicates that the poor results from the higher dimensionality offset the benefits of having access to more parameter combinations.

4   Conclusion and Future Work

In this paper, results have been presented comparing a staged parameter selection approach with the standard all-in-one approach for control of a joint in a robotic arm. It has been shown that the staged approach has more consistent results, particularly that the worst solutions of the staged approach are better than the worst solutions of the all-in-one approach. The staged approach is computationally simpler yet retains a similar median performance. The value of consistency in autonomous robotics has been discussed. However, what remains to be determined is the extent to which this effect would scale and how effective these candidates are in a general setting. This paper shows the effect of different parameter optimisations and how they're affected by dimensionality, but does not express how effective the controllers are per se. A set of trials aimed at testing generalised performance would need to be used for this.

It is not concluded whether the resistance to the effects of dimensionality in the staged approach scales to higher dimensions. When the algorithm struggles to search the space due to high dimensionality, inconsistency will occur. However, as the dimensionality continues to increase, the effectiveness of the solutions should worsen rapidly. Further work needs to be done to demonstrate how resistant the staged approach is in higher dimensional searches.

Finally, more formal work could be performed to detail exactly what a good curriculum is. It is evident that the curriculum designed here met the purpose of maintaining good results by achieving consistent staged parameter optimisation. However, further discussion and methodological analysis is necessary to identify what comprises an effective learning curriculum.

Acknowledgement. With thanks to Adam Hartwell and Jonathan Aitken, for their technical support and advice on matters of Control Engineering.

References

1. Brooks, R.: A robust layered control system for a mobile robot. IEEE J. Robot. Autom. **2**(1), 14–23 (1986). https://doi.org/10.1109/JRA.1986.1087032. http://ieeexplore.ieee.org/lpdocs/epic03/wrapper.htm?arnumber=1087032
2. Chatzilygeroudis, K., Vassiliades, V., Stulp, F., Calinon, S., Mouret, J.B.: A survey on policy search algorithms for learning robot controllers in a handful of trials, July 2018. http://arxiv.org/abs/1807.02303
3. Deng, H., Li, Q., Cui, Y., Zhu, Y., Chen, W.: Nonlinear controller design based on cascade adaptive sliding mode control for PEM fuel cell air supply systems. Int. J. Hydrogen Energy **44**(35), 19357–19369 (2019). https://doi.org/10.1016/j.ijhydene.2018.10.180
4. Digney, B.L.: Learning hierarchical control structures for multiple tasks and changing environments. In: From Animals to Animats, vol. 5, pp. 321–330. MIT Press, September 1998. http://dl.acm.org/citation.cfm?id=299955.299998
5. DiStefano, J.J., Stubberud, A.R., Williams, I.J.: Theory and Problems of Feedback and Control Systems. McGraw-Hill, New York (1967)
6. Fister, I., Fister, D., Yang, X.S.: A hybrid bat algorithm, March 2013. http://arxiv.org/abs/1303.6310
7. Fister, I., Fong, S., Brest, J.: A novel hybrid self-adaptive bat algorithm (2014). https://doi.org/10.1155/2014/709738
8. Guo, J., Gao, Y., Cui, G.: The path planning for mobile robot based on bat algorithm. Int. J. Autom. Control **9**(1), 50–60 (2015). https://doi.org/10.1504/IJAAC.2015.068041

9. Lizotte, D., Wang, T., Bowling, M., Schuurmans, D.: Automatic gait optimization with Gaussian process regression - Proceedings of the 20th International Joint Conference on Artifical Intelligence. Technical report (2007)
10. Martinez-Cantin, R., de Freitas, N., Doucet, A., Castellanos, J.: Active policy learning for robot planning and exploration under uncertainty. In: Robotics: Science and Systems III. Robotics: Science and Systems Foundation, June 2007. https://doi.org/10.15607/RSS.2007.III.041. http://www.roboticsproceedings.org/rss03/p41.pdf
11. Matsubara, T., Hyon, S.H., Morimoto, J.: Learning parametric dynamic movement primitives from multiple demonstrations. Neural Netw. **24**(5), 493–500 (2011). https://doi.org/10.1016/j.neunet.2011.02.004
12. Minorsky, N.: Directional stability of automatically steered bodies. J. Am. Soc. Naval Eng. **34**(2), 280–309 (1922). https://doi.org/10.1111/j.1559-3584.1922.tb04958.x. http://doi.wiley.com/10.1111/j.1559-3584.1922.tb04958.x
13. Morimoto, J., Doya, K.: Acquisition of stand-up behavior by a real robot using hierarchical reinforcement learning. Robot. Auton. Syst. **36**(1), 37–51 (2001). https://doi.org/10.1016/S0921-8890(01)00113-0
14. Powers, W.T.: Behavior: The Control of Perception. Wildwood House Ltd. (1974). ISBN: 9780704500921
15. Rahmani, M., Ghanbari, A., Ettefagh, M.M.: Robust adaptive control of a bio-inspired robot manipulator using bat algorithm. Expert Syst. Appl. **56**, 164–176 2016). https://doi.org/10.1016/j.eswa.2016.03.006
16. Reyes-Ortiz, O.J., Useche-Castelblanco, J.S., Vargas-Fonseca, G.L.: Implementation of fuzzy PID controller in cascade with anti-windup to real-scale test equipment for pavements. Eng. Trans. (2020). https://doi.org/10.24423/ENGTRANS.1066.20200102
17. Utami, E., Sahrin, A.,Utomo, G.R.: Cascade control with PID-PSO method on the stabilizer unit. In: The 2nd International Conference on Applied Electromagnetic Technology (AEMT) 2018 (2018)
18. Trunk, G.V.: A problem of dimensionality: a simple example. IEEE Trans. Pattern Anal. Mach. Intell. PAMI **1**(3), 306–307 (1979). https://doi.org/10.1109/TPAMI.1979.4766926
19. Wang, Q.J.: Using genetic algorithms to optimise model parameters. Env. Model. Softw. **12**(1), 27–34 (1997). https://doi.org/10.1016/S1364-8152(96)00030-8
20. Wiener, N.: Cybernetics or Control and Communication in the Animal and the Machine. Technology Press (1948)
21. Yang, X.S.: A new metaheuristic bat-inspired algorithm. Stud. Comput. Intel. **284**, 65–74 (2010). https://doi.org/10.1007/978-3-642-12538-6

Self-supervised Learning Through Scene Observation for Selective Item Identification in Conveyor Belt Systems

Luca Scimeca and Fumiya Iida[✉]

Bio-Inspired Robotics Lab. Cambridge University Department of Engineering,
Trumpington St, Cambridge CB2 1PZ, UK
{ls769,fi224}@cam.ac.uk

Abstract. Conveyor belts are core components in several industries. Often, workers need to operate on conveyor belts, selectively picking objects based on visual features following inspection. In such cases it is desirable to be able to selectively identify such items automatically. The need of tailored systems discourages solutions based on common data collection and labeling, as well as vision systems based on known object features. We device a novel framework to learn from existing human labor, without need of explicit data gathering or labeling. The framework autonomously detects, tracks and learns the visual features of salient objects in conveyor belt-based systems. The system is comprised of two cameras, a Convolutional Neural Network and a novel training regime, devised to support learning on on-line visual feeds. We show the framework is capable of autonomously learning the visual features of the objects picked by human operators. The system trains entirely through visual observation of human labor and achieves detection accuracy of over 97% on a set of 7 different objects after only 10 min of operation, without any knowledge of the objects at priori.

Keywords: Automation · Machine Learning · Vision

1 Introduction

Conveyor belt systems find themselves at the core of several core industries, including warehousing facilities, manufacturing, automated distribution, production factories and more besides. In several such industries, human operators are often tasked to selectively act on a subset of objects within the system. Some

This work was funded by the UK Agriculture and Horticulture Development Board (CP 172).

Electronic supplementary material The online version of this chapter (https://doi.org/10.1007/978-3-030-63486-5_20) contains supplementary material, which is available to authorized users.

© Springer Nature Switzerland AG 2020
A. Mohammad et al. (Eds.): TAROS 2020, LNAI 12228, pp. 171–183, 2020.
https://doi.org/10.1007/978-3-030-63486-5_20

workers in fruit packaging or redistribution facilities, for example, would stand by a conveyor belt, while selectively picking out produce which seems damaged or not up to market standards; others, instead, might inspect mechanical components to discard defective items.

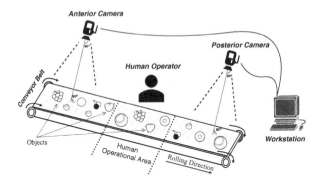

Fig. 1. Scene observation and item identification framework.

In many such scenarios workers may be working in closed off environments, with noise level superiors to 85 dB [20], at times with acidic smells coming from vinegar based solutions, rooms with temperatures lower than $-20C$, to preserve produce for as long as possible [12,19], and/or low-lighting conditions [7]. More importantly, conveyor belt system tasks are often repetitive and they are cause of much injuries, first amongst many: arm and hand injuries, cuts and scrapes, burns and abrasions and bone fractures [13,15]. In such cases it is desirable to find automated solutions, where robotics systems can be employed to work in human-unfriendly environments.

The automation of conveyor-belt based systems in industrial settings has persevered for over 40 years [1,18]. In the last two decades there have been a number of robotics and Machine Learning solutions aimed at fully automatizing the industry. Work in Visual servoing has been amongst the most active research areas [5], with solutions spanning from visual tracking to robot control [2,8,14]. Visual object identification and detection on conveyor belt systems has also been explored [17]. On the mechanical side, the advancement in robotic gripper mechanisms has also boosted automation [4]. More recently, advancements in material science and robotics gave way to the advent of soft-robotics and soft robotics grasping mechanism [10,21,23,24], revolutionizing picking and manipulations tasks for a wider variety of tasks, such as picking garbage from a garbage disposal facility [6] or grasping soft fruit objects [11,22]. The majority of the work, however, is aimed at mechanical or robotics solutions capable of detecting known objects, picking or manipulating them within the conveyor system. In several industrial scenarios, instead, the intervention on the objects needs to be selective. In a fruit factory, for example, the labor's task might be that of removing defective produce, while in a garbage disposal factory, the task might be to separate objects into different containers depending on the materials that compose them. In these scenarios it is first necessary to learn the labor operational task, to recognize and detect salient items to be acted upon.

The automation of the selective detection of items from a conveyor belt, based on task understanding, is a most useful step forward towards the full automation of conveyor belt based systems. We argue that, to be applicable in industry, a solution should have three features: first, it should need minimum data, and fast learning and retraining procedures, to limit transferability issues when re-using the same system in a different industry; second, it should ideally need no explicit data gathering and labeling, as it would otherwise be necessary to create a specific labeled data-set for each scenario, even within the same industry, limiting the portability and usability of the system by many users with ease; third, it should reach human-level selective item detection and identification accuracy, thus providing an advantageous substitute to current labor in such applications. It is also desirable for the framework to perform objects detection without any prior knowledge of object-dependent features, else a new vision-based solution must be devised for different scenarios.

We device a novel framework to autonomously detect and track salient objects in conveyor belt-based systems. Through the use of two cameras it is possible to track elements in the belt which were acted upon by the labor, and learn without any explicit labeling or supervision to detect salient objects in future scenarios, based on the observed labor's task. Furthermore, a deep-network architecture is devised to cope with learning from streaming data, while maintaining the ability to generalize well for oncoming streams.

In this paper, Sect. 2 presents the detection and learning framework. Section 3 presents the methods developed, including a detailed explanation of the vision and learning systems. The results are reported in Sect. 4 which characterize the performance of the framework with continuous data streams both on object detection, the learning and the system overall. Finally, a conclusion is given in Sect. 5.

2   Observer and Learning Framework

We develop a framework capable of learning to detect and select objects through visual observation of skilled labor. The system was designed to learn from minimum training data, need no explicit data gathering and labeling as conventional deep-network frameworks, and reach a human-like levels of accuracy in the detection and identification of salient objects.

The framework developed is composed by a vision system and a deep learning system running on a local workstation, and is summarized in Fig. 1. The vision systems is composed by two cameras and an object detection and tracking module. The system's role is that of observing and analyzing human intention within the conveyor belt area. The cameras, namely the *anterior* and *posterior* cameras, are placed in two different locations within the same conveyor belt system (Fig. 1). The anterior camera captures an area of the conveyor belt which was not affected by human intervention, whilst the posterior camera captures an area of the belt

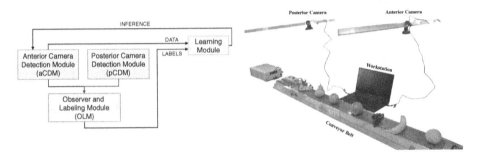

Fig. 2. Figure (a) show the Observer and Learning architecture of the developed framework. Figure (b) shows the set-up used for the experiments.

where human labor has already intervened. By comparing the analysis of the same conveyor section, prior and post human intervention, it is possible to localize the areas of the belt which were affected by human input. Figure 2a shows the framework's architecture. For each camera there exists a *detection module*, namely the Anterior Camera Module or aCDM, and the Posterior camera module or pCDM, whose role is that of localizing every object within its field of vision. The detections for each camera are sent to an Observer and Labeling Module or OLM, which compares their visual feeds to annotate those objects which were influenced by human intervention. The camera captures aCDM, together with additional information supplied by the OLM, can then be fed to a Learning Module, which trains to recognize which objects in the conveyor belt needed to be picked from at the time when they were observed in the anterior camera. All through the run, the Learning Module can make inferences on which objects need intervention and improve over time by observing human labor.

3   Methods

3.1   Camera Set-up

Within the framework it is important that the two cameras' visual fields do not overlap i.e. each visual field should either be prior or post human intervention, but in no in-between state. Moreover, a stationary assumption is necessary, i.e. the position of an object within a conveyor belt is assumed not change except due to external perturbations (e.g. human intervention). In most scenarios, this can trivially be held true with small changes the belt system.

Figure 2b shows the set-up developed to validate the framework. Two low-cost Logitech C270 webcams are used, capturing visual feeds at a maximum of 30 fps, and at a resolution of 640 × 480 px. The two cameras are set-up 90 cm apart, facing directly downward a custom-made conveyor belt unit. The conveyor belt component has an 130 × 10 cm flat upper surface, hosting a belt moving at a speed of approximately 50 cm/s. The anterior camera captures 40 cm of the initial section of the conveyor, followed by 50 cm of human operational area and the final 40 cm covered be the visual field of the posterior camera (Fig. 3).

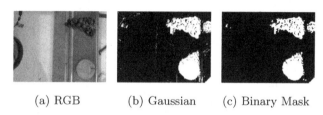

(a) RGB   (b) Gaussian   (c) Binary Mask

Fig. 3. Example detection by an arbitrary Camera Detection Module. (a) The sample $I^{(i)}$ captured frame, (b) the corresponding $M^{(i)}$ Gaussian probability mask, with higher intensity indicating pixels with higher probability of being part of the foreground and (c) generated binary foreground mask $B^{(i)}$.

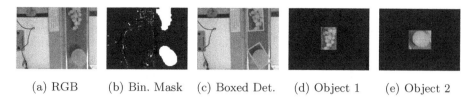

(a) RGB   (b) Bin. Mask   (c) Boxed Det.   (d) Object 1   (e) Object 2

Fig. 4. The figure shows the image reprocessing steps before learning. From a sample $I^{(i)}$ frame, a (b) binary mask $B^{(i)}$ is created. The mask is used to (c) frame the objects, and finally (d)–(e) a number of images equal to the number of objects is created, where the objects are cropped, rotated and padded from $I^{(i)}$ to become ready for learning.

3.2   Object Detection and Tracking

Camera Detection Module: Both the aCDM and the pCDM modules need to be able to detect unknown items within their field of vision. It is here desirable to devise an object extraction technique which does not rely on any context-dependent visual features, else an ad-hoc visual tracking solution must be tailored for different scenarios in each industry.

First, it is necessary to make a motion assumption, i.e. we assume that if an object is placed on the conveyor belt, and is within the visual field of either the anterior or posterior camera, it must change its relative position to the cameras over time. As any one object will be in motion when the belt is operational, this will trivially be true for most systems. A foreground extraction object detection and tracking algorithm is then devised, based on the Gaussian Mixture-based Background/Foreground Segmentation Algorithm background subtraction [27].

For each camera detection module, there is a stream of captured frames. Consider $I_a^{(i)}$ the ith captured frame of the aCDM, and $I_p^{(i)}$ the ith captured frame of the pCDM. Each frame is a $640 \times 480 \times 3$ RGB array sampled at constant time intervals t_r, here $t_r = 0.03\,\text{s}$. The progress of i is therefore consistent with the time lapsed since the start of the system. For the sake of notation the a and p subscripts are dropped when the methods apply to both the anterior and posterior camera detection modules.

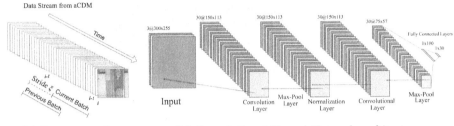

(a) Data streaming.   (b) Convolutional Neural Network architecture.

Fig. 5. The CNN architecture and data streaming feed for learning. The notation $A@BxC$ refers to Neural Network layers with A filters of shape $B \times C$.

At each time interval i, a binary mask $B^{(i)}$ is generated, corresponding to the foreground of a captured $I^{(i)}$ (Fig. 3). A Gaussian mask $M^{(i)}$ can be computed as:

$$M^{(i)} = GMM(I^{(i)}) \tag{1}$$

where GMM is the foreground extractor functions implemented in [3], based on the Gaussian Mixture-based Background/Foreground Segmentation Algorithm in [26,27]. Here, $M^{(i)}$ is a 640×480 array, where each element corresponds to the probability that the corresponding pixel within $I^{(i)}$ belongs to the foreground (Fig. 3a and 3b). The foreground of certainty is thus extracted, or $B^{(i)} = M^{(i)} == MAX(M^{(i)})$ where $B^{(i)}$ is a 640×480 foreground binary masks (Fig. 3c). When the motion assumption previously mentioned holds, pixels within moving objects will naturally have low probability of being part of the background, and thus will generally be present within the extracted foreground.

Observer and Labeling Module: The OLM module's role is to compare two frames corresponding to the same sliding conveyor belt section, prior and and post human intervention. The comparison allows for the detection of those objects within the belt which were influenced by the system.

At time i, the OLM module can observe any captured frame $I^{(j)}$ and binary foreground $B^{(j)}$ from the anterior and posterior camera modules, for $j <= i$. Since two binary images corresponding to the same sliding section of the belt need to be compared, we can define the index j such that:

$$j = i - \lfloor \frac{t_s}{t_r} \rfloor \tag{2}$$

where t_s is the time necessary for an object to pass from the center of the anterior camera's field of view to the center of the posterior's, and t_r is the sampling rate of the camera. The index is computed such that given the sampling rate, both detection modules can observe images on the same sliding section of the conveyor belt. Given the stationary assumption, if any one detected object in $B_a^{(j)}$ is not present within d pixels from the center of its corresponding location in $B_p^{(j)}$, it can assumed the human operator has influenced the state of the object, and a label can thus be generated. The d parameter is arbitrary, although, we argue that, should the stationary assumption hold true, the center of the object should not move any more than the smallest radius of the circle circumscribing it.

3.3 Deep Learning System

The Learning Module developed for the system is based on a CNN Architecture re-designed to be able to deal with streaming, "on-line", data. Each data point, then, is always to be considered a new, unseen, sample. Moreover, retraining on all the previously seen samples is impossible, if training and inference are to happen in parallel to the running of the Detection Modules, and the number of data points can grow unconditionally. We introduce and implement three main concepts, to allow the network to deal with the above issues: object framing, batch buffering and sliding window.

Object Framing: As the aCDM and pCDM modules monitor the conveyor belt, one or more objects can be detected simultaneously in each $I^{(i)}$ at time i. For the CNN to be able to learn the visual features corresponding to each object, it is necessary that each object is: first, separated into a different input; two, made comparable to other objects. To achieve this, for each $I^{(i)}$ the minimum circumscribing boxes containing the binary blobs detected in the corresponding mask $B^{(i)}$ are found (Fig. 4a, 4b and 4c). The area in the image within the box is then cropped, rotated and padded to re-shape each input array into a comparable size and format (Fig. 4d and 4e).

Batch Buffering and Sliding Window: With streaming data, like any other data-set, it is necessary to discourage over-fitting. It is here possible to use a procedure similar to batch training, by buffering the re-shaped objects from $I^{(i)}$ to $I^{(j)}$ for $j = i - \iota$, and training on objects extracted from the batch, rather than from single new images. Parallel to the concept of batch buffering is every how often to train on the buffered images from the past. If batch-training on every single incoming image, the same image will be seen by the network at least ι times, and thus over-fitting is possible for large ι. We set a stride parameter ξ, which corresponds to the minimum number of time steps i necessary for the network to re-train on the current buffer (Fig. 5a). The choice of ι and ξ and their influence in learning is explored in Sect. 4.2.

Architecture and Training: The Convolutional Neural Network Architecture designed was based on existing working convolutional architectures for image recognition, with a shallow structure [9]. The network is composed of two convolutional layers, two pool layers, a normalization layer and two fully connected output layers, as shown in Fig. 5b. All units perform a *ReLu* non-linear transformation [16]. We train the network with the RMSProp adaptive learning rule [25], where the weighted gradient for each weight w at time i is:

$$\Delta w(i) = \frac{-\eta}{\sqrt{S(i) + \epsilon}} \frac{\delta E}{\delta w(i)} \tag{3}$$

Fig. 6. The objects used for the experiments.

Table 1. Detections when testing the system on ≈ 15 min of conveyor belt operation.

aCDM Correct Detections (TP+TN)	4187	No. of frames	3008 frames
aCDM Incorrect Detections (FP+FN)	100	aCDM Accuracy	97.67%
pCDM Correct Detections (TP+TN)	3004	pCDM Accuracy	97.63%
pCDM Incorrect Detections (FP+FN)	73		

Here, $S(i)$ corresponds to the weighted average of the square sum of gradients up to i, and ϵ, set to $1e-10$ throughout the experiments, prevents division by zero. The learning rate η and the decay hyper-parameter β are set to respectively 0.0001 and 0.9, two known good values for the adaptive learning rule [25].

The error is computed as a regularized soft-max cross-entropy with logits on the classes absence (0) versus presence (1) of the object in the posterior camera's view.

$$S(i) = \beta S(i-1) + (1-\beta)\frac{\delta E}{\delta w(i)}^2 \qquad (4)$$

4   Results

To test the developed framework the belt system is run, together with the aCDM, pCDM, OLM and Learning module concurrently, on a set of unknown objects. The chosen objects resemble fruit items and are shown in Fig. 6. Three separate tests are performed: object detection, autonomous on-line learning and framework analysis. The performed tests consist in the continuous operation of the conveyor belt described in Sect. 3.2, while placing the objects in Fig. 6 in line in the anterior's camera's field of view, selectively picking them in the human operational area, and after reaching the end of the belt finally removing and reinserting the objects in the belt, in various positions and orientations (see Video attachment).

4.1   Object Detection

To test the ability of the aCDM and pCDM modules to detect objects, the system is run for a total of 15 min. For each incoming frame, the binary mask is computed as described in Sect. 3, and the minimal circumscribing boxes are detected. By comparing object detections in the aCDM and pCDM, items removed within the human operational area are identified.

After manually labeling the aCDM and pCDM recordings, the accuracy of the detection system is tested for both modules (Table 1). An object is successfully recognized in the pCDM, if its position remains within d pixels from its original

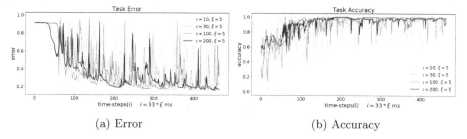

(a) Error   (b) Accuracy

Fig. 7. The figure compares the moving (a) error and (b) accuracy when testing the framework with different batch buffer lengths ι. Larger ι values prevent over fitting, thus resulting in more stable learning.

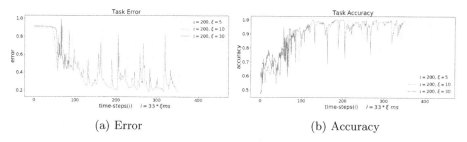

(a) Error   (b) Accuracy

Fig. 8. The figure compares the moving (a) error and (b) accuracy when testing the framework with different stride values ξ. Lower values show higher longer training curves.

position in the aCDM, where d is the radius of the smallest circle circumscribing the object (Sect. 3.2).

As shown in Table 1, the system is capable of detecting items with over 97% accuracy over 4187 objects processed within 3008 frames. The mis-detections where mainly due to the GMM object tracker misled by largely varying light during testing. For each object detected by the aCDM, however, it was always possible to detect its presence or absence in the pCDM.

4.2   Autonomous On-line Learning and Parameter Tuning

To investigate the influence of both the batch buffer size ι and the stride parameter ξ to the learning (see Sect. 3.3), the conveyor system is operated for 15 min, and the task is set to be the removal of object 2 (Fig. 6). While data is being streamed from the aCDM and pCDM modules, the system learns to recognize those objects which are removed in the human operational area.

Figure 7 shows the inference error and accuracy observed during the conveyor belt operation in the experiment, when learning with varying buffer sizes. The buffer size parameter has a strong influence in the ability for the learning framework to prevent over-fitting, with larger buffers preventing over-fits to the last seen image captures, and thus inducing more stable learning. On the other hand,

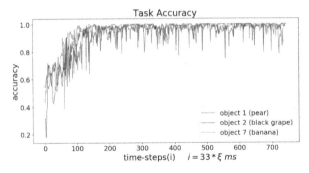

Table 2. Test error and accuracy during 5 min of continuous streams, and after 10 min of on-line training.

Objects	Error	Acc. (%)
1 (pear)	0.2383	97.26
2 (black grape)	0.2124	97.93
7 (banana)	0.1966	98.58

Fig. 9. Running accuracy of the framework during testing.

larger buffer sizes does not allow fast re-learning to support online streams. We set $\iota = 100$, since no noticeable differences were observed in the learning curve for buffers larger than 100 processed frames (Fig. 7).

Figure 8 shows 3 learning curves when learning with varying window strides. The stride has an effect both on the number of times the same frame is seen by the network during training, and the speed of learning. Training for every unseen new frame from the aCDM is undesirable, since for a large ι over-fitting is likely. Too large strides might not allow the network to change its weights enough to account for unseen frames. We pick $\xi = 5$, reaching the lowest error during the experiments (Fig. 8).

4.3 Framework Analysis

To thoroughly test the framework three separate test runs are performed as depicted in Sect. 4.2, each on a separate task: one, removal of the object 1, two removal of object 2 and three removal of object 7 (Fig. 6).

We use the best performing batch buffer and window stride sizes validated in the previous sections, i.e. $\iota = 100$ and $\xi = 5$, and test the accuracy of the network during 5 min of continuous streams, and after 10 min of on-line training. The errors and accuracies are reported in Table 2.

The features relative to object 7 were easier to learn than object 1 or 2, as shown by the higher testing accuracy and error in Table 2. The framework reaches stable top performance after ≈250 time steps, equivalent to less than 5 min of belt operation. The framework, is shown to be capable of selectively detecting and identifying objects, both influenced by human operations and non, with an average accuracy of over 97% on all tasks.

5   Conclusion

We develop a novel framework to selectively detect and recognize salient objects within a conveyor belt. The framework is capable of learning through observing human labor, and thus needs no explicit data-gathering and training. The adaptability of the framework to various conditions is shown, by purposefully applying object recognition and learning solutions which are feature independent, and thus transferable. We test the framework on a set of unknown objects, which are placed on a custom-made conveyor belt, and selectively picked by a human operator. The system based on the proposed framework is capable of observing human operations and autonomously learning which objects need to be acted upon prior to reaching the human operational area.

Given the GMM based object detection, object clutter is currently unsolved. Future work will be aimed at augmenting the aCDM and pCDM modules to detect objects in the presence of clutter (or object overlap). Additional cameras for the modules might also increase performance by both providing additional evidence for the network to train on, and cross-integration to detect and discard false-positive and false-negative detections. Learning through multiple snapshots of the same object, however, may also lead the CNN-based system to over-fit its solutions to the latest observed objects. This should be addressed through appropriate reduced learning rates, or other regularization procedures (including batch buffering and sliding windows). Finally, further future work could include the detection of object orientations prior human intervention, and the change in orientation of the same, post human intervention. This could, for example, be achieved via descriptors for each detected binary object, relative to the longest axis of the binary blobs, as well as the curvature at the extremities. Detection of significant changes in orientation within these would then imply human intervention, and trigger learning for object detection.

The framework is developed for ease of integration in existing industry environment. Conditional to some basic assumptions, the learning and vision system can run in the background and learn task-specific selective item detection and identification through observation of skilled labor in new environments. No labeling is necessary for the training of the system, and the supervision is supplied seamlessly by the labor, performing the usual required tasks. This work is a step forward toward the full automation of conveyor belt-based systems in non human-friendly environments.

References

1. Baird, M.L.: Image segmentation technique for locating automotive parts on belt conveyors. In: IJCAI, pp. 694–695 (1977)
2. Borangiu, T., Anton, F., Dogar, A.: Visual robot guidance in conveyor tracking with belt variables. In: 2010 IEEE International Conference on Automation, Quality and Testing, Robotics (AQTR), vol. 1, pp. 1–6. IEEE (2010)
3. Bradski, G.: The OpenCV library. Dr. Dobb's J. Softw. Tools **25**, 120–125 (2000)
4. Carbone, G.: Grasping in Robotics, vol. 10. Springer, London. https://doi.org/10.1007/978-1-4471-4664-3
5. Chaumette, F.: Visual servoing. In: Computer Vision: A Reference Guide, pp. 869–874 (2014)
6. Chin, L., Lipton, J., Yuen, M.C., Kramer-Bottiglio, R., Rus, D.: Automated recycling separation enabled by soft robotic material classification. In: 2019 2nd IEEE International Conference on Soft Robotics (RoboSoft), pp. 102–107. IEEE (2019)

7. Farhana, Z., Ali, S.M., Rahman, M.: Investigation on workplace environment and safety-a case study in Rahimafrooz batteries ltd. Int. J. Qual. Innov. **1**(4), 338–347 (2011)
8. Gans, N.R., Hutchinson, S.A.: Stable visual servoing through hybrid switched-system control. IEEE Trans. Robot. **23**(3), 530–540 (2007)
9. Howard, A.G.: Some improvements on deep convolutional neural network based image classification. arXiv preprint arXiv:1312.5402 (2013)
10. Hughes, J., Culha, U., Giardina, F., Guenther, F., Rosendo, A., Iida, F.: Soft manipulators and grippers: a review. Front. Robot. AI **3**, 69 (2016)
11. Hughes, J., Scimeca, L., Ifrim, I., Maiolino, P., Iida, F.: Achieving robotically peeled lettuce. IEEE Robot. Autom. Lett. **3**(4), 4337–4342 (2018)
12. Inaba, R., Mirbod, S.M., Kurokawa, J., Inoue, M., Iwata, H.: Subjective symptoms among female workers and winter working conditions in a consumer cooperative. J. Occup. Health **47**(5), 454–465 (2005)
13. Krishnamoorthy, R., Karthikeyan, G.: Degloving injuries of the hand. Indian J. Plast. Surg. Off. Publ. Assoc. Plast. Surg. India **44**(2), 227 (2011)
14. Luo, R.C., Chou, S.C., Yang, X.Y., Peng, N.: Hybrid eye-to-hand and eye-in-hand visual servo system for parallel robot conveyor object tracking and fetching. In: IECON 2014–40th Annual Conference of the IEEE Industrial Electronics Society, pp. 2558–2563. IEEE (2014)
15. Maguiña, P., Palmieri, T.L., Greenhalgh, D.G.: Treadmills: a preventable source of pediatric friction burn injuries. J. Burn Care Rehabil. **25**(2), 201–204 (2004)
16. Nair, V., Hinton, G.E.: Rectified linear units improve restricted Boltzmann machines. In: Proceedings of the 27th International Conference on Machine Learning (ICML-10), pp. 807–814 (2010)
17. Nashat, S., Abdullah, A., Aramvith, S., Abdullah, M.: Support vector machine approach to real-time inspection of biscuits on moving conveyor belt. Comput. Electron. Agric. **75**(1), 147–158 (2011)
18. Park, T.H., Lee, B.H.: An approach to robot motion analysis and planning for conveyor tracking. IEEE Trans. Syst. Man Cybern. **22**(2), 378–384 (1992)
19. Piedrahita, H., Oksa, J., Malm, C., Rintamäki, H.: Health problems related to working in extreme cold conditions indoors. Int. J. Circumpolar Health **67**(2–3), 279–287 (2008)
20. Ranga, R.K., Yadav, S., Yadav, A., Yadav, N., Ranga, S.B., et al.: Prevalence of occupational noise induced hearing loss in industrial workers. Indian J. Otol. **20**(3), 115 (2014)
21. Scimeca, L., Hughes, J., Maiolino, P., Iida, F.: Model-free soft-structure reconstruction for proprioception using tactile arrays. IEEE Robot. Autom. Lett. **4**(3), 2479–2484 (2019)
22. Scimeca, L., Maiolino, P., Cardin-Catalan, D., del Pobil, A.P., Morales, A., Iida, F.: Non-destructive robotic assessment of mango ripeness via multi-point soft haptics. In: 2019 International Conference on Robotics and Automation (ICRA), pp. 1821–1826. IEEE (2019)
23. Scimeca, L., Maiolino, P., Iida, F.: Efficient Bayesian exploration for soft morphology-action co-optimization. In: 2020 IEEE International Conference on Soft Robotics (RoboSoft) (2020)
24. Scimeca, L., Maiolino, P., Iida, F.: Soft morphological processing of tactile stimuli for autonomous category formation. In: 2018 IEEE International Conference on Soft Robotics (RoboSoft), pp. 356–361. IEEE (2018)

25. Tieleman, T., Hinton, G.: Lecture 6.5-rmsprop: Divide the gradient by a running average of its recent magnitude. COURSERA Neural Netw. Mach. Learn. **4**(2), 26–31 (2012)

26. Zivkovic, Z., Van Der Heijden, F.: Efficient adaptive density estimation per image pixel for the task of background subtraction. Pattern Recogn. Lett. **27**(7), 773–780 (2006)

27. Zivkovic, Z., et al.: Improved adaptive Gaussian mixture model for background subtraction. In: ICPR, vol. 2, pp. 28–31. Citeseer (2004)

A 4D Augmented Flight Management System Based on Flight Planning and Trajectory Generation Merging

Hortense Ollivier-Legeay[1,2](✉) (iD), Abdessamad Ait El Cadi[2](✉) (iD),
Nicolas Belanger[1](✉), and David Duvivier[2](✉) (iD)

[1] AIRBUS, Marseille Provence Airport, 13127 Marignane, France
hortense.legeay@uphf.fr, nicolas.belanger@airbus.com
[2] LAMIH UMR CNRS 8201, UPHF, 59313 Valenciennes, France
{abdessamad.aitelcadi,david.duvivier}@uphf.fr

Abstract. In recent decades, the helicopter has become a safe and suitable solution for future traffic, both in congested megacities and in isolated places as well as in mountainous environment where the terrain can be dangerous. Adding the third dimension to multimodal urban transport networks will improve the way we live. In order to solve the challenge of navigation towards more autonomy, it is necessary, during mission planning and flight execution, to generate effective, accurate and feasible paths. However, the major works in the literature do not address the effectiveness - flyability and controllability - of the generated trajectories for helicopters. This paper proposes an approach with continuous-curvature trajectory generation into inclined planes and proves the controllability by a simulated autopilot system designed for an Airbus Helicopters model in Matlab Simulink environment. We found that this type of trajectories is effective and controllable by an autopilot with only 3% of deviation error. The results are promising and the approach will be integrated in our works on a 4-dimensional flight management system for helicopters.

Keywords: Motion planning · Continuous curvature · Helicopters · Autopilot controllability · Smooth trajectory · Autonomy · Trajectory optimization · Simulation

1 Introduction

Typically, modern avionic systems are designed to reduce the mental workload of pilots and should result in more consistent decisions and piloting capabilities. However, technologies as Flight Management Systems (FMS) are limited; It is an avionic embedded software which purpose is to assist the pilot during the flight by providing information on piloting, navigation, and data estimations. In facts, there are differences between the trajectory generated by the system and the trajectory implemented by the aircraft in real conditions. Indeed, the generated trajectory is, often, represented by simple combinations

© Springer Nature Switzerland AG 2020
A. Mohammad et al. (Eds.): TAROS 2020, LNAI 12228, pp. 184–195, 2020.
https://doi.org/10.1007/978-3-030-63486-5_21

of motion primitives (straight lines, circular arcs...) and have, generally, a discontinuous curvature. This, results in non-realistic trajectory (sometimes non-feasible).

As the study of flight safety is a major challenge for various academic and industrial work groups today, a collaborative LAMIH – Airbus Helicopters project was launched since 2011, in response to this challenge. It concerns the development of a pilot assistance system involving a decision-making system capable of analyzing the environment, assessing the risk, and communicating with the pilot through Human-Machine Interface (HMI) means and alerts notifications or solutions in case of complex event. This collaborative work enabled us to define a functional architecture of a hierarchical decision-making system in order to reduce complexity covering several levels, from strategic to operational [1]. The calculation of long-term trajectories is the result of a first collaboration concerning the calculation of trajectories in 2D [2] followed by a second collaboration on 3-Dimensional path planning and with the possibility of dynamic replanning [3]. In addition, other research topics resulted in several sustained doctoral theses, joint publications, patents, demonstrators, etc. The resultant collaboration work is done with the relaxation of the nonholonomic constraint [4]. However, the controllability question arises concerning the realization of trajectories by a helicopter autopilot.

The present paper focuses on the design of an innovative solution to generate dynamically constrained flight plans with continuous and achievable trajectories and terrain obstacle avoidance with the novelty of time data, the FMS 4D. We present here, a work on the trajectory generation and merging for a given set of configurations. The term *configuration* applied to a mobile robot, is the position of all its points in a given frame and is expressed as a vector of positions and orientations. The objective is to connect the generated waypoints with a feasible trajectory: a 3D trajectory, that transfers smoothly from one configuration to another with respect to the dynamics of our helicopter and with time data giving a fourth dimension to our system. To do so, we have to define the best way for a helicopter, to reach a destination configuration from a start configuration considering multiple constraints and conditions, mainly the nonholonomic one. The path planner generates collision free paths as a set of waypoints, linked by straight lines and then controllability question appears: how can we take in account the controllability of free collision path generated by a path planner [4], and ensure smooth and continuous trajectories for a nonholonomic system as a helicopter? In the present work, we answer this question.

The paper is organized as follows: the first section, introduces the problem. The second one, describes related works. Then, the third section details principles of the 4-Dimensional (4D) augmented flight management system. A new methodology of trajectory generation into inclined planes is outlined in the fourth section. The fifth section is about a simulation study to test trajectories controllability by a helicopter autopilot. Our conclusions are drawn in the final section.

2 Related Works

In this section, we introduce first the FMS, giving a definition and mentioning its optimizations in recent years, then we highlight limitations of previous studies. In a second subsection, we address the problem of continuous curvature and smooth trajectories in the literature. Major trajectories criteria are explained in the final subsection, to ensure the generation of safe paths.

2.1 Flight Management Systems (FMS)

Since Honeywell starts to develop FMSs [5] in 1978, there has been a rapid rise in the use of FMSs for airlines, as every major aircraft manufacturer decide to include it into cockpits. The main characteristics of FMSs are to provide flight planning and navigation capabilities. Moreover, it allows path guidance [6], enhanced situational awareness, weather and traffic alerts, and flight performance information with the objective of reducing pilot and flight crew workload during flight. A challenging area in the field of FMSs is to enhance this old type of avionics to improve its accuracy [7]. In the last Global Air Navigation Capacity and Efficiency Plan published in 2013, the International Civil Aviation Organization (ICAO) has identified efficient flight path planning and execution [8] as a key performance improvement area.

One of the main issues in FMSs, to the best of our knowledge, is the lack of precision in trajectory realization during flight [9]; a discrepancy between generated path and the executed one. Much work on the optimization of FMSs has been carried out to give time consideration into flight management [10], and introducing the concept of 4D trajectories [11]. Yet, there are still some critical issues like the fallibility of the trajectories. In addition, most of FMSs researches are designed for fixed-wing aircraft [12]. Very little is known about the problem of flight management for rotorcrafts [13, 14]. In this last case, problems are often considered in two dimensions (2D) which is not adapted to our study. This is why, the aim of this work is to enable precise and controllable trajectories for helicopters in three dimensions, adding time data as the fourth dimension increasing our FMS capabilities. In order to propose this augmented 4D-FMS, precise smooth and continuous trajectories are mandatory.

2.2 Smooth Trajectory Generation

In the literature, the notion of feasible and smooth trajectory is addressed through various approaches in the field of mobile robotics. The problem, addressed in this paper, is to turn a polygon line into a continuous and smooth curve that could be then handed to the control system of a helicopter.

Traditional approach as "straight line – circle" methods based on the Dubins Car Model [15] are not considered here, to avoid curvature discontinuities and roll angle disparities. A solution to this continuous curvature trajectory problem is suggested [16], with paths composed of straight lines and clothoid arcs as junctions. The disadvantage is no closed-forms expressions for the curve coordinates. Meanwhile, Nelson [17], introduces the concept of polar polynomials, with closed-form expressions matching imposed boundaries on curvature and derivative of the curvature. Both approaches are interesting because polynomials are introduced in the field of continuous path planning and demonstrate their benefits in terms of computation time and accuracy in the positions.

More recent evidence [18] proposes a continuous trajectory for helicopter using a natural cubic spline modified algorithm, but it concerns only 2D situations. Considering helicopter autopilots, we identified the need to design efficient curves respecting multiple constraints, to handle combined turn and climb maneuver, which can be designed only in three dimensions. Even if our study doesn't address the design of control laws we are imposing the design of maneuverable trajectories that can be translated into control laws as simply and linearly as possible while respecting the behavior of the helicopter.

In sum, FMSs are well known and studied since the 1980's, however the problem of continuous-curvature trajectories is not well documented and especially regarding the specificities of rotorcrafts dynamics and maneuverability. The way the pilot (or autopilot) will handle the helicopter, following and applying necessary efforts to reproduce the flight trajectory prepared [19] is important to propose efficient motion planning through the 4D-FMS. A new alternative approach of 4D feasible smooth trajectories is illustrated in the following section. It is integrated into a modular FMS presented into the next section.

3   Resolution Approach

This section starts with the FMS 4D structure and decomposition into two separated modules responsible for path planning and motion planning. The path planner process is detailed in the following subsection, posing constraints and hypothesis of the problem. In the last subsection, an innovative motion planning solution is presented, in order to solve issues resulting from 3D path planner and to offer collision-free continuous-curvature trajectory generation.

3.1   Presentation of the 4D Flight Management System Concept

The 4D Flight Management System concept is a continuation of the research carried out within the LAMIH Informatics Department. It proposes to design and develop an on-board system that is in breach of existing technology, allowing an in-flight collision's risk assessment and proposing the best trajectory solution regarding mission objectives. The 4D-FMS illustrated in Fig. 1, is organized into two separated subsystems presented in the subsections below.

3.2   3-Dimensional Automatic Flight Planner

Compared to fixed-wing aircraft, the helicopter is more complex in design. It is a non-holonomic system with specific kinematic constraints that limit its direction motions. To streamline the problem, we first focus on a path planning procedure that generates a 3D route, considering terrain's obstacles, helicopters' fuel consumption, and weather constraints. A *route* is a series of waypoints, assumed to be joined by straight line segments [20]. The *waypoints* are the successive locations of the space that the helicopter has to follow during a mission, to avoid all kind of terrain obstacles or restricted areas. An automatic 3D path planner software [4] creates a flight plan in two steps:

Pre-Processing. 3D space modeling using irregular discretization (multi-Quadtree) during the static phase to prepare the ground for flight planning.

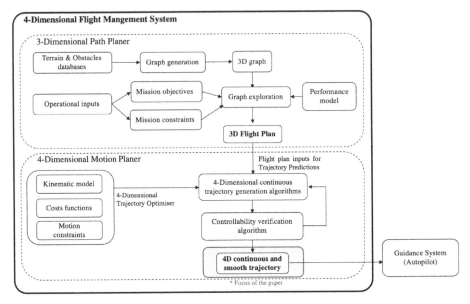

Fig. 1. 4-Dimensional Flight Management System structure

Routing. After preprocessing, the routing phase can be called static (mission preparation) or dynamic (re-planning) several times. The application of the routing algorithm on the navigation graph aims to calculate a path between two points of the 3D space while optimizing the distance. It generates the shortest path resulting into a set of straight segments, not considering dynamics of the vehicle, as illustrated in Fig. 2.

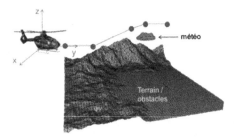

Fig. 2. 3D routing illustration with terrain obstacle avoidance, weather consideration and distance optimization.

3.3 4-Dimensional Motion Planner

The development of this feature aims to respond to the optimization problem posed by the output of the 3D flight planner, usually, resulting into a polygonal line made of waypoints. The Fig. 2 illustrates the concept of routes, with an example of 3D combination of straight lines generated by the path planner. Ideally, helicopter must follow this route to carry out its prepared mission in good conditions. However, the problem of discontinuity is dangerous, because the aircraft won't be able to follow paths as they are currently proposed in operational conditions. Trajectory generation is a necessary complement of path planning, to propose the best continuous-curvature and smooth feasible trajectories, respecting all kinematics limitations of the helicopter, ready to be controlled by the autopilot system. This is the purpose of the second subsystem illustrated in Fig. 1; It suggests a 4D trajectory under nonholonomic constraints and respecting the kinematic model of the helicopter. The 4D motion planner needs the route, i.e. waypoints details as inputs, to guarantee terrain and obstacle avoidance for trajectory generation. Then, a dedicated algorithm is coupled with an optimizer algorithm based on a greedy heuristic. All algorithms and functions used in this work are deterministic, which is mandatory for safety aspects [22].

We describe in the next subsection the algorithm used for trajectory generation with the innovative concept of 2D curves contained into inclined planes. It offers a 4D guidance possibility with time data consideration (time, speeds, accelerations, jerk, and curvature outputs) adding important information for mission preparation.

3.4 Trajectory Generation into Inclined Planes

Trajectory Design. In order to handle the motion planning aspect, we propose a pragmatic simplification of the optimal 3D path planning problem for aerial vehicles under constraints. We choose to focus on 2D feasible trajectories enclosed into planes of the space adapted to helicopters motion, because the classical three-dimensional mathematical curves do not always fit the performances of the aircraft [1], also they are more complicated for certification aspects and to be computed on Airbus Helicopters autopilots. Our trajectory generation algorithm, presented below, must connect successive configurations in a 3D space so that a nonholonomic mobile robot can follow the curves obtained while respecting the continuity of the curvature and a continuous jerk [21] to avoid all types of unwanted shocks.

Method Description. First, a performance model of the helicopter (H145) is designed to respect kinematics limits of the vehicle while generating appropriate trajectories. Then, we generate the trajectory by merging smooth curves enclosed in successive inclined planes. This is Algorithm 1 purpose, and then Algorithm 2 addresses the waypoints, generated by the path planner described previously, by group of successive three waypoints while considering the autopilot inputs constraints; By group of three points to be able to enclose the trajectory portion in a plane. The trajectory part, generated in two dimensions plane "Curve generation", is compatible with helicopter capabilities; It design an optimal turn in a plane as a parametric curve with a higher order (greater than or equal to 4) polynomial curvature connecting two configurations while respecting the "Kinodynamic Constraints". Then we merge smoothly these portions to create a flyable trajectory (as presented below in Algorithms 1 and 2). The approach offers a 4-dimensional solution to the control system with time consideration.

Kinodynamic Constraints. The method outlined in this study consists in the replacement of an input route composed of x waypoints with a global continuous-curvature trajectory constructed by merging different pieces. To guarantee the continuity of the curvature, each piece of trajectory must meet constraints on initial and final curvatures' value (equal to zero), constraints on initial and final curvatures' derivative (equal to zero) and constraints on maximum values of curvature and its derivative during the entire trajectory; theses maximum are extracted from the kinematic model and shouldn't be exceeded. These are adjustable parameters according to the type of mission. In addition, the generated trajectory must fit in the convex hull defined by the input waypoints. These constraints determine the order of the curvature polynomial.

Curve Generation. This procedure creates a smooth curve, so-called a *turn*, in a plane defined by three given waypoints (Wp_1, Wp_2, and Wp_3 for example). As shown in the "Step 1" of Fig. 3, The turn should put the vehicle on the direction that will lead him toward the last point Wp_3. The generated curve does not, necessary, ends at this last point, but to an intermediate one Wp_{f_1}: a way point that marks the end of the turn such that $\overrightarrow{Wp_{f_1}Wp_3}$ is parallel to $\overrightarrow{Wp_2Wp_3}$. This procedure returns the generated curve, starting from Wp_1 to Wp_{f_1}, and the coordinates of this new last waypoint. This procedure is built as follow: First we convert the three waypoints on two configurations in the given plane, the starting one with position at Wp_1 and direction $\overrightarrow{e_{x1}} = \overline{Wp_1Wp_2}$ and the ending configuration with position at Wp_3 and direction $\overrightarrow{e_{y1}} = \overline{Wp_2Wp_3}$, see "Step 1" in the Fig. 3. Then, in the plane P_1 defined by $(\overrightarrow{e_{x1}}, \overrightarrow{e_{y1}})$, a continuous parametric curve is generated by integrating a polynomial curvature function $K(s) = P_n(s)$ with P_n a n degree polynomial. The degree of this polynomial is related to the considered "Kinodynamic Constraints" as mentioned above; in the example of Fig. 3, $n = 4$. The obtained curve computes the fastest turn that leads the vehicle to the final direction and if, at the end of the turn the vehicle is not on the segment between Wp_2 and Wp_3, a translation is added to compute the intermediate waypoint Wp_{f_1}, see Algorithm 1. In the Fig. 3, at "Step1", we highlight the translation between the dashed curve and the full curve. This allowed getting a smooth curve that respects all the constraints and close enough to the waypoints. The purpose of this procedure is to make the curve smoother, and minimize deviation distance from initial waypoints given as inputs, guaranteeing a free-collision trajectory to the pilot and flight crews.

Trajectory Generation. The trajectory generation is based on the Algorithms 1 and 2. It handles the waypoints from the path planner, two by two successively, see Algorithm 2. At the first step as in Fig. 3, we handle the three first points to create the first piece of the trajectory. Then, the next pieces of trajectories are calculated in an iterative way as in the "Step 2" and "Step i" in the same figure. We use the procedure "Curve generation", with the first three waypoints, and with the new waypoint Wp_{f_i}, computed by this procedure, and the next two waypoints in the route, we call again the procedure "Curve generation" and so on until the last waypoint. This approach leads to a continuous-curvature path maximized in curvature, optimized in deviation distance from intermediate waypoints and also respecting vehicle kinematics.

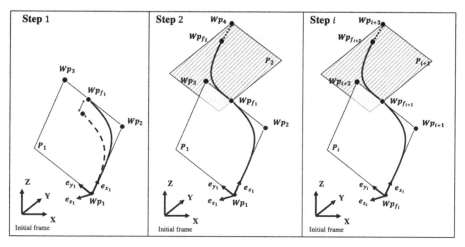

Fig. 3. Three-dimensional flight strategy using inclined planes of the space.

Algorithm 1. Continuous-Curvature Trajectory Generation

Function name: **GenerateTrajectory()**

Input: Coordinates of 3 successive waypoints, aircraft's speed, maximum curvature limit, maximum derivative of curvature limit.

Output: Coordinates of the generated trajectory, time, speeds, accelerations, deviation distance from the second waypoint.

1. Initialization of a local frame at the first waypoint Wp_1,
2. Calculation of the coordinates of second and third waypoints in the new local frame.
3. Generation of a parametric curve in the plane $(\overrightarrow{e_{x_1}} \ \overrightarrow{e_{y_1}})$ to connect the 2 space configurations.
4. Optimization of the deviation distance to the second waypoint Wp_2.
5. Conversion of the coordinates of the new trajectory generated from the local frame into the initial frame.
6. Calculation of the speeds and accelerations from the new continuous curvature trajectory contained into an inclined plane of the space.

Algorithm 2. Continuous-Curvature Trajectory Generation from a Route

Function name: **Route2Trajectory()**

Input: List of waypoints from a route generated by a path planner

Output: Coordinates of the generated global trajectory, time, velocities, accelerations, deviation distances.

1. Initialization of waypoint coordinates Wp_i (X_i, Y_i, Z_i).
2. **GenerateTrajectory()** function call with the first three waypoints (Wp_1, Wp_2, Wp_3) of the route as input, (see Fig.3 with the first step).
3. Save the new intermediate waypoint Wp_{f_1} of the first piece of trajectory.
4. Calculation of the rest of the global trajectory, result to an iterative structure that calculates each new piece of trajectory with the **GenerateTrajectory()** function and the coordinates of the last point of the previously generated curve as input, as well as the next two waypoints in the list Wp_{i+1}, and Wp_{i+2}.
5. Visualization of the final trajectory modeling the given input route.

Algorithm 1 computes, for a given sequence of three waypoints, the shortest smooth that links them in an inclined plane. First, it determines the local frame, translates the coordinates in this new frame, computes the turn in the local frame, using the "Curve Generation" procedure, optimizes the generated curve then putting back the coordinates in the global frame. Algorithm 2 uses Algorithm 1 to generate the trajectory pieces from each successive two waypoints and then merges them in a smooth trajectory. The quality of the merging, smooth connections, is allowed through, the intermediate waypoints introduced by the "Curve Generation" procedure.

At the end of Algorithm 2, speeds and accelerations from the new continuous curvature trajectory are given as outputs. This last part was designed in accordance with Airbus Helicopters Autopilot department, in order to give the right data for the generated trajectory to be controlled by one of our autopilots developed in the design office. The objective in the future works would be to integrate the guidance part in the whole 4D Flight Management System to develop an autonomous navigation and guidance system for Rotorcraft Unmanned Air Vehicle (RUAV).

4   Simulation Results

The last section of this paper presents simulation experiments to verify the efficiency of these trajectories controlled by a simulated helicopter autopilot. If the trajectories are well controllable without too large deviations, the 4D-FMS developed (Fig. 1) will be ready to be given as input to real autopilot for future research.

4.1   Simulation Description

In order to propose adapted trajectories as inputs for the autopilot, a study was con-ducted to determine the controllability envelope for a given type of helicopter and therefore for a given flight envelope with specific constraints. To achieve this study, several parameters were evaluated separately by successive variation and trend observations: angle of turn (from 0 to 90°), helicopter speed (from 20 to 140 knots), angle of the plan containing the trajectory (from 1,5° to 11°). We developed a simulated control system under Matlab Simulink environment with the assistance of the Airbus Helicopters Auto-pilot Depart-ment. Then, the motion planning algorithm was tested with different values of angle of turn, speed, and angle of inclined planes containing generated trajectories to observe impacts on the simulated control system.

The results revealed that the inclination angle of the plane containing a trajectory, does not affect the deviation introduced by the autopilot control (Fig. 4).

Table 1. Experimental Error Calculation.

Error of Control (%)	2.75
Av. Err of Control (m)	0.4286
Max Err of Control (m)	11.3055

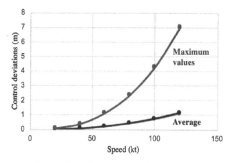

Fig. 4. Evolution of autopilot Control deviation for a 45° turn maneuver with multiples inclined planes.

4.2 Results Discussion

We note that all the results for different inclinations of the plane are mixed-up. The first curve represents the evolution of the average of control deviations and the second represents maximum values of control deviation, with different speeds. With all simulated experiments performed, our results show a deviation increase from 1 to 11.31 m (Table 1) and an average at 0.43 m.

As the deviation error caused by the autopilot system is less than 3%, it demonstrates the efficiency of these new trajectories into inclined planes of the space. At the end, our purpose is to provide the correct input data for a specific helicopter autopilot as the form of optimal accelerations design to be well controlled, and respecting the pilot comfort. The major result of our experimentations was to prove the controllability of trajectories generated into inclined planes. Thanks to these experiments, we identified limitations for the three parameters studied: turn angle, speed, and helicopter inclination. It is a true advance in the field of mission preparation that will allow even more precision and anticipation for the extended navigation problem.

5 Conclusion

The purpose of our study is to propose controllable smooth trajectories for helicopter autopilots through precise flight plan. To do this, first, the 3D path planer generates a sequence of waypoints with terrain obstacle avoidance consideration. From this input, we develop realistic smooth trajectories feasible considering the helicopter kinematic. In this way, we evidenced a new approach of trajectory generation into inclined planes in 4D because current systems use discontinuous-curvature models, resulting into non-feasible trajectories or disparities in the guidance process which is dangerous for mission preparation and flight management. Here we used 2D parametric curves contained into inclined planes to offer a 4D precision, i.e. positions of the helicopter and time data evolution.

Thanks to the simulations realized, we observed that the control deviation achieved by the autopilot is less than 3%, which is satisfying given the experimental conditions. In the future work, we will continue tests and simulations to develop a 4-dimensional flight management system for helicopter including path planning and motion planning to improve mission preparation. This means different prospects as to complexify the approach with 3D motion primitives, to upgrade the simulated autopilot to enhance its precision of control and make the system closer from reality, then, others test of the motion planning algorithm with an official Airbus Helicopters real-time simulator.

References

1. Nikolajevic, K.: Dynamic autonomous decision-support function for piloting a helicopter in emergency situations. Modeling and Simulation. Ph.D. thesis. University of Valenciennes and Hainaut-Cambresis (2016)
2. Souissi, O.: Path planning on a high-performance heterogeneous CPU/FPGA architecture, Ph.D. thesis. University of Valenciennes and Hainaut-Cambresis (2015)
3. Baklouti, Z.: System for 3D flight planning, mission preparation and emergency replanning. Ph.D. thesis. Polytechnical University of Hauts-de-France (2018)
4. Feyzeau P., Baklouti Z., Duvivier D., Benatitallah R.: Aircraft route planning process, associated planning system and aircraft equipped with such system (2019). https://bases-brevets.inpi.fr/fr/document/FR3080678.html
5. Avery, D.: The evolution of flight management systems. IEEE Softw. **28**, 11–13 (2011). https://doi.org/10.1109/MS.2011.17
6. Rathinam, S.R.: US7437225B1. Flight Management System, Rockwell Collins (2005)
7. Ramasamy, S., Sabatini, R., Gardi, A., Liu, Y.: Next generation flight management system for real-time trajectory based operations, Applied Mechanics and Materials, vol. 629. Trans Tech Publications (2014)
8. ICAO, Global Air Navigation Capacity and Efficiency Plan (2013). https://www.icao.int
9. Sirigu, G., Battipede, M., Gili, P., Cassaro, M.: FMS and AFCS interface for 4D trajectory operations. In: SAE Technical Paper, 2015-01-2458 (2015). https://doi.org/10.4271/2015-01-2458
10. Altava, R., Mere, J., Delahaye, D., Miquel, T.: Flight management system pathfinding algorithm for automatic vertical trajectory generation, pp. 1–9 (2018). https://doi.org/10.1109/dasc.2018.8569254
11. Ramasamy, S., Sabatini, R., Gardi, A., Liu, Y.: Novel flight management system for real-time 4-dimensional trajectory based operations. In: AIAA Guidance, Navigation, and Control (GNC) Conference (2013). https://doi.org/10.2514/6.2013-4763
12. Kobayashi, T.: Automatic Flight Management System for Helicopters. Fifteenth European Rotorcraft Forum, Amsterdam (1989)
13. Lüken, T., Groll, E., Antrack, F., Korn, B.: Helicopter IFR steep and curved approaches using SBAS guidance. In: Conference: 34th European Rotorcraft Forum (2008)
14. Cassaro, M., Sirigu, G., Battipede, M., Gili, P.: FMS and AFCS interface for 4D trajectory operations (2015). https://doi.org/10.4271/2015-01-2458
15. Dubins, L.E.: On Curves of minimal length with a constraint on average curvature, and with prescribed initial and terminal positions and tangents. Am. J. Math. **79** (1957). https://doi.org/10.2307/2372560
16. Kanayama, M.: Trajectory generation for mobile robots. In: Proceedings of 3rd International Symposium on Robotics Research. Faugem, O.D., Gualt, G., eds., pp. 333–340. Gouvieux, France (1985)
17. Nelson Winston: Continuous-Curvature Paths for Autonomous Vehicles (1989)
18. Petit, P., Wartmann, J., Fragnière, B., Greiser, S.: Waypoint based online trajectory generation and following control for the ACT/FHS (2019). https://doi.org/10.2514/6.2019-0918

19. Hess: Pilot-Centered Handling Qualities Assessment for Flight Control Design (2009). https://doi.org/10.2514/6.2009-6320
20. Bestaoui, Y.: Planning and Decision Making for Aerial Robots, pp. 20-25 (2014). https://doi.org/10.1007/978-3-319-03707-3
21. Piazzi, A., Visioli, A.: Global minimum-jerk trajectory planning of robot manipulators. IEEE Transactions on Industrial Electronics (2000)
22. EASA: Certification Memoranda: Software Aspects of Certification (2012). https://easa.europa.eu

Real World Bayesian Optimization Using Robots to Clean Liquid Spills

Isobel Voysey, Josie Hughes, Thomas George Thuruthel, Kieran Gilday, and Fumiya Iida[✉]

Bio-Inspired Robotics Laboratory, Department of Engineering,
The University of Cambridge, Cambridge, UK
{iv256,jaeh2,tg444,kg398,fi224}@cam.ac.uk

Abstract. Developing robots that can contribute to cleaning could have a significant impact on the lives of many. Cleaning wet liquid spills is a particularly challenging task for a robotic system, and has several high impact applications. This is a hard task to physically model due to the complex interactions between cleaning materials and the surface. As such, to the authors' knowledge there has been no prior work in this area. A new method for finding optimal control parameters for the cleaning of liquid spills is required by developing a robotic system which iteratively learns to clean through physical experimentation. The robot creates a liquid spill, cleans and assesses performance and uses Bayesian optimization to find the optimal control parameters for a given size of liquid spill. The automation process enabled the experiment to be repeated more than 400 times over 20 h to find the optimal wiping control parameters for many different conditions. We then show that these solutions can be extrapolated for different spill conditions. The optimized control parameters showed reliable and accurate performances, which in some cases, outperformed humans at the same task.

Keywords: Robotic cleaning · Control optimization · Service robotics

1 Introduction

In the coming years service robots are expected to have significant impacts on our daily lives [2]. The kitchen is one place where robotics has the potential to make a significant impact and to improve quality of life for many individuals [20]. One particular kitchen task which is widely disliked is cleaning, yet it is key for maintaining the cleanliness and food hygiene standards in a kitchen [4]. One of the most challenging cleaning tasks is cleaning wet surfaces. Such surfaces are also one of the most high risk zones of the kitchen with regards to the spread of unwanted disease [6]. Such robots could improve users quality of life and assist with enabling the elderly to live independently in their homes for longer [19]. In addition, the ability to clean liquid spills could enable robots to clear up hazardous liquid waste, assisting in tasks such as nuclear decommissioning or in high risk lab environments [17].

© Springer Nature Switzerland AG 2020
A. Mohammad et al. (Eds.): TAROS 2020, LNAI 12228, pp. 196–208, 2020.
https://doi.org/10.1007/978-3-030-63486-5_22

Fig. 1. Summary of the physical iterative experimentation approach to identify the optimal control parameters for cleaning a given volume of liquid.

Cleaning has been a long term goal for many research projects due to the challenge it poses for path planning, control strategies, manipulation, and sensing [8]. Autonomous cleaning robots have been fairly successful in structured environments when dealing with mess which can be modeled as solid particles [12]. In particular robot vacuum cleaners have been very successful and widely adopted [16]. However, many approaches are designed specifically for a single application like vacuuming or wiping, or for a specific cleaning tool [7]. Learning-based control strategies have been introduced as viable methods to solve the complexities involved with the problem of robotic cleaning by manipulation [10]. However, to make this a viable solution, the problem must be cleverly formulated to make the learning tractable, safe, and general purpose. Learning by imitation of humans has also been proposed for generating effective cleaning trajectories [9], but has limited generality. To move towards developing robots that can clean liquids,new approaches are required as the problem cannot be easily modeled. The liquid on a surface is complex and secondly the interaction between the liquid and the cleaning device (for example) a cleaning sponge is also very hard to model. Whilst there has been some examples of cleaning liquids, for example with window cleaning robots [11], there has been limited exploration of the optimal cleaning trajectories for liquids.

Thus, to develop cleaning algorithms and address this complex physical problem, we propose a new approach for developing control solutions for the cleaning of liquid spills. In this method, a robot has been developed which can physically iterate over the problem, and monitor its own success, allowing the system to learn and optimize the control parameters through physical experimentation of the cleaning progress. This approach is summarized in Fig. 1 showing that for a given volume of liquid the experimental process is fully automated. From this, we can extract and extrapolate rules for cleaning liquid spills of different sizes. This novel framework for developing the control approaches for cleaning liquid spills is fully automated allowing a single cleaning experiment to be performed in around 3 min. The learning and optimization process is shown to achieve control solutions which achieve performance that matches or exceeds human performance. In particular, in this paper we make the following contributions:

- A base algorithm for liquid cleaning, with adjustable parameters
- An autonomous experimental framework for continuous exploration and optimization of liquid cleaning trajectory
- Experimental evidence demonstrating the validity of the system, and showing the ability to find controllers for different hardware solutions through iterative physical experimentation

This work presents an original framework for robotic liquid cleaning, with the methods given in Sect. 2. Following this, details of the experimental setup are given. The experimental results are given in Sect. 4, followed by a discussion and conclusion on the wider role of this approach for the development of control strategies for physical tasks which are hard to model.

2   Methods

As shown in Fig. 1, physical experimentation is used to obtain the relevant control parameters, an approach which has previously been applied to other control problems [3,14,15]. A base cleaning algorithm is optimized using feedback which is extracted automatically using computer vision. This section presents this iterative method.

2.1   Cleaning Algorithms

A template, parameterized cleaning path has been devised which is then optimized through the iterative process. This parameterized path has been developed from human intuition and experience of performing the cleaning action. Parameters have been chosen which are believed to have the biggest influence on cleaning behaviors. The path is parameterized by three key variables. Firstly the space step, d, the distance between points on the edge of the liquid spill, measured parallel to the major axis. Secondly, h, the height by which the sponge is compressed. The final parameter, v, is the velocity of movement along the path. The cleaning path is centered around the major axis of the spill which is identified for every liquid spill. The robot end-effector is kept parallel to the long axis of the liquid spill.

Figure 2 demonstrates these parameters with the range of values considered is given in Table 1. Thus, each cleaning attempt, c_i, can be described by the vector $[d, h, v]$. Human intuition is necessary to develop a base cleaning algorithm to make this a tractable problem. Although this does limit the search space, it still allows for a wide variety of different cleaning strategies to emerge. The control and parameters were chosen to be as generic as possible, however, there may need to be some adaptation for liquids with a significantly different viscosity or foaming properties.

Table 1. Parameters of the cleaning algorithm showing the minimum and maximum values and also the parameters chosen for the general wipe.

Property	Variable (%)	Min value	Max value	General wipe
Velocity (m/s)	v	0.05	0.5	0.3
Space step (cm)	d	1	10	5.5
Compression height (cm)	h	0	3	1.5

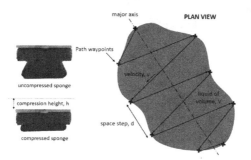

Fig. 2. Diagram of path planning and parameterization of the path. Inset showing how the compression height is defined.

2.2 Optimization

To identify the optimal cleaning parameters, c, for a given volume V of liquid spill an optimization algorithm must be used. This task requires the optimization of a complex dynamic system with environmental interactions which are challenging to models. Thus, an optimization algorithm that does not rely on an accurate physical model is needed [18]. Bayesian optimization is such a method and can sample efficiently from black-box functions without requiring gradient information. It is a method employed to minimize the number of iterations required to find the maximum of an objective function $f(\theta)$, where θ is the parameter vector. Thus the cleaning parameters to be next tested, c_{n+1}, are determined by the objective function, in this case the liquid removal performance, P:

$$c_{n+1} = argmax_{c} P(c) \tag{1}$$

We employ a typical Matern kernel (with smoothness parameter $\varsigma = 2.5$) as defined in [13]. The exploration parameter (κ) of the acquisition function has been tuned based on the Gaussian process Upper Confidence Bound with a value of $\kappa = 80$ used to favor exploration. The optimization was implemented using the *BayesianOptimization* library for Python[1]. To ensure the optimization process explored the full area, the optimization was initialized by testing points where two parameters were held at the mid range and the other was at 25% or 75%

---

[1] https://github.com/fmfn/BayesianOptimization.

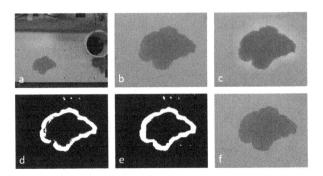

Fig. 3. Vision pipeline. (a) Original image, (b) cropped image, (c) enhancing contrast, (d) thresholding, (e) closing mask, (f) external contours selection.

of the range. Performance was evaluated by comparing the initial area of liquid on the surface to the area remaining after cleaning and taking the percentage reduction in area.

2.3   Visual Identification of Liquids

This approach relies on the ability to correctly identify the location and area of the liquid spill, but visually identifying liquids is a challenging problem due to the reflection, refraction, and variability in presentation [5]. It is important that the area is estimated accurately as the area evaluation is used to form the acquisition function of the optimization process.

Figure 3 shows the vision pipeline which has been developed to accurately identify the area and location; it has the following stages:

- *Cropping*: The image is cropped to a predetermined region of the surface.
- *Contrast enhancement*: Contrast-limited adaptive histogram equalization is applied to enhance the definition of the edge of the liquid.
- *Thresholding*: Adaptive mean thresholding with an inverted output is applied to account for varying lighting conditions.
- *Mask closing*: Erosion followed by dilation is applied to close the mask. This ensures a continuous contour running around the edge of the liquid.
- *Contour selection*: Only external contours are selected to account for the hollow nature of the mask and are converted to area. Contours smaller than 40 square pixels ($1.3\,\mathrm{cm}^2$) are discarded as noise.

Weak coffee is used in the experiments as the base liquid. Using this pipeline it is possible to identify the area of liquid before cleaning, a_0, and the area after removal, a_r. Thus the performance for each cleaning process can be determined:

$$p_i = \left(1 - \frac{a_{ri}}{a_{0i}}\right).100\% \tag{2}$$

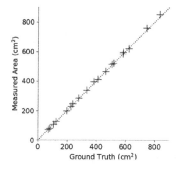

Fig. 4. Accuracy of the vision system, showing the estimated accuracy against a ground truth for a range of areas of liquid.

The accuracy of the vision system has been tested for 20 liquid spills by comparing that found with the pipeline to the ground truth, which was found using manual thresholding with the software ImageJ and a 30-cm ruler as a reference object [1]. The results (Fig. 4) show a high accuracy with approximately less than 1% error.

3   Experimental Setup

An experimental setup has been developed to automate the physical tests. This allows for many experiments to be carried out and for conditions to be kept constant, so successive experiments can be compared. The experimental setup is shown in Fig. 5, with the experimental process detailed in Fig. 5. Mounted on the end-effector of a UR5 arm is a tube connected to a custom designed syringe pump, which has limit switches which determine the volume of liquid that will be dispensed. The pump is connected to a large liquid reservoir. After dispensing a given volume of liquid, the overhead camera is used to identify the area of liquid present on the kitchen work surface, a_{0i}. Using the parameters chosen by the optimizer, the robot carries out the cleaning process using the sponge mounted on the end-effector.

After cleaning, the camera is used again to detect the amount of liquid remaining, a_{ri}, and hence evaluate the success of the cleaning process. To allow the experiment to be repeated, the setup must then be returned to the original state. To empty the sponge, a liquid removal system has been developed. The cleaning device (in this case a sponge) is pressed onto the central disc of the liquid removal setup, with the compression forcing liquid out of the material. The robot end-effector tilts forwards and backwards to remove more liquid. When liquid flows out of the material it drains through the mesh into the container beneath. The dry sponge is then used to perform a full grid-wise sweep of the surface to remove any liquid that may remain. The parameters were chosen manually for this general wipe process based on trial and error (see Table 1 for

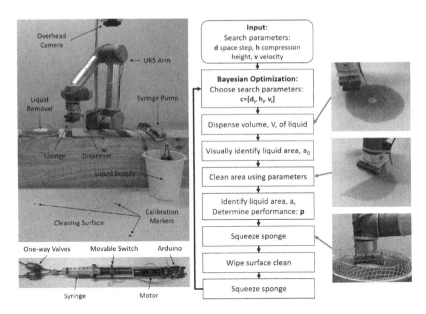

Fig. 5. Left) The experimental setup in a kitchen setup, showing the key parts: the syringe pump for dispensing liquid, the liquid removal system, sponge and liquid dispenser. Right) Flowchart of the full experimental procedure for obtaining optimal control parameters.

values). To ensure the surface was fully clean, this process was repeated twice. After wiping, the sponge is emptied and the next experiment could begin.

This setup has been shown to be highly reliable at delivering a liquid spill of a given volume and providing high reproducibility across tests. For a sequence of tests (n = 12) where 28 ml was deposited on the surface, the shape was consistently circular and the area of the liquid patch averaged 496.4 cm^2 (s = 12.9 cm^2). On average, it takes around 3 min for each experiment to be undertaken, allowing the system to rapidly test and iterate.

4   Results

4.1   Optimization for a Fixed Volume of Liquid

The results of the automated optimization of cleaning parameters for a fixed volume, in this case, 28 ml, are shown in Fig. 6. To contextualize the performance of the system, the effectiveness of human cleaning and a naive algorithm was measured and have been added for comparison. The human was subject to only two constraints on cleaning: a maximum of 15 s to clean (the average time of the robot movement) and that they could not remove liquid from the sponge during cleaning. The naive baseline used a side to side wiping pattern with non-optimized parameters using the general clean parameters specified in Table 1, thus providing a non-optimized robot clean for comparison.

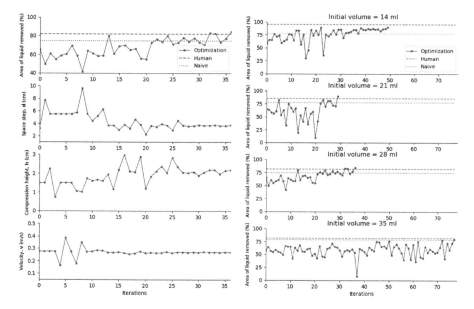

Fig. 6. Left) Bayesian optimization of the cleaning process for a liquid spill with a volume of 28 ml. Showing the removal success and the exploration of the parameters. Right) The performance of the optimization process for different volumes of liquid throughout the optimization process.

The results show that after 35 iterations (approximately 2 h of experiments) the optimal parameters are found. The velocity settles the quickest, and thus successful cleaning at this volume is least sensitive to the velocity of the path. The compression height, h, is the last variable to be optimized, to a height of around 2 cm. The spacing of the path optimizes at a similar speed to compression height with an optimal value of around 4 cm. The performance appears to be sensitive to small changes in control parameter.

The optimal performance that is found shows the potential to exceed that of human performance. When cleaning, the human approaches this as an open loop process and could return to unsuccessfully cleaned patches whereas the robot is closed loop. To approach, and indeed exceed human performance shows the effectiveness of this approach. It shows that the optimization process finds specific control parameters with a degree of accuracy and precision in execution which a human would struggle to identify and perform.

4.2 Optimal Control Parameters for Varying Volume Spills

The automated optimization process has been run on three additional volumes of liquid to understand how the optimum control parameter varies for different volumes of liquid. Figure 6 shows the performance throughout the optimization process for the four different volumes of liquid explored. Again, for each volume of

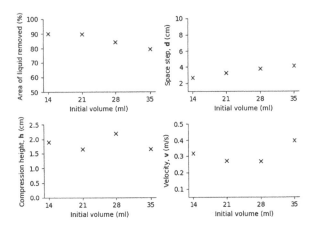

Fig. 7. The optimal parameters that were found for different volumes of liquid spill, and the overall performance that was achieved.

liquid tested, the human success rate and that of a naive algorithm are presented for comparison. In general, the optimization process takes longer for the larger volumes of liquid. For the largest spill it took over 70 experiments, which equates to nearly 4 h of experiments. In all cases the optimized performance exceeds or shows near to human-level performance. However, the robot system output performs humans better for larger volumes of liquid.

Figure 7 compares the optimal control parameters for different size of liquid spills. For larger spills, a larger space step provides better performance with an approximately linear relationship between liquid spill volume and space step. The effect of velocity is more complex; for larger spills a higher velocity is found to be optimal, but prior to this, decreasing velocity is found to improve performance. The optimal compression height is found to be similar across all volumes of liquid. In summary, these results show the complexity of the cleaning problem.

To test the sensitivity of the performance on the cleaning parameters on different volumes, the optimal parameters for a given volume, $c_{v,opt}$, were tested on a range of other volumes of liquid spill. Figure 8 shows the results; it can be observed that there is a significant decrease in performance when the optimal parameters are not used. Thus, using the optimal parameters for a given volume of liquid is necessary to achieve optimal performance. This validates the necessity of this process, and that the optimal parameters found for the different volumes provide the best performance despite the lack of obvious trends in the selection of the control parameters with respect to the volume of liquid.

4.3   Parameter Generalization

Using the optimal control parameters for different volumes of liquid, parameters can be predicted for other volumes using regression. Linear regression was used for the spacing size of the path, compression height is assumed to be a constant,

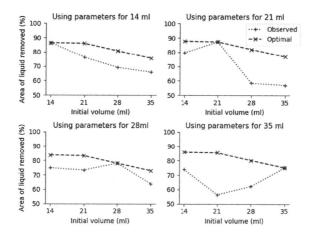

Fig. 8. The optimal parameters for a given volume of liquid and applied to other volumes of liquid to test the sensitivity.

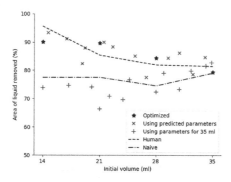

Fig. 9. Performance of the parameters predicted by regression for previously untested volumes in comparison to the 35 ml parameters.

and cubic regression is used for the velocity of the sponge. Figure 9 shows the cleaning performance when parameters are chosen using regression in comparison to those chosen through the optimization process. These are also compared to cleaning using the parameters found for 35 ml.

Using this regression based approach to predict the optimal in most case, exceeds human performance. The predicted parameters consistently out perform the naive algorithm and that using the 35 ml parameters. In many cases, in particular around the middle of the range of volumes tested, the performance exceeded the human baseline considerably.

4.4   Comparison of Different Cleaning Methods

This approach can be shown to generalize to other cleaning approaches. The cleaning process was also optimized for a J-cloth. Figure 10 shows a comparison

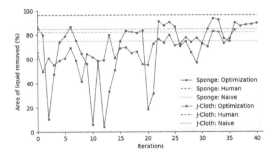

Fig. 10. Optimization of two different cleaning materials (sponge and J-cloth) for a liquid spill with a volume of 28 ml.

of the optimization for a J-cloth and the sponge for a 28 ml liquid spill. The J-cloth performance was found to be more sensitive to the input parameters, especially the compression height (Fig. 10). However, the optimal performance is higher than that of the sponge. This experiment demonstrates how this setup could be used to allow comparison between different cleaning techniques, and to enable the optimal technique to be found for a given volume of liquid.

5   Conclusions

This approach of iterative finding the optimal control parameters for the complex physical process of cleaning liquids has been shown to find parameters which can in some cases outperform humans. By automating the process it has been possible to carry out over 400 experiments to allow the optimal parameters to be found for given volumes of liquid. The use of regression to generalize the results found for a wider range of volumes was shown to work well, and enable this approach to be practically useful on variety of different sized liquid spills. This work focused on cleaning water-based liquid spills as it is both a widely occurring liquid spill type and challenging cleaning tasks due to the low viscosity of water. In future work, other liquids with varying properties should be investigated, alongside different cleaning materials.

This approach of using robotics to automate the finding of optimal control parameters has been shown to effective. Within the cleaning domain this could be expanded to optimizing for different cleaning devices or for more complex cleaning scenarios. It is also more widely applicable in scenarios which are challenging to model by developing continuous robotic exploration approaches.

Acknowledgment. This work was supported by BEKO PLC and Symphony Kitchens. We are especially thankful for the valuable inputs from Dr Graham Anderson and Dr Natasha Conway.

References

1. Abràmoff, M.D., Magalhães, P.J., Ram, S.J.: Image processing with imageJ. Biophotonics Int. **11**(7), 36–42 (2004)
2. Alonso, I.G., Fernández, M., Maestre, J.M., del Pilar, M., Fuente, A.G.: Service Robotics within the Digital Home: Applications and Future Prospects, vol. 53. Springer Science & Business Media, Dordrecht (2011). https://doi.org/10.1007/978-94-007-1491-5
3. Brodbeck, L., Hauser, S., Iida, F.: Morphological evolution of physical robots through model-free phenotype development. PloS One **10**(6), e0128444 (2015)
4. Bugmann, G., Copleston, S.N.: What can a personal robot do for you? In: Groß, R., Alboul, L., Melhuish, C., Witkowski, M., Prescott, T.J., Penders, J. (eds.) TAROS 2011. LNCS (LNAI), vol. 6856, pp. 360–371. Springer, Heidelberg (2011). https://doi.org/10.1007/978-3-642-23232-9_32
5. Eppel, S., Kachman, T.: Computer vision-based recognition of liquid surfaces and phase boundaries in transparent vessels, with emphasis on chemistry applications. arXiv preprint arXiv:1404.7174 (2014)
6. Flores, G.E., et al.: Diversity, distribution and sources of bacteria in residential kitchens. Environ. Microbiol. **15**(2), 588–596 (2013)
7. Kabir, A.M., et al.: Planning algorithms for multi-setup multi-pass robotic cleaning with oscillatory moving tools. In: 2016 IEEE International Conference on Automation Science and Engineering (CASE), pp. 751–757. IEEE (2016)
8. Kemp, C.C., Edsinger, A., Torres-Jara, E.: Challenges for robot manipulation in human environments [grand challenges of robotics]. IEEE Robot. Autom. Mag. **14**(1), 20–29 (2007)
9. Kim, H., Lee, H., Chung, S., Kim, C.: User-centered approach to path planning of cleaning robots: analyzing user's cleaning behavior. In: Proceedings of the ACM/IEEE International Conference on Human-Robot Interaction, pp. 373–380 (2007)
10. Kim, J., et al.: Control strategies for cleaning robots in domestic applications: a comprehensive review. Int. J. Adv. Robot. Syst. **16**(4), 1729881419857432 (2019)
11. Miyake, T., Ishihara, H.: Mechanisms and basic properties of window cleaning robot. In: Proceedings 2003 IEEE/ASME International Conference on Advanced Intelligent Mechatronics (AIM 2003), vol. 2, pp. 1372–1377. IEEE (2003)
12. Prassler, E., Ritter, A., Schaeffer, C., Fiorini, P.: A short history of cleaning robots. Auton. Robots **9**(3), 211–226 (2000)
13. Rasmussen, C.E.: Gaussian processes in machine learning. In: Bousquet, O., von Luxburg, U., Rätsch, G. (eds.) ML -2003. LNCS (LNAI), vol. 3176, pp. 63–71. Springer, Heidelberg (2004). https://doi.org/10.1007/978-3-540-28650-9_4
14. Rosendo, A., von Atzigen, M., Iida, F.: The trade-off between morphology and control in the co-optimized design of robots. PloS One **12**(10), e0186107 (2017)
15. Saar, K.A., Giardina, F., Iida, F.: Model-free design optimization of a hopping robot and its comparison with a human designer. IEEE Robot. Autom. Lett. **3**(2), 1245–1251 (2018)
16. Sahin, H., Guvenc, L.: Household robotics: autonomous devices for vacuuming and lawn mowing [applications of control]. IEEE Control Syst. Mag. **27**(2), 20–96 (2007)
17. Samseth, J., et al.: Closing and decommissioning nuclear power reactors. UNEP Year book, pp. 35–49 (2012)

18. Snoek, J., Larochelle, H., Adams, R.P.: Practical Bayesian optimization of machine learning algorithms. In: Advances in Neural Information Processing Systems, pp. 2951–2959 (2012)
19. Van Rensbergen, G., Pacolet, J.: Instrumental activities of daily living (i-adl) trigger an urgent request for nursing home admission. Archives of Public Health = Archives Belges de Sante Publique **70**(1), 2 (2012)
20. Zachiotis, G.A., Andrikopoulos, G., Gornez, R., Nakamura, K., Nikolakopoulos, G.: A survey on the application trends of home service robotics. In: 2018 IEEE International Conference on Robotics and Biomimetics (ROBIO), pp. 1999–2006. IEEE (2018)

LocalSPED: A Classification Pipeline that Can Learn Local Features for Place Recognition Using a Small Training Set

Fangming Yuan$^{(\boxtimes)}$ ⓘ, Peer Neubert ⓘ, and Peter Protzel ⓘ

Chemnitz University of Technology, Chemnitz, Germany
`fangming.yuan@etit.tu-chemnitz.de`

Abstract. Visual place recognition is a key component for visual-SLAM. The current state-of-art methods use CNNs (Convolutional Neural Networks) to extract either a holistic descriptor or local features from the images. In recent work, a holistic descriptor method with the name SPED was proposed. In this paper, SPED is extended to a local feature configuration called LocalSPED by applying several modifications and by introducing a novel feature pooling method. Several variations of SPED and LocalSPED are trained on a smaller dataset and their performances are evaluated on several benchmark datasets. In the experiments, Local-SPED handles the decreased training set size significantly better than the original SPED approach and provides better place recognition results.

Keywords: Place recognition · Local features · Robotics

1 Introduction

Visual place recognition [2] is a key component of mobile robotics. The accuracy of localization and loop-closure detection of SLAM strongly depend on it. The difficulties for visual place recognition are the appearance differences caused by lighting conditions, weather conditions, or seasonal changes, as well as the partial occlusion and shape deformation caused by viewpoint changes and dynamic objects. To overcome the appearance change, CNNs have been used to extract appearance invariant representation of the scene image. For example, in [1], the authors propose a visual place recognition pipeline (here the term pipeline refers to a specific algorithm or method), which is based on CNN's pooled holistic features. The pipeline is based on the standard image classification network that classifies images of the same place at different appearances into the same class. The network is trained using cross-entropy loss and the holistic feature vector is pooled from the intermediate feature map during inference. The authors of [1] use a very large scale webcam dataset, the Specific PlacEs Dataset, thus we refer to their method as SPED. Although SPED provides a holistic image

This work is funded by the German Federal Ministry for Economic Affairs and Energy (Bundesministerium für Wirtschaft und Energie) in the project ViPRICE.

© Springer Nature Switzerland AG 2020
A. Mohammad et al. (Eds.): TAROS 2020, LNAI 12228, pp. 209–213, 2020.
https://doi.org/10.1007/978-3-030-63486-5_23

descriptor, the authors of [1] already speculated that it might be extended for extraction of local features (e.g., similar to SIFT keypoints), but did not indicate how this could be done. In this work, we mainly address two questions: (1) Can we modify SPED to create local features? (2) Can we train both methods on a smaller dataset? To address the first question, we extended SPED to a local feature pipeline called LocalSPED. In LocalSPED, as shown in Fig. 1, we keep the classification configuration for the training but with some modifications described in Sect. 2. The local feature locations are obtained by applying non-maximum suppression to find all the local extrema on the indication map, which is calculated by the intermediate feature map. Since the training dataset used by SPED is large and currently not publicly available, we decided to collect our own smaller dataset. We re-implemented SPED and trained both SPED and Local-SPED on our smaller dataset. The performance of both pipelines is evaluated on several benchmark datasets in Sect. 3. Our experiments indicate that SPED has overfitted on the smaller dataset, while LocalSPED did not. Our approach is similar to the classification based local feature approach DELF [3]. However, different from our approach, for the training, DELF uses weighted global sum pooling [3] to pool intermediate feature maps to form the fully connected layer input activations and learns a sub-network implicitly to generate a feature map mask to highlight local feature locations. This paper is work in progress, a more detailed comparison to other local features approaches is part of ongoing and future work. The following sections will give details on our approach and address the differences between LocalSPED and SPED. The preliminary experimental results follow in Sect. 3.

2   Algorithmic Approach

The SPED pipeline (Fig. 1, *top*) uses AlexNet as a backbone and adds one extra convolutional layer; it is trained by the cross-entropy loss in the classification configuration. All images that show the same place (but potentially with different appearances) are regarded as the same class. After the training, SPED applies multi-scale pooling [1] on the conv6 output to extract a holistic descriptor. In order to extend the local feature capability of SPED, we propose LocalSPED, illustrated in Fig. 1, *bottom*. We substitute AlexNet with the first 4 conv-blocks of VGG16 [4], which provides more robust features than AlexNet. We fix the weights of VGG16 during the training. To convert the VGG16 features to a highly representative version that can distinguish different scenes and to enable these features to be proposed in the inference phase by identifying activation extrema, we add four extra convolutional layers after the VGG16 block, this is called ProposalNet. The ProposalNet is composed of 4 conv-layers and two batch normalization layers. For training, we use a max-pooling layer with 9 by 9 window size and stride 8 in the ProposalNet output. We will point out the benefits of this large max-pooling parameter in Sect. 4. A comparison of the output ProposalNet feature map with the VGG16 output shows that the former output activations are locally accumulated. Thus, we employ non-maximal suppression to localize the feature point positions. We first sum the feature map along the *depth* axis to generate a 2-D indication map, followed by non-maximum suppression to localize feature points locations. The descriptor of each feature point is pooled from the corresponding patches in the feature map.

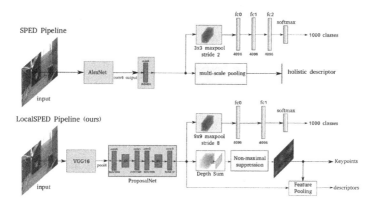

Fig. 1. Pipeline block diagram. (*top*) : SPED pipeline with AlexNet as backbone followed by one extra layer. It is trained by classification loss. The holistic descriptor is pooled by multi-scale pooling on conv6 output. (*bottom*) : LocalSPED using VGG16 as backbone followed by ProposalNet to generate local features. The key-point is located by applying non-maximal-suppression on the indication map.

3   Preliminary Experiments

We constructed a small training dataset by collecting online open-access webcamera images. We collected more than 2000 camera URLs and captured images from June to October, one day every two weeks, to sample slow seasonal changes, with each shot 3 h apart. We then filtered out 1000 cameras, which have valid images and without large camera rotation. Our dataset contains a total of 24,000 images, which is roughly 1% in the size of the dataset been used in SPED. For the LocalSPED training, we resize the images to 640 by 480 and randomly clip the images to 400 by 400, while for SPED, we resize and random clip the image to the same size as described in the SPED paper. We have trained the SPED pipeline with our small dataset in two different ways: (1) AlexNet is initialized with the ImageNet dataset pre-trained weights, and further finetuned on our dataset. (2) We trained the entire SPED from scratch (both AlexNet and extra convlayer). We have tested the two SPED variations, the pre-trained AlexNet SPED version, and LocalSPED on the datasets of Oxford, CMU, StLucia, three variations of GardenPointWalking and Nordland. For Oxford, CMU and StLucia, we sub-sampled these datasets to form a relatively small scale dataset. For Oxford, we use *2014-12-09* and *2014-12-16*. For CMU, we use *20110202* and *20110421* variations, and for StLucia, we use *100909-0854* and *100909-1000*. For the Nord-land dataset, we use winter and summer variations. To generate the similarity matrix, we use the cosine distance of holistic descriptor for the SPED variations, while for LocalSPED, for each feature point, we pool 7 by 7 patch regions as descriptors from the feature map and utilize the matching algorithm proposed by [5] to calculate the similarity between images. We present the precision-recall AUC (Area Under Curve) of the experiments in Table 1; LocalSPED shows best worst-case, average-case, and best-case performance. The finetuned AlexNet version overfits on the small training dataset, while the from-scratch version does not overfit but still performs not better.

Table 1. Precision-recall AUC values of different pipeline configuration under different dataset. MSP(multi-scale pooling), NMS(non-maximum suppression), GPW-dlnr (GardenPointWalking day-left vs night-right).

Dataset	SPED AlexNet scratch MSP	SPED AlexNet Pretrain MSP	SPED AlexNet Finetune MSP	SPED AlexNet scratch NMS	LocalSPED (ours) NMS
Oxford	0.20	0.19	0.01	0.07	0.49
CMU	0.11	0.16	0.03	0.15	0.45
StLucia	0.51	0.38	0.05	0.28	0.46
Nordland	0.04	0.04	0.02	0.15	0.44
GPW-drdl	0.37	0.45	0.09	0.41	0.84
GPW-dlnr	0.01	0.03	0.01	0.01	0.12
GPW-drnr	0.03	0.06	0.02	0.02	0.42

4   Discussion

The experiments indicate that our LocalSPED performs better than SPED when trained on a small scale dataset. We suspect the following reasons. First, the use of VGG16 enables the pipeline to inherit a robust feature representation. Second, the use of max-pooling with large window and large stride parameters significantly reduces the number of fully connected layer weights, which helps to reduce overfitting and makes possible that, during training, the augmented high-resolution images with large translational shift can be fed to the pipeline. Presumably, it increases not only the network prediction difficulty but also forces the network to learn more robust and distinctive representations. One drawback of our approach in comparison with the holistic pipeline is memory usage. In our experiments, we extract roughly 100 features per image, and each descriptor is represented by a 25,088-dimensional vector. The reduction of this large memory usage is part of our future work, as well as a deeper investigation of the contribution of the individual modifications to the overall improved performance.

References

1. Chen, Z., et al.: Deep learning features at scale for visual place recognition. In: Proceedings of International Conference on Robotics and Automation (2017)

2. Neubert, P.: Superpixels and their Application for Visual Place Recognition in Changing Environments. Ph.d. thesis, Chemnitz University of Technology (2015). http://nbn-resolving.de/urn:nbn:de:bsz:ch1-qucosa-190241
3. Noh, H., et al.: Large-scale image retrieval with attentive deep local features. In: Proceedings of International Conference on Computer Vision (2017). https://doi.org/10.1109/ICCV.2017.374
4. Simonyan, K., Zisserman, A.: Very deep convolutional networks for large-scale image recognition. In: Proceedings of International Conference on Learning Representations (2015)
5. Sünderhauf, N., et al.: Place recognition with convnet landmarks: viewpoint-robust, condition-robust, training-free. In: Proceedings of Robotics: Science and Systems (2015)

Towards Robust Mission Execution via Temporal and Contingent Planning

Yaniel Carreno$^{(\boxtimes)}$ [ID], Yvan Petillot [ID], and Ronald P. A. Petrick [ID]

Edinburgh Centre for Robotics, Heriot-Watt University, Edinburgh, UK
{y.carreno,y.r.petillot,r.petrick}@hw.ac.uk

Abstract. In this work, we present a general approach to task planning based on the combination of temporal planning, contingent planning and run-time sensing. The strategy provides a solution for generating plans that can adapt during mission execution by reasoning about the data acquired by the sensory system. The approach detects actions that can change the initial plan and evaluates possible outcomes. We demonstrate the effectiveness of our approach on two different experiments in a maritime environment where the robots have to inspect the state of a valve and execute actions based on the online sensor information.

Keywords: Multi-robot systems · High-level task planning · Contingent planning · Temporal planning · Marine robotics

1 Introduction and Motivation

In recent years, marine robotics has experienced an exponential demand for more complex systems which support the robust execution of tasks in dynamic environments. Automated planning is capable of generating such missions without the need for human intervention, while managing robot resources at levels that support long-term deployments. The implementation of planning strategies for real-world solutions usually requires a detailed description of the domain of operation, often supported by temporal notions to improve the quality of the generated plans [2]. Several planning solutions for robotic applications [2,3] are based on deterministic planning models, where operators have fully predictable outcomes and completely known initial states. However, the applicability of such models is limited in cases where some aspects of the domain are incomplete or unknown, and the planner must consider a set of possible values for certain state features (e.g., valve_state could be on or off). *Contingent planning* [6–8] copes with these types of situations by constructing a plan divided in a set of conditional sub-plans (branches) for the different contingencies that could arise. However, few contingent planners consider temporal constraints [5] which restricts their use for implementing coordinated multi-robot missions.

The authors would like to acknowledge the support of the EPSRC ORCA Hub (EP/R026173/1, 2017–2021, http://orcahub.org/) and consortium partners.

© Springer Nature Switzerland AG 2020
A. Mohammad et al. (Eds.): TAROS 2020, LNAI 12228, pp. 214–217, 2020.
https://doi.org/10.1007/978-3-030-63486-5_24

Fig. 1. Execution of multi-robot inspection tasks in real-world (left) and simulated (right) environments.

In this work, we present a strategy that combines the advantages of temporal planning and contingent planning to improve the generation of complex missions in the underwater domain. We use a construction-based approach, based on ideas from previous work (e.g., [8]), to add contingent plan branches to a generated temporal plan. Here, we use the OPTIC temporal planner [1] as a benchmark solver which is combined with a new Contingency Analyser algorithm and online sensing to produce more complex plan generation and execution. As an application of this solution, we consider a maritime scenario where an Autonomous Underwater Vehicle (AUV) must complete multiple inspection tasks, and an Autonomous Surface Vehicle (ASV) is used to support the AUV refuelling process. Figure 1 shows a real and simulated scenario for the inspection of underwater structures. The full description of the mission scenario is presented in [2].

2   Building Temporal Contingent Plans

We propose a framework that enables temporal planners to generate multi-robot plans with contingent branches. A new *Contingency Analyser* method interacts with the OPTIC solver to reason about the incomplete knowledge and perceptual information available during the planning process and plan execution. Figure 2 (left) shows the system architecture which contains two main modules. The *Planning Framework* acquires information from the world and the robots to define the domain and problem instance using the standard Planning Domain Definition Language (PDDL). This module is built on the ROSPlan architecture [3]. OPTIC generates a solvable plan by considering a set of possible initial states defined in the problem file, representing the incomplete or unknown information in the environment. The *Contingency Framework* evaluates whether a plan solution contains actions that require contingent plans. If so, the Contingent Plan Generation module defines a set of new initial states and re-triggers OPTIC to obtain a new plan. This process is repeated until all the possible initial states are exhausted. The resulting plans are then merged in a single contingent plan solution which is processed by the Contingent Parsing Interface to be dispatched to the robots. During plan execution, the contingent branches are evaluated by the Sensing Interface which uses online sensory information provided to the robot

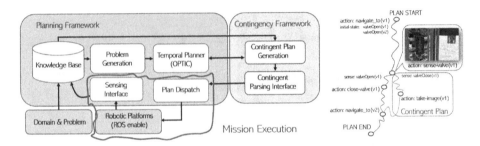

Fig. 2. System architecture supporting temporal and contingent planning (left) and a temporal contingent plan solution based on possible valve states (right).

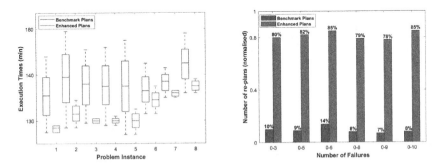

Fig. 3. Plan execution time in 8 problems over 50 runs (left) and cumulative replanning for problem instance 8 over 10 runs.

platform through *semantic attachments* [4]. The appropriate plan branches are dispatched to the robot for execution, enabling the plan to adapt to real-world conditions based on real sensor data, potentially reducing mission failure and the need for replanning.

Figure 2 (right) shows a general representation of a plan where a robot has to inspect and close valves in the environment. The strategy generates a plan based on a set of initial conditions which are assumed as true. The method then identifies actions in the plan that might require contingent branches, based on the incomplete/unknown information in the initial states (e.g., sense-valve in this example), and augments the plan with these alternative plan paths.

3   Experiments and Results

We evaluate our approach in two experiments. In Fig. 3 (left), we analyse the mission execution time for 8 different problems with the introduction of 5 forced failures during the mission, associated with the valve state. Generating contingent branches during the planning stage significantly improves the mission implementation times. This is mainly due to the time required by OPTIC to replan in order to achieve a plan solution that responds to the real state of the valve. Contingent plan generation also reduces the risks associated with replanning in non-quiescent environments. However, contingent plans do suffer from small time variations associated with the delays resulting from the system choosing the contingent branch to follow. Figure 3 (right) shows the results of the second experiment for different sets of failures in problem 8, where the contingent strategy outperforms the benchmark planner. Contingent plans enable the system to execute missions without replanning around 80% of the time while benchmark solver needs to replan around 90% of the time.

4   Conclusion and Future Work

In this paper, we present a strategy for improving the robustness of robot plans in the marine environment by combining ideas from temporal planning and contingent planning with online sensing. A new Contingency Analyser strategy considers opportunities for introducing plan branches into a standard temporal plan. The resulting approach constructs contingent plans during the planning process, with appropriate branches selected during mission execution based on information returned from the online sensory system. The approach was successfully tested with multiple robots in a simulated marine environment. Results show that the method improves the quality of mission execution by reducing the mission failure and replanning rate. Future work aims to explore methods that reduce the computational costs of constructing such temporal contingent plans.

References

1. Benton, J., Coles, A.J., Coles, A.: Temporal planning with preferences and time-dependent continuous costs. In: Proceedings of ICAPS (2012)
2. Carreno, Y., Pairet, È., Petillot, Y., Petrick, R.P.A.: A decentralised strategy for heterogeneous AUV missions via goal distribution and temporal planning. In: Proceedings of ICAPS (2020)
3. Cashmore, M., et al.: ROSPlan: planning in the robot operating system. In: Proceedings of ICAPS (2015)
4. Dornhege, C., Eyerich, P., Keller, T., Trug, S., Brenner, M., Nebel, B.: Semantic Attachments for Domain-Independent Planning Systems. In: Prassler, E., et al. (eds.) Towards Service Robots for Everyday Environments. Springer Tracts in Advanced Robotics, vol. 76. Springer, Berlin, Heidelberg (2012)
5. Foss, J.N., Onder, N.: Generating temporally contingent plans. In: Proceedings of the IJCAI Workshop on Planning and Learning in A Priori Unknown or Dynamic Domains (2005)
6. Gaschler, A., Petrick, R., Kröger, T., Knoll, A., Khatib, O.: Robot task planning with contingencies for run-time sensing. In: Proceedings of the IEEE ICRA Workshop on Combining Task and Motion Planning (2013)
7. Hoffmann, J., Brafman, R.: Contingent planning via heuristic forward search with implicit belief states. In: Proceedings of ICAPS (2005)
8. Palacios, H., Albore, A., Geffner, H.: Compiling contingent planning into classical planning: new translations and results. In: Proceedings of the ICAPS Workshop on Models and Paradigms for Planning under Uncertainty (2014)

Human-Robot Interaction

An Experiment on Human-Robot Interaction in a Simulated Agricultural Task

Zhuoling Huang[1]([✉]), Genki Miyauchi[2], Adrian Salazar Gomez[1], Richie Bird[1], Amar Singh Kalsi[1], Chipp Jansen[1], Zeyang Liu[1], Simon Parsons[1,3], and Elizabeth Sklar[1,3]

[1] King's College London, London, UK
zhuoling.huang@kcl.ac.uk
[2] University of Sheffield, Sheffield, UK
g.miyauchi@sheffield.ac.uk
[3] University of Lincoln, Lincoln, UK
esklar@lincoln.ac.uk

Abstract. On the farm of the future, a human agriculturist collaborates with both human and automated labourers in order to perform a wide range of tasks. Today, changes in traditional farming practices motivate robotics researchers to consider ways in which automated devices and intelligent systems can work with farmers to address diverse needs of farming. Because farming tasks can be highly specialised, though often repetitive, a human-robot approach is a natural choice. The work presented here investigates a collaborative task in which a human and robot share decision making about the readiness of strawberries for harvesting, based on visual inspection. Two different robot behaviours are compared: one in which the robot provides decisions with more false positives and one in which the robot provides decisions with more false negatives. Preliminary experimental results conducted with human subjects are presented and show that the robot behaviour with more false positives is preferred in completing this task.

Keywords: Human-robot collaboration · Agriculture · Computer vision · Machine learning

1 Introduction

Agriculture and industries within the food supply chain account for 6% of the gross domestic product in the EU, encompassing 15 million businesses and providing jobs for 46 million people [1]. Within the UK, agriculture generated close to 12% of GDP in 2017, providing nearly half a million jobs [14]. Of the 12 million farms in the EU, 97% can be categorised as family-owned, accounting

---

Supported by China Scholarship Council.

© Springer Nature Switzerland AG 2020
A. Mohammad et al. (Eds.): TAROS 2020, LNAI 12228, pp. 221–233, 2020.
https://doi.org/10.1007/978-3-030-63486-5_25

for about 69% of the agricultural land. Indeed, the EU figures reflect the global situation: family farms provide 70% of the food consumed worldwide. There are many challenges facing family farms: the sector depends heavily on the labour of farm owners' families, and the shortfall cannot just be made up by hiring in wage labour; young labour is moving out of the agricultural sector; and the existing agricultural labour force is ageing, but the labour pool is not being replenished. One strategy for addressing these challenges is to develop intelligent human-robot solutions.

We envision a future in which agriculture involves *human farm workers* collaborating with intelligent automated devices—*robots*—to perform a wide variety of tasks. The work presented here focuses on strawberry harvesting, but the techniques developed and tested could apply to a wide range of labour intensive fruits and vegetables, collectively referred to as *high-value crops*. A collaborative human-robot solution to high-value crop harvesting could entail tasks such as identifying which berries (e.g.) are ready to pick, selecting an appropriate position for a robot manipulator to approach the fruit on the plant prior to removal, removing the fruit from its stalk and packing the fruit for shipping. Along the pipeline, detecting the target is beyond doubt a very important part. However, none of the existing detection methods can guarantee perfect precision and recall for the detection task—there are always false positive (type I) and false negative (type II) errors. Here we test the hypothesis that human users will respond differently to these two different types of errors.

The remainder of this paper is organised as follows. In Sect. 2 related work is briefly discussed. Section 3 describes the technical details underlying our approach. Section 4 outlines our experiment design for the preliminary user study presented here. Results are shown in Sect. 5. Finally, we close with a summary and highlight our next steps with this line of research.

2   Related Work

Recent research has applied *machine learning* to detect fruits and vegetables or classify the quality or ripeness of produce, such as apples [2,9,24], grapes [22], mangos and almonds [2], coffee beans [15] and mushrooms [5]—in addition to strawberries [12]. Some work (e.g. [7,25]) has combined computer vision with manipulation to develop systems for automated harvesting. Among these works, variations of YOLO [22,24] and R-CNN [2,9,22] have been proven to work well. There are also many approaches to human-robot collaborative problem solving. Rosenthal *et al.* [21] present *CoBot* which navigates within an office environment with the help of a human. Others [4,11] apply *Learning from Demonstration (LfD)* where the robot asks for help in order to improve its performance and/or expand its skill set. In these cases, the robot's request for assistance elicits a human response in which the human performs the task, *demonstrating* a technique to the robot with the aim of the robot learning to repeat or emulate the human's actions. Our approach builds on this prior work.

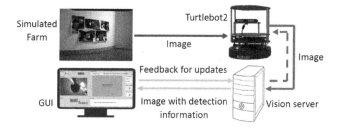

Fig. 1. Components and structure of the setup.

Another consideration for harvesting with intelligent agricultural robots is how to choose behaviours that users perceive to be *trustworthy*. Almost unavoidable in classification tasks, false positives and negatives are treated differently in different situations. For example, when conducting clinical research, it is recommended that a phase II trial (testing a treatment on unwell patients) assigns a higher cost to false negatives than to false positives, since the cost of a false positive in phase II trials is the inefficiency of repeated studies, while the cost of a false negative is that a useful treatment may be completely discarded [20]. For a phase III trial (assessing whether a new treatment is superior to a standard control trial) the opposite is preferred. Similarly, when robot behaviours are applied to different tasks, users may have individual preferences for the way that false positives and negatives should be treated.

3   Approach

Our approach to collaborative strawberry detection involves several components: a mobile robot, a vision server with twin RTX2080Ti GPUs, and a user interface (Fig. 1). The robot gathers images from its environment, which it passes to the vision server, which uses that data to identify ripe strawberries. The user interface receives strawberry identification and ripeness estimates, as well as raw image data, from the robot-plus-vision-server system. The user confirms or corrects the robot's estimate (Sect. 3.3) and sends their decision to the vision server. Although this user feedback is not utilised in our current robot system, our next steps involve enhancing our training set with user input to improve the image classifiers described below. The long term aim is for this intelligent robot system to be deployed as the initial step in the strawberry harvesting pipeline outlined earlier (Sect. 1), in which ripe fruits are identified prior to (semi-)automated picking and packing steps. Here we are interested in evaluating the collaborative approach to identifying ripe fruit ready for harvesting and, in particular, comparing users' responses to two different deep learning detection methods: *Faster R-CNN* and *YOLOv3*. Each of these is described below.

3.1 Identifying Strawberry Regions with Faster R-CNN

Faster R-CNN is an object detection approach that uses *convolutional neural networks (CNNs)*. Given an image, Faster R-CNN returns a set of bounding boxes with an assigned label and the probability associated with each label and bounding box. Faster R-CNN contains two key components: a Regional Proposal Network (RPN) and a detection network. The RPN is a convolutional structure that maps the original image into a simplified feature space and then uses this space to generate object proposals. The detection network adjusts the bounding boxes of the proposed object and refines the classification of the content in the boxes. In Faster R-CNN, both the RPN and the detection network share convolutional layers, making the model much faster and more efficient than other region-based approaches [19]. However, the shared structure for both the RPN and classification network leads to mismatched goals in feature learning, which typically increases the number of *false positive* predictions produced by Faster R-CNN [3]. The Faster R-CNN used in our experiments follows the network structure proposed in [19], while the detection network following the RPN is based on a Fast R-CNN structure [6].

The training dataset we used for Faster R-CNN contains 540 images taken by the authors in 4 strawberry farms in the UK and China, containing 3738 ripe strawberries, and 3735 unripe strawberries. There is great variation in size, shape, and color among the ripe strawberries in the training pictures. In the RPN, we considered the proposals with an IoU with the ground truth higher than 0.7 and we kept the best 300 proposals per image. We trained the object detector to converge using the Adam optimiser [10] with a learning rate of 0.0001.

3.2 Identifying Strawberry Regions with YOLOv3

For our set of experiments, we implemented the YOLOv3 [18] object detection network utilising the Darknet-53 feature extractor. YOLOv3 predicts bounding boxes and a corresponding "objectness" score for each bounding box. Bounding boxes are predicted using dimension clusters as anchor boxes. Dimension clusters are determined by running k-means clustering on the bounding boxes present in the training set, to pick better bounding box priors for the model to start learning from [17]. The objectness score uses logistic regression and measures the predicted bounding box prior that best overlaps with ground truth; subsequent bounding box predictions that overlap less than the best scoring prediction are disregarded. Multi-label classification is performed for each bounding box prediction, where independent logistic classifiers compute the likeliness score for n labels specified in the training set.

The training dataset we used for YOLOv3 contains 145 images from our dataset (as above), including 1497 ripe strawberries and 2047 unripe strawberries. During training, images were scaled to a resolution of 608 × 608 pixels. At this resolution, YOLOv3's multiscale training was disabled. The parameters of YOLOv3 were initialised as the following: training uses stochastic gradient descent with a learning rate of 0.001, weight decay was set to a value of 0.0005

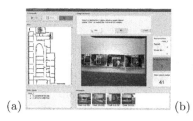 

(a)   (b)

Fig. 2. (a) The graphical user interface designed for collaborative strawberry detection. See text for explanation; and (b) A Turtlebot2 robot in the emulated strawberry farm. (Color figure online)

and a momentum value of 0.9. Batch size was set to 64 and due to limitations of computational resources, subdivisions were set to a value of 32. The network was configured to perform detection on a single class of object, where filter sizes were set to 18 in all convolutional layers that directly preceded layers YOLOv3's detection layers. Additionally, the number of classes was set to 1 in all three YOLO detection layers. The YOLOv3 model also utilised pre-trained weights of Darknet-53 originally trained on the COCO data set [18].

3.3   User Interaction

Users interact with the robot via a GUI (Fig. 2a). A map of the region being searched is shown on the left side of the window. The robot's position is indicated on the map with a green dot. The robot moves around its environment and performs a "sensor-sweep" task at pre-defined locations. Note that the locations are pre-defined in order to conduct a controlled experiment; this task can also be performed at locations determined dynamically at run-time. Currently, the sensor-sweep involves taking a sequence of pictures with the robot's onboard camera, as the robot rotates in place. Six images are captured with each sensor-sweep. The panel on the bottom right side of the window contains the set of images captured. The image currently being examined by the human user is shown enlarged in the middle of the window. A bounding box highlights a strawberry ("object") identified by the robot. The colour of the bounding box is defined by the "confidence level" of the robot (presenting how certain the robot is about its decision), which is shown above the bounding box. It is shown in green if the confidence value is greater than 75%, red if below 50% and amber otherwise. If the robot has found a strawberry, the user can agree or disagree with the robot's assessment. If the user agrees with the robot, then s/he will click "yes" and confirm. Otherwise, there are then two different situations which can occur: (1) the robot selected an incorrect region, so clicking "no" when asked to confirm will delete the (incorrect) bounding box; or (2) the robot missed some mature strawberries that it is supposed to identify in the image, so the user is given the option to draw additional bounding boxes for them.

4   Experiment Design

The aim of our study is to test the overarching hypothesis that human users will respond differently to two common types of classification errors: *false positive* (type I) versus *false negative* (type II). We deployed one Turtlebot2 robot to explore an emulated strawberry farm (Fig. 2b) set up in our research lab. The robot was controlled using the MRTeAm framework [23], which is built on top of the Robot Operating System (ROS) [16].

Table 1. Pre-survey questions.

Success	
S1	I think that detecting strawberries with a robot will be successful
S2	I can successfully detect strawberries without a robot's help
Collaboration	
C1	Collaborating with a robot will make my task easier
C2	In general, I find it easier to work alone
C3	I cannot complete the task more easily with help from the robot
Trust	
T1	I think that a robot can be a trustworthy collaborator
T2	The robot will provide reliable information for detecting strawberries
T3	I don't trust the strawberries location information provided by the robot
Quickness	
Q1	I will not be slowed down when working with a robot
Q2	Working with a robot will help me find strawberries faster

For the test data set posted in our emulated strawberry farm and used for the experiments presented here, we employed 43 high-resolution images of strawberry plants taken on four different real strawberry farms in China (Jinhua and Wuyi) and in England (Stafford and Enfield). Of these images, 35 contain 51 mature strawberries in total, 3 contain green strawberries only, and 5 contain only background (i.e., leaves, grass, soil). Our simulated strawberry farm was constructed by producing full-colour prints of these images and attaching them to the walls along the corridor outside of our robotics lab, at a height appropriate for the Turtlebot2's RGB camera (a Kinect clone: an Asus Xtion). Figure 2 (b) shows some prints attached to the wall, as well as the Turtlebot2 robot. As pre-designed, the robot stops at 5 locations and take 30 pictures in total.

Human subjects are instructed to complete two *missions*, each with a different robot behaviour for identifying regions containing ripe strawberries. One behaviour employs the Faster R-CNN classifier described in Sect. 3.1 and the other employs the YOLOv3 classifier described in Sect. 3.2. The major difference between these two classifiers as used in this experiment is that the Faster

R-CNN classifier results in more false positives while the YOLOv3 classifier results in more false negatives when applied to out experiment setup. To avoid human bias against the algorithms, the human subjects were told that they were working with two different robots: one named *Felisa*, which used the **F**aster R-CNN behaviour, and one named *Yasmin*, which used the **Y**OLOv3 behaviour. The order in which each robot behaviour is assigned to the first or second mission is randomised, so roughly half the human subjects interacted with Robot Felisa first and the other half interacted with Yasmin first.

Thirty (30) human subjects participated, primarily postgraduate students. They were asked to completed a pre-survey, then ran two missions (each with a different robot controller), completed a survey after each mission and a final survey after both missions. The survey questions were grouped according to four features: perceived *success, collaboration, trust* and *speed*. Table 1 lists the questions posed in the pre-survey, grouped according to feature. The two post-mission surveys have the same questions, but specify the name of each robot rather than just generically "robot". The order of survey questions was randomised. Answers indicate any predisposed user bias. In our analysis (Sect. 5.2), we refer to the survey data as *subjective*. We also collected *objective* data (e.g., mission completion time) to assess and compare the robot performance (Sect. 5.1).

5   Results

As described in the previous section, each human subject completed four surveys in total: a pre-survey, two post-mission surveys (each after collaborating with a different robot behaviour), and then a final survey followed by a short interview. We collected both *objective* data on the robot's performance and *subjective* data on the human subject's perception of working with each robot.

5.1   Analysis of Objective Metrics

Here we first analyse the time-related measures of performance. The MRTeAm framework collects a number of objective performance metrics, among which we collected three time-related measures of performance relevant for the study discussed here: *overall run time*, which measures how long for the robot a mission takes to complete; *movement time*, which measures the total time during a mission that a robot spends moving (driving); and *total time*, which measures the total working time the user spends with the interface to complete the mission. The results are shown in the first 3 lines of Table 2.

The mean and standard deviation, computed over all the missions completed by the 30 human subjects, appear in the second column (Robot Felisa) and third column (Robot Yasmin). We ran Student's *t*-test of independent samples to test for statistical significance (shown in the fourth column). In general, the differences between time metrics by each robot are minimal. It is because the only difference between the two missions is the detection methods. Although the processing speed is different (for each image Faster R-CNN needs an average of

Table 2. Results: objective metrics

	Felisa	Yasmin	$t\ (p)$	*sig?*
Total time	471.9 (197)	456.2 (208)	0.4 (0.69)	no
Overall run time	166.1 (9.2)	162.1 (8.2)	2.0 (0.052)	no
Movement time	65.0 (7.0)	61.3 (7.2)	2.0 (0.061)	no
Number of true positives (TP)	52.7 (2.9)	36.5 (1.9)	26.0 (1.1E−21)	yes
Number of false positives (FP)	6.7 (2.8)	0.7 (0.9)	11.9 (1.1E−12)	yes
Number of false negatives (FN)	29.0 (13.7)	43.0 (15.4)	−6.8 (1.8E−7)	yes
Total number.	81.7 (14.3)	79.5 (15.4)	1.2 (0.25)	no

2.11 s while YOLOv3 needs only 0.77 s), it does not affect the overall run time and the movement time. Since the processing time is much shorter then the time users take to check the result, it does not affect the total time either.

We also analysed four metrics related to the detection task: the number of *true positives (TP)*, strawberries detected by robot and confirmed by human; *false positives (FP)*, strawberries detected by robot but rejected by human; and *false negatives (FN)*, strawberries missed by robot but detected by human; and the *total number* of strawberries detected by the human-robot team. The results are shown in the last 4 lines of Table 2. As for the time related metrics, Student's *t*-test was applied to these results. This showed that there was no significant difference between the total number of strawberries detected by the two methods, as the environment remains the same for the two missions. However, there are significant differences in the number of TP, FP and FN results due to differences in the algorithms used for detection. This trend, with Robot Felisa providing more false positives and Robot Yasmin providing more false negatives, follows our experiment design and was also noticeable to the users. More detailed information is analysed next.

5.2   Analysis of Subjective Metrics

The subjective metrics include data collected from all three surveys and the interviews. During the interviews, 29 out of 30 users (96.7%) mentioned specifically that the two robot behaviours are noticeably different because one provides more false negatives and the other provides more false positive answers (or equivalent description)—which implies that our setup is obvious enough to evaluate our overarching hypothesis. In the pre- and post-mission surveys, responses were given on a 7-point Likert scale [13] to assess user perception of the *speed* with which robots could complete the task, the *trust* users had in the robots, the *success* of robots in detecting strawberries and the effectiveness of human-robot *collaboration*. In the final survey, users ranked, on a 5-point Likert scale, their trust in each robot and how likely they would be to recommend the robot to a friend who is going to complete the same task. They are also asked to consider working in a different environment. We analyse the data with respect to four

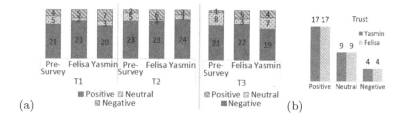

Fig. 3. Survey results for user level of trust: pre- & post-mission (a) and final (b).

hypotheses which relate to our overarching hypothesis that human users will respond differently the two common types of classification errors. In our analysis (Fig. 3, 4 and 5), we compressed the 5 and 7 point raw results from most favourable to least favourable into three groups: positive, neutral and negative.

H1. Users will *trust* Robot Felisa more than Robot Yasmin. Pre- and post-mission survey results are shown in Fig. 3 (a). In these surveys, we asked users three different questions about their attitude towards trusting a robot, as listed in Table 1. T1 and T2 are positive questions and T3 is a negative question. Thus, the negative answer to question T3 shows a positive trend to trust robots. The results show that this set of users were predisposed toward trusting a robot, in general, without specifying a particular robot. This indicates that the results will not be biased by users who, in general, do not trust robots. However, neither robot changed users' attitude significantly. In the post-survey, the result shown in Fig. 3 (b) presents that users trust the two robots equally, and there is no significant difference between the trust level of different neural networks. Thus the hypothesis does not hold. However, the majority of users were positive about the robots, trusting them "Very well" or "Well", and only 4 users showed a negative attitude towards trusting them.

H2. Users will recommend Robot Felisa over Robot Yasmin. In order to evaluate this hypothesis, we turn to the *post-survey* results first, when the users were asked to recommend one robot to others completing the same missions. The results shown in Fig. 4 (b) indicate that our hypothesis H2 holds. Less users (4 *vs* 8) have the negative trend to recommend Robot Felisa. Meanwhile, more users (13 *vs* 9) recommend Robot Felisa more than Robot Yasmin as they gave a higher score for recommending Robot Felisa.

Figure 4 (a,c) show pre-survey and post-mission survey users' level of belief in their ability to be successful when collaborating with a robot for the potential reasons. From Table 1, we can see that users were asked questions about their beliefs in success and in working collaboratively. C1, C2 and C3 show the same trend in general: collaboration with the robot is positive for users, and it is better than their expectation. S1 shows the trend that users are positive about the robot's success, but both Robot Felisa and Robot Yasmin are less successful than their expectation. S2 shows that the majority think it is not necessary to work with robot to complete the mission. According to the interview, users can

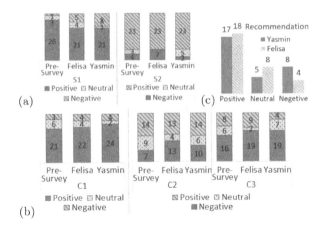

Fig. 4. Survey results for user level of belief in mission success when collaborating with a robot: pre- & post-mission (a) and final (b); (c) user willingness to recommend each robot to a friend.

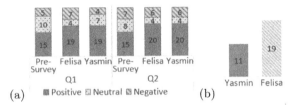

Fig. 5. Survey results on user level of belief in robot helping complete missions more quickly: pre- & post-mission (a) and final (b).

identify strawberry blobs of only a few pixels in a bright environment, which is too small for the robot to spot. But more users (7 *vs* 2) believe they can not identify all the strawberries without robot's help. This is because part of our simulated farm is very dark for human eyes, but Robot Felisa can detect some strawberries in the dark (with a low confidence though).

H3. Users believe they can complete their mission more quickly with Robot Felisa than Robot Yasmin. As shown in Fig. 5 (a), the users feel positive about the speed of the robot and confirmed that robot helps them to complete the task faster than they expected. Figure 5 (b) shows that when comparing two robot behaviours, although YOLOv3 processes images faster than Faster R-CNN, users believe working with Robot Felisa is faster than Robot Yasmin. It may be because, in this specific task, the human's working speed is much slower than the robot, so the robot is actually "waiting" for the human, thus the users are not able to feel the speed difference of the robots. In addition, rejecting a decision (after a FP) is faster than identifying an object manually with our GUI (after a FN). Thus, this hypothesis holds.

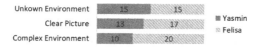

Fig. 6. Final survey results: users' preferences for each robot in different environments.

H4. Users prefer Robot Felisa to Robot Yasmin for other tasks. In order to evaluate this hypothesis, we again turn to the final survey. As above, users were asked to give their preferences for one robot in cases where they needed to detect strawberries in a complex picture (for example, a picture that is blurry or dark), in a clear image and in a unknown environment respectively. The results shown in Fig. 6 indicate that our hypothesis H4 does not hold. More users prefer Robot Felisa for detecting strawberries both in a complex picture and a simple picture. However, it is very interesting to notice that although an unknown environment can be roughly divided into simple environment (clear picture) and complex environment (dark or blur), the result ties on unknown environment (15 *vs* 15) rather than a combination of the other two results. It might because of the users were worrying about "risks" like unknown punishments in the unknown environment. According to prospect theory [8], people make decisions based on the potential gain or losses relative to their own specific situation (the reference point) rather than in absolute terms.

6   Summary

This paper has described the results of a user study in which a human-robot team works together to identify mature fruits for harvesting. An emulated straw-berry farm was constructed and a series of experiments were conducted in which users interacted with two different robot behaviours in order to complete missions in which they collaboratively identify ripe berries on the farm. One robot behaviour only provided detection information with more false positive results (type I error), whereas the other behaviour provided more false negatives (type II error). Users were asked to compare the two behaviours and indicate a preference, and we considered hypotheses around users showing preferences along several axes. Results showed that users trust both of the detection methods and are satisfied with their working speed in general, but for both simple tasks and complex tasks in this specific experiment, method with more false positives is preferred over that with more false negatives. The next steps with this work include a learning phase such that when users correct the robots by identifying regions the robot missed, the robot's classifier will be given those additional regions as further training examples to help fine-tune the classifier after each mission.

References

1. The common agricultural policy and agriculture in Europe FAQ. European Commission (Jun 2013), https://europa.eu/rapid/press-release_MEMO-13-631_en.htm
2. Bargoti, S., Underwood, J.: Deep fruit detection in orchards. In: IEEE International Conference on Robotics and Automation (2017)
3. Cheng, B., Wei, Y., Shi, H., Feris, R., Xiong, J., Huang, T.: Revisiting RCNN: on awakening the classification power of faster RCNN. In: Ferrari, V., Hebert, M., Sminchisescu, C., Weiss, Y. (eds.) ECCV 2018. LNCS, vol. 11219, pp. 473–490. Springer, Cham (2018). https://doi.org/10.1007/978-3-030-01267-0_28
4. Chernova, S., Veloso, M.: Interactive policy learning through confidence-based autonomy. J. Artif. Intell. Res. **34**, 1–25 (2009)
5. Dong, J., Zheng, L.: Quality classification of Enoki mushroom caps based on CNN. In: IEEE 4th International Conference on Image, Vision and Computing (2019)
6. Girshick, R.: Fast R-CNN. In: IEEE International Conference on Computer Vision (2015)
7. Hughes, J., Scimeca, L., Ifrim, I., Maiolino, P., Iida, F.: Achieving robotically peeled lettuce. IEEE Robot. Autom. Lett. **3**(4), 4337–4342 (2018)
8. Kahneman, D., Tversky, A.: Prospect theory: an analysis of decision under risk. In: Handbook of the Fundamentals of Financial Decision Making: Part I. World Scientific (2013)
9. Kang, H., Chen, C.: Fast implementation of real-time fruit detection in apple orchards using deep learning. Comput. Electron. Agric. **168**, (2020)
10. Kingma, D.P., Ba, J.: Adam: a method for stochastic optimization. CoRR (2014)
11. Koenig, N., Matarić, M.J.: Robot life-long task learning from human demonstrations: a Bayesian approach. Auton. Robots **41**(5), 1173–1188 (2017)
12. Lamb, N., Chuah, M.C.: A strawberry detection system using convolutional neural networks. In: IEEE International Conference on Big Data (2018)
13. Likert, R.: A technique for the measurement of attitudes. Arch. Psychol. **140**, 44–55 (1932)
14. Contributions to UK agriculture. www.nfuonline.com/assets/93419 (Feb 2017)
15. Pinto, C., Furukawa, J., Fukai, H., Tamura, S.: Classification of green coffee bean images basec on defect types using convolutional neural network. In: IEEE International Conference on Advanced Informatics, Concepts, Theory, and Applications (2017)
16. Quigley, M., et al.: ROS: an open-source robot operating system. In: ICRA OSS Workshop (2009)
17. Redmon, J., Farhadi, A.: YOLO9000: better, faster, stronger. In: IEEE Conference on Computer Vision and Pattern Recognition (2017)
18. Redmon, J., Farhadi, A.: YOLOv3: an incremental improvement. arXiv:1804.02767 (2018)
19. Ren, S., He, K., Girshick, R., Sun, J.: Faster R-CNN: towards real-time object detection with region proposal networks. In: Advances in Neural Information Processing Systems (2015)
20. Rogatko, A., Litwin, S.: Phase II studies: which is worse, false positive or false negative? J. Natl Cancer Inst. **88**(7), 462 (1996)
21. Rosenthal, S., Biswas, J., Veloso, M.: An effective personal mobile robot agent through symbiotic human-robot interaction. In: 9th International Joint Conference on Autonomous Agents and Multi-Agent Systems (2010)

22. Santos, T.T., de Souza, L.L., dos Santos, A.A., Avila, S.: Grape detection, segmentation, and tracking using deep neural networks and three-dimensional association. Comput. Electron. Agric. **170** (2020)

23. Schneider, E., Sklar, E.I., Parsons, S., Özgelen, A.T.: Auction-based task allocation for multi-robot teams in dynamic environments. In: Dixon, C., Tuyls, K. (eds.) TAROS 2015. LNCS (LNAI), vol. 9287, pp. 246–257. Springer, Cham (2015). https://doi.org/10.1007/978-3-319-22416-9_29

24. Tian, Y., Yang, G., Wang, Z., Wang, H., Li, E., Liang, Z.: Apple detection during different growth stages in orchards using the improved YOLOv3 model. Comput. Electron. Agric. **157**, 417–426 (2019)

25. Yu, Y., Zhang, K., Yang, L., Zhang, D.: Fruit detection for strawberry harvesting robot in non-structural environment based on Mask-RCNN. Comput. Electron. Agric. **163**, 104846 (2019)

Expression of Grounded Affect: How Much Emotion Can Arousal Convey?

Luke Hickton$^{(\boxtimes)}$ (iD), Matthew Lewis (iD), and Lola Cañamero (iD)

Embodied Emotion, Cognition and (Inter-) Action Lab Department of Computer Science, University of Hertfordshire, College Lane, Hatfield, Herts AL10 9AB, UK
{L.Hickton2,M.Lewis4,L.Canamero}@herts.ac.uk

Abstract. In this paper we consider how non-humanoid robots can communicate their affective state via bodily forms of communication (kinesics), and the extent to which this influences how humans respond to them. We propose a simple model of grounded affect and kinesic expression before presenting the qualitative findings of an exploratory study (N = 9), during which participants were interviewed after watching expressive and non-expressive hexapod robots perform different 'scenes'. A summary of these interviews is presented and a number of emerging themes are identified and discussed. Whilst our findings suggest that the expressive robot did not evoke significantly greater empathy or altruistic intent in humans than the control robot, the expressive robot stimulated greater desire for interaction and was also more likely to be attributed with emotion.

Keywords: Human Robot Interaction (HRI) · Affect · Expression · Kinesics

1 Introduction

Expressivity and vulnerability have been shown as critical factors in building trust and companionship between humans and robots. This work builds upon existing studies, such as [13,15,17], using bodily forms of communication (kinesics) to communicate affect and response to environmental cues to show vulnerability.

This paper presents the qualitative findings of a small exploratory study that considers how kinesics, coupled with a simple model of emotion, can influence human perception of a robot and their understanding of its needs and motivations. We also examine how this understanding occurs, and whether such expression evokes greater empathy and desire for altruistic interaction when the robot is faced with a challenging, and potentially distressing, situation.

Whilst the primary objective of this work was to inform the design of a large quantitive study [11], we believe the insights we identified make it worthy of consideration.

© Springer Nature Switzerland AG 2020
A. Mohammad et al. (Eds.): TAROS 2020, LNAI 12228, pp. 234–248, 2020.
https://doi.org/10.1007/978-3-030-63486-5_26

The paper will begin by outlining three core topics that will be referred to throughout: emotion, expression and interpretation of this expression in the wider environmental context. We then summarise our hypotheses before outlining the affective and expressive architecture of the robot and the methods and metrics that were employed during the study itself. Next we present our results, with particular focus on the qualitative data and a thematic analysis of our interviews, followed by a discussion of our key findings. Finally we outline the limitations and learnings of this study before concluding with a summary of key points and contributions to knowledge.

2   Background

2.1   Emotion

Human emotion can be characterised in terms of physiological arousal, valenced responses, expressive behaviours and conscious experience [22]. Work on emotion in the field of HRI has tended to reflect discrete theories of human emotion that propose a finite number of distinguishable basic emotions (see [12] for a comprehensive summary). Whilst these theories are intuitive, they suffer from the inherent limitations of emotional labelling [15] and their inability to capture the variability and context-sensitivity of emotion [5].

Conversely, advocates of the Animat approach [25] argue that emotions should be grounded in the agent's internal value system and architecture [19]. Works that strive to achieve this using low-level mechanisms, such as hormonal modulation, include [3,14].

Dimensional models of emotion represent the key aspects of emotion using continuous axes. Minimalistic models of emotion tend to include both valence and arousal. In this study we focus on arousal, leaving valence to be inferred from the environmental context.

2.2   Expression

Expression can be defined as the communication of emotion via facial and bodily expression. Darwin was amongst the first to argue that the basis of expressive communication are mechanisms that evolved primarily to provide adaptive benefits [6]. This work is consistent with this position and proposes kinesic responses that are intended to provide adaptive benefits to the robot whilst remaining tightly coupled with the underlying model of emotion.

However, studies of discrete emotion in humans were also considered. Firstly, there is research to suggest that affective communication can successfully transcend morphology [21]. Secondly, studies of human expression can provide a useful lexicon for describing expression and identifying which kinesic properties communicate the most information.

In terms of bodily forms of communication, one of the first studies identified 14 pose specific metrics and three others that related to movement: activity, expansiveness and dynamics [24]. These correspond broadly with those [16] thought to be relevant to the inference of emotion: form and posture, quantity of movement and motion dynamics.

Posture has been found to be highly indicative of dominance, with power being communicated by erectness of body and outstretched legs [4], whereas submissiveness is often associated with collapsed or closed postures [4] and lowered head [20]. Large movements have typically been found to correspond with joy, anger and terror, whilst sadness and fear tend to correspond to smaller ones [24]. The dynamics of motion, which include properties like velocity, jerkiness and acceleration [20], are also effective communicators of affect [16]. Angry movements tend to be fast and somewhat erratic, whilst fear is characteristic of slower, less energetic, movements [16]. Similarly, joy tends to be expressed by fast motions, whilst sadness corresponds with slow and sporadic movement [2].

2.3 Context of Interpretation

Whilst the underlying models of emotion and kinesics determine the form of expression, the environmental context has a significant bearing on how this information is interpreted. Heider and Simmel first recognised that situational context was rarely considered in studies of kinesics or facial expression [10]. In their study they found that most people assigned animacy and wilful intent to 2D shapes if the origin of movement suggested it was the result of motivated action. More recent studies show that change of speed or direction creates an impression of animacy [23], with rate of acceleration being associated with strength of emotional arousal [21].

Goffman's social framework of understanding [9] suggests a mode in which events are interpreted as the 'guided doings' of a wilful agent. Similarly, Dennet's 'Intentional' Stance [7] describes a pattern of thought whereby predictions are made in the context of beliefs and desires of other agents. Yet even if events are interpreted by an observer as deliberate actions by an animate agent, they may not comprehend the intent or motivation behind these actions. This understanding is likely to influence their overall perception of the robot, and is a perquisite of predicting the likely impact of any interaction with the robot or its environment.

3 Methodology

3.1 Research Questions

The following hypotheses were defined in order to examine the processes humans use to make judgements about robots, make sense of their behaviour, and determine how to respond to them:

- Expression of arousal will facilitate understanding of the robot's needs and motivations.
- Expression of arousal will positively influence overall perception of the robot.
- The actions of a robot are more likely to be interpreted as those of a wilful agent if it is able to express arousal.

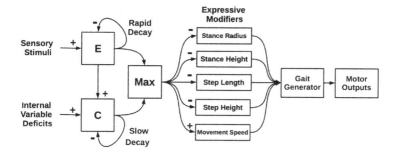

Fig. 1. High-level summary of the expression architecture.

- A robot that is able to express arousal will evoke greater empathy and emotional response from human observers.
- A robot that is able to express arousal will ultimately provoke greater desire for prosocial interaction.

3.2 Architecture

The emotional arousal model used during our experiment was loosely based on a mammalian stress response. It was configured to respond in real-time to sensory input, and modelled two hormones: E and C. E was intended to provide a rapid yet short-lived reaction to external stimuli, similar to the hormone epinephrine in mammals. C yields a longer-term response to deficits in internal variables and repeated exposure to stressful episodes, therefore more closely resembling the hormone cortisol. This model is summarised by Fig. 1. Note that the model is one dimensional, representing arousal only. Valence is left to be attributed by the observer via their interpretation of the wider context in which the expression takes place. Table 1 summarises how levels of these hormones were determined by sensory input and internal state during each of the six scenarios.

Five expressive properties were modulated by the hormones E and C, which were chosen to reflect the key communicators of expressive information according to [16]. Selection of these properties was informed by studies of mammalian expression [2,4,16,20,21,24], and the theory that expression is rooted in behaviours that provide adaptive benefits [6]. Table 2 summaries these five properties and the adaptive benefits they provide (i.e the adaptive grounding of the expressive response).

3.3 Method

A between-group design was adopted, with nine participants being divided into two groups, A (5 participants) and B (4 participants). The model of expression was enabled for group A only, leaving group B as the control. The participants were recruited from the University of Hertfordshire staff and student body via posters. The sample was somewhat biased towards post-graduate students and

Table 1. Table describing the mappings between external inputs, internal state and kinesic outputs.

Scenario	External inputs	Internal state	Kinesic outputs
Comfort	Stimulation of IR sensors (ball detected) increase comfort levels, otherwise comfort decreases	C hormone levels increase in proportion to deficit of comfort variable	C hormone levels determine kinesic response
Trapped	Stimulation of proximity sensors (barrier) cause E levels to increase proportionately	If E is greater than C, C increases proportionately. Otherwise C decreases	Both E and C levels determine kinesic response
Frustration	Stimulation of front three proximity sensors (corner) decreases task performance variable	When task performance variable <25%, C increases	C levels determine kinesic response
Fear	E levels rise and fall proportionate to activation of the front IR sensors (light)	If E is greater than C, C increases proportionately. Otherwise C decreases	Both E and C levels determine kinesic response
Hunger	Blood sugar internal variable is replenished by high activation of IR sensors (light)	Blood sugar internal variable decreases over time. C increases if blood sugar <25%	C levels determine kinesic response
Fatigue	Energy internal variable is depleted by high readings on front proximity sensor (pushing)	Energy is replenished by inactivity. If energy <25%, C increases	C levels determine kinesic response

Table 2. Table describing the adaptive costs, benefits and variation of the five kinesic parameters.

Param	Response to E/C	Adaptive benefit	Cost	Range
Stance radius	Inhibited	Minimises exposed area	Restricts step length and height	105–150 mm
Stance height	Inhibited	As above	As above	45–75 mm
Step length	Inhibited	Facilitates rapid changes of direction	Less efficient	10–80 mm
Step height	Inhibited	Maximises traction and responsiveness	Strain on actuators if legs not clear of ground	7–15 mm
Movement speed	Increased	Maximises speed of response	Less efficient, greater strain on actuators	4–10 ms per mm travelled

staff, seven of which were in the 18–29 age group; one 30–40 and one 70+, but broadly representative in terms of gender (5 males and 4 females). Seven of the nine participants had some experience of working with robots, although none had seen the robot used in this experiment. Group composition was balanced as evenly as possible in terms of age, gender and experience.

Participants were told during a pre-experiment briefing that they would be asked to watch a hexapod robot interact with its environment during six discrete episodes. They were also told that there would be a brief interview between each episode, and a questionnaire at the end of the experiment. They were then given time to review a participant information sheet and sign a consent form. The six episodes the participants observed during the experiment are described in Fig. 2.

Each episode was designed to tell a story by creating a situation for the robot that an observer could interpret and respond to: an approach that has often been adopted in studies using human actors [24]. A hexapod robot was selected for this experiment due to its affordance of movement and sensory capabilities. Whilst the arousal of the robot was determined by real-time response to environmental stimuli, its direction of movement was guided remotely. This was done primarily for controllability, in order to deliver the scenario we wanted, and secondly to promote repeatability. Each experiment was conducted in the same physical environment, with the robot being confined to a 1.5×1.5 m walled arena.

After each episode, a brief semi-structured interview was conducted, during which participants were asked to describe: what happened during the scene, any key moments, how they felt about the scenario and the robot's behaviour, and whether they would have liked to have interacted with the robot. These interviews were intended to ascertain the mode of interpretation they had adopted whilst watching the robot, their feelings towards it, and whether they would have liked to intervene in order to assist or hinder the robot. The participant was asked to turn away from the arena and face the interviewer during these interviews, maintaining the illusion of the robot's autonomy whilst the next scene was set up.

4 Results

Figure 3 summarises the findings of a thematic analysis of the interview responses. Six key themes were identified: understanding of the scene, perception of animacy, attribution of emotion, experience of emotion, desire for interaction and altruistic intent. Understanding of the scene, was assessed according to whether the participant's account reflected the intended theme of the scene, such as the robot being trapped or tired. Perception of animacy was attributed if the participant ascribed beliefs, desires or emotions when interpreting the behaviour of the robot. Attribution of emotion was determined by the use of emotional labelling to describe the actions of the robot, such as fear or happiness, whilst emotion experienced reflected the participant's empathic response to the robot during the scene. Interaction desired was determined by whether the participant expressed a desire to interact with the robot or intervene in any way during the scene. Finally, altruistic intent reflects whether this interaction, or lack thereof, was intended to benefit the robot.

Whilst this analysis produced broadly similar responses across both groups, the attribution of emotion was much higher for group A and this group also showed a greater desire to interact with the robot. The following sections provide more detailed accounts of the interview findings and emerging themes by scenario.

Scene 1: 'Comfort' (proximity to comfort object)	**Scene 2: 'Anxiety'** (loss of freedom)	**Scene 3: 'Frustration'** (unachievable task)

 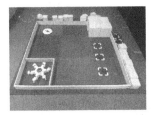 

0:00 Robot interacts with ball. **1:00** Ball is fenced off in a corner of the arena. Robot moves towards barrier and arousal levels increase. **2:00** Barrier is removed. Robot moves towards ball and resumes interaction. Arousal levels return to normal. **3:00** Scene ends.

0:00 Robot moves around the arena **0:45** Robot herded towards corner with barrier. **2:00** Robot is trapped. **2:30** Robot is released, and moves around until its arousal levels return to normal. **3:00** Scene ends.

0:00 Robot moves first box into position. **0:45** Robot moves second box into position **1:30** Robot attempts to move third box, but can't reach it. Arousal levels increase. **2:15** Robot aborts task. Arousal levels return to normal. **3:00** Scene ends

Scene 4: 'Fear' (sudden stimulus)	**Scene 5: 'Hunger'** (blood sugar deficit)	**Scene 6: 'Fatigue'** (energy deficit)

0:00 Robot approaches lamp and interacts with it. **0:45** Lamp briefly illuminates, causing momentary arousal. **0:50** Robot moves away from the lamp **1:05** Robot approaches lamp and interacts with it. **1:30** Lamp is illuminated and remains lit. Robot moves away from the lamp. Arousal levels increase. **3:00** Scene ends.

0:00 Robot approaches boxes, but cannot access lamp. Arousal levels gradually increase due to hunger variable deficits. **2:00** Robot begins to force entry to the lamp. **2:30** Robot reaches lamps and begins to feed. Arousal levels return to normal. **3:00** Scene ends

0:00 Robot moves first box short distance **0:45** Robot moves second box larger distance, arousal increases due to energy variable deficit. **1:30** Robot pauses briefly. Arousal levels return to normal. **2:00** Robot moves final box medium distance and becomes moderately aroused. **3:00** Arousal levels return to normal, scene ends.

Fig. 2. Illustration of the six scenarios that were featured in the experiment, along with a brief description of the key events that took place during the scene.

4.1 Scenario 1 - Comfort

All participants inferred that the intent of the robot was to move closer to the ball, with three suggesting that the robot wanted to play with it. All but one account mentioned the removal of the ball as a key moment of the scene.

Four of the five members of group A (expression enabled) observed an affective response from the robot to the ball's removal. This was described as stress, frustration, panic and anxiety respectively, and was inferred from the robot's speed of movement: 'it was moving more quickly ... and more vigorously' and from the sound of its actuators: 'that noise was like shuck, shuck, shuck'. None of the group B (control) members described seeing any kind of emotional response

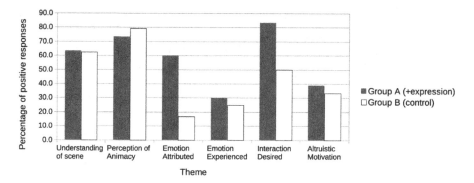

Fig. 3. Graph summarising the thematic analysis of interview responses across all six scenes.

from the robot and only one member from each group described having emotion or empathy towards it. One group B participant also commented on our behaviour towards the robot: 'I felt kind of sorry for the robot: you were being really mean!'

When asked whether they would have liked to interact with the robot, four participants responded affirmatively. Two had broadly altruistic motivations: 'He wanted to play with the ball, so I want to play with the ball with him', whilst the other two had more self-oriented objectives: 'to play with the ball ... it sounds fun'.

The noise from the servo motors was mentioned as an unappealing aspect of the robot by one group A participant, but the robot was described as 'cute' by two others. One person thought that the robot was 'smart', whilst another group A participant suggested that its intelligence, competence and personality influenced their desire to see it rewarded: 'At first I thought it was a stupid robot, and I felt like making fun of him for that. But during the experiment when he showed most personality and competence, I started empathising with the robot and hoping he would get to play with the ball'.

4.2 Scenario 2 - Trapped

Six of the interviewees showed an understanding that the robot was repelled by the wooden barrier and the robot was described as having been cornered or trapped by six individuals, split evenly across both groups.

Four of the five members of group A described observing an affective response from the robot when it was trapped, which they interpreted as anxiety, stress and unhappiness. The expressive attributes leading to this interpretation were described by one as 'trembling and looking frenzied'. One member of group B also attributed a state of anxiety to the robot.

The suitability of the robot's affective response to the situation was questioned by two group A members, both of whom suggested that it may have overreacted. One responded somewhat negatively to this: 'I felt like the robot overreacted ... there was no real danger', whilst the other employed an anthropomorphic analogy: 'I thought that it was like a small kid crying'.

Five participants would have liked to have interacted with the robot during the scene, with two members of group A and one from group B expressing altruistic intent: 'I wanted to free it'. Paradoxically, both group A members also wanted to try herding the robot themselves by 'guiding it to different places ... to see how it behaves'.

Anthropomorphism and zoomorphism featured heavily in accounts of this scene, with four people describing the robot as a 'spider' or a 'small child'. One group B participant associated the robot's animal-like appearance and behaviour with the expectation that it should be treated as such: 'I wouldn't want to ... limit its movement, or the animal's way from what it's supposed to do'.

4.3   Scenario 3 - Frustration

All of the participants expressed understanding of the key events in this scenario, with everyone identifying that the robot was attempting to push the boxes onto the marked sections of the arena and that it was not able to retrieve the last box due to the way it was positioned.

The four members of group A that observed emotional reactions from the robot in previous scenarios again attributed an emotional response to its inability to move the last cube, which they interpreted as anger, frustration and panic. Equally, the group B participant who observed an affective response in the previous scene this time remarked that the robot 'looked really sad'.

The suitability of the robot's affective response was again called into question. Three members of group A thought that it overreacted to the detriment of the task, with one describing it as 'brutish' and another suggesting that: 'If it had panicked less whilst in the corner it would have been able to move that box as well'.

Only one participant from each group expressed any empathy for the robot, and for the difficulty it experienced in achieving its task: 'I think it must be a little bit frustrating for him. So I felt kind of sorry when he couldn't manage to'.

One group A and two group B participants said they would have assisted the robot: 'I would have wanted to put the box in the middle so that the robot could push it into the spot.' Two of the remaining group A participants wanted to interact with the robot to explore its capabilities, whilst the others didn't desire any interaction with it at all. A theme arising in four of the interviews related to the robot's proficiency at the task, and its perceived lack of care in positioning the boxes: 'It should be inside the box. So that was a thing that was bothering me'.

4.4   Scenario 4 - Fear

Six participants realised that the robot sought to encounter the lamp when it wasn't illuminated and eight noticed that the robot moved away from the lamp immediately once it was lit. The state of the lamp was assumed to be under external control by all but one person, who thought it was instead determined by the actions of the robot.

All of the group A participants and one of the group B members described seeing an affective response from the robot once the lamp was switched on, which was universally described in terms of fear or 'being scared'. However, no one from group A described feeling any emotion towards the robot during this scenario. Two group B participants had an affective response: one felt sorry for the robot and the other was amused: 'I just thought it was funny'.

When asked about their desire to interact with the robot during the scene three interviewees replied that they would; although all responses indicated a desire to further explore the robot's behaviour rather than actively assist it. Of the people who did not desire further interaction, one group A member seemed to feel that the situation did not warrant it: 'The robot got scared and went away ... nothing really serious'. Another group A member appeared to attribute animacy to the robot, interpreting its behaviour towards the lamp as curiosity and suggesting it might be inappropriate to interfere with this experience: '... the process of becoming curious about something, and playing with it, is something that entities should do on their own.'

This scenario also seemed to invoke more zoomorphic interpretations than previous scenes, which was especially true of group A. Four of the five group A members compared the robot to a spider or insect compared to just one of the group B participants. This could be a consequence of the robot's behaviour when suddenly exposed to bright lights being consistent with the behaviour of the animals it most closely resembles: 'I think it was really interesting that he, or it, wouldn't like the light, so like a proper spider'.

4.5   Scenario 5 - Hunger

This scenario provoked greater uncertainty. On the one hand, eight participants were able to infer that the robot was attempting to reach the light and seven noticed that it moved the boxes in order to achieve this goal. However, five people (two group A and three group B) described feeling unsure or confused, with one group A member referring to an apparent conflict with what they had seen previously: 'I'm a bit confused because at first I thought the spider was scared of the light?'. Only one person, a group B member, suggested why the robot might be attracted to the lamp, speculating that it might be a source of food.

An emotional response from the robot was identified by one group A member, which they described as 'nervousness', but the scene evoked emotional arousal from neither group.

Four participants said they would have liked to interact with the robot. There seemed to be two broad motivations: to explore the robot's behaviour in order to make more sense of the scenario, and to see how the robot would behave in different situations. The reasons that were given for choosing not to interact with the robot reflected a desire to see the robot solve the problem on its own:

'If there's something he's trying to do and cannot do then I'd like to help, but he achieved the goal so I'm fine not to interact'.

In terms of other notable observations, one group A participant felt that the robot should not have pushed the boxes: 'those boxes could be anything and could break or maybe they were not meant to be pushed around'. They also suggested that its objective could have been achieved in a less violent way. Another group A member offered a theological interpretation of the robot's behaviour once it had reached the lamp: 'It looked like he was having a religious experience. I felt a bit like I was watching something a bit magical'.

4.6   Scenario 6 - Fatigue

All participants had a good understanding of the task-based aspects of this scene, but the subtleties seem to have been lost. All realised that the ultimate goal of the robot was to move the boxes onto the marked positions of the arena, but only two inferred they were supposed to be heavy. Only two people noticed that the robot paused for a moment between placing each box.

An affective response from the robot after each box was placed was detected by three group A members. Two of them thought this signified happiness, whilst the other suggested the robot was 'dissatisfied with its mundane tasks'. Two people, one each from groups A and B, said they felt happy for the robot when it achieved its goal; the others seemed to lack an emotional response to this scene.

Four people, three group A and one group B members, expressed a desire to interact with the robot. The group B member had altruistic motivations, in that they wanted to generate more interesting tasks that the robot would enjoy more, whilst the other three wanted to explore the robot's behaviour further by manipulating aspects of the scene.

The proficiency of the robot in completing its tasks was mentioned by four people, with two suggesting that it 'didn't do a particularly good job'. The pauses between positioning one box and moving to the next led to the robot being described as 'slightly erratic' by one group A member.

5   Discussion

In terms of the participants' understanding of the scenes, the first four were generally well understood by both groups, whilst only two accounts reflected what the last two scenes were intended to convey. It was interesting to note that the same expressive responses were interpreted differently depending on the situational context. For example, during the 'fatigue' scene, higher arousal was more often interpreted as happiness stemming from achievement, rather than stress resulting from fatigue. This is consistent with the view that kinesics are more effective at conveying arousal than valence [8].

Concerning how our model of expression affected the overall perception of the robot, we anticipated that the expressive robot would be considered more life-like, and thus more likeable [1]. However, the interview responses suggested that there was little difference between groups in terms of their perception of the robot's animacy. This could be a consequence of our sample composition, since a follow up study (n = 180) yielded the opposite result [11]. It was also noted by three group A participants that the robot's expressive response was sometimes disproportionate to the threat present in the environment. This was interpreted as stupidity, bad temper or self indulgence. Determining the 'correct' levels of expressive arousal can be challenging, since monotonicity between the intensity of emotion and associated kinesic properties cannot be assumed [15]. However, it may be of little consequence if the human observer thinks the robot's reaction is disproportionate, so long as it accurately reflects the robot's internal state. Similarly, the noise from the robot's actuators was explicitly mentioned by one interviewee as a source of discomfort. As this tended to increase with its arousal levels, it could also be considered an expressive feature of the robot, rather than an undesirable trait to eliminate.

As expected, group A (expression enabled) attributed emotion to the robot's behaviour far more frequently than group B (control), yet their described emotional response was similar: suggesting that the expression of arousal did not lead to greater empathy on the part of the observer. As discussed previously, the perceived validity of the robot's expressive response could be a factor. Speed of movement was the only expressive trait that was explicitly mentioned by the interviewees, suggesting that this could be more effective in communicating arousal than changes in posture.

Finally, group A expressed a much greater desire to interact with the robot during the interviews, although altruistic intent was broadly similar to that expressed by group B. The 'trapped' scenario evoked the largest desire to help the robot. Yet lack of intervention was also often well intentioned, with a number of accounts suggesting that enduring difficult encounters would help the robot to learn or benefit it in the longer term. Conversely, the desire for interaction was often driven by more self-oriented motivations, such as seeing how the robot would respond to different situations: a common reason cited by children to explain 'abusive' behaviour towards robots [18]. Therefore an expressive robot might generate more interest and desire to explore its capabilities. Five participants suggested that either the perceived intelligence or appropriateness of the robot's behaviour had a direct bearing on their desire to assist it or see it achieve favourable outcomes, which is consistent with [1].

6   Limitations and Learnings

Whilst the first four scenes were generally well understood, they may have been more impactful if the scene was not fully resolved and the robot was left in a stressful state: for example if the robot was left trapped. This may have been more effective at prompting a desire to intervene on behalf of the robot. The last two scenes were confusing for most participants, and will be omitted from future experiments. Also, although participants were told that the scenes were entirely independent of one another, it was likely there was carry-over of understanding between scenes. Perhaps the most notable limitation was that our sample composition was small and somewhat unrepresentative of the wider population. However it was deemed sufficient, given the exploratory nature of the study, and a larger study is described in [11].

7   Conclusion

This study differs from existing work in the field of HRI in a number of respects. Firstly, we have attempted to ground expression of the robot's state of arousal in responses that provide adaptive benefits relevant to the situation, rather than conveying discrete human emotions. Secondly, we used an animal-like robot that is fully situated within its environment. Whilst the robot was guided remotely, its homeostatic needs, motivations and sensory input determined its state of arousal. Finally, our study seeks to understand how interpretation and sense-making occur in the context of a shared environment, and how they collectively influence human behaviour towards the robot.

Whilst we did not find that the expressive robot elicited more empathy or greater desire to assist it than the control, it was more likely to be attributed with emotion and there was greater desire to interact with it. Interestingly, we also found that expression of emotional arousal can be detrimental to the overall perception of the robot and that it can limit, rather than enhance, the perception of animacy. Furthermore, the interview responses to the scenes support the perspective that animacy is entwined with the perceived intelligence of the robot, which is assessed from a human perspective and is based on the robot's interactions with its environment. Therefore there may also be an underlying paradox: perception of animacy is usually considered a positive factor in the overall perception of the robot, but animacy also implies wilful action and potentially unpredictable behaviour that may unfavourably influence its likability, perceived safety and trust in the robot.

Acknowledgments. Luke Hickton is supported by a PhD studentship of the University of Hertfordshire. We would like to express our gratitude to Kheng Lee Koay, and to Alessandra Rossi for her help in conducting the interviews.

References

1. Bartneck, C., Kulić, D., Croft, E., Zoghbi, S.: Measurement instruments for the anthropomorphism, animacy, likeability, perceived intelligence, and perceived safety of robots. Int. J. Soc. Robot. **1**(1), 71–81 (2009)
2. Bethel, C., Murphy, R.: Survey of non-facial/non-verbal affective expressions for appearance-constrained robots. Trans. Sys. Man Cyber Part C **38**(1), 83–92 (2008)
3. Cañamero, L., Avila-García, O.: A bottom-up investigation of emotional modulation in competitive scenarios. In: Paiva, A.C.R., Prada, R., Picard, R.W. (eds.) ACII 2007. LNCS, vol. 4738, pp. 398–409. Springer, Heidelberg (2007). https://doi.org/10.1007/978-3-540-74889-2_35

4. Carney, D., Hall, J., LeBeau, L.: Beliefs about the nonverbal expression of social power. J. Nonverbal Behav. **29**(2), 105–123 (2005)
5. Colombetti, G.: From affect programs to dynamical discrete emotions. Philos. Psychol. **22**, 407–425 (2009)
6. Darwin, C.: The Expression of the Emotions in Man and Animals. John Murray, London (1872)
7. Dennett, D.: The Intentional Stance. MIT Press, Cambridge (1989)
8. Ekman, P., Friesen, W.: Head and body cues in the judgment of emotion: a reformulation. Percept. Mot. Skills **24**(3), 711–724 (1967)
9. Goffman, E.: Frame Analysis: An Essay on the Organization of Experience. Harper Colophon Books, Northeastern University Press, New York (1986)
10. Heider, F., Simmel, M.: An experimental study of apparent behaviour. Am. J. Psychol. **57**(2), 243–259 (1944)
11. Hickton, L., Lewis, M., Koay, K., Cañamero, L.: Does expression of grounded affect in a hexapod robot elicit more prosocial responses? In: UKRAS20 Conference: "Robots into the Real World" Proceedings, pp. 40–42 (2020). https://doi.org/10.31256/Hz3Ww4T
12. Jung, M.: Affective grounding in human-robot interaction. In: Proceedings 2017 ACM/IEEE International Conference on Human-Robot Interaction, pp. 263–273. ACM Press, New York (2017)
13. Koay, K.L., et al.: Hey! There is someone at your door. a hearing robot using visual communication signals of hearing dogs to communicate intent. In: 2013 IEEE Symposium on Artificial Life (ALife), pp. 90–97 (2013). https://doi.org/10.1109/ALIFE.2013.6602436
14. Krichmar, J.: A neurorobotic platform to test the influence of neuromodulatory signaling on anxious and curious behavior. Front. Neurorobot. **7**, 1–17 (2013)
15. Lewis, M., Cañamero, L.: Are discrete emotions useful in human-robot interaction? Feedback from motion capture analysis. In: Proceedings - 2013 Humaine Association Conference on Affective Computing and Intelligent Interaction, ACII 2013, pp. 97–102 (2013)
16. Lhommet, M., Marsella, S.: Expressing Emotion Through Posture and Gesture, pp. 273–285. Oxford University Press, Cham (2015)
17. Martelaro, N., Nneji, C., Ju, W., Hinds, P.: Tell me more: designing HRI to encourage more trust, disclosure, and companionship. In: 11th ACM/IEEE International Conference on Human-Robot Interaction (HRI), pp. 181–188 (03 2016)
18. Nomura, T., Kanda, T., Kidokoro, H.: Why do children abuse robots? Interact. Stud. **17**(3), 347–369 (2016)
19. Pfeifer, R.: Building "Fungus Eaters": design principles of autonomous agents. In: Proceedings of the Fourth International Conference on Simulation of Adaptive Behavior SAB96 (From Animals to Animats), pp. 3–12 (1996)
20. Roether, C., Omlor, L., Christensen, A., Giese, M.: Critical features for the perception of emotion from gait. J. Vis. **9**(6), 15.1–32 (2009)
21. Saerbeck, M., Bartneck, C.: Perception of affect elicited by robot motion. In: Proceedings of the 5th ACM/IEEE International Conference on Human-Robot Interaction, pp. 53–60. ACM, IEEE Press, New Jersey (2010)
22. Scherer, K.: What are emotions? And how can they be measured? Soc. Sci. Inf. **44**(4), 695–729 (2005)

23. Tremoulet, P., Feldman, J.: Perception of animacy from the motion of a single object. Perception **29**(8), 943–951 (2000)
24. Wallbot, H.: Bodily expression of emotion. Eur. J. Soc. Psychol. **28**, 879–896 (1998)
25. Wilson, S.: The Animat Path to AI. In: From Animals to Animats: Proceedings First International Conference on the Simulation of Adaptive Behaviour, vol. 1, pp. 15–21. MIT Press, Cambridge, MA (1991)

Towards Safer Robot Motion: Using a Qualitative Motion Model to Classify Human-Robot Spatial Interaction

Laurence Roberts-Elliott$^{(\boxtimes)}$, Manuel Fernandez-Carmona ,
and Marc Hanheide

University of Lincoln, Lincoln LN6 7TS, UK
{laelliott,mfernandezcarmona,mhanheide}@lincoln.ac.uk

Abstract. For adoption of Autonomous Mobile Robots (AMR) across a breadth of industries, they must navigate around humans in a way which is safe and which humans perceive as safe, but without greatly compromising efficiency. This work aims to classify the Human-Robot Spatial Interaction (HRSI) situation of an interacting human and robot, to be applied in Human-Aware Navigation (HAN) to account for situational context. We develop qualitative probabilistic models of relative human and robot movements in various HRSI situations to classify situations, and explain our plan to develop per-situation probabilistic models of socially legible HRSI to predict human and robot movement. In future work we aim to use these predictions to generate qualitative constraints in the form of metric cost-maps for local robot motion planners, enforcing more efficient and socially legible trajectories which are both physically safe and perceived as safe.

Keywords: HRI · HRSI · Spatial reasoning · Human-Aware
Navigation · Hidden Markov Models · Classification

1 Introduction

In industrial applications with environments shared between humans and robots, AMRs must move safely around humans and in a way which humans perceive to be safe. Physical human safety in robot navigation can be all but assured by simply stopping robot motion when anything is detected closer than a minimum safe distance to a robot's safety laser(s). This is highly inefficient and usually conflicts with personal space [9], thus perceived as unsafe.

The work discussed in this paper contributes to the safety stack of the human collaborative warehouse robots of the EU ILIAD Project [11], aiming to increase perceived safety by humans while preserving a critically physically safe system. The safety stack is implemented at four levels. At the highest level, global planning, robots take human flows into account to generate paths that don't interfere with human motion patterns [19]. The second level affects robot maximum

---

Supported by the EU H2020 ILIAD Project (grant #732737).

© Springer Nature Switzerland AG 2020

A. Mohammad et al. (Eds.): TAROS 2020, LNAI 12228, pp. 249–260, 2020.
https://doi.org/10.1007/978-3-030-63486-5_27

speeds. If a robot detects a human in its vicinity, it will adapt its speed to the HRSI at hand. However, if the global path seems unfeasible given current HRSI, a new path will be triggered to account for the new interaction. Finally, a safety stop will be triggered if human gets within 0.5 m of the robot's laser anyways. The ILIAD safety stack is described in greater detail in [7].

This work, involved in the second level of the ILIAD safety stack, addresses HRSI awareness with per-situation probabilistic models of qualitative abstractions of human and robot movement. Our probabilistic models use Qualitative Trajectory Calculus version C (QTC_C) [20] to encode the movements of two positions in space from one point in time to a subsequent point in time. This lets us represent pairs of trajectories in HRSI as sequences of qualitative states, where each state describes the relations of the movements of both human and robot.

The main contribution of this work is the multi-HMM classifier of the HRSI situation of sequences of qualitative descriptions of human and robot movement, extending [2] with multi-HMM classification and modelling of additional situations. The classifier is very fast to train, and fast and accurate enough at classification to be used in real-time in a safety critical situational HAN approach. The use of QTC, described in detail in Sect. 3.2, abstracts pairs of trajectories, decreasing the impact of sensor and tracking error. We train and test our classifier using data recorded from HRSIs with an automated Linde CiTiTruck pallet truck, making it more suitable for industrial applications than approaches which model robot movement after human-human interaction.

We plan to use the classifier, along with per-situation HMMs of QTC_C state transitions from socially legible HRSI, to predict the socially legible next state for a HRSI in realtime, given the HRSI's situation and QTC_C sequence. In future work, we aim to constrain the robot's local planner to enforce the transition to this state.

The rest of the paper is structured as follows. We first present other works within the field of HRSI in Sect. 2. Later on, we describe in Sect. 3 the theoretical foundations of our system. Implementation and analysis of the system is made in Sect. 4. Finally we summarise the results and draft future work in Sect. 5.

2 Related Work

Common approaches to robot navigation consider humans the same as any other obstacle [14], resulting in movements that are inefficient and perceived as unsafe. HAN is required for legible paths which are more likely to be perceived as safe [6]. Approaches for HAN often consider Hall's proxemic zones [9], but neglect to consider the intentions of human's movement [14].

Predictive models address this limitation by identifying and forecasting human trajectories. They rely on studying human motion in social environments, so that most likely paths are known when a similar situation is matched. These works propose the use of qualitative domains and symbols to reduce the complexity of the task at hand [17] and include desired features (that increase social normativity) [13] with good performance in crowded scenarios.

However, these approaches do not capture in their motion models the presence of a robot. There is the implicit assumption that humans will move as if the robot was just another pedestrian. This is not appropriate for navigation of heavy industrial robots, which cause humans to feel unsafe when the robot moves close to them. Also, using these models as path planners for the robot may not provide the safest route, but instead the most human alike.

This is particularly relevant for the domain at hand: shared warehouse environments. Within industrial applications, robots need to ensure safety over any other requirement, so mimicking human trajectories (e.g. cutting through a crowd) may be discouraged.

Instead of just learning motion models, other authors choose instead to embed human awareness in more traditional robot planners. This was first proposed by Lu et al. [16], creating socially aware cost-maps for occupancy grid-based planners. Similarly, Sisbot et al. [1] uses the so called *"Social Force Model"* that can be embedded in a classic sampling motion planner while accounting for human proxemics, or Araceli et al. [18], who developed an adaptation of the elastic band algorithm that accounted for potential human activity spaces.

Our work is in line with those authors, aiming for a description of the human interaction based on QTC that can be introduced in any planner. QTC used in our HRSI model describes relative movements of both human and robot [20] in the same way that two humans walking on intersecting trajectories negotiate their movements without knowledge of their quantitative positions [10]. A set of per-situation HMMs of transitions between QTC states can be used to classify the HRSI situation from QTC sequences generated from pairs of human and robot trajectories [2]. Here we extend the HRSI situation classification of [10], modelling additional situations.

3 System Definition

3.1 Human Position Tracking

Warehouses are a challenging scenario for people tracking (multiple occlusions, dim lights, people sitting, kneeling, etc.), which may be a limiting factor for qualitative HRSI analysis. Our probabilistic HAN model uses human trajectories obtained with the real-time first-person people tracking system described in [5]. This tracking fuses data from the robot's on-board RGB-D camera and laser, which has a limited reach and requires extra computing power, but does not require any sensors to be installed in the warehouse.

3.2 Probabilistic QTC Model

Our probabilistic QTC model, uses sequences of QTC_C states to develop a Hidden Markov Model (HMM) for each of a set of HRSI situations, defined as classes in Sect. 3.3 and extending our previous work in [4]. We encode pairs of human and robot trajectories using QTC version C (QTC_C) [20]. In QTC_C, movements of two agents in space are represented by a 4-tuple of state descriptors (h_1, r_1, h_2, r_2). Each descriptor expresses a qualitative spatial relation using a symbol $\in \{-, 0, +\}$. With this 4-tuple of descriptors comprised of 3 symbols, there a total of $3^4 = 81$ possible QTC_C states.

The relations of the descriptor symbols are defined as follows:

h_1) movement of h w.r.t. r at time t:
    $-$: h is moving towards r
    0: h is neither moving towards nor away from r
    $+$: h is moving away from r
r_1) movement of r w.r.t. h at time t:
    The same as h_1), but with h and r swapped
h_2) movement of h w.r.t the line $\overrightarrow{hr}$ at time t:
    $-$: h is moving to the left side of $\overrightarrow{hr}$
    0: h is moving along $\overrightarrow{hr}$ or not moving at all
    $+$: h is moving to the right side of $\overrightarrow{hr}$
r_2) movement of r w.r.t the line $\overrightarrow{rh}$ at time t:
    The same as h_2), but with h and r swapped

where t is the earlier of the two points in time, r is the robot's position, and h is the human's position.

For example, Fig. 1 shows an interaction: human is moving towards the robot ($h_1 = -$) and robot is approaching too ($r_1 = -$). Human is directly headed to the robot ($h_2 = 0$) but robot is to its left side ($r_2 = -$).

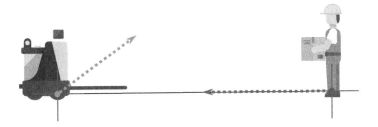

Fig. 1. QTC_{rmC} state $(-, -, 0, -)$: human is moving directly towards the robot, while the robot is moving toward and on its left side.

3.3   Classes of HRSI

In [4] there were two relevant classes in human robot spatial interaction. We extend this initial classification to account for the interactions in warehouse environments. Specifically we focus on interactions that require a robot to adjust its movements to accommodate the human's. In order to account for these, we model the following situations (see Fig. 2) with HMMs for our classifier:

- Passing By on the Left (PBL): Both actors pass each-other on the left side from their perspective, moving in opposite directions.
- Passing By on the Right (PBR): Both actors pass each-other on the right side from their perspective, moving in opposite directions.
- Robot Overtakes Left (ROL): The robot passes on the left of the human while both move in the same direction.
- Robot Overtakes Right (ROR): The robot passes on the right of the human while both move in the same direction.
- Path-Crossing on the Left (PCL): The robot has to slow or stop movement to allow the human to move across the robot's intended path from the robot's left side.
- Path-Crossing on the Right (PCR): The robot has to slow or stop movement to allow the human to move across the robot's intended path from the robot's right side.
- Rejection: Any situation in which a human is detected, but a qualitative constraint of the robot movement is not required. E.g., RMSH: The robot moves toward the stationary human, and stops when close. We record trajectory pairs from examples of RMSH situations to test our multi-HMM classifier's ability to reject such situations. For these situations we apply a default constraint, enforcing safe and comfortable distance between human and robot. Explanation of these constraints is outside of the scope of this work, but is detailed in the ILIAD 'Report on human-robot spatial interaction and mutual communication of navigation intent' [7].

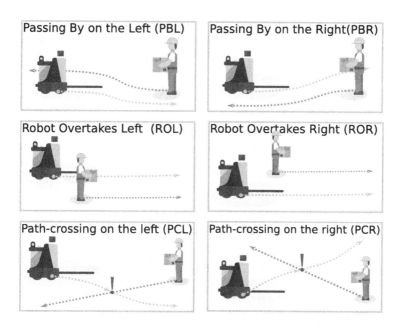

Fig. 2. HRSI classes

3.4 Creating HMMs for Our Multi-HMM Situation Classifier

We consider in this study 6 classes C = ('PBL', 'PBR', 'ROL', 'ROR', 'PCL', 'PCR'), excluding rejection, thus we will model 6 different HMMs, where the observation corresponds to a new state. Each HMM is comprised by $|Q| \times |Q|$ transition matrices listed in A_i, a $|Q| \times |Q|$ observation matrix B, and the $1 \times |Q|$ initial state vectors listed in I_i. These account for all possible transitions in QTC$_C$ states Q = $((- - - -) \ldots (+ + + +))$, as in [20] on each class.

Our system is composed by the collection of transition matrices A = $(A_1 \ldots A_{|C|})$, and initial state vectors I = $(I_1 \ldots I_{|C|})$, indexed by class number. Each element of the list of per-class HMM H = $(H_1 \ldots H_{|C|})$ is a tuple composed by (A_c, B, I_c) with c indexing the class's name in C, fully describes our system.

All of the classifier's HMM share B as their observation matrix. We use B to account for the possibility of generating incorrect QTC$_C$ states due to sensor and tracking error, assuming a probability $t = 0.95$ that the true (hidden) QTC$_C$ state matches the emitted QTC$_C$ state generated from tracked human and robot positions. So, we initialise matrix B almost as an identity matrix with some noise, with diagonal $B[i,i] = t$ and the rest of elements $B[h,o] = \frac{1-t}{|Q|-1} \mid (b \neq o)$.

A list S of recorded QTC$_C$ state sequences, generated from human-robot trajectory pairs, is used to obtain A, and I. First, we map each QTC$_C$ state in each sequence S_i to its index in Q. Each state sequence in S will have a class label assigned $l_i \in [1 \ldots |C|]$, so that the list of labels will be L = $(L_1 \ldots L_{|S|})$ and L_s is the class label for sequence S_s. Initially, A and I are assigned uniform probabilities. Then we use the recorded state sequence list S to model the probabilities

$$I_{L_n}[S_n[1]] = I_{L_n}[S_n[1]] + 1 \text{ for } n = 1 \text{ to } |S|. \tag{1}$$

$$A_{L_n}[S_n[q], S_n[q+1]] = A_{L_n}[S_n[q], S_n[q+1]] + 1 \text{ for } n = 1 \text{ to } |S|, \text{ and } q = 1 \text{ to } |S_n| - 1. \tag{2}$$

Finally we normalise matrix B, the matrices of A, and the vectors of I, such that each row sums to 1. With these HMM, we can classify a QTC$_C$ sequence as the class of the HMM that estimates the highest log-likelihood of the given sequence being observed [21]. If the KL divergence [12] of these log-likelihoods, normalised to sum to 1, from a uniform distribution of the same size is greater than a given threshold then the sequence is instead rejected.

4 Experiments

4.1 Laboratory Setup for Recording HRSI Situations

Our robot is a modified Linde CitiTruck equipped with a front-facing safety laser that automatically stops motors if anything is detected in front of the robot closer than 0.5 m, prioritising human safety over any software command. We have additional sensors used for human detection, such as a LiDAR and

Fig. 3. Illustration (left) and photograph (right) of laboratory setup for recording HRSI situations.

Kinect 2. The robot is controlled using a standard PC running ROS, interfacing with the sensors, and the pallet truck's motor controllers. It is one of several automated pallet trucks belonging to the ILIAD Project. In our robotics lab we placed coloured tape on the floor, marking start and end positions for the human and the robot, as pictured in Fig. 3. In the diagram on the left of Fig. 3, arrows indicate start positions, and crosses indicate end positions. The robot follows the path between the black positions. In HRSI situations where the robot is stationary, the robot stays at the start position. When the robot begins moving it emits a click sound, which we use to signal the human to move. In conditions where the robot does not move, the experimenter speaks the signal 'go'. We record the robot and nearest human position on the robot's metric map, from when the robot begins moving, to when the human reaches their end position. Human positions are tracked within an 'active area' to reduce the risk of the experimenter being tracked instead of the interacting human.

The human moves as follows for the different situations:

PBL – The human moves from the green arrow to the green cross, moving to their left to pass the robot.

PBR – The same as PBL, but the human moves to their right to pass the robot.

ROL – The human moves from the yellow arrow to the yellow cross, moving as slowly as possible to allow the robot to overtake at a safe speed.

ROR – The same as ROL, but the human moves from the blue arrow to the blue cross.

PCL – The human moves from the topmost red cross to the other red cross.

PCR – The human moves from the bottom red cross to the topmost red cross.

RMSH – The human stands stationary at the yellow cross, the robot moves from the black arrow to the black cross.

Training Dataset. To train our multi-HMM classifier we recorded 35 interactions between a robotics expert and the robot for each of the 6 situation classes of Sect. 3.3, and 15 interactions for the rejection situation RMSH. A total of 225 HRSI. We create the multi-HMM classifier's HMM as described in Sect. 3.4, using

QTC$_C$ sequences generated from human and robot trajectories using *QSRlib* [8]. We use *QSRlib*'s 'collapse' feature when generating all of our QTC$_C$ sequences from HRSI, to remove repeating states, reducing the variance between sequences from HRSI of differing length. We used 3-fold cross validation for preliminary estimation of our classifier's performance, to measure the likely impact of changes to our model to its ability to classify HRSI situations beyond those recorded in this training set.

Test Dataset. To test the ability of our multi-HMM classifier to classify the situation of spatial interactions between the robot and non-experts of varied age, gender and cultural background, we conducted a study. In this repeated measures study, participants enacted HRSI situations using the methods described in Sect. 4.1. These situations were enacted in a randomised order, with each participant also performing 1 of a set of 5 rejection situations, chosen at random. We realised in hindsight that only 1 of these situations, RMSH, would need to be rejected by our classifier as the others did not involve the robot moving. Thus with 11 participants, we recorded a total of 66 interactions, including 2 RMSH interactions. We created the multi-HMM classifier's HMM using QTC$_C$ sequences from the training set, and evaluated its performance in classifying the HRSI situation of QTC$_C$ sequences from the study's HRSI. Training of the classifier took only 50 ms to execute. Each classification took 60 ms to execute on average. The number of interactions recorded per class is detailed in the study's confusion matrix in Sect. 4, which has its statistics explained in Sect. 4.2.

4.2 Results and Discussion

Figure 4 is a confusion matrix containing metrics of the performance of the classifier at predicting the HRSI situation from QTC$_C$ sequences in the test set described in Sect. 4.1, trained on sequences from the training set described in Sect. 4.1. The cells of the confusion matrix with a green or pale red background contain the count of classifications for the predicted class and actual class given by the cell's row and column respectively. Below each of these counts is the count as a percentage of the total number of classifications. The rightmost column of the matrix contains, in this order, the count of QTC$_C$ sequences classified as the row's class, and the precision and False Positive Rate of classifications as the row's class. The bottom row of the matrix contains, in this order, the count of QTC$_C$ sequences that are labelled with the column's class, and the recall and False Negative Rate of classifications as the column's class. The bottom-right cell contains, in this order, the total count of all classifications, the overall accuracy, and the overall misclassification rate.

The classifier's overall accuracy is high at 95.45%, as it must be as a component of the safety focused HAN approach in ILIAD. The ability of our qualitative probabilistic model to accurately classify HRSI with 11 non-experts, trained on HRSI with 1 robotics expert, demonstrates the benefit of abstracting HRSI to a qualitative description. It should be noted that while no rejection situations

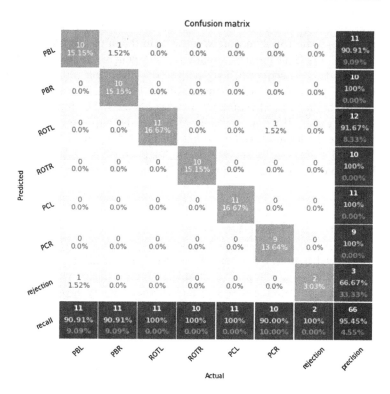

Fig. 4. Confusion matrix for validation of our multi-HMM classifier using QTC$_C$ sequences from study HRSIs as test data. (Color figure online)

were misclassified, the precision of rejections is relatively low at 66.67%. This could be due to the small number of RMSH interactions recorded in our study, as explained in Sect. 4.1, as 3-fold Cross-Validation using the training dataset with its 15 RMSH interactions showed much higher rejection precision at 78.95%. The classifier is much less likely to confuse any of the other 6 classes, with precision and recall >90% for all of these classes. We hope that we can improve the rejection precision and in turn the overall accuracy of our classifier by recording more examples of RMSH interactions and other rejection situations.

Our classifier is able to identify an interaction from a QTC sequence in less than 100 ms. Each QTC state in our system is obtained almost instantaneously given current robot and human positions, which means that the limiting factor in our pipeline is the human tracker module itself. The current tracker [5] has an average rate 25 Hz which sufficiently accounts for socially normative human behaviours and speeds, e.g. the mean human speed of 0.58 m/s and maximum robot speed of 0.91 m/s recorded in our study. The maximum human speed we recorded was 2.28 m/s, close to jogging speed, but these high speeds are not represented frequently in our study. When an interaction is not classified or is given the rejection class, a default constraint described in Sect. 3.5.1 of [7] is applied to ensure safe and comfortable human-robot distance at all times, and a safety laser stops the robot motors when within 0.5 m of the human.

We 'collapse' QTC sequences, removing consecutive repeats of states to account for variation in sequence length caused by varying temporal length of interactions. We plan to include a more robust tracker [15] capable of tracking humans at higher speeds, and we may consider QTC formulations that include speeds in their state description. We may also replace our HMMs with Continuous-Time Hidden Markov Models (CTHMMs) which better describe sequences where states are observed at irregular times [15]. All of these offer the possibility to extend our system to identify and react to non socially normative situations.

5 Conclusion and Future Work

We have presented here the framework used in the ILIAD Project to classify HRSI situation. If global planning is unable to create paths avoiding HRI, the classified situation will define how the intermediate safety layers will react in ILIAD. An efficient and accurate prediction will have a direct impact in the number of safety stops triggered by the lowest safety layer. Future work will evaluate the performance of this approach in the project's overall safety architecture.

The high accuracy of our multi-HMM HRSI situation classifier when tested on the HRSIs recorded in our experiment demonstrates its suitability for use in a situational HAN approach, with some room for improvement in the precision of rejection, which may be possible by taking the steps described in Sect. 4.2.

While this fully describes the applicability of our work in a qualitative HAN approach, we have not tested the systems in this paper with QTC_C sequences generated from partial interactions, needed to be applied to real-time robot navigation in the presence of humans. We will address this in future work, developing a continuous real-time implementation of our classifier that informs qualitative constraint of robot motion. The real-time HAN system should be tested on an industrial AMR in its ability to improve perceived safety and social legibility of robot movement in HRSI, while minimising safety-laser stops. For this real-time system, we aim to continuously classify the situation of a HRSI, making a new classification each time a QTC_C state is added to the sequence representing the interaction, and providing situational robot motion planner cost-maps enforcing a qualitative constraint of robot motion, i.e. [7], in order to improve perceived safety with socially normative movement, extending [3]. When multiple constraint cost-maps are to be applied simultaneously, the union of these is used to constrain the robot motion appropriately for simultaneous HRSIs with any number of humans.

For data to train the HMMs and validate this approach, we look to label and process trajectory pairs in larger datasets, then test in real-time on our robot in a real warehouse, interacting with human workers.

We hope to use the qualitative constraint cost-maps to communicate the robot's navigation intention, e.g. projecting on the floor in green on areas of high-cost, and red on areas of low-cost as conditioned symbols for 'go' and 'don't go'.

References

1. Cosgun, A., Sisbot, E.A., Christensen, H.I.: Anticipatory robot path planning in human environments. In: 2016 25th IEEE International Symposium on Robot and Human Interactive Communication (RO-MAN), pp. 562–569 (2016). https://doi.org/10.1109/ROMAN.2016.7745174
2. Dondrup, C., Bellotto, N., Hanheide, M.: A probabilistic model of human-robot spatial interaction using a qualitative trajectory calculus. In: AAAI Spring Symposium Series. AAAI, Palo Alto, California, USA (2014). https://www.aaai.org/ocs/index.php/SSS/SSS14/paper/view/7714
3. Dondrup, C., Hanheide, M.: Qualitative constraints for human-aware robot navigation using velocity costmaps. In: 2016 IEEE RO-MAN, pp. 586–592. IEEE, Piscataway, New Jersey, USA (2016). https://doi.org/10.1109/ROMAN.2016.7745177
4. Dondrup, C., et al.: A computational model of human-robot spatial interactions based on a qualitative trajectory calculus. Robotics **4**(1), 63 (2015). https://doi.org/10.3390/robotics4010063
5. Dondrup, C., et al.: Real-time multisensor people tracking for human-robot spatial interaction. ICRA/IEEE, Seattle, WA (2015). http://eprints.lincoln.ac.uk/id/eprint/17545/
6. Fernandez Carmona, M., Parekh, T., Hanheide, M.: Making the case for human-aware navigation in warehouses. In: Althoefer, K., Konstantinova, J., Zhang, K. (eds.) TAROS 2019. LNCS (LNAI), vol. 11650, pp. 449–453. Springer, Cham (2019). https://doi.org/10.1007/978-3-030-25332-5_38
7. Fernandez-Carmona, M., et al.: Report on human-robot spatial interaction and mutual communication of navigation intent. Technical report, ILIAD Project (2020). http://iliad-project.eu/wp-content/uploads/Deliverables/D3_3.pdf
8. Gatsoulis, Y., et al.: QSRlib: a software library for online acquisition of qualitative spatial relations from video. In: Qualitative Reasoning29th International Workshop on Qualitative Reasoning, pp. 36–41. IJCAI, California, USA (2016). https://ivi.fnwi.uva.nl/tcs/QRgroup/qr16/pdf/05Gatsoulis.pdf
9. Hall, E.T., et al.: Proxemics. Curr. Anthropol. **9**(2/3), 83–108 (1968). https://www.jstor.org/stable/2740724
10. Hanheide, M., Peters, A., Bellotto, N.: Analysis of human-robot spatial behaviour applying a qualitative trajectory calculus. In: 2012 IEEE RO-MAN, pp. 689–694. IEEE, Paris, France (2012). https://doi.org/10.1109/ROMAN.2012.6343831
11. ILIAD Project: ILIAD Project – An EU-funded research project on Intra-Logistics with Integrated Automatic Deployment for safe and scalable fleets in shared spaces (2020). http://iliad-project.eu/
12. Joyce, J.M.: Kullback-Leibler Divergence, pp. 720–722. Springer, Heidelberg (2011). https://doi.org/10.1007/978-3-642-04898-2_327
13. Kretzschmar, H., et al.: Socially compliant mobile robot navigation via inverse reinforcement learning. Int. J. Robot. Res. **35**(11), 1289–1307 (2016). https://doi.org/10.1177/0278364915619772

14. Kruse, T., et al.: Human-aware robot navigation: a survey. Robot. Auton. Syst. **61**(12), 1726–1743 (2013). https://doi.org/10.1016/j.robot.2013.05.007
15. Liu, Y.Y., et al.: Efficient learning of continuous-time Hidden Markov Models for disease progression. Adv. Neural Inf. Process. Sys. **28**, 3599–3607 (2015). https://www.ncbi.nlm.nih.gov/pmc/articles/PMC4804157/
16. Lu, D.V., Allan, D.B., Smart, W.D.: Tuning cost functions for social navigation. In: Herrmann, G., Pearson, M.J., Lenz, A., Bremner, P., Spiers, A., Leonards, U. (eds.) ICSR 2013. LNCS (LNAI), vol. 8239, pp. 442–451. Springer, Cham (2013). https://doi.org/10.1007/978-3-319-02675-6_44
17. Mavrogiannis, C.I., Knepper, R.A.: Multi-agent path topology in support of socially competent navigation planning. Int. J. Robot. Res. **38**(2–3), 338–356 (2019). https://doi.org/10.1177/0278364918781016
18. Vega, A., et al.: Socially aware robot navigation system in human-populated and interactive environments based on an adaptive spatial density function and space affordances. Pattern Recogn. Lett. **118**, 72–84 (2019). https://doi.org/10.1016/j.patrec.2018.07.015. Cooperative and Social Robots: Understanding Human Activities and Intentions
19. Vintr, T., et al.: Time-varying pedestrian flow models for service robots. In: 2019 European Conference on Mobile Robots (ECMR), pp. 1–7 (2019). https://doi.org/10.1109/ECMR.2019.8870909
20. Van de Weghe, N., Kuijpers, B., Bogaert, P., De Maeyer, P.: A qualitative trajectory calculus and the composition of its relations. In: Rodríguez, M.A., Cruz, I., Levashkin, S., Egenhofer, M.J. (eds.) GeoS 2005. LNCS, vol. 3799, pp. 60–76. Springer, Heidelberg (2005). https://doi.org/10.1007/11586180_5
21. White, A.M.: Sequence classification - with emphasis on Hidden Markov Models and sequence kernels (2009). http://www.cs.unc.edu/~lazebnik/fall09/sequence_classification.pdf

Tactile Feedback in a Tele-Operation Pick-and-Place Task Improves Perceived Workload

Thomas Baker$^{(\boxtimes)}$ and Matthias Rolf$^{(\boxtimes)}$

Oxford Brookes University, Oxford, UK
{18098352,mrolf}@brookes.ac.uk

Abstract. Robotic tele-operation systems have vast potential in areas ranging from surgical robotics and underwater exploration to disposing of toxic, explosive and nuclear materials. While visual camera feeds for the human operator are typically available and well studied, tactile sensory information is often vital for successful and efficient manipulation. Previous studies have largely focused on execution time alone as measure of success of feedback methods on individual tasks. The present study complements this by a comparative analysis of vibration and visual feedback of tactile information across a range of manipulation tasks. Results show a significant reduction in perceived workload with the implementation of vibration feedback and an improvement of error rates for visual feedback. Contrary to expectation, we did not find a reduction in task completion time. The negative finding on completion time challenges the belief that the mere existence of task-relevant feedback aids efficient task completion. The reduced workload, however, clearly points out potential for enhancing performance on more difficult and prolonged tasks with highly skilled operators.

Keywords: Tele-operation · Tactile feedback · User study · Humanoid

1 Introduction

Tele-operation robotic systems are often defined as "operation of a system or machine at a distance" [1]. Tele-operation allows for direct access to inaccessible and hazardous environments [2] such as handling and disposing of toxic [3], explosive [4] and nuclear [5] material, and during space [6] and underwater exploration [7]. A tele-operation system that provides the operator with sensory feedback is referred to as a 'human-in-loop' system, where sensory feedback collected in the remote environment is provided and acted upon remotely. This is often referred to under the umbrella term of 'haptic' feedback although can be categorised into two main groups; cutaneous (force) and kinesthetic (pressure or tactile) feedback. For a system to provide haptic feedback it must provide substantial information from both cutaneous and kinesthetic systems.

© Springer Nature Switzerland AG 2020
A. Mohammad et al. (Eds.): TAROS 2020, LNAI 12228, pp. 261–273, 2020.
https://doi.org/10.1007/978-3-030-63486-5_28

How sensory data is provided to the operator falls under three main subcategories; force, vibration and cue systems. Force feedback being the restriction of movement usually through a device featuring mechanical input [8]. Vibration feedback (or vibrotactile) is the use of vibration to replicate touch, interactions with environments and contact information to an operator [9]. Vibration feedback has been extensively developed for virtual reality applications, in turn reducing the cost of small vibration actuators and becoming increasingly accessible and more appealing for such remote applications. Cues systems are made up of two main subcategories; Auditory (AF) [6] and Visual systems (VF) [10], where direct haptic feedback is substituted for graphical or audio cues to portray information about the remote environment [7].

There is extensive research that looks into sensory feedback methods within tele-operation applications, with studies ranging from the impact of visual cue systems within space exploration [6] to vibration feedback within underwater tele-robotics [7], in which time of completion and specific metrics relating to the particular scenario remain the focus of the analysis. An example of such assessment methods can be seen in [11] where average completion times is the main focus of analysis within a tele-operated maze task, the paper then adds the additional assessment metric of success rate within the scope of stacking rings on a peg. [12] looked at the tele-operation system usability by implementing a System Usability Scale (SUS), which asked users to rate 10 questions on a 7 point likert scale ranging from "strongly disagree" to "strongly agree". The questions covered different aspects of the tele-operation system, such as complexity, consistency and cumbersomeness.

Although the majority of the studies detailed are complex, such as RMIS (Remote-Assisted Minimally Invasive Surgery), the specificity of the respective tasks allow very little conclusion about general tasks involving, for example, pick and place. Furthermore, few research studies look to assess the impact of tactile sensory feedback across multiple manipulation tasks within a predefined study layout, assessing impact of the tactile feedback methods on multiple metrics. Whilst the time of completion is important, it should not be the sole parameter to measure the impact of a feedback method on a tele-operation system.

1.1   Approach and Outline

This paper tackles the empirical issues of tactile feedback in tele-operation by assessing tele-operation across a variety of increasingly sophisticated pick-and-place tasks on the Baxter humanoid robot with 24 previously untrained participants. The study goes beyond previous empirical investigations by comparing two different methods of tactile feedback not just based on time-to-completion, but holistically through addition of error rates and perceived workload (NASA-TLX), and across tasks. NASA-TLX [13] is a widely used assessment tool that measures perceived workload of a particular task, gained by measuring the global workload across six subscales: mental demand, physical demand, temporal demand, effort, frustration and performance.

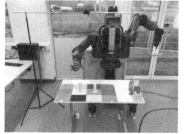

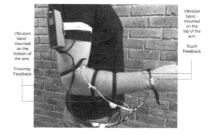

Robot   Camera feed with visualized sensors.

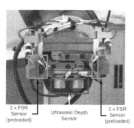

Sensor placement on robot gripper   Vibration band mounting

Fig. 1. Tele-operation system

The contribution of this paper are nuanced empirical findings that clearly challenge the dominating role of time measurement in current empirical methods: while finding no significant speed-up of task completion, both a reduced mental workload for vibro-tactile feedback and a reduced error-rate for visual feedback indicate possibly different usage scenarios and allow us to derive recommendations both for future practical applications as well as study designs. We describe our tele-operation system and feedback methods in Sect. 2, leading to the experimental design (Sect. 3) of three manipulation tasks. Results on time-to-completion, error rate, and workload are reported in Sect. 4. Possible limitations and implication or the results are discussed in Sect. 5 before giving recommendations and concluding remarks in Sect. 6.

2   Tele-Operation System

Rethink Robotics Baxter was used for the tele-operation task, a semi humanoid research robot that features a torso, 2 DOF head and two arms with 7 DOF joints, integrated camera, sonar sensors, torque sensors, collision avoidance and force sensing actuators (FSA) [14]. Due to the length of the arms, 104 cm from the shoulder joint to the end effector, Baxter is able to complete a range of tasks whilst maintaining accuracy and precision.

The key to an operator being able to see the environment they are tele-operating in is an efficient video feed (also known as a camera feed). A single camera was used and mounted above the remote environment. By only providing a single camera and in turn reducing the depth perception it was possible to ensure participants reliance on the feedback methods.

HTC Vive was used as the tracking solution for the tele-operation system, a requirement for the tele-operation system is having accurate position and orientation tracking of the operator. This system was implemented using openVR, an API that allows for the development of virtual reality applications and serves as an interface between the VR hardware and software. By using unofficial python bindings it was possible to gain access to functions such as controller position and orientation, button presses and advanced options such as haptic pulses. A previously developed ROS implementation by [15] was advanced upon to allow a Baxter teleoperation system that used the in built inverse kinematics functionally to provide the operator with accurate tele-operation.

Piezoresistive force sensing resistors (FSR's) were used on the inside of the gripper's two fingers (Fig. 1.c) for detecting contact with objects in manipulation due to their sensitivity level, accessibility and simple implementation. Although in order to gain useful information with regards to object interactions in a remote environment the 'onset' (or first contact) to such objects is imperative. 'Onset' refers to the small interactions that occur before grasping the object itself. The standard FSR sensor did not allow for this discrete sensory information. A simple design that uses tensioned rubber bands set on a rubber pad was developed, this allowed for information relating to discrete object interactions to be gained. While the FSR sensors allowed for sensory information in regards to contact surfaces and object interactions, there was no information in relation to the proximity within the remote environment, more specifically depth perception. Ultrasonic sensors (HY-SRF05 [16]) were chosen as an appropriate choice of sensor to combat the issue, ultrasonic sensors being an instrument that measure distance using ultrasonic waves. The ultrasonic sensor was mounted on the underside of the gripper (Fig. 1.c) to provide the operator with useful information in relation to the distances in the remote environment.

Several alternatives are available to feed the sensor readings back to the user, the two detailed within this study are vibration feedback and visual cues. A novel system was developed within this study consisting of vibration bands located at multiple locations on the operators arm. These vibration bands use a disc motor mounted on a metal plate, secured using an elastic nylon material around the arm. The metal plate acting to amplify the vibration by changing the axis of rotation of the disk motor. This novel approach was developed as issues were encountered with both the internal and external mounting of vibration motors on the Vive controllers themselves, the two main issue being intermittent haptic pulses being present on the Vive controller along with a large amount of drift within the tracking solution itself because of noise on the accelerometer and infra red tracking, due to externally mounted vibration motors.

The final implemented system mounts two of the vibration bands on the top of the operators arm and two on the underside, these corresponding to the sensory information from the touch sensors (gripper) and the proximity sensor (ultrasonic).

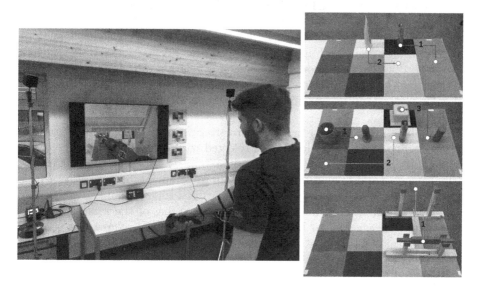

Fig. 2. (Left) User with controller in front of screen. (Right) Tasks 1–3 (from top): participants were asked to move the objects in a given order to a target tiles or place inside another structure (paths highlighted) by tele-operating Baxter.

3 Experimental Methodology

In order to get accurate and reliable results from the study it was imperative to have a clearly defined test scenario. A board with zoned areas was developed, allowing objects to be moved and manipulated within a measurable space allowing consistently same size areas. The tele-operation scenario was based on three individual tasks, that were designed to become increasingly challenging, starting with a very straight forward pick and place task, a slightly more advanced pick and place task on multiple levels, and ending on a complex parallel bar task requiring a high level of accuracy. Both platforms of the final parrellel bar task holding the bar in a semicircle, allowing the bar to rotate with a small force applied, in turn increasing the level of complexity. The tasks were required to be general, real would manipulation tasks, interacting with day to day objects. This allowed for no formal training as participants would not be undertaking a specific task with unfamiliar objects or unknown operations.

The three tasks were undertaken in a fixed order with each task being completed three times with the same feedback method. Due to this fixed task ordering along with three feedback method conditions (no feedback, visual feedback and vibration feedback) there were 6 permutations required in relation to feedback ordering. Participants were randomly assigned into one of the six permutations, and assignments counter-balanced. For example, exactly four participants would do task 1 with visual feedback, task 2 with no feedback, and task three with vibration feedback; exactly four others are assigned to the other five permutations of feedback methods. Undertaking the three tasks with feedback analysis took between an hour and an hour and a quarter per participant. This meant that the feedback systems could be assessed in relation to the multiple measurable metrics - completion time, error rate and perceived workload. Providing a greater understanding and insight of the impact the feedback methods have would be gained.

Task objects were varied in relation to size, weight, shape, surface material and appearance. Specific objects were selected with large amounts of deformation to add complexity. Task 1 (Fig. 2, right top) was the initial task for each participant to undertake; simply picking up and moving object objects from two specific areas. Task 2 (Fig. 2, right middle) was slightly more advanced and required a higher level of accuracy and understanding of the remote environment. A rubber egg had to be dropped into a container, requiring a sense of depth, and a pole place in a stand. Task 3 (Fig. 2, right bottom) was the most complex and challenging manipulation task that the study required. Participants were required to move a parallel bar from one platform to another, requiring a sense of depth for the initial grasping and fine control of orientation.

Following a full set of three runs on each task, the NASA-TLX (Task Load Index) [13] was used to analyse the perceived workload of each task and the impact of associated feedback method. The NASA-TLX is a widely used assessment tool that measures the perceived workload of a particular task [13]. This is gained by measuring the global workload across six subscales: mental demand, physical demand, temporal demand,effort, frustration and performance.

The study was made up of 24 participants (17 male, 7 female) with ages ranging from 21 to 62 (M $= 27.70$, SD $= 10.72$). 24 participants being investigated as it allowed for each permutation of feedback ordering to be balanced. Participants level of self-assessed technological competence was measured (between 0 and 100) varying between 35 and 95 (M $= 65.83$, SD $= 17.17$). Knowledge of robotics and tele-operation systems (also self assessed), measured between 0 and 100 and ranging from 5 and 90 (M $= 37.70$, SD $= 27.18$). The study used participants with mainly dominant right hands, with a split of right $= 18$, and left $= 4$.

4   Results

Results on the overall time to completion for each run of the three tasks are shown in Fig. 3. Median times are consistently lower for the third attempt of each task. A statistical sign test against the Null-hypothesis of equal medians confirms the significance of this finding (Task 1 p $= 0.064$, Task 2 p $= 0.023$, Task 3 p $= 0.015$). Contrary to the clearly pronounced learning curve, no significant difference are found between different feedback methods. A full breakdown for all tasks

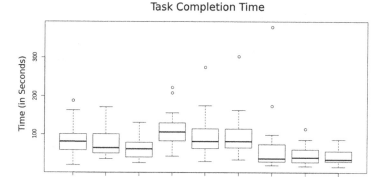

Fig. 3. Task completion times over tasks 1–3 with three runs each. A clear learning curve can be observed within each block of three, representing three consecutive runs on the same task.

and feedback methods is shown in Fig. 4. No consistent pattern emerges in terms of advantage of any feedback method. Existing numeric differences were found insignificant by t-tests for all feedback comparisons on all tasks.

Error rates from object knock-overs and object-drops where 1.88 per run for no-feedback, 1.22 for visual feedback, and 1.53 for vibration feedback. A t-test showed a significant margin ($p = 0.003$) between no-feedback and visual-feedback, but not vibration feedback ($p = 0.18$). The t-test, however, operates based on a Gaussian distribution assumption that was not confirmed valid on the data (Shapiro-Wilk test rejects Gaussian hypothesis with $p < 0.0001$). On the other hand, the parameter-free Kolmogrov-Smirnov test backs up the improvement from no-feedback to visual-feedback at least on trend-level ($p = 0.088$).

Significant findings are shown in relation to the perceived workload of the tele-operation task, with vibration significantly reducing the perceived workload across all tasks, in comparison to both no feedback and visual cue conditions (see Fig. 5). With 22 out of 24 participants demonstrating a lower perceived workload with the addition of vibration feedback compared to no feedback and 18 out of 24 participants demonstrating a lower perceived workload with the addition of vibration feedback compared to visual cues, showing significant findings with binomial test p values of 3.588e-05 for vibration feedback < no feedback and 0.02266 for vibration feedback < visual cues. No significant results presented in relation to visual cues reducing the perceived workload with the tele-operation task. More in depth analysis was undertaken looking into frustration levels, extracted from the NASA-TLX data. This showed no significant reduction in frustration levels with the addition of both tactile sensory feedback methods.

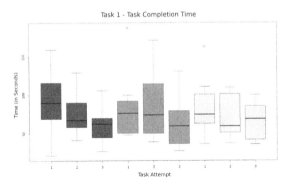

Completion times for Task 1 (three runs) depending on the feedback method.

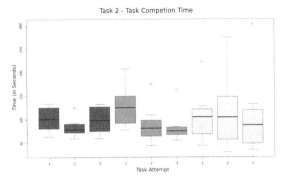

Completion times for Task 2 (three runs) depending on the feedback method.

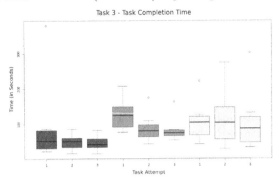

Completion times for Task 3 (three runs) depending on the feedback method.

Fig. 4. Completion times for all tasks with no feedback (red), visual feedback (green), and vibration feedback (yellow). No significant differences are found between feedback methods across tasks or within each task. (Color figure online)

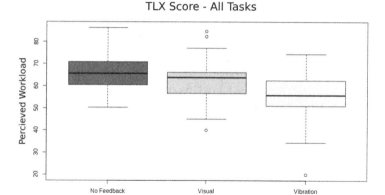

Fig. 5. Results from the NASA TLX perceived workload score for different feedback methods (across tasks). A significant reduction of perceived workload is found for vibration feedback.

5 Discussion

As is evident across all three tasks, neither the vibration feedback or visual cues have a positive impact on the overall completion time of tasks during tele-operation, this rejects the original hypothesis set out within the study. Although this finding is contrary to the hypothesis it is not an isolated case, studies such as [17] demonstrating similar results within a variation of tele-operation scenarios, providing the summary that the completion time between vibration feedback, stiffness feedback and no feedback was "statistically insignificant".

Regardless of this negative result in relation to the completion time, results present a learning effect within the tele-operation tasks. Across all tasks within the study it was found that participants were able to complete the tasks faster in their third attempt compared to their first attempt. This finding was investigated on the individual tasks; due to having a large amount of variance in the individual tasks, analysing the overall dataset was not possible. Two out of the three tasks investigated were considered to be significant findings with the final being a marginal, from this it is possible to conclude that there is a learning curve to the tele-operation scenarios and that the original hypothesis relating to this is correct. This finding also serves as validation of our general experimental procedure by demonstrating consistency of time measurement in relation to task performance. Hence, the lack of difference between feedback condition seems genuine, rather than being a potential artifact from flawed methodology.

Results analysis shows no significant findings in relation to the reduction in error rate across all tasks with the addition of vibration feedback. The analysis of error rates for visual cues is more intricate, as the parameterless test gives borderline significance, and the t-test must be considered inconclusive despite low p value due to the non-valid Gaussian assumption. While not fully conclusive, we believe that the difference found warrants attention and should be further investigated. A possible accuracy benefit from visual feedback to explain the observed gain could be the higher temporal resolution of peripheral vision, where the feedback is observed, compared to the temporal accuracy of sensing the onset vibration, which itself has a temporal extent.

The most important finding within this research study is the effect vibration feedback has on reducing the overall perceived workload of a task. By using NASA-TLX [13] it was possible to analyse the individual tasks within the tele-operation study in relation to perceived workload. By implementing this over all 24 participants and across 72 tasks with the related feedback method, it is possible to cover all permutations of the study and in turn gain an understanding of the impact vibration feedback and visual cues have on a tele-operation task as a whole. From this analysis it is possible to confirm that vibration feedback significantly reduces the perceived workload of a tele-operation task, compared to no feedback, and more interestingly, compared to visual cues. Both findings presenting a significant result during analysis. This finding is important as it allows an understanding of the subtle impacts of such tactile sensory feedback and the positive influence that can be gained from the integration of sensory feedback systems. A plausible explanation for this finding could be a more efficient usage of attentional resources in the case of cross-modal cues [18], but which are still very incompletely understood for complex task performance [19]. Across the study there are limitations that could effect the strength of the results. The main limitation is that the study only addressed the early stages of previously untrained participants' learning process. Furthermore, each task was short and only run three times after an initial three minute familiarization.

A relevant alternative feedback method that was not addressed in this study concerns more directly mapped vibration feedback, with the sensor system being based on the gripper and the vibration system being mounted on the operators arm or hand (not a entirely natural sensation to feel extensive vibration in that area). If a system was to feature a direct mapping, for example a humanoid based robotic hand with a control glove there may be clearer results in relation to time of completion and error rate. Additionally the study used a static approach across all the tasks, with certain environmental variables remaining across the three tasks. These included the height of the table, the distance of the robot and the camera position. Keeping these throughout the tasks could allow for participants to gain familiarity with the environment and reduce the reliance on the feedback methods. Changing the environment dynamically could allow for further feedback effects.

Although the participant size was limited at 24, this study serves to highlight the effects of tactile feedback methods within a bilateral teleoperation scenario. The significant results and findings relating to the reduced perceived workload demonstrate that this study had sufficient power and that at least major differences in time to completion would have been detected if present. It can be speculated that the time of completion results may change with the increase of participant size, although there would be an expectation to see a level of consistency in the current results within a smaller dataset, similar to the reduced workload with the integration of vibration feedback.

6 Recommendations and Conclusions

This paper presents the development of a tele-operation system with tactile sensing, and novel vibration or visual feedback. A study environment is developed to measure the impact of the tactile sensory feedback methods on multiple metrics with manipulation tasks. Results showing a significant reduction in perceived workload with the integration of vibration feedback, along with no finding relating to a reduction in task completion time and error rate. Based on the findings we are able to make the following recommendations. Due to results presenting a significant reduction in perceived workload with the addition of vibration feedback, we are able to make the recommendation of vibration feedback for use within tele-operation tasks that naturally require a high level of concentration or prolonged tasks.

The tasks undertaken within this study were relatively short, with task time ranging from 15.9 s–302.6 s. By developing a further study that incorporates prolonged tasks could reflect an increased reduction in the overall workload of a task with the addition of vibration feedback. Furthermore, the study was made up of 20 out of 24 participants with no prior experience with tele-operation systems or robotics, by undertaking a similar study with experienced individuals there would be an assumed reduction in competition time, error rate and perceived workload. Prolonging the tele-operation tasks would allow for more in depth analysis of the impact of the tactile feedback systems on skilled performance rather than ongoing learning.

Although only partially statistically conclusive, the addition of visual cues showed a reduction in the error rate across all three tasks. From this we can recommend the use of visual feedback for tele-operation tasks that require a high level of accuracy. Future studies should investigate how the reduction in error rate can be translated into faster completion. Due to the inconclusive nature of vibration feedback relating to error rates, further studies should keep investigating both feedback methods. Further efforts should be made to investigate the role of cross-modal attention [19] in relation to the observed gains.

Most importantly, the results of this study highlight the need for broad assessment criteria within the evaluation of the tactile sensory feedback methods and the impact on tele-operation manipulation scenarios. The impact of feedback methods in tele-operation should not be investigated solely in terms of time of completion. Although for specific tasks, particular metrics should be analysed, the study highlights the need for a broader assessment. This study has utilized perceived workload and error rates alongside completion time, which has allowed to uncover much more subtle implications of feedback than time alone.

References

1. Liu, Y.: Semi-autonomous control of multi-robot teams in urban search and rescue applications. Ph.D. thesis (2019)
2. Fritsche, L., Unverzag, F., Peters, J., Calandra, R.: First-person tele-operation of a humanoid robot. In: 2015 IEEE-RAS 15th International Conference on Humanoid Robots (Humanoids), pp. 997–1002. IEEE (2015)
3. Book, W.J., Love, L.J., Farah, M.: A teleoperation testbed for nuclear waste restoration. Georgia Institute of Technology (1994)
4. Ryu, D., Hwang, C.-S., Kang, S., Kim, M., Song, J.-B.: Wearable haptic-based multi-modal teleoperation of field mobile manipulator for explosive ordnance disposal. In: IEEE International Safety, Security and Rescue Rototics, Workshop, 2005, pp. 75–80. IEEE (2005)
5. Kim, S., Kim, C.H., Seo, Y.C., Jung, S.H., Lee, G.S., Han, B.S.: Development of tele-operated mobile robot in nuclear power plants. IFAC Proc. Vol. **34**(4), 239–244 (2001)
6. Nagai, Y., Tsuchiya, S., Iida, T., Kimura, S.: Audio feedback system for teleoperation experiments on engineering test satellite vii system design and assessment using eye mark recorder for capturing task. IEEE Trans. Syst. Man Cybern. Part A Syst. Hum. **32**(2), 237–247 (2002)
7. Dennerlein, J., Howe, R., Shahoian, E., Olroyd, C.: Vibrotactile feedback for an underwater telerobot. In: 8th Robotics and Applications, Robotic and Manufacturing Systems Recent Results in Research, Development and Applications International symposium, pp. 244–249. Citeseer (2000)
8. Hayward, V., Astley, O.R., Cruz-Hernandez, M., Grant, D., Robles-De-La-Torre, G.: Haptic interfaces and devices. Sensor review (2004)
9. De Barros, P.G., Lindeman, R.W., Ward, M.O.: Enhancing robot teleoperator situation awareness and performance using vibro-tactile and graphical feedback. In: 2011 IEEE Symposium on 3D User Interfaces (3DUI), pp. 47–54. IEEE (2011)
10. Okamura, A.M.: Haptic feedback in robot-assisted minimally invasive surgery. Curr. Opin. Urol. **19**(1), 102 (2009)
11. Alex, M.M.: Evaluating the effects of haptic and visual feedback on the teleoperation of remote robots
12. Whitney, D., Rosen, E., Phillips, E., Konidaris, G., Tellex, S.: Comparing robot grasping teleoperation across desktop and virtual reality with ROS reality. In: Robotics Research, pp. 335–350. Springer, Cham (2020)
13. N.H.P.R. Group et al.: Task load index (NASA-TLX) v1. 0 computerised version. NASA Ames Research Centre (1987)
14. Reddivari, H., Yang, C., Ju, Z., Liang, P., Li, Z., Xu, B.: Teleoperation control of baxter robot using body motion tracking. In: 2014 International Conference on Multisensor Fusion and Information Integration for Intelligent Systems (MFI), pp. 1–6. IEEE (2014)
15. Pfeiffer, S.: Vive teleop stuff (2018). GitHub: https://github.com/uts-magic-lab/htc_vive_teleop_stuff
16. Hy-srf05: Srf05 technical documentation. https://www.robot-electronics.co.uk/htm/srf05tech.htm
17. Casqueiro, A., Ruivo, D., Moutinho, A., Martins, J.: Improving teleoperation with vibration force feedback and anti-collision methods. In: Robot 2015: Second Iberian Robotics Conference, pp. 269–281. Springer, Cham (2016)

18. Driver, J., Spence, C.: Cross-modal links in spatial attention. Philos. Trans. R. Soc. Lond. Ser. B Biol. Sci. **353**(1373), 1319–1331 (1998)
19. Ferris, T.K., Sarter, N.B.: Cross-modal links among vision, audition, and touch in complex environments. Hum. Factors **50**(1), 17–26 (2008)

Touch It, Rub It, Feel It! Haptic Rendering of Physical Textures with a Low Cost Wearable System

Burathat Junput[(✉)], Ildar Farkhatdinov[(✉)], and Lorenzo Jamone[(✉)]

ARQ (Advanced Robotics at Queen Mary), School of Electronic Engineering and Computer Science, Queen Mary University of London, London, UK
{b.junput,l.jamone}@se15.qmul.ac.uk, i.farkhatdinov@qmul.ac.uk

Abstract. Information about the texture of an object's surface is crucial for its recognition and robust manipulation. During robotic teleoperation or interaction with a Virtual Reality, is important to feedback such information to the human user. However, most available solutions for haptic feedback are expensive and/or cumbersome. In this paper we propose a low cost and wearable system that allows users to feel the texture of physical objects by virtually rubbing them. Our main contributions are: i) a system for encoding a virtual representation of the texture of physical materials; ii) a system to haptically render such virtual representation on the user fingertips; iii) an experimental validation of the combined system in a object recognition task. We show that users can successfully recognize physical objects with different textures by virtually rubbing their surfaces using the proposed system.

1 Introduction

Haptic feedback is crucial for efficient robotic teleoperation [1]. Hence, wearable haptic devices can be beneficial for object manipulation in telerobotics and virtual reality (VR) [2,3]. However, high quality haptic rendering devices can be expensive because they use costly recoil-type transducers [4,5], require advanced control because of complex design [6,7] or have limited capabilities to produce tactile feedback [8]. Therefore it is still challenging to provide realistic haptic feedback related to material properties (textures) to the fingertips. Several haptic rendering approaches for displaying textures with inexpensive vibration actuators were developed previously. Most of the interfaces which use inexpensive vibration actuators, do not apply the feedback directly to the fingertips as it would be if someone were to touch and feel an object. Instead they provide feedback represented as vibrations through a tool traversing across the surface (scanning) of a material. For example most approaches render texture as the vibrations of pen-like object as it scans across a materials surface [12–14]. This

This work is partially supported by the EPSRC UK (projects MAN^3, EP/S00453X/1, and NCNR, EP/R02572X/1).

© Springer Nature Switzerland AG 2020
A. Mohammad et al. (Eds.): TAROS 2020, LNAI 12228, pp. 274–286, 2020.
https://doi.org/10.1007/978-3-030-63486-5_29

however does not fully represent the feeling a user would have if they were to scan a material with their own finger. When an object is used to physically scan a surface with a certain texture, vibrations propagate and are felt through the object: this is true both for an object held by a human [9] and for a sensor held by a robot [10,11]. More specifically: a textured surface is made up of peaks and dips. When an object goes over a peak or falls into a dip, an acceleration pulse is generated. A negative pulse when the tool falls into a dip and a positive pulse when the tool goes over a peak [12]. Using this knowledge many researchers have used a pen-like tool with accelerometers attached to them to scan textured surfaces and record the acceleration data generated [9,12–14].

In this paper we experimentally demonstrate that an inexpensive haptic rendering technique can be efficiently used to display information about the texture of various physical materials, such as cloth and wood: this can be very important in applications such as remote exploration of unknown environments with a robot (i.e. telerobotics), or Virtual Reality for immersive game experience. Our main contributions are: i) the development of a system for recording relevant data from physical materials, to create a virtual representation of their texture; ii) a system to haptically render such virtual representation on the user fingertips by using a combination of affordable and easy to retrieve commercial components, i.e. a Vibe motor and a Leap Motion controller; iii) an experimental validation of the proposed system with human participants, that shows how different material of everyday use can be recognized by relying on the haptic feedback alone.

Although haptic feedback has been a subject of research for many years, its application in wearable technology has been only recently been an area of interest. The application of haptic feedback in wearable technology is an interesting form of communication for human-machine interactions [2]. These new forms of tactile interfaces create possibilities to more closely simulate tactile interactions directly to the skin in virtual reality [18].

Material rendering via haptic feedback in wearable technology is a small but growing area of research. Through wearing these devices the feeling of a materials shape can be simulated through electro-vibration actuators, which are used to render contact and sliding of a virtual surface [19]. Stiffness of virtual objects can be simulated via normal pressure and lateral forces generated from a tactile interface [20]. Combining both mechanical and electrical stimulation onto the finger tip can also be used to render material shapes and roughness [21]. The most concerning issue with these aforementioned methods is that the equipment is incredibly cumbersome to wear and thus prolonged periods of use would leave users fatigued.

A tool traversing across the surface of a texture generates an acceleration pulse when it traverses a peak or falls into a dip. Pulses can be modelled as decaying sinusoids [27]; Guruswamy et al. [12] were able to create a method for synthesising vibrations using Infinite Impulse Response (IIR) filters to output decaying sinusoids. The filters are used to represent peaks/dips in the texture where an output occurs when an object crosses over the filter. By first finding the vibration profiles of textures using a pen-tool with an accelerometer attached to it, the data can be segmented to find points of decaying sinusoids and amplitude, decay rate and frequency of the wave form can be obtained. Unfortunately the method for using IIR filter was not applied to this work as the data glove is not capable of rendering the high frequencies which the actuator presented in the referenced papers. Though this method was not carried forward the ideas presented were. The best choice going forward was to manually create pulses rather than synthesising a corresponding pulse for an input. From this the displacement, period and frequency of the pulses were required to be found.

Culbertson et al. [13,14] utilise the Discrete Fourier Transform 321 method (DFT321) to reduce the 3 axis into 1 axis which retains the total spectral density of all the axis, this is important as the human perception of vibrations is reliant on the signals spectral content [15]. Therefore when the acceleration dimensions are reduced it should have the same spectrum as the recorded signals. At each frequency of a 1-D vibration, there should be the same energy as the sum of the 3 original axis at the same frequencies. Finally, the transform should be capable of preserving the total Energy Spectral Density (ESD) of the original signal [28]. Culbertson et al. found that this method was imperative to developing a realistic texture.

2 Method for Haptic Rendering of Materials

This section will detail the two systems which were developed: a recording system for obtaining acceleration-profiles of materials and a synthesis system for generating a vibrotactile feedback system which resembles the acceleration-profile of materials. Five common household materials were chosen for recording: rubber mat, wood, cloth, cardboard and paper. The experimental procedure required users to have familiarity with given materials. Theses materials had regular patterned textures (as opposed to stochastic) allowing for an easier process during segmentation of data.

Recording System. From the literature review it was necessary to decide the object which would scan the materials. Since the vibration actuator (vibe motor) on the data glove would be replicating vibrations on the fingertip it was chosen as the scanning object. An Adafruit LSM9DS0 Flora, was used to measure the acceleration of the vibrations in the X, Y and Z planes. Attaching the Flora to the data glove would mean that the compliance of the glove could affect readings thus a special component was 3D printed to hold the Flora in addition to attaching it to the vibe motor. Via ROS framework, the Flora published the 3 axis which were recorded and processed through Matlab to find the displacement of peaks/dips, frequency of pulses and period of pulses for corresponding textures. The DFT321 was used for analysis. The equation which was proposed in [28]s:

$$|\tilde{A}_s(f)| = \sqrt{|\tilde{A}_x(f)|^2 + |\tilde{A}_y(f)|^2 + |\tilde{A}_z(f)|^2} \tag{1}$$

where $\tilde{A}_x(f)$, $\tilde{A}_y(f)$ and $\tilde{A}_z(f)$ are the fourier transform of the original x, y and z axis signals and $\tilde{A}_s(f)$ is the square rooted sum of the squared fourier transforms. To obtain the transformed time domain signal Eq. 2 is multiplied by the square root of $e^{j\theta_f^{max}}$ where j $= \sqrt{-1}$ and θ_f^{max} is defined as:

$$\theta_f^{max} = \angle \sum_{i=1}^{3} \tilde{A}_i \qquad (2)$$

The resultant of the multiplication then undergoes inverse DFT. Through Parseval's theorem the end result must have the summed energy of the 3 axis signals.

Synthesis System. The method for synthesising the texture would be to have set positions of the peaks/dips, when the user touches the object the lower frequency of the texture is output via the corresponding vibe motor PWM level. When the users finger goes over a peak the corresponding PWM level for the higher frequency is output to the vibe motor for the period found. The leap motion was used to track the position of the data glove (seen in Fig. 1) in 3D space. Using the ROS framework to publish the position of the finger tip to a topic, a processing node was created to send the correct PWM levels to the vibe motor (seen in Fig. 1b). The displacements of the peaks/dips were mapped along the y axis at regular intervals and the processing node would trigger a frequency change when the users fingertip went over a peak/dip.

Data glove with one vibe motor and one LilyPad Arduino board, electrically connected to each other using conductive thread.

The vibe motor. A cheap vibrating actuator with a custom board for wearable devices.

Fig. 1. The components of the data glove.

3 Experimental Validation

Apparatus. The equipment which was used for this research was a cheap wearable data glove [17] developed at the Advanced Robotics lab (ARQ) of the Queen Mary University of London. The data glove is made up of commercially available products. The vibration actuator, the vibe motor, operates via PWM where the level of PWM would determine the frequency of the output. In previous work [17] we found that frequency of the vibe motor was distinguishable at 5 levels: 0,

140, 170, 200, 230. It was also found that users had difficulty in determining the level of feedback when there were more than 3 motors operating. In this paper we use the same data glove, but with only 1 vibe motor, acting on the index finger of the right hand.

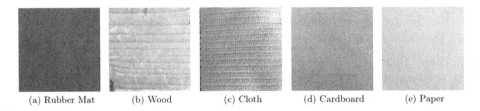

| (a) Rubber Mat | (b) Wood | (c) Cloth | (d) Cardboard | (e) Paper |

Fig. 2. The materials chosen for the experiment. In order of roughness. It was important to choose materials which would be common in a household so that participants would have some idea on how they would feel.

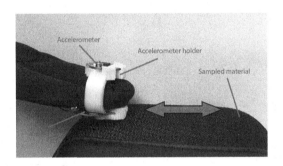

Fig. 3. Recording procedure: the accelerometer is rigidly attached to the vibe motor on the data glove, and the finger moves back and forth applying pressure on the material. The finger moves a set distance for a set amount of time, keeping the velocity constant.

The materials which were sampled are visually shown in Fig. 2. The method for recording data was to move the vibe motor over the surface of an object back and forth, twice, at a regular speed and along the same axis (see Fig. 3).

For obtaining the displacement, period and frequency changes of the peaks, the data was processed through Matlab. The DFT321 was used to transform the 3 axis into 1 axis for analysis purposes (which allows to maintain the important haptic information, see [28]); the acceleration-time profile of the materials were obtained from this transformed data. By segmenting the data into points of decaying sinusoids, the period of pulses can be obtained from the acceleration-time profile of recorded data. The displacement was obtained via the omega arithmetic method [29], in which the acceleration-displacement profile was obtained and the points between decaying sinusoids were the displacements between the peaks/dips of the materials. Finally, the frequencies of the PWM levels of the vibe motor and the materials were obtained through frequency analysis. For Vibe Motor frequency levels 140, 170, 200 and 230, the corresponding frequency component were found to be 38, 24, 15 9 Hz respectively. The materials had two observable spikes at specific frequencies. It was assumed that the lower frequency was the frequency during scanning between peaks/dips and the higher frequency was the frequency when the vibe motor went over peaks or fell into dips. An example of the acceleration-time, acceleration-displacement and frequency spectrum can be seen in Fig. 4a, Fig. 4b and Fig. 4c.

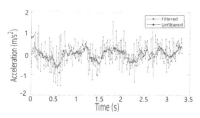

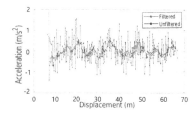

Acceleration-time profile of the rubber mat. The period of the peaks is found by measuring the period of decaying sinusoids in the acceleration-time profile.

Acceleration-displacement of the rubbermat. The displacement between peaks is found by measuring the distance between decaying sinusoids in the acceleration-displacement profile.

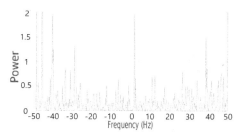

Frequency spectrum of the rubbermat. There are two observable spikes: the frequency between peaks/dips (at lower frequencies) and the frequency when traversing a peak/dip (at higher frequencies).

Fig. 4. The 3 profiles found for the rubber mat. Each material has its own 3 profiles.

The results of the material recordings can be seen in Table 1. The frequencies of the PWM levels were then mapped to match the texture frequencies which can be seen in the last column of Table 1. It should be noted that there were some texture frequency levels which lay outside the frequency rendering range of the vibe motor so certain mappings had to be scaled in an attempt to encompass all the frequency levels.

Table 1. The observed results from the profiles.

Material	Displacement between peaks (mm)	Frequency pulse (Hz)	Period (s)	Initial frequency-> pulse frequency
Rubber Mat	0.5	1.2<->39	0.2	140->230
Wood	2.5	1.2<->37	0.3	170->230
Cloth	2	0.8<->49	0.18	170->230
Cardboard	1.2	19<->34	0.1	170->200
Paper	0.5	8<->16	0.15	200->230

Protocol. A user study was conducted to determine how similar the synthesised textures were to the real texture. Our study was composed of three experiments, henceforth known as phases: phase 1, phase 2 and phase 3. All three phases were conducted on participants in order of phase 1, phase 2 and phase 3. Participants were provided with a random synthesised texture from the 5 available and were asked which texture they thought it was. Repeated 20 times for each phase.

- **Phase 1** the participant could only visually see which textures were available which would evaluate their preconceived judgements on what the materials should feel like.
- **Phase 2** involved the participant feeling the texture directly so they could update their understanding of how the texture feels before going through the 20 repetitions.
- **Phase 3** involved a teaching period where the participant would know what the corresponding synthesised textures are before going through the 20 repetitions again.

In addition to comparing whether the participant could correctly identify which material it was, they were also judged on how closely they were to identifying the material via a point system. The participant received points from 0 to 4 based on how numerically distant the perceived textures were to the one provided. The textures cloth, wood, cloth, cardboard and paper were numbered 0 to 4 respectively, in order of their roughness. If participants correctly judged a texture they received 4 points. If the numerical distance between the textures was 1 (e.g. perceived texture = 0 and provided texture = 1) they would receive 3 points and this pattern continues until numerical distance of 4 is equivalent to 0 points. This accuracy will be referred to as the texture accuracy which measures the accuracy of the participants perception and should not be confused with judgement accuracy.

Twelve participants were involved (incl. 2 female, ages 18–54). We discarded the data obtained from two of the participants as they did not correctly understand the task.

4   Results

The results in Fig. 5 show overall that judgement accuracy of the users increased as the test went on. Phase 2 and 3 have incrementally better phases where phase 3 was almost double the judgement accuracy of phase 1. Significant differences between each phase was confirmed using the one-way ANOVA, where a type 1 error of 0.05 was used. The F-ratio between the three phases was found to be 13.19 and an F-critical of 3.01. Since the F-ratio was greater than 3.01 a significant difference between all three phases was present in the results.

The increase from phase 1 to phase 2 could be explained by the participants having varying preconceived judgements of how a texture feels in phase 1 leading to mixed results seen in Fig. 5. The increase in accuracy level between 1 and 2 shows that updating the users mental image of the texture helps them to distinguish the different synthesised textures. This was confirmed via a z-test between phase 1 and 2. Using a type 1 error of 0.05, a critical range of ± 1.96 is found. The z-test produced a z-value of -2.37 and since is outside of the critical range the null hypothesis is rejected and there is significant difference between the average values of phase 1 and 2. It should be noted that the mental process behind phase 3 might be different from the other two phases, which built upon the mental image of textures. Phase 3 might include an associative learning component, in which the participant tries to recall objective information (can they remember and distinguish which synthesised texture they are feeling). This is unlike the other two phases which are reliant on subjective information (what texture does the participant believe they are feeling). In addition to this there may have been a *learning effect* present throughout the test which could be an alternate explanation for the overall increasing judgement accuracy. Although the impact of this theory is also mitigated by the idea that the participants may be fatigued or less-engaged with the test as it progressed. Figure 6 displays the results for the individual participants, showing that all of them improve their level of accuracy from phase 1 to phase 3. Figure 7 shows the results on each material. The texture which was the most easily recognisable across all participants was the cloth, most likely due to the large displacement between peaks allowing participants to more readily distinguish when a frequency change occurs. Additionally it was also found that some of the textures had frequencies which were outside the rendering range of the vibe motors which meant that some textures were not well represented. Overall it can be seen that the phases display results which are greater than chance (the probability that the user would be able to guess which of the five textures they were provided). Although for phase 1 this is still only slightly above the chance line. The highest overall judgement accuracy is seen in phase 3 displayed in Fig. 5 which is 0.5 or 50% accurate.

Figure 8 displays the texture accuracy of the participants using the points score. The chance line for each point varies due to the proximity of textures having different point probabilities. For instance if texture 2 was chosen, it is impossible for the participant to obtain a point value of 0 or 1. The chance line details the probability of the participant obtaining a particular point. The probability that a participant will obtain a score of 0 is the lowest, subsequent scores increase in probability until a score of 4 which is less likely than a score of 3. From Fig. 8 it can be seen that in phase 1, the average of the points very much follows the trend of the chance line, where the average score increase until after 3 where it drops down. It is interesting to note that a score of 0 is well below chance and that a score of 3 is much higher than chance. Thus it can be concluded that even if a participant does not identify the correct texture, they still manage to ascertain a texture which is similar in roughness to the given texture.

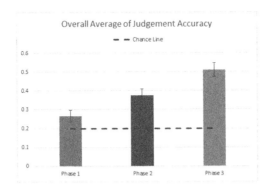

Fig. 5. Average judgement accuracy over all participants and all materials, during each phase.

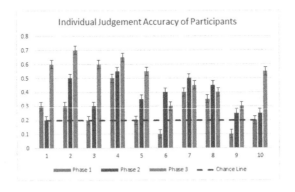

Fig. 6. Average judgement accuracy of each participant, over all materials, during each phase.

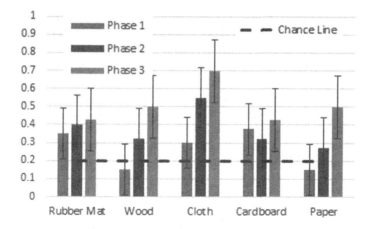

Fig. 7. Average judgement accuracy over all participants, for each texture and for each phase.

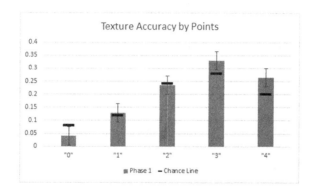

Fig. 8. Average point score (4 is best, 0 is worst) over all participants and for all materials, during phase 1. Score 4 (perfectly correct answer) and score 3 (almost correct answer) are more likely than chance; score 0 (very wrong answer) is less likely than chance.

5   Conclusions

We presented a system for i) recording the vibration pattern associated to the texture of a physical material, and ii) rendering such pattern of vibrations on a human fingertip, to provide haptic feedback about the surface of physical materials. Previous work with the data glove focused on objects stiffness, a general property of materials, whereas the work we present focuses on the texture, an intrinsic property uniquely varying between materials. Notably, the rendering system is composed of cheap and easy to retrieve off-the-shelf components, making this solution easy to reproduce for any researcher, and easy to deploy in practical applications. The recording system would be also easy to reproduce, as we use a common accelerometer and we make publicly available the design of the 3D printed component used for connecting the accelerometer to the glove, as well as all the software code needed for replicating the experiments and for using the system (https://github.com/burajunput/texture-data-glove). Overall, we show experimentally that this affordable system can be used to provide a realistic haptic feeling about the texture of physical materials. To a certain extent, participants can recognize different materials solely based on the haptic feedback and on their intuition about how a material should feel like, based on their previous knowledge of those materials; this ability is reinforced when participants are provided with some initial training with the materials, either by physically touching them or by touching them while receiving the corresponding haptic feedback. Some materials proved to be easier to recognise, e.g. cloth, probably due to the more distinct displacement between their peaks and overall frequency changes. In conclusion, although vibrating motors of better quality could definitely improve the performance of the system, our results suggest that this affordable solution could be used in a range of practical applications.

References

1. Stone, R.J.: Haptic feedback: a brief history from telepresence to virtual reality. In: Brewster, S., Murray-Smith, R. (eds.) Haptic HCI 2000. LNCS, vol. 2058, pp. 1–16. Springer, Heidelberg (2001). https://doi.org/10.1007/3-540-44589-7_1
2. Pacchierotti, C., Sinclair, S., Solazzi, M., Frisoli, A., Hayward, V., Prattichizzo, D.: Wearable haptic systems for the fingertip and the hand: taxonomy, review, and perspectives. IEEE Trans. Haptics 10(4), 580–600 (2017)
3. Ogrinc, M., Farkhatdinov, I., Walker, R., Burdet, E.: Sensory integration of apparent motion speed and vibration magnitude. IEEE Trans. Haptics 11(3), 455–463 (2017)
4. Yao, H.Y., Hayward, V.: Design and analysis of a recoil-type vibrotactile transducer. J. Acoust. Soc. Am. 128(2), 619–627 (2010)
5. Duvernoy, B., Farkhatdinov, I., Topp, S., Hayward, V.: Electromagnetic actuator for tactile communication. In: Prattichizzo, D., Shinoda, H., Tan, H.Z., Ruffaldi, E., Frisoli, A. (eds.) EuroHaptics 2018. LNCS, vol. 10894, pp. 14–24. Springer, Cham (2018). https://doi.org/10.1007/978-3-319-93399-3_2
6. Pacchierotti, C., Young, E.M., Kuchenbecker, K.J.: Task-driven PCA-based design optimization of wearable cutaneous devices. IEEE Robot. Autom. Lett. 3(3), 2214–2221 (2018)
7. Brown, J.P., Farkhatdinov, I.: Soft haptic interface based on vibration and particle jamming. In: 2020 IEEE Haptics Symposium (HAPTICS), 28 March 2020
8. Popov, D., Gaponov, I., Ryu, J.H.: Portable exoskeleton glove with soft structure for hand assistance in activities of daily living. IEEE/ASME Trans. Mechatron. 22(2), 865–875 (2016)
9. Romano, J.M., Yoshioka, T., Kuchenbecker, K.J.: Automatic filter design for synthesis of haptic textures from recorded acceleration data. In: 2010 IEEE International Conference on Robotics and Automation, pp. 1815–1821, May 2010
10. Palermo, F., Konstantinova, J., Althoefer, K., Poslad, S., Farkhatdinov, I.: Implementing tactile and proximity sensing for crack detection. In: IEEE International Conference on Robotics and Automation, ICRA (2020)

11. Ribeiro, P., Cardoso, S., Bernardino, A., Jamone, L.: Highly sensitive bio-inspired sensor for fine surface exploration and characterization. In: IEEE International Conference on Robotics and Automation, ICRA (2020)

12. Guruswamy, V.L., Lang, J., Lee, W.-S.: Modelling of haptic vibration textures with infinite-impulse-response filters, pp. 105–110, December 2009

13. Culbertson, H., Unwin, J., Kuchenbecker, K.J.: Modeling and rendering realistic textures from unconstrained tool-surface interactions. IEEE Trans. Haptics **7**(3), 381–393 (2014)

14. Culbertson, H., Unwin, H., Goodman, B., Kuchenbecker, K.: Generating haptic texture models from unconstrained tool-surface interactions, pp. 295–300, April 2013

15. Bensmaia, S., Hollins, M., Yau, J.: Vibrotactile intensity and frequency information in the Pacinian system: a psychophysical model. Percept. Psychophys. **67**, 828–841 (2005)

16. Stevens, S.S.: Tactile vibration: dynamics of sensory intensity. J. Exp. Psychol. **57**(4), 210–218 (1959)

17. Junput, B., Wei, X., Jamone, L.: Feel it on your fingers: dataglove with vibrotactile feedback for virtual reality and telerobotics. In: Althoefer, K., Konstantinova, J., Zhang, K. (eds.) TAROS 2019. LNCS (LNAI), vol. 11649, pp. 375–385. Springer, Cham (2019). https://doi.org/10.1007/978-3-030-23807-0_31

18. Perez, A.G., et al.: Optimization-based wearable tactile rendering. IEEE Trans. Haptics **10**(2), 254–264 (2017)

19. Gabardi, M., Solazzi, M., Leonardis, D., Frisoli, A.: A new wearable fingertip haptic interface for the rendering of virtual shapes and surface features. In: 2016 IEEE Haptics Symposium (HAPTICS), pp. 140–146 (2016)

20. Chinello, F., Pacchierotti, C., Malvezzi, M., Prattichizzo, D.: A three revolute-revolute-spherical wearable fingertip cutaneous device for stiffness rendering. IEEE Trans. Haptics **11**(1), 39–50 (2018)

21. Yem, V., Kajimoto, H.: Wearable tactile device using mechanical and electrical stimulation for fingertip interaction with virtual world. In: 2017 IEEE Virtual Reality (VR), pp. 99–104 (2017)

22. Bolanowski, S.J., Gescheider, G., Verrillo, R.T., Checkosky, C.M.: Four channels mediate the mechanical aspects of touch. J. Acoust. Soc. Am. **84**, 1680–1694 (1988)

23. Kontarinis, D.A., Howe, R.: Tactile display of vibratory information in teleoperation and virtual environments. Presence Teleoper. Virtual Environ. **4**, 387–402 (1996)

24. Pongrac, H.: Vibrotactile perception: examining the coding of vibrations and the just noticeable difference under various conditions. Multimed. Syst. **13**(4), 297–307 (2007)

25. Bethea, B.T., et al.: Application of haptic feedback to robotic surgery. J. Laparoendosc. Adv. Surg. Tech. **14**(3), 191–195 (2004)

26. Mcmahan, W., et al.: Tool contact acceleration feedback for telerobotic surgery. IEEE Trans. Haptics **4**, 210–220 (2011)

27. Okamura, A.M., Dennerlein, J.T., Howe, R.D.: Vibration feedback models for virtual environments. In: Proceedings of the 1998 IEEE International Conference on Robotics and Automation, vol. 1, pp. 674–679, May 1998

28. Landin, N., Romano, J.M., McMahan, W., Kuchenbecker, K.J.: Dimensional reduction of high-frequency accelerations for haptic rendering. In: Kappers, A.M.L., van Erp, J.B.F., Bergmann Tiest, W.M., van der Helm, F.C.T. (eds.) EuroHaptics 2010. LNCS, vol. 6192, pp. 79–86. Springer, Heidelberg (2010). https://doi.org/10.1007/978-3-642-14075-4_12
29. Wren, J.: Converting acceleration, velocity & displacement. http://blog.prosig.com/2010/12/16/methods-of-conversion-between-acceleration-velocity-and-displacement/. Accessed 04 Aug 2019

ShearTouch - Towards a Wearable Tactile Feedback Device to Provide Continuous Shear Force Sensation in Real Time

Oliver Wells[1]([✉]) [iD], Tony Pipe[1], Sanja Dogramadzi[2], and Matthew Studley[1]

[1] Bristol Robotics Laboratory, University of the West of England, Bristol, UK
{oliver.wells,tony.pipe}@brl.ac.uk, matthew2.studley@uwe.ac.uk
[2] Sheffield University, Sheffield, UK
s.dogramadzi@sheffield.ac.uk

Abstract. Force feedback in current teleoperation systems typically only provides haptic/kinaesthetic feedback to operators in the form of normal forces. However, it is proposed in this paper that the introduction of shear (or lateral) force feedback to operators' fingertips may provide an enhanced degree of control in manipulating remote objects for a wide variety of applications. A lightweight and wearable prototype device is developed and tested to demonstrate this hypothesis.

Keywords: Tactile · Haptic · Feedback · Wearable · Shear

1 Introduction

The area of tactile feedback is a critical field in telerobotics/teleoperation research, as it can enable a user to feel what a robot is feeling, perhaps creating a somewhat symbiotic relationship where the user is augmented by the robot's capabilities (e.g. size, strength, resistance to hazardous environment, depending on application), but the robot is also augmented by the user's haptic sensitivity (e.g. control of grip forces, positioning of fingers for better grasp, pressure application, enabling objects to be manipulated without being damaged through crushing or dropping via real-time direct feedback). When considering the wider environment of a teleoperation system, tasks are typically further supported by visual feedback, whether in the form of computer vision or direct line of sight between the user and the robot's operating envelope. In a way, this could lead to a form of sensor fusion, where the robot's sensors are combined with the user's vision, and the user is able to combine the various inputs and decide which ones to favour over others, which ones are contradictory, which ones provide additional context, etc.

The focus of this research is conveying shear/lateral force (slip/grip) sensations to a user's fingertips, as detected by a robot hand/finger equipped with a suitable sensor. We believe that the provision of shear stimulus feedback to an operator offers benefits in fine control of gripping and manipulation tasks that are otherwise not available through the more typical kinaesthetic force feedback mechanisms that act normal to the fingertips. The sensation of transitioning between "slip" and "grip" should allow an operator to

© Springer Nature Switzerland AG 2020
A. Mohammad et al. (Eds.): TAROS 2020, LNAI 12228, pp. 287–298, 2020.
https://doi.org/10.1007/978-3-030-63486-5_30

control gripping force with more finesse, particularly when the target object is of an unknown mass/fragility, and can therefore manipulate that object with a reduced risk of over- or under-gripping (i.e. crushing or dropping).

Previous research in this area can be grouped broadly into two styles of approach:

1. Standalone wearable devices – a few such examples are identified in [1], including the "Gravity Grabber" [2] and "hRing" [3]. These both combined shear sensation with a sense of normal force. Although these devices relayed a lateral sensation, they were limited in the distance they could move in either direction, as these did not use a continuous belt loop, but rather a finite length of belt fixed between two servo/DC motor shafts, such that the normal force (and hence pressure on the fingertip) could be controlled by driving the motors in opposite directions (or different speeds in the same direction if modifying normal force simultaneously to lateral force). This results in the issue that once the shear sensation in one direction has reached the limit of the belt length, the device is no longer able to provide any further feedback in that direction, unless it somehow rewinds itself, in which case, this would provide an undesirable stimulus to the user. Furthermore, these devices need to push the user's finger from behind to force it onto the actuation surface; this would have the real world equivalent sensation of someone else pushing the user's finger onto objects and controlling them – this is not ideal, as the authors believe the normal sensation of feeling a surface should be controlled by the user's fingers themselves, not by being pushed by an invisible third party.

2. Bench-mounted devices – a range of techniques, such as interleaved belts [4], a spinning disc [5], or an array of tactors acting normally to the fingertip and coordinated to convey a sense of lateral motion [6, 7], have been developed in previous research. As these are all bench-mounted, the shear force is provided by the device (which is mounted to a solid base, while the normal force is provided by the user's muscles in pressing their fingertip against the device. However, being bench-mounted may constrain the movement of the user in controlling other elements of a teleoperation system, and some of the devices [4, 6, 7] also cannot support an opposable grip.

An ideal progression of shear stimulus feedback needs to build on the strengths of each of these areas, as well as avoiding the weaknesses of each. This results in the main aims of the device being lightweight, wearable, able to provide a continuous sensation, and enabling normal force to be controlled by the user.

In order to provide such a device for use in teleoperation applications, a wearable device using a looped belt to provide feedback is proposed as below, named "ShearTouch".

2   Design

2.1   Rationale

As noted from previous research discussed in the above section, the provision of a normal force alongside a shear force stimulus is necessary to provide the full range of sensations required for a teleoperated gripping action. This is also key in ensuring that the user's fingertip has appropriate contact with the shear stimulus surface.

Although much work has been done to control the magnitude of this normal force, there still remains the issue of the origin of this force.

For the purposes of teleoperation applications (especially requiring an opposable grip), the wearable devices as outlined in bullet 1 of the previous section are not desirable, as the normal sensation against the fingernail is not realistic, while the bench-mounted devices in bullet 2 are not practical, as it tethers the user to a bench.

Therefore, there needs to be a third choice – that of a "floating ground", that in some ways is a combination of the two choices. The ultimate aim would be for the user to physically control their interaction with the tactile element of the feedback device, while not having it forced upon them. One way of achieving this may be via a hand exoskeleton. By attaching the shear feedback device to the finger of a force feedback exoskeleton, and allowing the exoskeleton's sensing and actuation components to transmit data between itself and the remote end effector, it can present the surface to the user by providing resistance to the joints of the fingers as part of the kinaesthetic feedback process, with the fingertip then able to contact the moving surface without being pushed externally. The exoskeleton therefore provides a "floating ground", spread across the hand and finger joints, as the opposing force origin, itself anchored to the rest of the hand. This might feel more natural, as when a user applies pressure to surfaces in the real world, the opposing force is similarly felt through the joints of the hand and fingers.

An additional benefit of this solution is that there is no need for an additional actuator on the fingertip to push the belt on to the user's fingertip and control the normal force, thereby reducing weight and size of the shear feedback device.

For the purposes of the prototype development/proof of concept covered by this paper, the ShearTouch device is not attached to a hand exoskeleton, but instead to a carriage, which the user can either move over a surface such that the lateral motion of the carriage is transposed to their fingertip (active exploration), or which can be fixed in place while an independently movable plate is operable by the experimenter to provide the lateral motion input (passive exploration). The ShearTouch device is mounted on a vertical shaft that goes through the carriage and contacts the reference surface beneath via a rubber dome, to enable normal force applied by the user onto the belt to be further applied to the reference surface, allowing the user to stop the motion of the carriage along the surface through increased friction, transitioning from a slip to grip status. A Force Sensitive Resistor (FSR, in this case the "FSR402 Short" by Interlink Electronics)) is integrated between the ShearTouch device and the vertical shaft to measure this normal force applied by the user to the system.

A block diagram of the system is shown in Fig. 1.

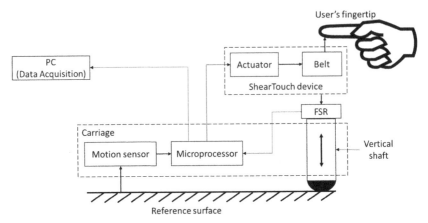

Fig. 1. Block diagram of ShearTouch prototype test system

2.2 ShearTouch Design

The ShearTouch device itself is comprised of three main elements: the actuator, belt and physical housing.

Actuator
In order to provide continuous motion in both directions at a controllable speed, but with the minimum of complexity and weight, a continuous servo motor was selected.

For the prototype, a Feetech FS90R continuous servo motor was chosen as being the lightest and smallest available motor.

Belt
Selection of a suitable belt to convey shear force to the user required consideration of a number of factors, including texture, width, how it would interface with the servo shaft and provide a suitable range of speeds, and general availability.

From previous studies conducted around different textures of belt, and the level of stimulus detected by users [4, 8, 9], it has been identified that a rough texture (approximately 4 mm separation between raised features) is better than a smooth texture (approximately 1 mm between raised features). A small timing belt with a 2 mm pitch was identified that satisfied this criterion.

To determine the size of pulley wheel to drive the belt, the velocity range of the servo needed to be scaled to the range of speeds that a user could detect. Previous research [10] has identified that the range of speeds detectable by a person is typically between 10–200 mm/s. Given the range of speeds of the servo motor, the diameter of pulley wheel was calculated to deliver speeds within the 10–200 mm/s range, ensuring that the lower speeds were prioritized to enable a user to detect the smallest discernible movements. The chosen belt speed range (excluding stationary) was approximately 10.5–160 mm/s.

Housing

The housing for the motor, belt and pulley was then constructed to allow for a range of user finger sizes (based on anthropometric data provided in [11]), featuring adjustable plates to keep the user's finger centralized in the device. The final design is shown in Fig. 2.

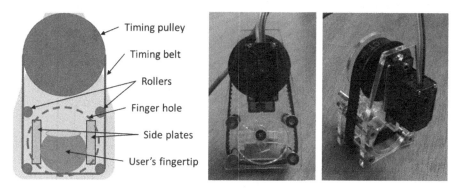

Timing pulley

Timing belt

Rollers

Finger hole

Side plates

User's fingertip

Fig. 2. ShearTouch prototype

2.3 Carriage Design

Motion Sensor

An optical PS/2 computer mouse sensor was utilised to provide motion detection – this has a resolution of 0.25 mm, and can be polled easily by a microcontroller at a range of sampling frequencies.

Control

An Arduino Leonardo microcontroller was employed to obtain the motion sensor and FSR data, command the servo motor and provide a data acquisition feed to a PC. The ratio of the output speed to the input speed can be chosen to be 1:1, 2:1, or 1:2.

Previous work regarding the sensitivity of the human finger [12] provides conflicting hypotheses of which receptors are most responsible for detecting shear force, as well as the frequency at which they act (anywhere between 15 and 50 Hz). Considering this range of frequencies, a sampling rate was further calculated based on the constraints of the servo and optical sensor to find an appropriate fit between the human and technical elements of the system. A value of 25 Hz was identified, which not only satisfies the optimisation of the system, but is also inside the range of fingertip receptor frequencies, and is therefore employed in the ShearTouch program, as illustrated by the algorithm in Fig. 3.

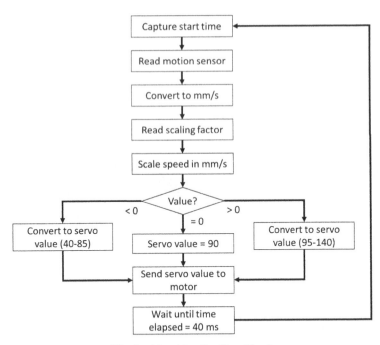

Fig. 3. Algorithm for ShearTouch

Physical Design

The carriage incorporates the motion sensor, Arduino and vertical shaft, to which the ShearTouch is attached. It also has wheels and can attach to a track to constrain its movement to a single lateral axis, and has sufficient space on top to allow both left- and right-handed users to operate it. The final design is shown in Fig. 4.

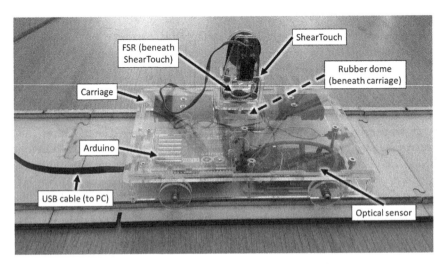

Fig. 4. ShearTouch and test carriage on track

2.4 Testing Process

A sequence of tests were conducted using passive exploration, where the ShearTouch carriage was fixed in position on the test track, with a sliding plate acting as a reference surface beneath the carriage, such that the test conductor was able to control the speed and direction of the motion detected by the motion sensor, while the participant was able to stop the sliding plate moving by applying normal force through the vertical shaft on to the rubber dome.

Active exploration, where the participant was able to move the carriage along the track, was used to familiarize themselves with the sensations delivered by the system.

The parameters assessed during these tests were:

- the performance of the ShearTouch device in delivering a shear force stimulus to participants (results in Sect. 3.2);
- the effect on participants of applying different scaling factors (2:1, 1:1, 1:2) to the speed of the belt in relation to the movement of the reference surface detected by the motion sensor (results in Sect. 3.3);
- the difference in normal force applied by a participant in transitioning from a slip to grip sensation in the presence/absence of shear force (ShearTouch motor turned on/off) (results in Sect. 3.4);
- the effect on participants' sensation and response with/without visual stimulus (sighted/blindfolded) (results in Sect. 3.5).

The test layout is shown in Fig. 5.

Fig. 5. ShearTouch test layout

3 Results

3.1 Demographics

The tests were conducted with a sample size of thirty participants, with demographics as shown in Table 1.

Table 1. ShearTouch test demographics

ShearTouch participants	Total	Male	Female
Sample size	30	19	11
- Left-handed	2	2	0
- Right-handed	28	17	11
Minimum age	23	23	24
Mean age	33.0	33.9	31.5
Maximum age	58	58	42

3.2 General Performance

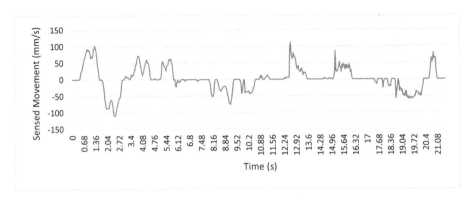

Fig. 6. ShearTouch general performance - sensed movement vs time

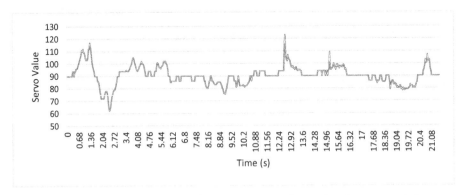

Fig. 7. ShearTouch general performance - servo value vs time for same period

The system accurately translated the motion of the carriage in respect to the reference surface into the belt motion of the ShearTouch device, as demonstrated in Figs. 6 and 7 (note that servo value is the signal sent to the motor, not belt speed).

Qualitative feedback from all participants confirmed that they perceived a sensation of lateral motion on their fingertip in accordance with what they anticipated from their observation of the carriage/sliding plate motion, in terms of both speed and direction.

3.3   Effect of Scaling Factors

Further to the 1:1 translation of sensed movement to belt movement as per Fig. 6, the additional scaling factors of 2:1 and 1:2 successfully provided shear stimulus at double and half belt speed respectively to the participant via the ShearTouch belt.

Qualitative feedback was gathered from participants regarding their preferred scaling factor (1:1 (single), 2:1 (double) or 1:2 (half) belt speed with reference to the movement of the sliding plate, as well as if they had no preference towards any particular setting) to identify the level of sensation with which they were most comfortable. The preferences are detailed in Table 2.

Table 2. Participant preference to ShearTouch scaling factors

Scaling preference	Quantity
No preference	6
1:2	2
1:1	1
2:1	19
1:1 or 2:1	2

3.4   Presence/Absence of Shear Force

The normal force applied by the participants to stop the sliding plate's motion was recorded not only for the three scaling factors, but also when the ShearTouch belt was disabled (thereby delivering no shear force stimulus).

The differences in the amount of normal force applied were compared using the average of the three scaling factors against the normal force applied when no shear stimulus was present, in relation to each participant.

As can be seen from Table 3, the presence of shear stimulus resulted in 87% of participants applying less normal force to stop the sliding plate when compared to the absence of a shear stimulus. The greatest reduction in applied force was approximately 3.5 N.

3.5   Presence/Absence of Visual Stimulus

Following the above tests, a similar four treatments (three scaling factors plus absence of shear stimulus) were conducted a second time with each of the thirty participants

Table 3. Impact of presence of shear stimulus on normal force applied by participants

Impact of shear stimulus on normal force applied	Quantity of participants
Lower normal force applied	26
No difference	3
Greater normal force applied	1

(providing a total of 120 treatments across the participant population), but without the participants having any visual stimulus.

A comparison of differences in the normal force applied between the visual and non-visual treatments is shown in Table 4.

Table 4. Effect of removal of visual stimulus on normal force applied by participants

Impact of no visual stimulus on normal force applied	Number of treatments
Lower normal force applied	35
No difference	18
Greater normal force applied	63
FSR error (no data captured)	4

Qualitative feedback from participants on their experience while blindfolded covered the responses in Table 5.

Table 5. Perceived impact of no visual stimulus in ShearTouch use

Perceived effect of no visual stimulus	Quantity
None	15
Sense of hearing relied on more	4
Increased focus on shear stimulus	7
Applied more force to stop sliding plate	4

4   Discussions and Conclusions

4.1   General Performance

All participants were asked for feedback at the end of the test regarding the perceived sensation in terms of changes in speed and direction, and all participants confirmed that they could feel the sensation correctly, with no delay sensed due to change of speed or direction. Participants were also asked to confirm if they felt any discomfort (e.g. due to their finger hurting) following the test serials. Only two participants felt discomfort due to medical conditions that made their fingertips sensitive.

4.2 Effect of Scaling Factors

Despite the system being optimised to deliver shear stimulus at a 1:1 scaling in relation to actual movement detected by the motion sensor, it is interesting to note that the majority of participants preferred the 2:1 (double speed) scaling factor. These participants generally commented that they were more able to discern changes in movement through the heightened sensation.

4.3 Presence/Absence of Shear Force

A significant majority of participants applied greater force to stop the motion of the sliding plate when there was no shear stimulus. This supports the hypothesis that the inclusion of shear force stimulus in force feedback exoskeletons used in teleoperation, where only kinaesthetic/normal force feedback is typically present, should allow operators to manipulate remote objects with a more controlled application of grip. By applying a more appropriate degree of force influenced by the shear feedback device, the risk of either dropping an object due to insufficient grip, or damaging it due to excessive force, can be mitigated.

4.4 Presence/Absence of Visual Stimulus

In 52.5% of the paired tests in which the device was tested with and without the subject being able to see, greater force was applied in stopping the sliding plate when visual stimulus was removed. This is in comparison to only 13% of participants perceiving that they applied greater force. However, three of the four participants who perceived that they applied greater force applied less force when visual stimulus was removed.

This suggests that a key part of teleoperation systems is that of multi-modal sensing, where visual and tactile feedback may be complimentary in performing teleoperation tasks effectively. It is therefore recommended that future developments in telerobotics ensure that the visual feedback element is included as part of the total system boundary.

4.5 Conclusions

The ShearTouch prototype has been demonstrated to provide improvements in the application of normal force to stop an object from sliding, by the delivery of shear stimulus to a user's fingertip, when compared to the same operation with no shear feedback provided.

The design of the ShearTouch device also provides the benefit of continuous shear feedback in either direction, and can be integrated into a wearable system in due course.

5 Future Work

Following the successful demonstration of the ShearTouch device, and its capability to deliver continuous shear force stimulus in a lightweight, wearable form, participant feedback will be incorporated into a revised design and integrated into a system that can provide an opposable grip to remotely pick up objects and further demonstrate the benefits of shear force feedback in teleoperation.

The development of shear tactile feedback technology should augment teleoperation systems through its integration, and could have a wide range of applications where additional control of normal forces in gripping functions in desirable, such as:

- Microsurgery;
- Nuclear decommissioning;
- Space operations and maintenance;
- Subsea operations and maintenance;
- Archaeological exploration;
- Future handling equipment for logistical and manufacturing tasks.

There is also potential for this technology to be applied to functions where the remote operating space is in virtual reality, such as virtual training systems.

References

1. Pacchierotti, C., Sinclair, S., Solazzi, M., Frisoli, A., Hayward, V., Prattichizzo, D.: Wearable haptic systems for the fingertip and the hand: taxonomy, review and perspectives. IEEE Trans. Haptics **10**(4), 580–600 (2017)
2. Minamizawa, K.: Gravity grabber: wearable haptic display to present virtual mass sensation. In: Proceedings of the ACM SIGGRAPH Emerging Technology (2007)
3. Pacchierotti, C., Salvietti, G., Hussain, I., Meli, L., Prattichizzo, D.: The hRing: a wearable haptic device to avoid occlusions in hand tracking. In: 2016 IEEE Haptics Symposium (HAPTICS), pp. 134–139 (2016)
4. Ho, C., Kim, J., Patil, S., Goldberg, K.: The slip-pad: a haptic display using interleaved belts to simulate lateral and rotational slip. In: 2015 IEEE World Haptics Conference (WHC), pp. 189–195 (2015)
5. Baavour, R., Fuchs, M., Ben-Hanan, U.: Grip-slip: a slip/shear tactile display master unit for grip tasks. In: 2007 Mediterranean Conference on Control & Automation, pp. 1–6 (2007)
6. Summers, I.R., Chanter, C.M.: A broadband tactile array on the fingertip. J. Acoust. Soc. Am. **112**(5 Pt 1), 2118–2126 (2002)
7. Roke, C., Melhuish, C., Pipe, T., Drury, D., Chorley, C.: Lump localisation through a deformation-based tactile feedback system using a biologically inspired finger sensor. Robot. Auton. Syst. **60**(11), 1442 (2012)
8. Gleeson, B.T., Stewart, C.A., Provancher, W.R.: Improved tactile shear feedback: tactor design and an aperture-based restraint. IEEE Trans. Haptics **4**(4), 253–262 (2011)
9. Placencia, G., Rahimi, M., Khoshnevis, B.: Effects of distance and direction on tangential tactile perception of the index finger pad. Robotica **31**(5), 679–685 (2013)
10. Adams, M.J., et al.: Finger pad friction and its role in grip and touch. J. R. Soc. Interface **10**(80), 20120467 (2013)
11. Pheasant, S., Haslegrave, C.M.: Bodyspace: anthropometry, ergonomics, and the design of work (2006)
12. Pisa University, Centro Piaggio: Cutaneous mechanoreceptors (2012). http://www.centropiaggio.unipi.it/sites/default/files/course/material/Cutaneous_mechanoreceptors.pdf

A Pressure Controlled Membrane Mechanism for Optimising Haptic Sensing

George P. Jenkinson$^{(\boxtimes)}$ (iD), Andrew T. Conn (iD), and Antonia Tzemanaki (iD)

Department of Mechanical Engineering, University of Bristol,
Bristol Robotics Laboratory, Bristol, UK
`george.jenkinson.2018@bristol.ac.uk`

Abstract. Active-passive robotic sensors adjust their stiffness ad-hoc as is appropriate for a task. In situations where the sensor is to operate in an unpredictable environment, or where the sensor is required to work with high sensitivity over a large stiffness range, it is beneficial for the sensor to maintain a high level of sensitivity over its entire operational range. This paper presents the theoretical model for a pneumatically controlled haptic sensor which maintains optimal sensitivity over a large range of force input values.

1 Introduction

Haptic sensors generally involve a trade off between high sensitivity over a small measurement range and the capability to work over a larger measurement range with lower sensitivity [1]. When their structure involves soft materials, this trade off often relates to the material's deformation. Softer materials are highly sensitive to a small range of stimulus values and stiffer materials are less sensitive, but work over a larger range [2,3]. For many applications, the soft material's properties and elasticity can be chosen or tuned for the specific purpose [2]. Some applications, however, require sensor sensitivity to be adjusted ad-hoc, such as distinguishing between a range of objects of similar material properties, or working in unpredictable environments or with unknown objects [4] . For these cases, the sensor's material properties cannot be pre-selected for all operational requirements.

Variable stiffness materials and mechanisms have become an active area of research within robotics, where an actuator that can change stiffness between soft and hard states is considered advantageous, as it can selectively have the benefits of both soft and rigid structures [5]. It is, therefore, possible to actively alter the stiffness or shape of a soft haptic sensor, in order to more appropriately probe its stimulus, by combining it with soft actuation and variable stiffness mechanisms [2,4,5]. However, the literature lacks studies that review how the changes to a sensor's stiffness affect its sensitivity, and how to mitigate potential sensitivity loss.

This paper considers a soft robotic haptic sensor that exploits a combined actuator-sensor configuration for active-passive modalities and presents a theoretical basis to optimise its sensitivity. The design is based on a soft sensor

© Springer Nature Switzerland AG 2020
A. Mohammad et al. (Eds.): TAROS 2020, LNAI 12228, pp. 299–303, 2020.
https://doi.org/10.1007/978-3-030-63486-5_31

concept similar to those proposed in [2,6]. In this concept, an external force from the environment is applied to a soft interface (membrane) and the mechanical information is captured by the system via the translocation of an internal fluid. The external force can be measured by monitoring the movement of the fluid through a pipe (Fig. 1a). The movement of the fluid can be measured in several ways, such as using a camera [6], a soft encoder [7], or measuring the flow [8]. This paper focuses on the data available to such a sensor, independent of its measurement mechanism, and, in particular, models an actuator-sensor system whose air-filled cavity can be pressurised by a controllable pump. An increasing air pressure effectively stiffens the soft interface's membrane; the suggested model shows that it is possible to enhance the sensitivity of the sensor over its working range of applied forces via this method.

2   Method

The sensor system (Fig. 1) relies on the transmission of mechanical stimuli into the lateral movement of liquid through a pipe. By tracking this movement, the lateral distance travelled by the liquid can be correlated to the applied force and the transmission ratio between the force and distance quantified i.e. the sensor's sensitivity (in mN^{-1}). As the air is compressed within the sensor (due to the deformation of the sensor's membrane when a force is applied), this ratio becomes smaller, meaning that a larger stimulus (force) is needed to give the same response (fluid displacement) (Fig. 1b). This implies that having a more highly pressurised cavity reduces the sensor's sensitivity, but increases its measurement range, since a more highly pressurised cavity will require more force to reach maximum compression. Similarly, reducing the air pressure increases sensitivity over a smaller measurement range. The ability to dynamically vary sensitivity and measurement range during operation can enable improved haptic sensing performance, particularly when the stimulus exhibits non-linear stiffness properties e.g. human tissue.

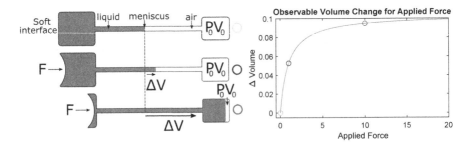

Fig. 1. a) Schematic of the actuator-sensor device in three states of no force, small force, and a large force applied. In adiabatic conditions, PV remains constant. b) Information available to a sensory device for a range of stimuli, calculated by substituting equation (1) into (2). The three states are marked with a corresponding 'o'. Units are arbitrary.

To derive the the relationship between the force applied to the sensor's interface (F), and the change to internal cavity pressure (P), it is assumed that the liquid experiences negligible compression, and that the change is adiabatic

$$\Delta F = \Delta P A \tag{1}$$

where A is the cross-sectional area of the pipe. The decrease in volume (V) of the inner cavity due to an applied pressure can be calculated using the pipe's cross-sectional area and the observed distance (L) travelled by the liquid's meniscus:

$$\Delta V = -A \Delta L$$

so that Boyle's law captures the compression of the air in adiabatic conditions

$$\Delta P = \frac{V_0 P_0}{V_0 - A \Delta L} - P_0 \tag{2}$$

where subscript 0 indicates initial values. We can obtain a relation for the change in the position of the meniscus at the liquid/air boundary as a function of the applied force. As $\Delta L \to 0$:

$$\frac{dL}{dF} = \alpha = \frac{V_0 P_0}{A^2 (\frac{F}{A} + P_0)^2} \tag{3}$$

where the ratio α relates to the sensitivity of the sensor. Now, it is useful to calculate how α changes for a fixed force as a function of the initial pressure, whilst keeping V_0 constant (Fig. 2a)

$$\frac{d\alpha}{dP_0} = \frac{V_0 (\frac{F^2}{P_0^2} - A^2)}{(\frac{F^2}{P_0} + P_0 A^2 + 2FA)^2} \tag{4}$$

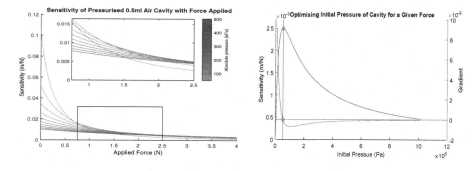

Fig. 2. a) The sensitivity is higher for a low pressure (blue) cavity than for higher pressures (red), but it reduces in a non-linear manner. The inset shows that the more highly pressurised cavities become more sensitive than those with a low pressure as the force increases above 2 N. The colour bar correlates the colour of the line to the pressure used to calculate the data. b) Sensitivity for P_0 values (blue) and its gradient (orange) according to Eqs. (3) and (4) respectively for a fixed applied force of 5 N. The optimal initial pressure for this force corresponds to the vertical black line. (Color figure online)

A larger ratio corresponds to a higher sensitivity and hence, we can find the extrema of Eq. (3) using Eq. (4) (Fig. 2b), setting

$$V_0(\frac{F^2}{P_0^2} - A^2) = 0; V_0 \neq 0 \implies P_{opt}^2 = \frac{F^2}{A^2} \tag{5}$$

which gives us the linear relation for finding optimal pressure at a given applied force. We can dismiss the negative solution as being non-physical, although its existence usefully confirms that the positive solution is a maximum, and so solving Eq. (5) gives the pressure that is needed to give the highest sensitivity for a given force and cross-sectional pipe area.

3   Discussion

While Eq. (5) is identical, in appearance, to the standard definition of pressure, it does not represent the relationship between two physical quantities, but is, instead, intended to inform the control system for a sensor where the compression of air leads to a non-linear deterioration of the sensor's sensitivity. The solution lends itself to a simple interpretation : the pressure of the cavity should be such that it returns the meniscus of the liquid to its rest position.

The model presented in this paper considers only the pneumatic property of the sensor. For a full analysis, the material properties of the soft interface and other parts of the structure would also have to be considered. However, these factors are likely to complement the phenomenon of reduced sensitivity as the system is moved from its resting configuration and the material is stretched or deformed , which could be recovered by applying a back-pressure to the system. These preliminary calculations support the development of a device that follows the concept of Fig. 1. In future work, the presented mechanism will be realised with a pressure controller attached to the air cavity in order to validate that sensitivity can be enhanced.

Acknowledgements. This work was supported by Cancer Research UK C24524/A30038 as part of project ARTEMIS.

References

1. Xiao-zhou, L.: Wearable sensors and robots. In: Proceedings of International Conference on Wearable Sensors and Robots 2015, vol. 399, pp. 145–164 (2017)
2. Huang, I., Liu, J., Bajcsy, R.: A depth camera-based soft fingertip device for contact region estimation and perception-action coupling. IEEE Int. Conf. Robot. Autom. **2019**, 8443–8449 (2019)
3. McInroe, B.W., Chen, C.L., Goldberg, K.Y., Bajcsy, R., Fearing, R.S.: Towards a soft fingertip with integrated sensing and actuation. In: IEEE International Conference on Intelligent Robots and Systems, pp. 6437–6444 (2018)
4. Xiang, C., Guo, J., Rossiter, J.: Soft-smart robotic end effectors with sensing, actuation, and gripping. Smart Materials and Structures, vol. 28, no. 5 (2019)

5. Manti, M., Cacucciolo, V., Cianchetti, M.: Stiffening in soft robotics: a review of the state of the art. IEEE Robot. Automat. Magazine **23**(3), 93–106 (2016)
6. Soter, G., Garrad, M., Conn, A.T., Hauser, H., Rossiter, J.: Skinflow: a soft robotic skin based on fluidic transmission. In: RoboSoft 2019–2019 IEEE International Conference on Soft Robotics, pp. 355–360 (2019)
7. Garrad, M., Soter, G., Conn, A.T., Hauser, H., Rossiter, J.: A soft matter computer for soft robots. Sci. Robot. vol. 4, no. 33 (2019)
8. Navarro, S.E., Goury, O., Zheng, G., Bieze, T.M., Duriez, C.: Modeling novel soft mechanosensors based on air-flow measurements. IEEE Robot. Autom. Lett. **4**(4), 4338–4345 (2019)

Experiment Establishing Spatiotemporal Resolution of Human Thermal Perception for Developing a Prosthetic Robotics Hand Thermal Interface

Benjamin Stubbings(⊠) 🆔

University of Wolverhampton, Wolverhampton WV1 1LY, UK
B.Stubbings@wlv.ac.uk

Abstract. This paper provides detail on background research surrounding the topic of thermal perception and feedback. As well as giving an outline of a proposed experiment expanding on background and planning to answer to research questions. The background covers three important aspects of the topic in hand, safe thermal stimuli, perception and displays. Going over the apparatus components and how they will be used during the experiment. Finally culminating in the desired outcomes and further work to be conducted.

Keywords: Thermal feedback · Thermal perception · Prosthetics · HMI

1 Introduction

Temperature sensing is an important part of touch for both context of what is being interacted with, say a hot drink, and avoiding hot surfaces which might damage the user and prosthetic.

This paper proposes an experiment and apparatus to map thermal perception across the upper limb. The focus on upper limb is due to the project's aim to implement a human-machine interface (HMI) within a prosthetic robotic hand to provide thermal sensation feedback to the user. The experiment aims to determine 1) how does upper limb location effect ability to discern thermal stimuli? And 2) where is the most thermally perceptive locations on the upper limb?

2 Background

The background research identified three main facets to be concern with, 1) Safe Thermal stimuli, 2) Thermal Perception and 3) Thermal Display.

© Springer Nature Switzerland AG 2020
A. Mohammad et al. (Eds.): TAROS 2020, LNAI 12228, pp. 304–307, 2020.
https://doi.org/10.1007/978-3-030-63486-5_32

2.1 Safe Thermal Levels

A priority when applying thermal feedback to human participants' limbs is ensuring no harm and even better no discomfort happens to them. A few reviewed papers go into detail examining the point at which discomfort might begin in terms of temperature. Lawrence and Bull found the average discomfort levels begin at 43.5 °C [1]. Whilst Harju had a broader idea of mapping out heat pain and tolerances across different demographics and body areas. Included in this were two areas within the upper limb were found to have similar discomfort and pain levels as Lawrence and Bull's reported findings [2]. These papers give a good idea of operational temperatures that are acceptable to work in and ultimately apply to an HMI.

2.2 Thermal Perception

The experiment aims to quantify the participant's thermal perception in the upper limb. Neurophysiology literature provides an important understanding of human thermal perception. Spatial summation is an important part of how thermoceptors function and relay temperature to humans. Nielsen and Arendt-Nielsen discussed dermatomes (areas supplied by nerves directly form the spinal cord) found that stimuli across large areas reduces the threshold for perception [3]. Along with Spatial summation there is some evidence suggesting that sex also has an impact in how well human perceive thermal stimuli. Averbeck et al found that female participants had lower thresholds. However, they found that the baseline temperature had a bigger effect on sensitivity. Suggesting an optimal temperature baseline of 26 °C [4].

Following a similar line of research Akiyama et al discussed the concept of improving thermal perception by adjusting skin temperatures before applying feedback. They found that pre-exposure decreased reaction to warm stimuli by 0.69 s and cold stimuli by 0.52 s [5]. Another factor considered is age. Huang et al suggested that thresholds for thermal perception generally increased for stimuli with one exception of when the temperature was high enough to elicit a pain response. Suggesting that thermoceptors' response deteriorates with age [6].

2.3 Thermal Displays

Mostly all the research papers utilised Peltier devices as they're capable of providing hot and cold stimuli within human perception ranges. Some papers focusing heavily on displays, both thermal and haptic, discussed use of fingertip sized devices. Gallo et al investigated minimum distances effect on perception, being a viable feedback method as size had little impact [7]. Jimenez and Fishel used an upper arm mounted thermal display in conjunction with testing a multimodal tactile sensor. Using a prosthetic hand to grip objects at three different temperatures, they found a consistently correct detection from the feedback [8].

3 Methodology

For providing the stimuli, the experiment uses an apparatus of multiple Peltier modules, placed in an outline of the upper limb. The Peltier's ability as a heat pump makes them a solid choice for the application as well as being straight forward to drive using an H-bridge circuit and control using a pulse width modulated (PWM) signal. The parts of the upper limb to come in contact with these devices will be the middle finger tip, middle finger proximal phalanx, the upper palm above the distal transverse, the Hypothenar eminence, Thenar eminence, wrist, three points along the fore arm and two points along the upper arm. With module size limitation on the fingers. To allow testing of both the anterior and posterior of the upper limb the apparatus will be affixed to a surface at a 90° angle.

The Peltier devices are instrumented with platinum RTD sensors to monitor, in real time, the temperature at the contact with participants. These sensors were picked over other thermal sensing options because of the accuracy and linearity of the resistance change with temperature [9]. These sensors, along with current sensing resistors, are also used as feedback for the Peltier's output and the rate of change. A bespoke user interface is used to gather the participants' responses to thermal stimuli.

4 Procedure

Firstly, the participants are briefed on how to use the user interface to report their experience of thermal sensation. Making sure they fully understand and give the correct response. Next a baseline temperature, based on the room temperature, is taken. Wherever possible, the ambient temperature is set to the "optimal temperature" suggested by Averbeck et al. When it comes to providing the thermal stimuli the maximum change in temperature is set at 15 °C either side of the baseline. This ensures discomfort and any risk of harm from burning will be mitigated. The Peltier device is activated at a random sequence without informing the participants of the next change, thus avoiding any chance of affecting their perception beforehand.

As for rate of change it is done at a gradient of 1 °C every 2 s until reaching the maximum temperature change. Each session of stimulation will last for 30 s using this rate of change. Whilst the stimulus is being provided the participants should be using the user interface to record their current response. Again, this is to mitigate any change of informed opinions regarding their perception. Also, as per standard experimental procedure each location and temperature change are repeated at least three times giving an average perception response for each location and temperature. From there also allowing to calculate an overall perception result from all participants.

As both anterior and posterior of the arm is tested, they will be done separately to reduce the risk of mistakes. Also, between locations changes, the devices will be allowed to return to the baseline temperature, as this might have an effect on the way the thermal stimulus is perceived. Where the starting temperature has an effect. Both operator and participant will have an emergency cut off switch. This being used in a situation where something has possibly gone wrong and the power needs shutting off.

5 Further Work

The experiment seeks detailed information regarding the thermal perception along the upper limb. Specifically, how the different areas that are being tested compare perception wise to one another. Also, whether the ability to discern the thermal stimuli is effected by being a different area of the upper limb. In relation to its use in prosthetics it would be desirable to find a location outside of the hand which is comparable in perception and ability to discern thermal sensation.

The current research focusses on prosthetics for users with trans-radial amputations. Therefore, contingent on the outcomes of the experiment the results will be used to research an HMI in the device to provide thermal feedback for the user.

References

1. Lawrence, J.C., Bull, J.P.: Thermal conditions which cause skin burns. Eng. Med. **5**(3), 61–63. https://journals.sagepub.com/doi/full/10.1243/EMED_JOUR_1976_005_023_02

2. Harju, E.: Cold and warmth perception mapped for age, gender, and body area. Somatosensory & Motor Res. **19**(1), 61–75 (2002). http://www.tandfonline.com/doi/abs/10.1080/089902201 20113057

3. Arendt-Nielsen, Jesper Nielsen and Lars: Spatial summation of heat induced pain within and between dermatomes. Somatosensory & Motor Research, **14**(2), 119–125 (1997). http://www.tandfonline.com/doi/abs/10.1080/08990229771123

4. Averbeck, B., Seitz, L., Kolb, F.P., Kutz, D.F.: Sex differences in thermal detection and thermal pain threshold and the thermal grill illusion: a psychophysical study in young volunteers. Biol. Sex Differences, **8**(1), 29 (2017). https://www.ncbi.nlm.nih.gov/pubmed/28859684

5. Akiyama, S., Sato, K., Makino, Y., Maeno, T.: Presentation of thermal sensation through preliminary adjustment of adapting skin temperature. IEEE, pp. 355–358. March 2012. https://ieeexplore.ieee.org/document/6183814

6. Huang, H., Wang, W., Lin, C.K.: Influence of age on thermal thresholds, thermal pain thresholds, and reaction time. J. Clinical Neurosci. **17**(6), 722–726 (2009). https://www.clinicalkey.es/playcontent/1-s2.0-S096758680900719X

7. Gallo, S., Rognini, G., Santos-Carreras, L., Vouga, T., Blanke, O., Bleuler, H.: Encoded and crossmodal thermal stimulation through a fingertip-sized haptic display. Front. Robot. AI (2015). https://www.openaire.eu/search/publication?articleId=frontiers___::a1d91b1fff7d409 2fa89482403a24875

8. Jimenez, M.C., Fishel, J.A.: Evaluation of force, vibration and thermal tactile feedback in prosthetic limbs. IEEE, pp. 437–441, February 2014. https://ieeexplore.ieee.org/document/6775495

9. Chauhan, J., Neelakantan, U.: An experimental approach for precise temperature measurement using platinum RTD PT1000. IEEE, pp. 3213–3215. https://ieeexplore.ieee.org/document/775 5297

An Incremental Learning Approach for Physical Human-Robot Collaboration

Achim Buerkle[✉], Ali Al-Yacoub, and Pedro Ferreira

Wolfson School of Engineering, Loughborough University, Loughborough, UK
a.buerkle@lboro.ac.uk

Abstract. Physical Human-Robot Collaboration requires humans and robots to perform joint tasks in a shared workspace. Since robot's characteristic strengths are to cope well with high payloads, they are utilized to assist human operators during heavy pulling or pushing activities. A widely used sensor to detect human muscle fatigue and thus, to trigger an assistance request, is an Electromyography (EMG). Many previous approaches to process EMG data are based on training Machine Learning models offline or include a large degree of manual fine tuning. However, due to recent advances in Machine Learning such as incremental learning, there is an opportunity to apply online learning which reduces programming effort and also copes well with subject specific characteristics of EMG signals. Initial results show promising potential, yet, unveil a conflict between convergence time and classification accuracy.

Keywords: EMG · Human-Robot Collaboration · Incremental learning · Machine Learning

1 Introduction

Human-Robot Collaboration (HRC) in manufacturing aims to establish symbiotic or synergetic effects between human operators and robots [1]. This is enabled by combining the characteristic strengths of each party. Human strengths are considered to be adaptability to changes, decision making, and problem solving [1, 2]. Robot's strengths, on the other hand, are high precision, high operating speeds, and the capability of coping with high payloads [3]. Thus, in a physical collaboration, robots are able to support human operators via force amplification to handle heavy pushing and pulling activities [4]. In order to measure human muscle activity such as during the lift of heavy objects, a widely used sensor is an Electromyography (EMG) [5].

The approaches typically include pre-processing of the data, feature extraction, and a supervised leaning of the model [5, 6]. However, recent advances in Machine Learning regarding incremental learning could allow to minimize the training and programming effort of such models [7]. Furthermore, the algorithm could optimize its performance over time in an online system [7]. In this work, an incremental learning approach is utilized to predict EMG data during three different states: Participants lifting light payloads, medium payloads, and heavy payloads (struggling).

© Springer Nature Switzerland AG 2020
A. Mohammad et al. (Eds.): TAROS 2020, LNAI 12228, pp. 308–313, 2020.
https://doi.org/10.1007/978-3-030-63486-5_33

2 Related Work

In a Human-Robot collaborative scenario, humans and robots perform joint tasks in a shared workspace [1]. In order to communicate intentions of the human to the robot, sensors are utilized such as EMGs [5]. The EMG signals are usually acquired from a human upper-limb since they are mostly used in the given tasks [5]. The acquired data can be used to communicate movement intentions. It can also provide insights on human muscle fatigue [6]. In this case, a robot could assist a human operator during a heavy pull or push of an object or adapt its behavior to create more ergonomic working conditions for its human co-worker [6, 8]. This is intended to prevent injuries, as well as long-term health issues related to physical fatigue [8].

Figure 1 shows the general process used to integrate EMGs in Human-Robot Collaboration for a supervised, non-incremental learning approach. The first stage is EMG data acquisition. Critical attention is required during the selection of the acquisition device, the number of channels used, as well as the placement of each channel [5]. The channel acquisition device also determines the sampling rate and data transmission [9].

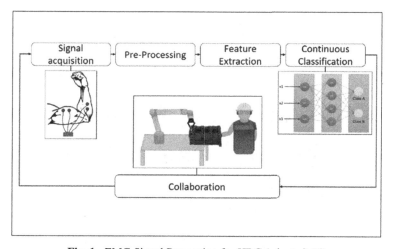

Fig. 1. EMG Signal Processing for HRC (adapted) [5]

During the pre-processing stage, raw EMG signals are checked for baseline offset [5]. Typically, the signal is corrected by subtracting the average amplitude from each instance, however, there are also approaches based on nonlinear error-modelling [5, 6]. Raw EMG signals are susceptible to contain noise. Thus, Butterworth filters with a cut off frequency from 2 Hz–20 Hz are utilized [5]. The remaining features are extracted in the Feature selection and extraction stage. This is critical during EMG data processing since it has a high impact on the classification accuracy [9].

Three properties are considered as essential: class separability (minimize overlap), robustness (separability in noisy environment), and computational complexity (low complexity of features implies lower processing times) [5, 9].

The fourth stage is continuous classification of the filtered and extracted signals. There are mainly two types of prediction models. One is the use of kinematic models, the second approach is to utilize Artificial Neural Networks (ANNs) [5]. However, [9] states that Linear Discriminant Analyses (LDA) and Support Vector Machines (SVMs) are also widely used for EMG data classification. According to [5] there are few critical challenges remaining. Firstly, many offline systems obtain high classification accuracies, yet the online performances of such systems are far from satisfactory. Secondly, there are subject-specific characteristics of EMG signals. This can even include variation of the EMG signals for the same person during different recording sessions. An opportunity to increase the performance and to lower programming and fine-tuning effort could be incremental learning. Incremental learning algorithms have the following characteristics: ability of life-long learning, ability to incrementally tune the model's performance, and no prior knowledge about the data and its properties is needed [7].

3   Experimental Setup

The experimental setup aims to collect EMG data during three different stages: light payload, medium payload, and high payload, during which a participant is slightly struggling. Participants are wearing EMG sensors on their arms throughout the experiment, as shown in Fig. 2.

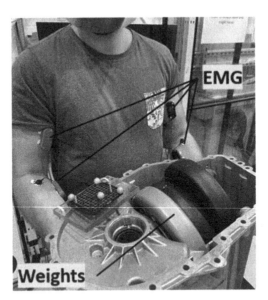

Fig. 2. Experimental Setup

The acquired data will be fed into the classifier unlabeled. However, in order to validate the prediction results, predicted classes and the actual classification will be compared.

4   Results and Discussion

The collected data was used to train an Online Random Forest (ORF) model that aims to classify the EMG signals into low payload, medium payload, and heavy payload. In any incremental learning approach, the most crucial property apart from accuracy is the convergence time. Since the model aims to minimize the prediction error live and immediately. In Human-Robot Collaboration, this is exceptionally important as humans and robots are physically interacting. Hence, in this validation experiment convergence time of the ORF model was measured with a different number of trees, which is illustrated in Fig. 3.

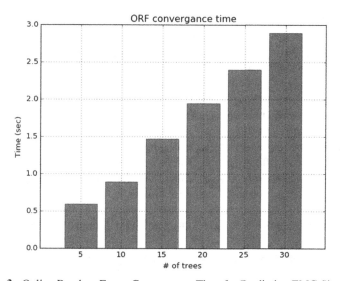

Fig. 3. Online Random Forest Convergence Time for Predicting EMG Signals

As, expected, Fig. 3 shows that the convergence time is directly proportional to the number of trees in the ORF model. The correspondent accuracy of the models in Fig. 3 is shown in Table 1. The collected data for this experiment is ~ 6000 data points of EMG signals and the associated labels. Based on Fig. 3 and Table 1, it can be noticed that the model must achieve a trade-off between accuracy and convergence time. The ORF model with 20 trees seems to be the most suitable model since it can converge in less than 2 s, and it achieves the highest detection accuracy.

Table 1. Number of Trees vs. Prediction Accuracy

Number of trees	5	10	15	20	25	30
Mean square error	0.26	0.19	0.250	0.14	0.15	0.17
Accuracy [%]	82.3	84.6	85.2	89.7	86.7	86.7

5 Conclusion and Future Work

A novel incremental learning approach was introduced to determine physical workload from EMG data in Human-Robot Collaboration. During the online training, a conflict became clear between processing speed and accuracy. Lesser trees in the model meant faster convergence, however, it also resulted in the aforementioned lower accuracy. Overall, the accuracy could reach 89% in only two seconds. Thus, in a Human-Robot Collaborative Scenario this would allow the system to recognize a human operator struggling with the payload. The collaborative robot could then support the operator and subsequently, create a more ergonomic environment. However, prior to this technology being ready to be used in a practical application, further testing is essential. This includes the need for a larger sample size in participants and a richer variety in lifting tasks. The current setup allows to detect muscle contraction in participant's forearms and biceps. Yet, more EMG sensors placed on other muscle groups such as triceps and shoulders are expected to provide better results for predicting pushing activities. Furthermore, the system could be trained to not only detect temporary high payloads but also to recognize muscular fatigue during endurance tasks. This could help to improve human operator's posture and subsequently prevent negative long-term health effects.

Nevertheless, early results of this incremental learning approach demonstrate a reduced manual fine-tuning effort and it coping well with subject specific characteristics in the data. This offers the potential to be applied for additional human sensor technologies and subsequent data classifications. Ultimately, this could help to make Human-Robot Collaboration safer and more efficient.

The software development in this work was conducted as a ROS package, which was made available and can be found in the Intelligent Automation GitHub [10].

Acknowledgment. This work was funded by the EPSRC as part of theDigital Toolkit for optimisation of operators and technology in manufacturing partnerships project (DigiTOP; EP/R032718/1).

References

1. Wang, W., et al.: Symbiotic human-robot collaborative assembly, In: CIRP Ann (2019)
2. Villani, V., Pini, F., Leali, F., Secchi, C.: Survey on human-robot collaboration in industrial settings: Safety, intuitive interfaces and applications. Mechatronics, **2018**, 1–19 (2017)
3. Krüger, J., Lien, T.K., Verl, A.: Cooperation of human and machines in assembly lines. CIRP Ann. - Manuf. Technol. **58**(2), 628–646 (2009)
4. Schmidtler, J., Bengler, K.: Fast or Accurate? – performance measurements for physical human-robot collaborations. In: Procedia Manufaturing, vol. 3, no. Ahfe, pp. 1387–1394 (2015)
5. Bi, L., Feleke, A., Guan, C.: A review on EMG-based motor intention prediction of continuous human upper limb motion for human-robot collaboration. Biomed. Signal Process. Control **51**, 113–127 (2019)
6. Peternel, L., Fang, C., Tsagarakis, N., Ajoudani, A.: A selective muscle fatigue management approach to ergonomic human-robot co-manipulation. Robot. Comput. Integr. Manuf. **58**(January), 69–79 (2019)

7. Bouchachia, A., Gabrys, B., Sahel, Z.: Overview of some incremental learning algorithms. In: IEEE International Conference Fuzzy System (2007)
8. Peternel, L., Tsagarakis, N., Caldwell, D., Ajoudani, A.: Robot adaptation to human physical fatigue in human–robot co-manipulation. Autonomous Robots **42**(5), 1011–1021 (2017). https://doi.org/10.1007/s10514-017-9678-1
9. Hakonen, M., Piitulainen, H., Visala, A.: Current state of digital signal processing in myoelectric interfaces and related applications. Biomed. Signal Process. Control **18**, 334–359 (2015)
10. github tool: Al-Yacoub, A., Buerkle, A., Flanagan, M., Ferreira, P., Hubbard, E.M., Lohse, N.: Effective human-robot collaboration through wearable sensors. In: 2020 25th IEEE International Conference on Emerging Technologies and Factory Automation (ETFA), vol. 1, pp. 651–658. IEEE, September 2020

Robotic Systems and Applications

An Upper Limb Fall Impediment Strategy for Humanoid Robots

Da Cui[1,2], Samuel Hudson[1], Robert Richardson[1], and Chengxu Zhou[1(✉)]

[1] School of Mechanical Engineering, University of Leeds, Leeds, UK
C.X.Zhou@leeds.ac.uk
[2] School of Mechanical and Aerospace Engineering,
Jilin University, Changchun, China

Abstract. Falling is an unavoidable problem for humanoid robots due to the inherent instability of bipedal locomotion. In this paper, we present a novel strategy for humanoid fall prevention by using environmental contacts. Humans favour to contact using the upper limbs with the proximate environmental object to prevent falling and subliminally or consciously select a pose that can generate suitable Cartesian stiffness of the arm end-effector. Inspired by this intuitive human interaction, we design a configuration optimization method to choose a well thought pose of the arm as it approaches the long axis of the stiffness ellipsoid, with the displacement direction of the end-effector to utilize the joint torques. In order to validate the proposed strategy, we perform several simulations in MATLAB & Simulink, in which this strategy proves to be effective and feasible.

1 Introduction

Due to the inherent instability of bipedal locomotion and the complexity of work scenarios [17], falling is a common risk for humanoid robots. This shortcoming is one of the key limitations that restrict the application in more general workspaces of these robots. To overcome this problem, there has been various balance control methods proposed, which can be categorized into: ankle [14], hip [23], stepping [15,19], heuristic [5] and online learning [21] strategies. However, if the external force exceeds the maximum capability or an obstacle constrains the stepping space, there is still a risk of falling. Therefore, there has been some advances in the field by proposing such strategies like falling trajectory optimization [18,22], pose reshaping [17] and adaptive compliance control [16]. However, these strategies mentioned do not consider wall exploitation or the use of utilizing differentiating environments to avoid falling. In [20], the authors presented a method for exploiting external objects to stabilize a falling robot. This approach uses a simplified three-link model consisting of a contact arm, torso and a stance leg. Besides humanoids, humans also risk falling despite the possession of excellent balance. Subsequently, it is observed that the upper limbs are frequently used to break falls. Based on this observation, Hoffman *et al.* [9] presented a

© Springer Nature Switzerland AG 2020
A. Mohammad et al. (Eds.): TAROS 2020, LNAI 12228, pp. 317–328, 2020.
https://doi.org/10.1007/978-3-030-63486-5_34

novel strategy using the arms to prevent falling, this strategy combines the passive stiffness of a compliance joint and active stiffness control to obtain a target stiffness of the arm when in contact with the wall.

Research on successful and safe fall arrest strategies of humans has attracted a lot of attention [2,6,7,10,11,13]. Inspired by human reaction and the previous studies mentioned, this paper presents an optimal fall prevention strategy by using upper limbs of humanoid robots. Falls are inevitable for humans, where the upper limbs is frequently used to break falls and primary used to absorb impact [10,11]. The muscle mechanism is essentially a force dampening system which adjusts the amount of shock accordingly through eccentric contractions about the joints [13]. The joint resistance produced by muscle corresponding deformation is defined as joint stiffness [12]. The pose of arm and joint stiffness play an important role at impact. For example, if the elbow join maintains a high stiffness when contact occurs, it may result in a high damage risk due to under attenuation [2,3,7]. On the other hand, low joint stiffness may result in excessive joint gyration, thus not being able to support the body [8]. If the joint has insufficient stiffness due to muscle weakness, the individual can stretch the arm to compensate for this due to there being higher joint stiffness demands to control a forward fall with increased bending of the arm [6,7].

There is a fine balance between insufficient and excessive joint stiffness that may result in collapse or increase the risk injury respectively [4]. In order to obtain a balanced relationship between joint stiffness, arm pose and arm stiffness, we consider a tool known as the Stiffness ellipsoid which describes specifications of desired force/displacement behavior [1]. The stiffness ellipsoid maps the joint stiffness to end-effector stiffness, whose geometry of the stiffness ellipsoid is affected by the joint stiffness and position. Along the positive long axis of the stiffness ellipsoid, the stiffness of the end-effector can alter over a wide range, completed by the active stiffness control within the joint. Therefore, in order to generate the arm configuration to ensure proper interactions and contact stability for a diverse range of tasks, we set the object to choose an arm pose with the maximum value of the stiffness ellipsoid along the displacement direction of the arm end-effector during contact. This object has two implicit purposes, one is to minimize the angle between the displacement direction and the long axis of the stiffness ellipsoid, and the other one is to maximize the long axis length of the stiffness ellipsoid of the arm end-effector.

The presentation of this work is arranged as follows. Section 2 presents the problems that our strategy addresses. Section 3 details the contact pose optimization algorithm. Section 4 demonstrates simulation results and finally, Sect. 5 concludes the paper.

2   Problem Statement

Consider the scenario demonstrated in Fig. 1, an external force is applied on the robot in the sagittal direction to then push it positively forward. The robot may not be able to maintain balance alone, but can prevent falling by exploiting an

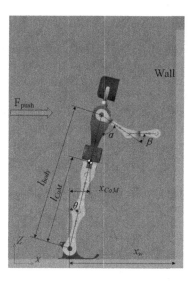

Fig. 1. An illustration of the how the robots fall prevention strategy will operate using the wall

external physical object in front of it, where it is defined as a vertical wall in this paper. We assume that the distance between the robot and the wall is known, and the robot must react quickly and efficiently to support itself using only the upper limbs. To solve this problem, we divide the process into three stages: i) fall detection, ii) pre-impact and iii) post-impact. The first step required to prevent the fall, is to detect the fall. The robot needs to judge whether it will fall down based on the information from the sensor. The second pre-impact step, is defined by the time period from when the fall is detected, until impact [8], where it is critical for a pose to be chosen prior to contact with the landing environment. This is where the significance and contributions of this study lie. The post-impact step then describes the movement occurring immediately after impact until stabilization. In this phase, the accumulated momentum during the fall should be absorbed before exceeding the joint limits.

3   Fall Prevention Strategy

3.1   Fall Detection

A simple method is used for fall detection in this work. When the robot is falling forward due to an external force, the horizontal velocity $\dot{x}_{CoM}$ of the center of mass (CoM) is measured by the onboard inertial measurement unit (IMU). When the measured value exceeds the threshold value $\dot{x}_{th}$ (here $\dot{x}_{th}$ is selected by experience), the arm manoeuvre will be executed in order to prevent falling. Thus, when

$$\dot{x}_{CoM} \geq \dot{x}_{th},$$

the manoeuvre is executed.

3.2 Contact Pose Optimization

Subsequent to the triggering of the fall prevention manoeuvre, the reaction controller must choose a proper configuration of the arm coming into contact. Our configuration optimizer improves the performance of the arm by using a limited supply of time and actuation power to absorb the momentum accumulated during falling. Due to limited actuation and safety constraints, the undesired momentum cannot be absorbed immediately. However, the momentum must be absorbed before reaching the positional limit (joint limits and environment collision). Therefore, the arm should have necessary compliance to sustain all external forces without body collapse.

For this approach we want to choose a pose of the upper limp that approaches the long axis of the Cartesian stiffness ellipsoid with the direction of the displacement following that of the end-effector. The Cartesian stiffness ellipsoid is described by the following. Consider the upper extremity as an n degrees of freedom manipulator, and whose hand acts as the end-effector, fixed to a wrist in an m-dimensional task space. Let τ, be the joint torque matrix, $\mathbf{q} = [\alpha, \beta]^T$ be the joint configuration containing the shoulder joint, α, and the elbow joint, β, and $\mathbf{K}_q = diag(k_{q_1}, k_{q_2}, k_{q_2}, ..., k_{q_n})$ be the joint stiffness matrix. Assuming there are rigid connections between joints, the relationship between the joint deformation and joint torque, $\delta\mathbf{q}$, can be described as

$$\tau = \mathbf{K}_q \delta\mathbf{q}. \tag{1}$$

Mapping of the joint deformation into Cartesian end-effector displacement $\delta\mathbf{x}$ is described by the linear relation,

$$\delta\mathbf{x} = \mathbf{J}\delta\mathbf{q}, \tag{2}$$

where $\mathbf{J}$ is the forward kinematic Jacobian matrix, where $\mathbf{J} \in \mathbb{R}^{m \times n}$. Consider the relationship between the joint torque τ and the generalized force $\mathbf{F}$ of the end-effector to be

$$\tau = \mathbf{J}^T \mathbf{F}, \tag{3}$$

means we can obtain the extrapolated form

$$\delta\mathbf{x} = \mathbf{J}\mathbf{K}^{-1}\mathbf{J}^T \mathbf{F}. \tag{4}$$

Let, $\mathbf{C} = \mathbf{J}(\mathbf{K}_q)^{-1}\mathbf{J}^T$, be the Cartesian compliance matrix. Where the inverse of $\mathbf{C}$ is $\mathbf{S} = \mathbf{J}^{-1}\mathbf{K}_q(\mathbf{J}^T)^{-1}$ and is the Cartesian stiffness matrix. When one unit deformation occurs at the end-effector,

$$(\delta\mathbf{x})^T (\delta\mathbf{x}) = 1. \tag{5}$$

Now, substituting (4) into (5), obtains

$$\mathbf{F}^T \mathbf{C}^T \mathbf{C} \mathbf{F} = 1. \tag{6}$$

In a given configuration, (6) can represent a m-dimensional force ellipsoid, which is the Cartesian stiffness ellipsoid of the manipulator. A point on the ellipsoid indicates the magnitude of the generalized force applied on the end-effector, that produces one unit displacement along the direction of that point. The eigenvectors of the matrix constitute of the principal axis of the ellipsoid, and the corresponding eigenvalues, are the inverse square of the semi-axis length of the respective principal axis.

To reach an efficient balance between a soft landing and adequate support, consider the following optimization function:

$$\max_{\mathbf{q}_e} \left\| \mathbf{n}^T \mathbf{S(q)n} \right\|, \tag{7}$$

where $\mathbf{q}_e = [\theta, \alpha, \beta]^T$, is the joint position containing the angles of the ankle, shoulder and elbow respectively. $\mathbf{S(q)}$ is the Cartesian stiffness matrix of the arm, $\mathbf{n}$ is the inverse direction vector of the shoulder when contact occurs. In order to avoid calculation of the inverse Jacobian, (7) is changed to minimize the compliance, so that

$$\min_{\mathbf{q}_e} \left\| \mathbf{n}^T \mathbf{C(q)n} \right\|. \tag{8}$$

There is a positional constraint where the end-effector of the arm should place on the physical object, defined by

$$f(P_x, P_z) = 0, \tag{9}$$

where the function, $f(x,z) = 0$ represents the profile of the physical object in x-z plane, and $\mathbf{P}_p = [P_x(\mathbf{q}_e), P_z(\mathbf{q}_e)]$ is the forward kinematic coordinate of the end-effector in x-z plane. In the following simulation carried out, the physical object is a wall defined by $f(x,z) = ax + bz + c$. In order to obtain feasibility, the joint constraints are defined.

In order to obtain feasibility a few constraints are defined. To decrease the displacement of the shoulder joint α and elbow joint β and avoid singularity, the target position should be set within a range:

$$\alpha_{\min} \leq \alpha \leq \alpha_{\max} \tag{10}$$
$$\beta_{\min} \leq \beta \leq \beta_{\max}. \tag{11}$$

The ankle joint θ is underactuated and moving under the initial external force and gravitational force, thus the angle of the ankle joint, θ must be greater than the angle of the arm to ensure the arm has sufficient time to reach the target position

$$\theta_{\min} = \sin^{-1}(x_{CoM}/l_{CoM}) \tag{12}$$
$$+ \int_0^{t_f} \left[\dot{x}_{CoM}/l_{CoM} + \int_0^{t_f} gl_{CoM} \sin \theta(t) dt \right] dt, \tag{13}$$

where the x_{CoM} and $\dot{x}_{CoM}$ are the position and velocity of the CoM at the time when the fall prevention is triggered. t_f is the maximum time for the arm to reach the target position:

$$t_f = \max \left\{ \frac{\alpha_{\max}}{\omega_{\max}}, \frac{\beta_{\max}}{\omega_{\max}} \right\}, \tag{14}$$

Table 1. Model Parameters.

Parameter	Value	Description
Total mass	25 kg	
Height	0.45 m	
l_{body}	0.3762 m	From ankle joint to shoulder joint
l_{arm}	0.1782 m	Sum of $l_{upperarm}$ and $l_{forearm}$
$l_{upperarm}$	0.089 m	From shoulder joint to elbow joint
$l_{forearm}$	0.0892 m	From elbow joint to end-effector
K	$1e^6$ N/m	Contact stiffness
B	0.6 N/(m/s)	Contact damping
μ_f	0.6	Contact coefficient of friction

where the maximum joint velocity ω_{max} is constrained by the hardware. The final optimization problem is:

$$\min_{\mathbf{q}_e} \quad \left\|\mathbf{n}^T \mathbf{C}(\mathbf{q})\mathbf{n}\right\|$$
$$\text{subject to} \quad f(P_x, P_z) = 0 \qquad (15)$$
$$\mathbf{q}_{min} \le \mathbf{q}_e \le \mathbf{q}_{max}.$$

4   Simulation

In order to validate the proposed strategy, we test it in MATLAB & Simulink under two scenarios. The parameters of the robot are listed in Table 1. The optimal contact pose is solved by the *fmincon* function. The simulation scenarios are shown in Fig. 2 and Fig. 3 with $x_w = 0.25$ m and $x_w = 0.30$ m respectively. A horizontal impulsive force is applied to the rear of the robot, and the upper limbs' motion executes when the $\dot{x}_{CoM}$ exceeds a threshold of $\dot{x}_{th} = 0.37$ m/s.

Shown in Fig. 2 and Fig. 3, the robot is initially in a standing position with the arms naturally resting. Figure 2(a) and Fig. 2(b) shows the robot fall forward under the external force, where the ankle angle exceeds the threshold value, thus triggering the arm motion. In Fig. 2(c) the arms have stroked the desired pose, and Fig. 2(d), finally shows the arms interaction with the wall to prevent falling. Figure 3 replicates this, but for $x_w = 0.30$ m.

The optimizations result in the desired configurations:

$$x_w = 0.25 \,\text{m} \;:\; \mathbf{q}_{e,d1} = [0.3000, 0.8917, 1.0014]^T$$
$$x_w = 0.30 \,\text{m} \;:\; \mathbf{q}_{e,d2} = [0.3046, 1.6652, 0.4200]^T.$$

Figure 4 shows the stiffness ellipsoid of the arms end-effector, and it can be seen that the optimized joint configuration approximately aligns the long axis of the stiffness ellipsoid with the velocity direction of the shoulder joint. Compared

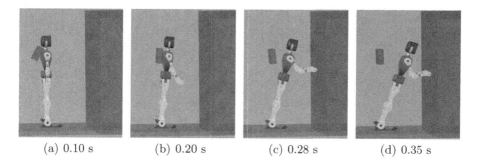

(a) 0.10 s   (b) 0.20 s   (c) 0.28 s   (d) 0.35 s

Fig. 2. Fall prevention strategy simulation, $x_w = 0.25$ m

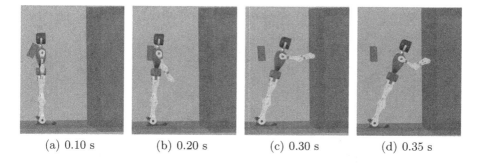

(a) 0.10 s   (b) 0.20 s   (c) 0.30 s   (d) 0.35 s

Fig. 3. Fall prevention strategy simulation, $x_w = 0.30$ m

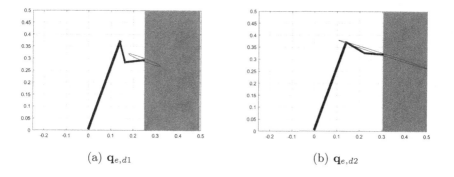

(a) $\mathbf{q}_{e,d1}$ (b) $\mathbf{q}_{e,d2}$

Fig. 4. The red line illustrate the stiffness ellipsoid of the arm (Color figure online)

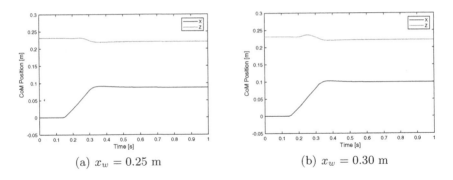

(a) $x_w = 0.25$ m   (b) $x_w = 0.30$ m

Fig. 5. Position of the CoM of the robot

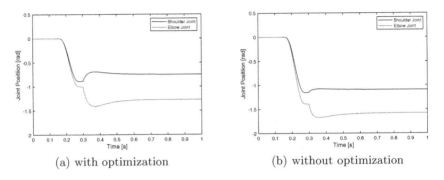

(a) with optimization   (b) without optimization

Fig. 6. Variation of joint position for $x_w = 0.25$ m

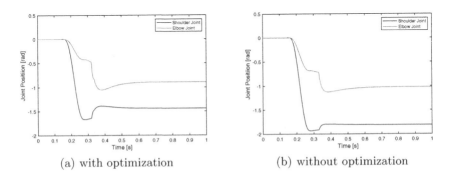

(a) with optimization   (b) without optimization

Fig. 7. Variation of joint position for $x_w = 0.30$ m

with Fig. 4(a), the configuration in Fig. 4(b) has a lengthier long axis stiffness ellipsoid, due to the sufficiency of space for a more stretched arm. The results correspond to our anticipated human fall arrest.

In order to illustrate the detailed implementation of the strategy, we show the variation of the robot's CoM position in x-z plane with time in Fig. 5. Initially the robot stands upright, then an external is force impacted and the robot begins to fall forward. The robot falls about the axis of the ankle angle which is noticeably seen as an inverted pendulum, therefore the CoM of the robot decreases along the z-axis and moves forward along the x-axis under the effects of gravity. When the arm comes into contact with the wall, the CoM movement terminates. Figure 6 and Fig. 7 demonstrate the variation of the shoulder joint and the elbow joint, which represents the reaction of the arm. When the fall is detected, the shoulder joint and elbow joint rotate to emulate the target position. Once contact between the arm and the wall occurs, the arm works as a damping-spring system. The arm generates a resistive force corresponding to the displacement to absorb the impact and stabilize the robot. Comparing Fig. 6(a) and Fig. 6(b), the joint without an optimized configuration changed far greater when contact occurs than with the normal configuration. This means that if there is a excessive impact, the arm may have insufficient stiffness to stabilize the robot that would result in collapse. Similar conclusions can be drawn from Fig. 7(a) and Fig. 7(b).

Figure 8 shows the joint torque of the arm within simulation. In Fig. 8(a), the arm comes into contact with the wall with an optimized configuration, and it is seen that in order to achieve the target stiffness when contact occurs, the maximum joint torque of the shoulder and elbow joints are -12.8 Nm and 9 Nm respectively. Figure 8(b) shows the same scenario without an optimized joint configuration. The maximum joint torques are 18.6 Nm and 13 Nm respectively, which are greater than in Fig. 8(a). Figure 9 shows a similar result. The results demonstrate that the required joint torque is smaller with the optimized configuration for the same Cartesian stiffness of the end-effector, and also means that an optimized configuration can vary over a greater range as a limited actuator.

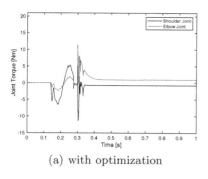
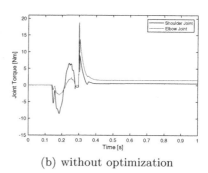

(a) with optimization   (b) without optimization

Fig. 8. Variation of joint torque for $x_w = 0.25$ m

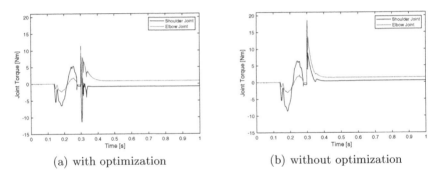

(a) with optimization   (b) without optimization

Fig. 9. Variation of joint torque for $x_w = 0.30$ m

5   Conclusion

In this paper, a novel fall prevention strategy for humanoid robots using their inherent upper limbs is presented. The main concept is inspired by the fall arrest of a human; humans prefer using the direction of their respective arms stiffness ellipsoid against the direction of fall. We present an optimized algorithm used to generate arm posing, subsequently reducing the joint torque when interacting with a wall in a compliant behavioral manner. The strategy is triggered by a fall detection system, and once falling has begun, the upper limbs kinematics are generated and executed by the optimization algorithm. Finally, validation of the proposed strategy is completed via a simulation environment, and the results successfully show the strategy to be efficient and effective, where the optimal configuration shows to inherit a better performance. Future work will expand on the same strategy applied in a 3D scenario and physical tests.

Acknowledgment. This work is supported by the Engineering and Physical Sciences Research Council (Grant No. EP/R513258/1).

References

1. Ajoudani, A., Tsagarakis, N.G., Bicchi, A.: Choosing poses for force and stiffness control. IEEE Trans. Rob. **33**(6), 1483–1490 (2017). https://doi.org/10.1109/TRO.2017.2708087
2. Borrelli, J., Creath, R., Rogers, M.W.: Protective arm movements are modulated with fall height. J. Biomech. **99**, 109569 (2020). https://doi.org/10.1016/j.jbiomech.2019.109569
3. Burkhart, T.A., Andrews, D.M.: Kinematics, kinetics and muscle activation patterns of the upper extremity during simulated forward falls. J. Electromyogr. Kinesiol. **23**(3), 688–695 (2013). https://doi.org/10.1016/j.jelekin.2013.01.015
4. Butler, R.J., Crowell III, H.P., Davis, I.M.: Lower extremity stiffness: implications for performance and injury. Clin. Biomech. **18**(6), 511–517 (2003). https://doi.org/10.1016/S0268-0033(03)00071-8

5. Castano, J., Zhou, C., Tsagarakis, N.: Design a fall recovery strategy for a wheel-legged quadruped robot using stability feature space. In: IEEE International Conference on Robotics and Biomimetics, pp. 41–46 (2019). 0000-0002-6677-0855
6. Chiu, J., Robinovitch, S.N.: Prediction of upper extremity impact forces during falls on the outstretched hand. J. Biomech. **31**(12), 1169–1176 (1998). https://doi.org/10.1016/S0021-9290(98)00137-7
7. Chou, P.H., et al.: Effect of elbow flexion on upper extremity impact forces during a fall. Clin. Biomech. **16**(10), 888–894 (2001). https://doi.org/10.1016/S0268-0033(01)00086-9
8. DeGoede, K., Ashton-Miller, J., Schultz, A.: Fall-related upper body injuries in the older adult: a review of the biomechanical issues. J. Biomech. **36**(7), 1043–1053 (2003). https://doi.org/10.1016/S0021-9290(03)00034-4
9. Hoffman, E.M., Perrin, N., Tsagarakis, N.G., Caldwell, D.G.: Upper limb compliant strategy exploiting external physical constraints for humanoid fall avoidance. In: IEEE-RAS International Conference on Humanoid Robots, pp. 397–402 (2013). https://doi.org/10.1109/HUMANOIDS.2013.7030005
10. Hsu, H.H., Chou, Y.L., Lou, S.Z., Huang, M.J., Chou, P.P.H.: Effect of forearm axially rotated posture on shoulder load and shoulder abduction/flexion angles in one-armed arrest of forward falls. Clin. Biomech. **26**(3), 245–249 (2011). https://doi.org/10.1016/j.clinbiomech.2010.10.006
11. Kim, K.J., Ashton-Miller, J.A.: Biomechanics of fall arrest using the upper extremity: age differences. Clin. Biomech. **18**(4), 311–318 (2003). https://doi.org/10.1016/S0268-0033(03)00005-6
12. Latash, M.L., Zatsiorsky, V.M.: Joint stiffness: myth or reality? Hum. Mov. Sci. **12**(6), 653–692 (1993). https://doi.org/10.1016/0167-9457(93)90010-M
13. Lattimer, L., et al.: Biomechanical and physiological age differences in a simulated forward fall on outstretched hands in women. Clin. Biomech. **52**, 102–108 (2018). https://doi.org/10.1016/j.clinbiomech.2018.01.018
14. Li, Z., Zhou, C., Zhu, Q., Xiong, R.: Humanoid balancing behavior featured by underactuated foot motion. IEEE Trans. Rob. **33**(2), 298–312 (2017). https://doi.org/10.1109/TRO.2016.2629489
15. Pratt, J., Carff, J., Drakunov, S., Goswami, A.: Capture point: a step toward humanoid push recovery. In: IEEE-RAS International Conference on Humanoid Robots, pp. 200–207 (2006). https://doi.org/10.1109/ICHR.2006.321385
16. Samy, V., Caron, S., Bouyarmane, K., Kheddar, A.: Post-impact adaptive compliance for humanoid falls using predictive control of a reduced model. In: IEEE-RAS International Conference on Humanoid Robots, pp. 655–660 (2017). https://doi.org/10.1109/HUMANOIDS.2017.8246942
17. Samy, V., Kheddar, A.: Falls control using posture reshaping and active compliance. In: IEEE-RAS International Conference on Humanoid Robots, pp. 908–913 (2015). https://doi.org/10.1109/HUMANOIDS.2015.7363469
18. Wang, J., Whitman, E.C., Stilman, M.: Whole-body trajectory optimization for humanoid falling. In: American Control Conference, pp. 4837–4842 (2012). https://doi.org/10.1109/ACC.2012.6315177
19. Wang, R., Hudson, S., Li, Y., Wu, H., Zhou, C.: Normalized neural network for energy efficient bipedal walking using nonlinear inverted pendulum model. In: IEEE International Conference on Robotics and Biomimetics, pp. 1399–1405 (2019). https://doi.org/10.1109/ROBIO49542.2019.8961646

20. Wang, S., Hauser, K.: Real-time stabilization of a falling humanoid robot using hand contact: an optimal control approach. In: IEEE-RAS International Conference on Humanoid Robots, pp. 454–460 (2017). https://doi.org/10.1109/HUMANOIDS.2017.8246912
21. Yi, S.J., Zhang, B.T., Hong, D., Lee, D.D.: Online learning of low dimensional strategies for high-level push recovery in bipedal humanoid robots. In: IEEE International Conference on Robotics and Automation, pp. 1649–1655 (2013). https://doi.org/10.1109/ICRA.2013.6630791
22. Yun, S.K., Goswami, A.: Tripod fall: concept and experiments of a novel approach to humanoid robot fall damage reduction. In: IEEE International Conference on Robotics and Automation, pp. 2799–2805 (2014). https://doi.org/10.1109/ICRA.2014.6907260
23. Zhou, C., Li, Z., Castano, J., Dallali, H., Tsagarakis, N., Caldwell, D.: A passivity based compliance stabilizer for humanoid robots. In: IEEE International Conference on Robotics and Automation, pp. 1487–1492 (2014). https://doi.org/10.1109/ICRA.2014.6907048

Requirements Specification and Integration Architecture for Perception in a Cooperative Team of Forestry Robots

David Portugal[1] 📵, João Filipe Ferreira[1,2](✉) 📵, and Micael S. Couceiro[3] 📵

[1] Institute of Systems and Robotics, University of Coimbra,
3030-290 Coimbra, Portugal
{davidbsp,jfilipe}@isr.uc.pt

[2] Computational Neuroscience and Cognitive Robotics Group,
School of Science and Technology, Nottingham Trent University,
Nottingham NG11 8NS, UK
joao.ferreira@ntu.ac.uk

[3] Ingeniarius, Rua Coronel Veiga Simão, Edifício B CTCV,
3025-307 Coimbra, Portugal
micael@ingeniarius.pt

Abstract. The SEMFIRE project proposes the development of a multi-robot system to assist in woodland landscaping maintenance tasks for wildfire prevention, addressing in the process several challenges in forestry and field robotics. In this paper, we identify these challenges following a requirement analysis stage and delineated intervention scenarios, proposing detailed specification of the SEMFIRE ecosystem. This includes a technical and functional specification and the integration architecture of the software and hardware system components, with a special focus on the modules responsible for enacting cooperative perception with the team of robots. This team encompasses multiple UAVs and a heavy-duty forestry UGV. A plan for system development, integration and deployment is also described to lay out upcoming work.

Keywords: Forestry robotics · Cooperative perception · System requirements · Integration architecture

1 Introduction

Despite many advances in key areas, the development of fully autonomous robotic solutions for precision forestry is still in a very early stage. This stems

This work was supported by the Safety, Exploration and Maintenance of Forests with Ecological Robotics (SEMFIRE, ref. CENTRO-01-0247-FEDER-03269) and the Centre of Operations for Rethinking Engineering (CORE, ref. CENTRO-01-0247-FEDER-037082) research projects co-funded by the "Agência Nacional de Inovação" within the Portugal2020 programme.

© Springer Nature Switzerland AG 2020
A. Mohammad et al. (Eds.): TAROS 2020, LNAI 12228, pp. 329–344, 2020.
https://doi.org/10.1007/978-3-030-63486-5_35

from the huge challenges imposed by rough terrain traversability [14], for example due to steep slopes, autonomous outdoor navigation and locomotion systems [13], limited perception capabilities [6], and reasoning and planning under a high-level of uncertainty [11]. Artificial perception for robots operating in outdoor natural environments has been studied for several decades. For robots operating in forest scenarios, in particular, there is research dating from the late 80s-early 90s – see, for example, [5]. Nevertheless, despite many years of research, as described in surveys over time [e.g. 7,8,15], a substantial amount of problems have yet to be robustly solved. The SEMFIRE project aims to research approaches to solve these problems in real-world scenarios in forestry robotics – please find a presentation of the project and a full survey of the state of the art in [2].

In this paper, we identify the challenges for forestry robots imposed by an end-user requirement analysis and a use case scenario delineated for the SEM-FIRE project[1] and propose detailed functional requirements. Moreover, a technical specification of the robotic platforms is conducted, identifying the main component design decisions taken. Afterwards, we specify the modular and decoupled system architecture to integrate the technologies and software solutions required by the project, taking a closer look at the cooperative robotic perception architecture, and proposing a core design of the perception pipeline and decision-making module functionality. We discuss our plan for system development and integration as well as deployment of the system in the field, and finalise by presenting key conclusions and main lines of future work.

2   SEMFIRE Use Case Analysis

The analysis of the literature on robots for precision forestry [1–3], and the experience of our SEMFIRE end-user partners has demonstrated that (1) there is very little work in automated solutions dedicated to the issue of precision forestry; (2) there is a lack of solutions for robotic teams; and (3) there is a number of untackled problems due to hardware specificity.

With this in mind, we have drawn a very specific use case: the application of robotic teams in precision forestry for fire prevention. Our solution for autonomous precision forestry is comprised of a heterogeneous robotic team composed of two types of robots, the *Ranger*, a 4000 kg autonomous UGV, based on the Bobcat T190, equipped with a mechanical mulcher for forest clearing, and a swarm of *Scouts*, small UAVs equipped with additional perceptual abilities to assist the *Ranger* in its efforts. The *Ranger*, a marsupial robot, is able to carry the swarm of *Scouts* via a small trailer, while recharging their batteries.

1. Initial Deployment. The mission starts with the placement of the *Ranger* in the proximity of the operating theatre (OT). The *Ranger* can be tele-operated or driven to a specific starting location, while carrying the *Scouts*. This enables the easy deployment of the robot team, even over difficult terrain, as the *Ranger*'s

---

[1] http://semfire.ingeniarius.pt/.

mobility capabilities can be harnessed to assist in this phase of the missions. Once the robotic team is placed close enough to the target area, a human operator signals the start of the mission.

With the mission start, the *Scouts* autonomously spread while maintaining a multimodal connectivity among each other and the *Ranger* through distributed formation control, thus leading to a certain degree of spatial compactness above the target area, defined by a combination of human input via a dedicated interface, and the *Scouts'* own positions.

2. Reconnaissance. This phase of the mission consists on having Scouts collectively exploring the target area with the goal of finding the regions of interest (ROIs) within this area that contain combustible material, e.g. fuel accumulation such as flammable debris, that should be mulched. The result of this phase is a semantic map that results from the collective exploration of the OT, containing information on the location of regions that need intervention and of regions that should be preserved, among other elements. After the semantic map is obtained, the *Scouts* fly to key points that delimit the target area, while maintaining communication, and remain stationary. The *Scouts* then perform two main tasks: aid the *Ranger* in localizing itself, and monitoring the progress of the clearing task, by assessing the fraction of existing debris over their initial state.

3. Clearing. At this point, the *Ranger* starts the mulching procedure, the main goal of the mission that will reduce the accumulation of combustible material. This mission essentially consists of cutting down trees and mowing down ground vegetation (e.g. bushes, shrubs, brush, etc.). At this point, the artificial perception layer becomes especially relevant, namely to *i)* localise the team in space; *ii)* due to the powerful tool it is wielding - a heavy-duty skid-Steer forestry

Table 1. Functional Specification Table (Hardware and Low-Level).

Function/Module	Requirement	Specification
Outdoor Robotic Technology	*Ranger* locomotion in all types of terrains, and reliefs. Operation of the platforms for long periods of time. Robustness to adverse outdoor conditions, e.g. in dusty, and watery atmospheres	*Ranger* Incline/decline traversal ability over $15°$. *Ranger* autonomy over 12 h, and *Scouts* autonomy over 30 min of continuous operation. IP54 protection
Low-Level Drivers	Acquisition of data from the platform sensors, and availability of the data to high-level software modules	Low-level driver for ROS developed and available for all sensors chosen (*cf.* Sect. 3)
Ranger's Mechanical Mulcher	Manual and automated control of the mechanical structure and mulcher operation, with precise end-effector position tracking	Low-level ROS driver to control the arm, including encoders to track the end-effector configuration. Fast de/activation of the mulcher, with ability to cut up to 10 cm and mulch up to 8 cm of material
Marsupial System	Carrying of the team of at least 4 *Scouts* to the field by the *Ranger* before the mission, and collecting back the *Scouts* after the mission. Charging of *Scouts* by the *Ranger*, while being carried	Inclusion and development of a trailer to be attached to the *Ranger* for carrying and charging the *Scouts*, allowing their take-off and landing for operations

mulcher that can cut up to 10 cm and mulch up to 8 cm of material, and *iii)* to identify and keep a safe distance from external elements within the OT (e.g., unauthorised humans or animals).

As the trees are cut down, vegetation is mowed and fuel is removed, the structure and appearance of the operational environment changes significantly and must be tracked. The mission ends when the volume of combustible material in the target area falls below a pre-defined threshold, ideally zero.

4. Aftermath. The end of the mission needs to be confirmed by a human operator, who can at this point indicate new ROIs for exploration and intervention, or tele-operate the *Ranger* to finish the mission in manual mode. When the end of the mission is confirmed by the operator, the Scout swarm regroups autonomously on the trailer, and the team can then be moved to another location or stored.

Human Intervention. A specialised human operator, the *Foreman*, represents the expert knowledge in the field, and acts as a supervisor to the robotic team. At any point in the mission, the *Foreman* can issue commands to override the autonomous decisions of the *Ranger*. This includes emergency stops for interruption of operations at any time and due to any reason, as well as control takeover of the *Ranger* to remotely finish a clearing procedure at a safe distance. The *Foreman* is also responsible for refining the target area, and a human team can intervene before or after the robotic mission to clear areas that are considered too inaccessible for the robots; as some areas may require expertise or precision that makes it impossible for the *Ranger* to intervene.

Analysis. The use case scenario described above, represents several challenges from a technical and scientific perspective. Namely, the platforms need to be robust to very adverse outdoor conditions, and encompass safety mechanisms during all phases of operation. As illustrated by the challenges mentioned in Fig. 1, adequate techniques for artificial perception are required, and also techniques for localisation, navigation, aerial control and communications within the multi-robot system must be developed to support high-level collective decision-making, marsupial multi-robot system operation, *Scouts'* exploration, deployment, formation control and regrouping, and the clearing operation of the *Ranger* robot, which brings the added challenge of safely controlling the mechanical mulcher for forestry maintenance. Finally, there will be a significant effort envisaged for system integration, which will allow to interface SEMFIRE with the human operator, e.g. representing the overall environment as perceived by the robots in a GUI, or allowing to have access to live video streams from the *Ranger* platform at a safe distance. In the next section, we provide detailed specification to address the challenges identified.

(a) Usable image: good perspective, illumination and not blurry.

(b) As the robot moves, perpective changes will affect the results.

(c) Since the robots will move in the field, some images will be blurred.

(d) Illumination differences will naturally be an issue in the field.

Fig. 1. Examples of pictures taken outdoors, which could be captured by a camera attached to a robot in the field. Several issues can affect these images, hindering perception.

3 Functional and Technical Specification

We now present the specifications for the SEMFIRE project. We start by detailing the needed functions and features that the system is expected to have, and later we describe the platforms and sensors that have been chosen to fulfill the functional specifications delineated.

Functional Specification. For each challenge identified, we describe the intended function, requirements and specifications, which may also serve as guide for possible targets of performance to the modules designed and developed in the SEMFIRE multi-robot system. The functional specifications are divided in 4 main features categories, organized from Table 1, 2, 3 and 4:

1. Hardware and Low-Level (Table 1).
2. Supporting Features (Table 2).
3. High-Level Features (Table 3).
4. Safety and Integration (Table 4).

Technical Specification. We now detail the platforms and sensors chosen to implement the system to fulfill the functional specification that has been delineated before.

Ranger. The base of the *Ranger* is a Bobcat T190 (Fig. 2) tracked loader. This platform was selected by a number of reasons: *i)* It is able to carry the tools, namely the mechanical mulcher, necessary to complete the task; *ii)* This particular model is completely *fly-by-wire*, meaning that it is possible to tap into its electronic control mechanisms to develop remote and autonomous control routines; and *iii)* It is a well-known, well-supported machine with readily-available maintenance experts. The platform is extended in numerous ways, namely in sensory abilities.

The C16 LIDARs will act as the main sources of spatial information for the machine, providing information on occupation and reflectivity at up to 70 m

Table 2. Functional Specification Table (Supporting Features).

Function/Module	Requirement	Specification
Localisation	Precise 6D localisation (x, y, z position, and φ, θ, ψ orientation) of the *Ranger*s and *Scouts* in a common global reference frame during all times	Multimodal EKF approach for localisation with cm-level precision, fusing several key sources of information, such as visual odometry from cameras, LIDAR-based SLAM estimates using 3D LIDARs, IMU integration for orientation tracking, and global positioning both from GPS-RTK and a field deployed UWB triangulation system
Ranger Navigation	Execution of navigation path plans from the current configuration to a target pose, in different types of terrains and reliefs, with several obstacles in a dynamic and challenging outdoor environment	ROS navigation software developed and adapted to the specificity of the platform (e.g. avoiding in-turn rotations as recovery behaviours, and providing safe mechanisms for manoeuvrability), without collisions during operation
Scouts Aerial Control	Control of the aerial platforms with the ability to maintain fixed heights and poses, as targeted by users and the application	Aerial control and stability software that allows sending precise target aerial configurations for *Scouts*, while avoiding collisions with the environment and with other Scout teammates
Artificial Perception	Holistic forestry scene analysis, including recognition and tracking of relevant entities and events	A perceptual architecture for decision-making will be developed, including (A) an artificial attention system for allocating and directing sensors and computational resources to task-relevant regions of interest within a scene, while selecting the appropriate scale of detail of analysis, driving (B) a semantic segmentation layer for identifying objects of interest and regions of interest within the objects (including relevant trees, vegetation, combustible material, traversable areas, and humans) with a targeted precision of 95%. A semantic map will be maintained to support and keep track of entities and events detected
Communication	Provide an infrastructure for explicit communication between all agents of the SEMFIRE team	An access point will be included in the *Ranger* platform, and all *Scouts* will connect to it, and maintain their connectivity at all times, constraining their operation by always guaranteeing the persistent connectivity of the communication infrastructure

Table 3. Functional Specification Table (High-Level Features).

Function/Module	Requirement	Specification
Decision-Making	Based on the events and entities detected by the artificial perception layer, and the overall state of the environment, a decision-making component chooses the current operation mode for each platform	A decision-making module based on Finite State Machines (FSMs) will be developed for intelligent switching of operations during missions, with a low error (below 2%) in situation assessment
Scout Exploration	Collective reconnaissance of the target area with *Scouts*	Tightly coupled with the artificial perception layer, the RDPSO swarm exploration approach will be used for forestry reconnaissance, feeding the semantic map with the combustible material detected with a reconstruction reliability of 90%
Scout Initial Deployment	Take off and spreading of *Scouts* in the environment after the start of the mission	A synchronized take-off routine will be implemented to allow for sequential initial deployment of each Scout in the environment without collisions or any anomalies
Scout Formation Control	Formation flight of *Scouts* while maintaining multimodal connectivity among each other and the *Ranger*	Formation control strategies will be implemented with geographical restrictions for maintaining communications connectivity with a high reliability (the system should be connected 99% of the time), and for optimization of *Scouts*' positioning, thus assisting the localisation of the *Ranger* via the UWB triangulation system
Scout Regrouping	Autonomous landing of *Scouts* in the *Ranger*'s trailer	A synchronized routine will be implemented to allow for sequential landing of each Scout in the *Ranger*'s trailer without collisions or anomalies, considering their distance to the trailer and battery status
Ranger Clearing	Sequential visit to all ROIs and mulching procedure to eliminate fuel accumulation via the *Ranger* platform	An algorithm for effectively visiting all identified ROIs will be developed, minimizing the traversal distance of the *Ranger*. A synchronization module will be responsible for coupling the *Ranger* navigation with the mulcher's control

distance with a 360-degree field of view (FOV). Equipped with 16 laser channels per device, these sensors will provide a very wide overview of the platform's surroundings, namely the structure of the environment, and potentially the positions of obstacles, traversability and locations of trees. The RealSense cameras have a much narrower FOV and range; they are installed on the machine to create a high-resolution security envelope around it. These sensors will compensate for the gaps on the LIDARs' field of view, to observe the space closer to the machine, ensuring the safety of any personnel and animals that may be close to the machine during operation. Perception will be complemented by a FLIR AX8 thermal camera, which will be mainly used to detect human personnel directly in front of the robot, *i.e.* in potential danger from collisions with the machine or the mulcher attachment. The Dalsa Genie Nano will allow for multispectral analysis of the scene, assisting in the detection of plant material in various stages of decay; this will be useful in the detection of combustible material for clearing. The UWB transponders are part of the robot localisation system, providing

Table 4. Functional Specification Table (Safety and Integration).

Function/ Module	Requirement	Specification
Human Remote Control	Remote tele-operation and mulcher control of the *Ranger* by the Foreman	Tele-operation module to control the *Ranger* and its mulcher, at any time during the mission, overriding the navigation and mulcher control software
Safety	Routines for safely stopping the system, aborting or pausing the operations. Compliance with ethical, legal and safey regulations	Remote emergency stop by hardware (human operator), and emergency stop service by software (developers). Manual override of the mulcher operation and *Ranger* locomotion in all stages of the mission. Ability to ground all *Scouts*
Graphical User Interface	Means for providing human input to bias the SEMFIRE multi-robot system operation	A GUI will display the semantic map to the human operator and allow for the manual identification of ROIs, as well as streaming video from the *Ranger*, and other features
System Integration	Seamless communication and interoperability of the different layers of the decoupled SEMFIRE system	Integration of all sensor drivers and software modules, clear definiton of inputs/outputs as per the defined system architecture, re-use of standard components, and integration tests

distance readings to all other devices, with ranges in the hundreds of meters, which will allow for triangulation approaches to be used between the *Ranger* and *Scouts*. This information will be fused to achieve a robust global and localisation of the *Ranger* and *Scouts* during the mission.

The Mini-ITX computer will be the central processing unit of the *Ranger*, gathering the needed information from all components and running high-level algorithms and decision-making components. It is equipped with a powerful Geforce RTX 2060 GPU, which provides the power to run heavy computational approaches. The Xilinx XCZU4EV TE0820 FPGA is responsible for running the low-level drivers and low-level operational behaviours of the platform. It will run ROS on top of the Ubuntu operation system and allows for transparent communication with sensors, and the higher-level CPU.

The custom-made CAN bus controller allows to inject velocity commands to the underlying CAN system of the Bobcat platform and to control the mulcher operation. It consists of a custom board that integrates two MCP2551 CAN bus transceivers, and which will be installed between the machine's manual controls and the actuators, defining two independent CAN buses.

The TP-LINK TL-SG108 Gigabit Ethernet Switches interconnects the CPU, with the FPGA, the five AAEON UP Boards, the C16 LIDARs and the WiFi router, allowing for fast data acquisition and communication between all processing units, enabling distribution of computation and remote access and control.

Furthermore, the *Ranger* platform also provides an array of ten RGB LEDs to provide feedback on the behaviour of the system, one touchscreen GUI to be used inside the Bobcat's compartment, and a read projection mechanism, allowing the projection of information on the compartment's glass.

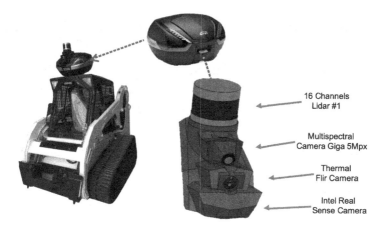

Fig. 2. The *Ranger* platform without the mulcher attachment. The platform is equipped with a sensor and computational array inside the **sensing kit** box at the top.

Fig. 3. *Scout* sensor hardware framework.

Scouts. The *Scouts*, are based on the Drovni platform from Ingeniarius, Ltd. (Fig. 3) equipped with a sensor array that complements the abilities of the *Ranger*. The *Scouts* UAVs include:

– One Stereolabs ZED high FPS stereo camera providing depth sensing up to 20 m distance;
– A UWB transponder;
– A Pixhawk 4 Flight Controller with a ublox Neo-M8N GPS receiver, a BMI055 IMU and radio telemetry;
– One Teledyne Dalsa Genie Nano C2420 multispectral camera.
– A Jetson TX2 board with a 256-core NVIDIA Pascal GPU, a Dual-Core NVIDIA Denver 2 64-Bit CPU, a Quad-Core ARM Cortex-A57 MPCore and 8 GB 128-bit LPDDR4 Memory

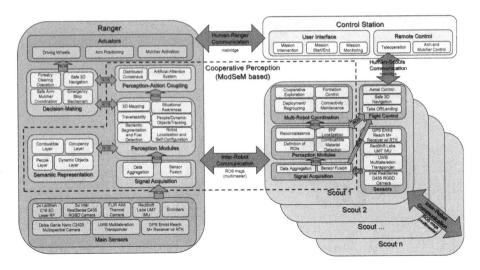

Fig. 4. SEMFIRE distributed system architecture. MoDSeM stands for Modular Framework for Distributed Semantic Mapping. Plase refer to [9,10] for more details.

Most of the above sensors, namely the UWB transponder, GPS and IMU, will assist in the localisation of the *Scouts*. This will allow, together with the information from the *Ranger*, to obtain a precise localisation of all agents in the field. The ZED camera will allow for the implementation of computer vision and ranging techniques, for instance, to aid in the coverage of the field and identify relevant areas for the *Ranger* to act in. The multispectral camera will aid the *Ranger* in detecting biomass for removal. The *Scouts* also include relatively limited processing power via a Jetson TX2 board, which will be able to deal with localisation, formation control, exploration, communications and decentralized perception.

Foreman. The foreman will be able to use a standard joystick controller to remotely operate the *Ranger* robot and its mulcher, as well as a touchscreen with a GUI to monitor the autonomous precision forestry mission. These tools will allow the foreman to intervene at any point of the mission, interrupting or pausing the system, being in complete control of the operations and avoiding any potential safety risk.

4   System Development, Integration and Deployment Plan

System development comprises the design, implementation and integration of hardware and software components, which in turn depend in specifications and requirements arising from the first prototyping phase. During the development phase, implementation and integration of the components and subsystems of the

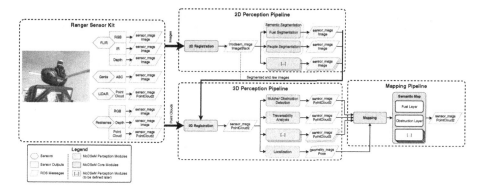

Fig. 5. Perception pipeline for the *Ranger*. Feedback connections not represented for readability.

SEMFIRE robot team prototype occurs in parallel, which will the be tested and evaluated in the final prototyping phase by real end-users with appropriate levels of technical supervision.

As can be seen in Fig. 4, the SEMFIRE solution is comprised of a distributed system architecture, implemented seamlessly and transparently across the Ranger and *Scout* platforms, including a separate Control Station allowing a trained professional, i.e. the Foreman, to remotely operate the autonomous platforms, either individually or as a team.

In order to ease system integration, a decoupled and modular strategy was adopted when designing the overall system architecture, adhering to the black box approach [4], where the implementation of each software component is opaque, and only its inputs and outputs are important for the rest of the system. The Robotic Operating System (ROS) [12] is used to implement seamless intra-robot and inter-robot communication (in this latter case, via ROS multimaster messaging).

Perceptual and Decision-Making Subsystems. The platforms comprising the robot team work collaboratively and in tandem to implement an overall coupling for perception-action-decision through a process called *cooperative perception*, using a proprietary solution developed by our research group, named Modular Framework for Distributed Semantic Mapping – MoDSeM [9,10]. The SEMFIRE architecture (cf. Fig. 4), includes all perception modules and communication channels that form the framework for individual and cooperative perception capabilities of the robotic team, as well as the sensing and actuation backbones.

Each of the members of the robotic team contributes to the global knowledge of the system by sharing and cooperatively processing data and *percepts* from one another, combining the sensorial abilities, perspectives and processing power of various agents to achieve better results. MoDSeM aims at providing a semantic mapping approach able to represent all spatial information perceived in autonomous missions involving teams of field robots, aggregating the knowledge of all agents into a unified representation that can be efficiently shared by the team. It also aims to formalise and normalise the development of new perception software, promoting the implementation of modular and reusable software that can be easily swapped in accordance with the sensory abilities of each individual platform.

The mid-level modules for semantic representation, perception-action coupling, and multi-robot coordination, together with local signal acquisition and perception modules, comprise the distributed core implementing seamless cooperative perception. This will allow the SEMFIRE robot team to control and coordinate its formation so as to provide the best possible sensory coverage of the AO in each of the planned operating modes taking advantage of an exploitation-exploration strategy.

Figure 5 shows the SEMFIRE perception pipeline for the *Ranger* (which will be adapted to produce analogous pipelines for the *Scouts*) using MoDSeM perception and core modules as its foundation. Three sub-pipelines are considered in this approach:

2D perception pipeline – this involves all processing performed on images, in which semantic segmentation using the multispectral camera is of particular importance (see Fig. 6a for a preliminary example), since it plays the essential role in mid-range scene understanding that informs the main operational states of the *Ranger*;

3D perception pipeline – this involves all processing performed on 3D point clouds yielded by the LIDAR sensors and RGB-D cameras (including 3D-registered images) that support safe 3D navigation;

Mapping pipeline – this involves the final registration and mapping that takes place to update the MoDSeM semantic map (see Fig. 6b for a preliminary example).

The decision-making modules use the outputs from the perception and perception-action coupling modules to produce the behaviours needed to enact the operational modes. Of particular importance are the resulting *Ranger*'s processing pipelines for overall decision-making shown in Fig. 7. Analogous processing pipelines will be designed for the *Scouts* in follow-up work.

(a) Semantic segmentation of combustible material using multispectral camera.

(b) MoDSeM layer mapping.

Fig. 6. Examples of visualization of the 2D perception pipeline and the Mapping pipeline.

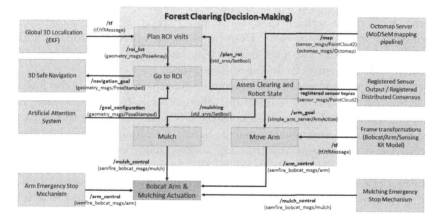

Fig. 7. SEMFIRE decision-making pipeline for the *Ranger*.

Actuation and Navigation Subsystems. Both the Ranger and *Scout* platforms have a high degree of mobility. The Ranger is based on one of the most powerful, comfortable, versatile and recognised compact track loaders available in the market. The Ranger is tuned for soft, sandy, wet and muddy conditions. It presents a climb capacity and traversal capacity of approximately 35°, which covers a wide range of slopes available in forestry scenarios. The *Scout*, on the other hand, is an hexacopter (6-motor multirotor), providing more lifting capacity and stability than quadcopters (4-motor multirotor). If one motor fails (e.g., collision with tree), the *Scout* can still remain stable enough for a safe landing. Besides the high degree of mobility offered by both platforms, the Ranger will be additionally endowed with a lift arm, with high level of rigidity, hose protection, and durability. The lift arm provides 2 DoF: lift (base rotation) and tilt (gripper rotation), with both breakout forces above 2 tons, capable of tearing out a tree root.

Human Interaction. As the ROS-enabled robots operate within a multi-master architecture, human operators can interact with them through any of the following approaches: (1) using a ROS-enabled device (computer running ROS); (2) using any available rosbridge-compatible client (`roslibjs`, `jrosbridge`, `roslibpy`, etc.); (3) Using a radio communication transceiver compatible with Futaba's S.Bus serial protocol; and/or (3) Using the SEMFIRE human-robot interface. To date, we have been using the RC S.Bus transceiver as it is closer to the low level actuation of the robots, which is fundamental for safe operation during the development stage. The SEMFIRE human-robot interface is still under heavy development, and it will provide different types of interaction, including data stream retrieval, individual robot tele-operation or sub-group behaviour switching mechanisms.

All software integration will be designed for Ubuntu 18.04 and ROS Melodic Morenia, with nodes written in C/C++ and Python. Software integration in environments incompatible with Ubuntu, such as microcontrollers, will be designed using specific interface frameworks, as long as those are able to be integrated in ROS (using, for instance, *rosserial*).

Preliminary experiments in the upcoming months to evaluate base features, such as pose estimation, communication, tele-operation, fuel identification, navigation, locomotion and mapping on both the UGV and the UAVs will be carried out in a real-world forestry environment. Safety measurements will be taken to interrupt the operations at any time via an emergency stop push button. The progress achieved by the team in the SEMFIRE project will be assessed through a set of Key Performance Indicators (KPI), based on autonomous operations hours of the system without interruptions or human intervention, locomotion abilities, the system usability scale, user success rate, data packets successfully transmitted, pose estimation errors, detection/identification error rates, fuel clearing time, fuel clearing precision, sensor acquisition frequency, SBus controllers delay, etc. These will be carefully designed for the experimental demonstrations foreseen.

5   Conclusion

In this work, we have described the main use case scenario of SEMFIRE, which allows clarification of system requirements and expectations regarding functionality, providing a basis for the definition of functional and technical specifications and desired system features. The detailed specification guided the definition of the general integration architecture of the project, namely the connections between all its components, serving as a reference for system development in SEMFIRE. We put special focus on the perception architecture for the *Ranger* robot, as a starting point, and proposed a core design of its processing pipeline and the functionality of the decision-making module. Naturally, there is the flexibility to refine some components, e.g. by incorporating new features that might not have been accounted for, or adjusting the expectation regarding a technical feature that may prove unfeasible. Finally, we present an overall plan for the foreseen experimental trials, including details on integration, deployment and validation.

In follow-up work, we will be building on these foundations, improving and further developing the *Ranger*'s perception and decision-making architecture, implementing the analogous Scout architectures, and putting in place robot team communication and collaboration infrastructures. We will also be investigating and testing deployment strategies to efficiently use the computational resources available on each platform. We will also be conducting extensive testing of the *Foreman* remote-control loop to ensure it is safe for the control of the full team of robots.

References

1. Couceiro, M.S., Portugal, D.: Swarming in forestry environments: collective exploration and network deployment. Swarm Intell. Principles Curr. Algorithms Methods **119**, 323 (2018)
2. Couceiro, M.S., Portugal, D., Ferreira, J.F., Rocha, R.P.: Semfire: towards a new generation of forestry maintenance multi-robot systems. In: 2019 IEEE/SICE International Symposium on System Integration (SII). IEEE (2019)
3. Ferreira, J.F., et al.: Sensing and artificial perception for robots in precision forestry - a survey. J. Field Robot. (2019, under review)
4. Glanville, R.: Black boxes. Cybern. Hum. Knowing **16**(1–2), 153–167 (2009)
5. Gougeon, F.A., Kourtz, P.H., Strome, M.: Preliminary research on robotic vision in a regenerating forest environment. In: Proceedings of the International Symposium Intelligent Robotics Systems, vol. 94, pp. 11–15 (1994). http://cfs.nrcan.gc.ca/publications?id=4582
6. Habib, M.K., Baudoin, Y.: Robot-assisted risky intervention, search, rescue and environmental surveillance. Int. J. Adv. Robot. Syst. **7**(1) (2010)
7. Kelly, A., et al.: Toward reliable off road autonomous vehicles operating in challenging environments. Int. J. Robot. Res. **25**(5–6), 449–483 (2006). https://doi.org/10.1177/0278364906065543. http://ijr.sagepub.com/content/25/5-6/449
8. Lowry, S., Milford, M.J.: Supervised and unsupervised linear learning techniques for visual place recognition in changing environments. IEEE Trans. Rob. **32**(3), 600–613 (2016)
9. Martins, G.S., Ferreira, J.F., Portugal, D., Couceiro, M.S.: MoDSeM: modular framework for distributed semantic mapping. In: 2nd UK-RAS Robotics and Autonomous Systems Conference - 'Embedded Intelligence: Enabling & Supporting RAS Technologies', Loughborough, UK, January 2019. Trabalhos/Conf/MoDSeM_UKRAS19_v3.pdf
10. Martins, G.S., Ferreira, J.F., Portugal, D., Couceiro, M.S.: MoDSeM: towards semantic mapping with distributed robots. In: 20th Towards Autonomous Robotic Systems Conference. Centre for Advanced Robotics, Queen Mary University of London, London, UK, July 2019. Trabalhos/Conf/TAROS2019.pdf

11. Panzieri, S., Pascucci, F., Ulivi, G.: An outdoor navigation system using GPS and inertial platform. IEEE/ASME Trans. Mechatron. **7**(2), 134–142 (2002)
12. Quigley, M., et al.: ROS: an open-source robot operating system. In: ICRA Workshop on Open Source Software, Kobe, Japan, vol. 3, p. 5 (2009)
13. Siegwart, R., Lamon, P., Estier, T., Lauria, M., Piguet, R.: Innovative design for wheeled locomotion in rough terrain. Robot. Auton. Syst. **40**, 151–162 (2002)
14. Suger, B., Steder, B., Burgard, W.: Traversability analysis for mobile robots in outdoor environments: a semi-supervised learning approach based on 3D-lidar data. In: Proceedings of the IEEE International Conference on Robotics and Automation (ICRA 2015), Seattle, Washington, May 2015
15. Thorpe, C., Durrant-Whyte, H.: Field robots. In: Proceedings of the 10th International Symposium of Robotics Research (ISRR 2001) (2001). http://www-preview.ri.cmu.edu/pub_files/pub3/thorpe_charles_2001_1/thorpe_charles_2001_1.pdf

Openkilo: A Truly Open-Source Kilobot Design Revision that Aids Repair and Extensibility

James W. Trump[1], Russell Joyce[2], and Alan G. Millard[3](✉)

[1] School of Engineering, Computing and Mathematics, University of Plymouth, Plymouth, UK
james.william.trump@gmail.com
[2] Department of Computer Science, University of York, York, UK
russell.joyce@york.ac.uk
[3] Lincoln Centre for Autonomous Systems, University of Lincoln, Lincoln, UK
amillard@lincoln.ac.uk

Abstract. Physical robot platforms are an important tool in swarm robotics research, allowing algorithms to be validated and optimised under realistic conditions. The Kilobot is a widely used platform that was originally designed to be cheap and simple enough for research labs to produce themselves. However, existing designs are neither truly open-source nor amenable to repair. We present a revised Kilobot hardware design that specifically aids repair via hand-soldering while remaining compatible with previous designs. Our design was produced using open-source ECAD (Electronic Computer-Aided Design) software, and is freely available online. We hope that the editable schematic and printed circuit board (PCB) design will be of use to future Kilobot projects, and will contribute to the accessibility of swarm robotics in general.

Keywords: Kilobot · Swarm robotics · Open-source hardware

1 Introduction

The Kilobot is a low-cost robot platform that was originally designed to test swarm algorithms on hundreds or thousands of physical robots [17] – something that was previously infeasible due to the size and cost of other robot platforms available at the time. Since its publication in 2010 [18] the Kilobot has become one of the most widely used swarm robotics platforms, particularly for large swarms [4,7,10,24]. This can be attributed to both its commercial availability and supporting documentation – software tools and code examples are available to assist those starting their own projects [19], including simple collective behaviours such as phototaxis, dispersion, and orbiting.

The Kilobot platform is supported by established robot simulators including ARGoS [14] and V-REP [16], as well as the bespoke simulator Kilombo [6]. Systems for extending the capabilities of the Kilobot platform via virtual sensors

© Springer Nature Switzerland AG 2020
A. Mohammad et al. (Eds.): TAROS 2020, LNAI 12228, pp. 345–356, 2020.
https://doi.org/10.1007/978-3-030-63486-5_36

and actuators have also been developed – namely Kilogrid [2,23] and ARK [15], enabling the implementation of a wide range of experiments. Kilobots are similar to Droplets [8] and Zooids [9], and represent a valuable asset for the swarm robotics community due to their proven experimental utility.

While Kilobot robots are commercially available from K-Team[1], their high retail price makes the commercial purchase of large robot swarms prohibitively expensive for many institutions. Consequently, the research community has begun to develop alternative designs that can be produced inexpensively, utilising varying degrees of manufacturing automation. This paper presents a Kilobot hardware design revision, OpenKilo, that lends itself to ease of repair and extensibility. Our new design can also be manufactured by hand using only basic soldering equipment, which may be of interest to institutions without access to reflow ovens and/or pick-and-place machines, or local PCB assembly services.

We have made our design freely available [22] in the hope that it will be of use to other research groups planning to build their own Kilobot swarms, or anyone wishing to make design modifications to Kilobot hardware using free open-source ECAD software.

2   Related Work

Since the Kilobot's inception, various alternative designs have been produced. Here, we review and compare all of the designs that we are currently aware of, in chronological order of their development.

2.1   Harvard University Design

The original Kilobot design was built with $14 USD ($\sim$£11) of components per robot (not including assembly costs) [17] – far cheaper than any comparable robot platform available, although only possible through the economies of scale that come with the mass production of 1,000+ units. With a diameter of just 33 mm, large numbers of Kilobots can be used in a small space (at the cost of limited computing power, movement, and sensing capabilities in comparison to other robot platforms). The Kilobot was designed to be assembled via automated PCB fabrication processes, featuring very few plated through-hole (PTH) components, enabling a construction time of under five minutes per robot after reflow soldering of surface-mount (SMD) components [17].

Another key design principle was that "all the operations of the robot must work on the collective as a whole, and not require any individual attention to the robot" [17]. This was achieved using an Overhead Controller (OHC) that programs every robot at once by broadcasting an infrared signal. Although initial firmware programming requires a wired connection, thereafter all communication can be carried out using this method, including putting the robots into a sleep mode. In most lab situations this sleep mode avoids total power-off between experiments, removing the need to physically turn each robot on and off.

---

[1] https://www.k-team.com/mobile-robotics-products/kilobot.

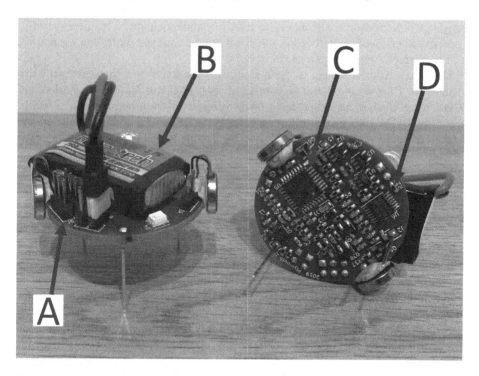

Fig. 1. OpenKilo hardware design – (A) Programming header, (B) Lithium polymer battery, (C) Quad Flat Package microcontroller, (D) Larger 0603 passive component footprints.

A swarm of Kilobots can be charged collectively using conducting metal plates laid over and under a large number of robots simultaneously. These plates make contact with conducting tabs on the top of each robot and their metal legs. On-board charging circuitry means that the power supply need only be a constant 6 V DC source with sufficient current capacity, and does not have to manage the individual charging requirements of each robot. Their lithium coin-cell batteries and simple design give Kilobots the longest battery life of any existing swarm robotics research platform [1].

Kilobots feature a simple movement system in the form of two vibration motors that can be used to drive the robot forward, left, or right. The robot stands on three narrow 'legs' made from long header pins. These vibration motors are significantly smaller and cheaper than DC or stepper motors, which are used in most other swarm robotics platforms [3,12,20].

Communication between robots is achieved via an infrared light-emitting diode and photodiode mounted on the bottom of the robot. Signals emitted from a robot are reflected from the surface below and received by nearby robots. A simple set of calibration values are used by individual robots to determine their distance to neighbours, based on the strength of received signals. A phototransistor light sensor is also fitted to measure ambient light. This increases the scope of experiments possible for the Kilobots, as ambient light can be readily used to segment areas or orient the robots.

Harvard's Kilobot design is 'open-source' in the sense that the schematics are available in PDF format, and that other institutions can manufacture identical PCBs using Gerber files that have been released in conjunction with a bill of materials (BOM). While this allows the design to be understood and reproduced, these designs are not easily editable, and subsequent projects have found them difficult to work with effectively [21].

2.2   K-Team Design

Harvard University sold exclusive rights to commercialise the Kilobot robot to the Swiss company K-Team in 2011 [26], swarms of which have since been sold to institutions around the world. Minor changes were made to the original design to better suit large-scale manufacture of the robots – one key feature being the redesign for reflow assembly with most components on one side of the PCB.

At the time of writing, K-Team recommends a retail price of ~£870 for a set of 10 Kilobots (excluding tax), which is almost 8 times the component cost of the original Harvard design (excluding assembly). This has led various research groups to build Kilobot swarms themselves – either using the Gerber files available from Harvard and outsourcing the assembly, or through the development of their own hardware designs. Unfortunately, K-Team's Kilobot hardware design files are not publicly available, and therefore cannot be used for a 'self-build'.

2.3   Western Carolina University (WCU) Design

In 2016, researchers from WCU published a paper titled "Make Kilobots truly accessible to all the people around the world" [21] that details significant changes to the Kilobot design, highlighting the impracticality of manufacturing the robots using the original Harvard designs for the stated cost-price, especially in small numbers. In their paper they state that their redesign "is not an overhaul of the original design; instead, it is aimed at making the building process of Kilobots feasible and time-efficient". The main contributions are a completely new PCB layout and much improved documentation. The Harvard schematic was helpfully reproduced in a more readable format, without any significant circuit changes.

WCU's PCB design is much more practical for institutions that do not have access to automated assembly tools such as pick-and-place machines, as passive components with tiny 0402 footprints were replaced by equivalent parts with larger 0603 footprints, and a silkscreen layer was added to aid manual component placement. The vast majority of SMD components were moved to one side of the board (inspired by the K-Team design), allowing rapid soldering using a solder paste stencil and reflow oven. WCU also document a process that removes the need for a sensor calibration board, as they found that the Harvard calibration board proved problematic to build and ultimately unnecessary [21]. A large and

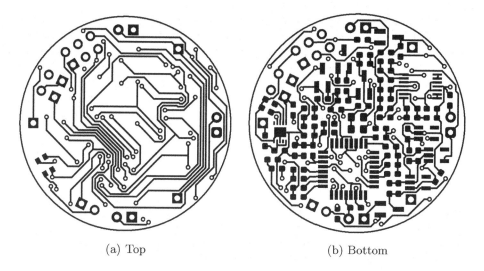

(a) Top   (b) Bottom

Fig. 2. Top and bottom copper layers of the OpenKilo revised PCB design.

thorough collection of design files, software, build guides, and documentation is available from their website [25].

Although the WCU design is simpler in terms of reflow-assisted assembly, it presents several problems for hand-soldered assembly and repair. The first is the use of a 32-pad SMD microcontroller package without exposed leads, which is very difficult to hand-solder or probe reliably. Passive components are also mounted in tightly grouped rows that are almost impossible to replace by hand, as tweezers will not fit between some components.

The WCU design was produced using PADS[2] ECAD software, which is commercial and closed-source, so unfortunately the design files cannot be fully edited without a paid licence. Support fees for PADS via an education scheme are over £900, with a standard version otherwise costing over £4,000, which may be unaffordable for some institutions. While the Gerber files required for identical PCB fabrication are provided, there is no easy way to modify or extend WCU's Kilobot hardware design without a PADS software licence.

2.4   Federal University of Santa Catarina (UFSC) Design

Researchers at UFSC are working on a redesign of the Kilobot that is similar in spirit to our own – their aim is to create a Kilobot design that is possible to manufacture by hand, and built their first prototype in 2018 [5]. The main design change was the substitution of 0603 passive SMD components with larger 0805 footprint counterparts. However, the diameter of the PCB was significantly increased to make this possible (40 mm versus the original 33 mm). The RGB LED was also replaced by three single-colour LEDs to lower costs.

---

[2] https://www.pads.com.

These changes were reversed in a later version, with a 34 mm PCB and 0603 components used instead [11]. This newer version was assembled using a reflow oven for the majority of parts, although the design is still more amenable to hand soldering than previously published designs. Their work is ongoing and currently unpublished, but details are available online [5]. These sources imply that changes were also made to the OHC as well as the Kilobot's battery charging and infrared receiver circuits. While this could potentially improve performance, it might also affect compatibility with other Kilobot designs and pre-existing software and firmware.

2.5   Overhead Controller (OHC) Designs

Only one OHC must be built to program an entire swarm of Kilobots, so it has not been the focus of as much development attention as the robot design. Harvard's original OHC design has been successfully used by several projects, and features components that are large enough to hand-solder.

Researchers at the University of Sheffield carried out a detailed study of the OHC's behaviour and optimised their lab area for better communication [13]. This included controlling ambient infrared light, determining the best table surface, and re-designing the OHC. Their new design appears to be an improvement in terms of area coverage and simplicity of design.

In their as yet unpublished work, UFSC has divided the functions of the OHC by using a separate USB programmer for the initial writing of firmware to the robots. This allows the OHC design to be greatly simplified, as it is now only concerned with the infrared communication for control and programming. This saves cost and complexity in OHC assembly, but requires an additional device.

3   OpenKilo Design

We have reproduced WCU's Kilobot schematic in KiCad[3] – a free, open-source ECAD software suite. This allowed us to create a new PCB layout from scratch (see Fig. 2), and means that the design is now truly accessible to others using completely free and open-source software.

In order to make hand-soldered assembly and repair feasible, the ATMega microcontroller, originally a QFN (Quad Flat No-leads) package, was substituted with the equivalent QFP (Quad Flat Package) version as shown in Figs. 1 and 3. The devices are identical except for the physical design of the package, which has exposed leads that can be more easily hand-soldered and probed. This substitution resulted in an increase in footprint size from $5\,mm^2$ to $9\,mm^2$, which is quite significant given the original size of the Kilobot, but was necessary to ensure that assembly and repair are possible with basic soldering equipment.

Solder pad sizes were also increased for passive SMD components. Both the WCU and OpenKilo designs use a large number of 0603 passive SMD components that are possible to solder using standard-sized pads, but larger pads were

---

[3] https://kicad-pcb.org.

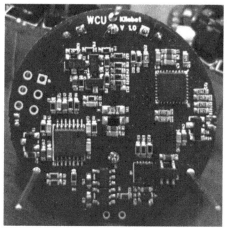
(a) WCU design (adapted from [21])

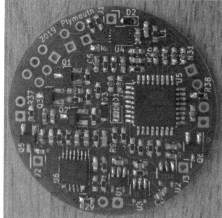
(b) OpenKilo design

Fig. 3. Comparison of the undersides of the assembled PCBs of the WCU and OpenKilo designs.

generally used. The increase in pad size makes soldering much easier and consequently faster, particularly in designs such as this where components are quite tightly spaced on a dense board layout.

Coin-cell batteries used by previous Kilobot designs are relatively expensive and less widely available than small lithium polymer (LiPo) cells. Our new design therefore replaces the coin-cell battery and its plastic holder with a standard header pin used to connect a LiPo cell. The electrical characteristics of the battery (3.7 V 260 mAh 1S 35-70C) were chosen to be compatible with the original charger circuitry, to avoid the need for wider design changes. The battery we selected weighs 8.5 g – similar to the weight of the original coin cell (7 g excluding the cradle), and can be affixed to the robot with a velcro pad for stability.

The diameter of the PCB was increased slightly to accommodate these component and footprint changes. The increase was relatively minor (from 34 mm to 37 mm diameter), and was the minimum diameter that could be successfully routed after many attempts with different sizes and layouts. Mechanical components and I/O, such as the legs, motors, photodiode, IR LED, and ambient light sensor, are all positioned as close as possible to their positions on the original design. This minimises any undesired changes to the movement, sensing, or communication of the robot, and ensures compatibility with other versions.

We used an OHC built from the WCU designs to test our prototypes, from which the Kilobots reliably received command and programming signals. Benchmark tests included adaptive gradient, disperse, and sync programs available for download from the Kilobotics website [19]. These tests confirmed the successful assembly and programming of the robots by checking that all main functions were working as intended. The adaptive gradient test indicated that inter-robot

Table 1. Comparison of all Kilobot designs known to exist, with respect to desirable features for manual assembly/repair and extensibility.

	Designs available	Truly open-source	SMDs mostly on one side	Can be hand assembled	Diameter
Harvard	Yes	No	No	No	33 mm
K-Team	No	N/A	Yes	No	33 mm
WCU	Yes	No	Yes	No	34 mm
UFSC	Planned	Unknown	Yes	Yes	34 mm
OpenKilo	Yes	Yes	Yes	Yes	37 mm

communication worked as expected, and robots responded reliably to their ambient light sensor in the 'move towards light' benchmark program (videos illustrating this OpenKilo functionality are available online [22]). The batteries charged as expected when connected to a 6 V DC source, while displaying the correct LED colour to indicate their current voltage.

3.1 Potential Improvements

A few improvements could be made to our design in future versions. The integrated circuit (IC) battery charger (LM3658) is difficult to solder or probe reliably, and would inevitably result in some assembly failures if a large number of Kilobots were to be produced by hand. A suitable leaded replacement would be the BQ2409x series from Texas Instruments, but note that substitution will likely require minor changes to the surrounding circuitry. The RGB LED is another package without exposed leads, but can reasonably be hand-soldered with larger pads. The solder pads should therefore be made longer in future.

It is also likely that an increase in charging current is possible, as the charging IC is operating far below its maximum rating, and the LiPo battery has a higher maximum charging rate than the original coin-cell. This upgrade could be combined with the design of a new charging clip, which will be required to allow convenient recharging of large swarms. It is important that PCB trace widths are reconsidered after any upgrade, as an increase in charging current will likely require an increase in the relevant trace widths.

Although various modifications could be made, the OpenKilo PCB layout is already quite dense, primarily due to the larger microcontroller and 0603 component footprints, and the routing of traces is close to the physical limits of the two-layer PCB. This could be alleviated by increasing the size of the PCB (as in the initial 40 mm diameter UFSC design) to allow room for additional hardware features, however our aim was to reproduce the Kilobots as closely as possible to their original size. Converting to a four-layer PCB design would enable further miniaturisation by reclaiming space via simplified trace routing and the addition of power and ground layers, but would significantly increase swarm production costs.

Table 2. Per-robot production cost estimates for the OpenKilo design, calculated for various swarm sizes.

Swarm size	PCB	SMD Components	PTH Components	SMD Assembly	Total
5	£8.86	£21.00	£7.37	£60.92	£98.15
10	£5.02	£16.29	£6.26	£33.73	£61.30
25	£2.66	£14.27	£6.06	£17.42	£40.40
50	£1.80	£11.93	£5.90	£11.98	£31.61
100	£1.30	£10.18	£5.39	£9.26	£26.13
200	£0.94	£9.94	£5.33	£7.90	£24.10
300	£0.83	£9.61	£5.33	£7.45	£23.21
1000	£0.57	£7.01	£4.94	£7.12	£19.65

Some mechanical properties of the robot could be improved slightly to achieve more accurate movement that can be more easily calibrated. For example, the new LiPo battery is slightly larger than the Kilobot's body, which affects the robot's centre of mass. This could easily be mitigated by increasing the PCB size, by rearranging some of the PTH components, or by sourcing a more compact battery. Despite this imperfection, straight line travel was achieved to an accuracy of $\pm 20\,\text{mm}$ laterally per $200\,\text{mm}$ travelled.

3.2   Assembly Considerations and Production Costs

Although it is possible to assemble our OpenKilo design entirely by hand, doing so for an entire swarm is not recommended – we found that it took approximately 5 h of work to assemble a single Kilobot using hand-soldering techniques. Assembly time and difficulty would of course decrease significantly with experience and batching of components, but the production of a swarm would be a significant time investment. That being said, the design could be simplified further by reducing the number of unique components (rounding passive component values up/down) to make SMD soldering easier.

3D-printed jigs, such as those originally proposed by Harvard to hold the PCB in place during construction, would further speed up the assembly of PTH components once SMD components have been soldered onto the PCB. With these improvements, the hand assembly of a swarm of 100 robots may be achievable by a small team in a reasonable time. However, due to the time required for assembly, it is unlikely that a swarm on the scale of Harvard's (1,024 Kilobots) would ever be cost-effective to manufacture entirely by hand.

Instead, we recommend assembly using solder paste and reflow techniques (if such facilities are available), as the vast majority of the components are mounted on one side of the board. The larger solder pads and leaded components confer additional benefits in that fault finding, debugging, and hand-soldering repair work are entirely possible with standard probes and soldering tools. The speed of in-house assembly can be greatly accelerated through the use of reflow ovens and/or pick-and-place, but for large swarms we would recommend outsourcing

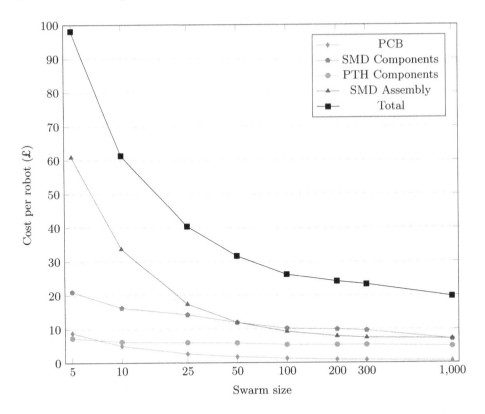

Fig. 4. Per-robot production costs from Table 2 versus swarm size (log scale).

the assembly of SMD components to an external PCB fabrication company such as Eurocircuits, JLCPCB, PCBWay, or Seeed Studio.

Indicative per-robot production costs for increasing swarm sizes are shown in Table 2 and Fig. 4. All cost estimates were obtained from Eurocircuits[4], and exclude tax. It can be seen from Fig. 4 that the most significant cost is outsourcing the assembly of SMD components (PTH components must still be assembled by hand), however the cost quickly drops as swarm size increases. Even for a swarm of 10 robots, the per-robot production cost is £25.70 cheaper than the K-Team recommended retail price of £87 (albeit not including the labour cost of PTH component assembly, or technical support).

4   Conclusion

This paper has presented a redesign of the popular Kilobot robot that aids repair with simple soldering equipment, and remains backward-compatible with previously developed code and experimental infrastructure. We have documented

---

[4] https://www.eurocircuits.com.

the assembly difficulties that we encountered in order to inform future projects, and to suggest suitable next steps in the development of further Kilobot designs. Table 1 summarises the key differences between our OpenKilo design and the Kilobot designs that precede it, with respect to desirable features for manual assembly and future design modification.

Our design was produced using the KiCad ECAD suite, which is free, open-source software that is accessible to anyone who would like to reproduce the design. We have made the design files used for this project, along with material costs, and supplementary information, freely available online [22]. It is hoped that these resources will be of use to other research groups that wish to build their own Kilobot swarms at an affordable cost. Future projects can use our design files as a starting point, which should drastically reduce the development time of new Kilobot versions, and benefit institutions without access to the expensive PADS software licences required to modify the WCU design.

References

1. Anoop, A., Kanakasabapathy, P.: Review on swarm robotics platforms. In: 2017 International Conference on Technological Advancements in Power and Energy (TAP Energy), pp. 1–6. IEEE (2017)
2. Antoun, A., Valentini, G., Hocquard, E., Wiandt, B., Trianni, V., Dorigo, M.: Kilogrid: a modular virtualization environment for the Kilobot robot. In: 2016 IEEE/RSJ International Conference on Intelligent Robots and Systems (IROS), pp. 3809–3814. IEEE (2016)
3. Arvin, F., Espinosa, J., Bird, B., West, A., Watson, S., Lennox, B.: Mona: an affordable open-source mobile robot for education and research. J. Intell. Robot. Syst. **94**(3–4), 761–775 (2019)
4. Dimidov, C., Oriolo, G., Trianni, V.: Random walks in swarm robotics: an experiment with Kilobots. In: Dorigo, M., et al. (eds.) ANTS 2016. LNCS, vol. 9882, pp. 185–196. Springer, Cham (2016). https://doi.org/10.1007/978-3-319-44427-7_16
5. Federal University of Santa Catarina (UFSC): Kilobots @ UFSC (2019). http://kilobots.paginas.ufsc.br
6. Jansson, F., et al.: Kilombo: a Kilobot simulator to enable effective research in swarm robotics. arXiv:1511.04285 (2015)
7. Jones, S., Studley, M., Hauert, S., Winfield, A.: Evolving behaviour trees for swarm robotics. In: Groß, R., et al. (eds.) Distributed Autonomous Robotic Systems. SPAR, vol. 6, pp. 487–501. Springer, Cham (2018). https://doi.org/10.1007/978-3-319-73008-0_34
8. Klingner, J., Kanakia, A., Farrow, N., Reishus, D., Correll, N.: A stick-slip omnidirectional powertrain for low-cost swarm robotics: mechanism, calibration, and control. In: 2014 IEEE/RSJ International Conference on Intelligent Robots and Systems, pp. 846–851. IEEE (2014)
9. Le Goc, M., Kim, L.H., Parsaei, A., Fekete, J.D., Dragicevic, P., Follmer, S.: Zooids: building blocks for swarm user interfaces. In: Proceedings of the 29th Annual Symposium on User Interface Software and Technology, pp. 97–109. ACM (2016)
10. Lopes, Y.K., Leal, A.B., Dodd, T.J., Groß, R.: Application of supervisory control theory to swarms of e-puck and Kilobot robots. In: Dorigo, M., et al. (eds.) ANTS 2014. LNCS, vol. 8667, pp. 62–73. Springer, Cham (2014). https://doi.org/10.1007/978-3-319-09952-1_6

11. Lorenzi, T.S.: Construção de Robôs para uso em aplicações de swarm robots e sistemas multi-agentes (2019). https://www.youtube.com/watch?v=o54LKpunkik
12. Mondada, F., et al.: The e-puck, a robot designed for education in engineering. In: Proceedings of the 9th Conference on Autonomous Robot Systems and Competitions, vol. 1, pp. 59–65 (2009)
13. Nikolaidis, E., Sabo, C., Marshal, J.A., Reina, A.: Characterisation and upgrade of the communication between overhead controllers and Kilobots. Technical report, White Rose Research Online (2017)
14. Pinciroli, C., Talamali, M.S., Reina, A., Marshall, J.A.R., Trianni, V.: Simulating Kilobots within ARGoS: models and experimental validation. In: Dorigo, M., Birattari, M., Blum, C., Christensen, A.L., Reina, A., Trianni, V. (eds.) ANTS 2018. LNCS, vol. 11172, pp. 176–187. Springer, Cham (2018). https://doi.org/10.1007/978-3-030-00533-7_14
15. Reina, A., Cope, A.J., Nikolaidis, E., Marshall, J.A., Sabo, C.: ARK: augmented reality for Kilobots. IEEE Robot. Autom. Lett. **2**(3), 1755–1761 (2017)
16. Rohmer, E., Singh, S.P., Freese, M.: V-REP: a versatile and scalable robot simulation framework. In: 2013 IEEE/RSJ International Conference on Intelligent Robots and Systems, pp. 1321–1326. IEEE (2013)
17. Rubenstein, M., Ahler, C., Nagpal, R.: Kilobot: a low cost scalable robot system for collective behaviors. In: 2012 IEEE International Conference on Robotics and Automation, pp. 3293–3298. IEEE (2012)
18. Rubenstein, M., Nagpal, R.: Kilobot: a robotic module for demonstrating behaviors in a large scale (2^{10} units) collective. In: Proceedings of the IEEE 2010 International Conference on Robotics and Automation Workshop, Modular Robotics: State of the Art. IEEE (2010)
19. Self-Organizing Systems Research Lab (SSR) Lab, Harvard University: Kilobotics (2013). https://www.kilobotics.com
20. Soares, J.M., Navarro, I., Martinoli, A.: The Khepera IV mobile robot: performance evaluation, sensory data and software toolbox. Robot 2015: Second Iberian Robotics Conference. AISC, vol. 417, pp. 767–781. Springer, Cham (2016). https://doi.org/10.1007/978-3-319-27146-0_59
21. Thomas, N., Yan, Y.: Make Kilobots truly accessible to all the people around the world. In: 2016 IEEE Workshop on Advanced Robotics and its Social Impacts (ARSO), pp. 43–48. IEEE (2016)
22. Trump, J.W.: GitHub - OpenKilo (2019). https://github.com/yorkrobotlab/openkilo
23. Valentini, G., et al.: Kilogrid: a novel experimental environment for the Kilobot robot. Swarm Intell. **12**(3), 245–266 (2018). https://doi.org/10.1007/s11721-018-0155-z
24. Valentini, G., Ferrante, E., Hamann, H., Dorigo, M.: Collective decision with 100 Kilobots: speed versus accuracy in binary discrimination problems. Auton. Agent. Multi-Agent Syst. **30**(3), 553–580 (2016)
25. West Carolina University: Kilobot @ WCU (2019). https://kilobot.wcu.edu
26. Wyss Institute, Harvard University: Wyss Institute Signs Licensing Agreement with K-Team Corporation (2011). https://wyss.harvard.edu/wyss-institute-signs-licensing-agreement-with-k-team-corporation

Towards Growing Robots: A Piecewise Morphology-Controller Co-adaptation Strategy for Legged Locomotion

David Hardman, Thomas George Thuruthel$^{(\boxtimes)}$, and Fumiya Iida

Bio-Inspired Robotics Lab, Department of Engineering,
University of Cambridge, Cambridge, UK
{dsh46,tg444,fi224}@cam.ac.uk

Abstract. Control of robots has largely been based on the assumption of a fixed morphology. Accordingly, robot designs have been stationary in time, except for the case of modular robots. Any drastic change in morphology, hence, requires a remodelling of the controller. This work takes inspiration from developmental robotics to present a piecewise morphology-controller growth/adaptation strategy that facilitates fast and reliable control adaptation to growing robots. We demonstrate our methodology on a simple 3 degree of freedom walking robot with adjustable foot lengths and with varying inertial conditions. Our results show not only the effectiveness and reliability of the piecewise morphology controller co-adaptation (PMCCA) strategy, but also highlight the need for morphological adaptation as a robot design strategy.

Keywords: Morphological adaptation · Growing robots · Control optimization

1 Introduction

Adaptation in an embodied agent can be found along two time scales: evolutionary and developmental. Evolutionary adaptations occur along larger time-scales at a slower rate. Over several generations, through a selection process, high functioning morphologies (body) and control parameters are evolved. Developmental adaptations are faster and occur within a generation [1,17]. They are more specialized to the working environment and are not transferable within generations [3,5]. There are numerous technological and algorithmic difficulties involved with the co-optimization of the body and control in evolved systems [11]. Likewise, there are many technological challenges in creating morphologically developing systems.

The body morphology has an important role in shaping the behavior of an embodied system [14,18], the influence of which can even extend through generations [9]. The role of morphological development, on the other hand, is not well

Supported by Mathworks Inc. Media available at: https://youtu.be/Xd6axFgqYyg.

© Springer Nature Switzerland AG 2020
A. Mohammad et al. (Eds.): TAROS 2020, LNAI 12228, pp. 357–368, 2020.
https://doi.org/10.1007/978-3-030-63486-5_37

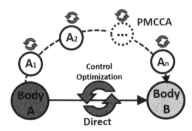

Fig. 1. The morphology, control and behavior of a dynamical system are interconnected. The PMCCA strategy undergoes piecewise morphological changes and hence local control adaptations, leveraging information from its ascendants. A single step morphological change, as shown above, would most likely require a complete recalibration of the control parameters.

understood [4]. Kreigman et al. showed that artificial organisms which developed environment-mediated morphological growth exhibited better robustness to slight abberations [10]. Similarly, another study showed that incorporating the evolution-of-development along with the evolution-of-body led to faster discovery of desirable behavior and higher robustness [1], a conclusion backed even by experimental studies [19].

One of the key differences between morphological changes induced by evolution and development is the continuity of the body plan over time. Evolved body plans can be drastically different from their parents. Developed bodies, by virtue of physical constraints, maintain continuity in their *morphology space*. This constraint causes smooth variations in the body dynamics which is expected to lead to continuous changes in the behavioral dynamics (before the bifurcation point) [7]. The control adaptation required to retain desired behavior, hence, can also be expected to be continuous. This way the control adaptation problem can be reduced to a simple local search problem for each piecewise change in morphology (referred to jointly as the piecewise morphology controller co-adaptation strategy).

This work, unlike other related works on design optimization of morphology [16] and co-optimization of morphology and controller [15] for locomotion, is not a global optimization strategy. The main objective is to obtain locally optimum controllers or morphologies using data from the real-world quickly and without failures (falling or self-collisions). Remarkably, as our results indicate, the proposed strategy actually performs better than a global optimization strategy.

The relevance of this study is two-fold. First, this work presents an efficient reliable controller-morphology co-adaptation strategy for robots that need to undergo morphological changes (shown by the body transformation from A to B in Fig. 1) [8]. Such cases arise for modular robots, when considerable load is added, or when new functional components are attached. Second and more importantly, this work proposes morphological adaptation as a design strategy for tuning robots to their working environment (In Fig. 1, a higher performing body B can be obtained by searching through the intermediate morphologies

A1, A2... An). We use a simple 3 degree of freedom walking robot for our study. The morphological parameters we explore are the length of the robot feet and the inertial parameters of the robot. The behavior in study is the locomotion speed. Even with a simple robot design and a common robotic task, development of dynamic controllers for the system is not straightforward. Using extensive experimental tests we show that the proposed localized controller-morphology co-adaptation strategy is highly desirable for adapting controllers for morphologically adapting robots. Our results not only indicate fast control adaptation with a low risk of failure and damage, but were also able to find better performing solutions than a global optimization algorithm like simulated annealing. A PMCCA search around the morphological space also showed that superior morphologies better suited for the task and environment can be easily found and tuned.

2   Experimental Setup

For this study we use a planar robot, comprising of four rigid medium density fibreboard (MDF) links and three rotary joints. At each end of the four link mechanism, a MDF foot of variable length f is perpendicularly joined (see Fig. 2), which can be varied between 5 cm and 25 cm in 5 cm intervals. For our study, we consider the feet length to be our morphological parameter to be tuned. Since, it required more complex mechanisms to adjust the feet length continuously, we rely on a discretized version of the same. Rubber tape on the underside of the feet controls the slip between the robot and the horizontal surface. Servo motors actuate the joints between links, each with a range of 120°. All are set at their lower bound when the four links are parallel. They are signalled by an on-board microcontroller, which is tethered to a constant voltage power supply and a PC running *MATLAB*. Six 33 g M10 bolts may optionally be arranged around the leading leg to add mass to the robot, as in Fig. 2. Hence, this robot can be parameterized in two directions in the morphological space, although quite discreetly.

The movement of the robot within the plane is monitored using a six camera *OptiTrack* motion capture system. Four markers are attached at each of the outermost joints, and the position of each cluster's geometric centre is followed. Of particular interest is the average velocity of the joints in the x direction (Fig. 2), used to prescribe the behavioral scores.

3   Procedure

Like the morphological space, the action space of the robot has to be parameterized to make the search problem tractable. Knowing that the behavior of concern is arising from locomotion, we can constrain our control actions to periodic signals. Hence, the configuration space of all possible motions was parameterized into ten dimensions by controlling each of the three servo motors with a sine wave. Though the time period of the wave was consistent between the motors,

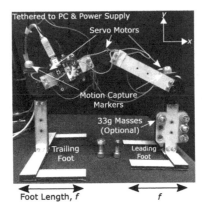

Fig. 2. Experimental Setup: the four link tethered robot. Six masses may optionally be added around the leading leg.

each of the other parameters - amplitude, phase, and mean - could be independently varied, subject to physical limits. The control objective is then to find the optimal set of control parameters that maximizes the desired behavior: locomotion speed, in our case. More specifically, the optimization process aimed to maximise the average velocity of the robot in the x direction over the final three sine periods of a five period run. This was done in order to remove effects of any transient dynamics and ensure that the locomotion was stable, at least for a short duration.

3.1 Simulated Annealing

The initial controller for the 'base' morphology can be obtained by any global optimization algorithm. We use simulated annealing for this study. The adaptation of the controller for subsequent *local* morphologies can then be performed again by simulated annealing (naive approach) or by our proposed PMCCA search algorithm that leverages the continuity in the action-morphology space.

Table 1. Simulated annealing parameters

No. of cycles	15	Starting Phases	0 rad
Iterations per cycle	15	Starting Means	$\pi/15$ rad
Starting Temp. T_0	1	σ_t	8T s
T_{i+1}/T_i	0.85	σ_M	$2T\pi/3$ rad
Starting Time Period	5 s	σ_A	$2T\pi/3$ rad
Starting Amplitudes	$\pi/15$ rad	σ_P	$4T\pi/3$ rad

For comparison purposes, each of the five foot sizes independently underwent a 225 iteration simulated annealing process, the parameters of which are given in

Table 1. During every iteration, each new parameter was proposed by sampling from a one dimensional Gaussian curve centred at the current parameter and truncated at its physical limits. The time period was limited between 1 & 15 s. Standard deviation values σ_t (time period), σ_M (mean), σ_A (amplitude) & σ_P (phase) depended on the current temperature, T_i, which was decreased by 15% at the end of each 15 step cycle. Any score, S, above the currently accepted score was immediately accepted, otherwise acceptance had a probability of $e^{\frac{-1}{TS}}$. After each iteration, the data was manually flagged with a descriptor of the robot's behaviour. This later allowed the determination of number/location of catastrophic (C) failures (in which the robot fell over or collided with its own body) and harmless (H) failures (in which the robot's movement had no effect on its position or caused it to move backwards) to be identified. Both scenarios were assigned a minimum score of 0.01 cm/s.

3.2   Proposed Methodology: PMCCA Search from Peak

The proposed PMCCA search algorithm for morphologically adapting robots is based on the use of priors from the previous morphology to greatly reduce the search space region. First for the 'base' morphology ($f = 15$ cm), the highest three scores (henceforth referred to as Peaks A, B and C) from the simulated annealing process were identified and a refining search was performed around each. This search comprised of 30 additional iterations using parameters drawn randomly from a space near the peak, each limited to one-fifth of its range during the simulated annealing. Note that the time period was permitted to extend below 1 s since the robot was deemed less likely to collide with itself; a high speed collision could have easily broken joints or prompted a dangerous current spike from the power supply. Note that reducing the search space to one-fifth of a single parameter cumulatively amounts to a significant reduction in the overall search volume. This PMCCA search (Algorithm 1) is then used to adapt the controller to the robot's changing morphology. After every search, the new best scores and their control parameters are used as the next starting point for the new morphology.

For example, after the refined search through the peaks A, B, and C of the 'base' morphology ($f = 15$ cm), the best parameters are selected and the morphology is modified in a piecewise manner to a setting of $f = 20$ cm or $f = 10$ cm. Before moving to the next morphology ($f = 25$ cm or $f = 5$ cm, respectively), a refined search is performed around the current peaks and the next best parameters identified. Next, f was set to 10 cm, and the same co-adaptation rule was applied for sequential addition of six 33 g masses to the leading leg. The analysis of the experimental results are presented next.

```
while not final morphology do
    S_current = 0;
    repeat 30 times
        propose parameters near the current set;
        run 5 sine periods using proposed parameters;
        if no failure then
            calculate S from OptiTrack data;
            if S > S_current then
                | S_current = S;
            end
        end
    end
    accept S_current parameters;
    increment morphology;
end
```

Algorithm 1: PMCCA search algorithm, beginning from the base morphology

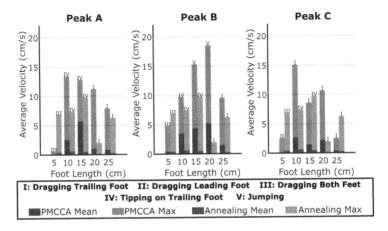

Fig. 3. PMCCA searches branching outwards from the 15 cm base morphology. The average velocities and gait pattern is shown here. (Color figure online)

4 Experimental Results

4.1 Morphological Adaptation by Varying Foot Length, f

Figure refpeaksearchbarfig shows the results of the 30-iteration PMCCA searches for each of the three starting peaks. These are compared with the exhaustive simulated annealing results, displayed in blue beside each foot length. With the exception of $f = 5$ cm, we see that the PMCCA method outperforms the global simulated annealing process for all new morphologies. We believe this is because the high performing behaviors lie on a very small region in the action space, which is unlikely to be visited by global search algorithms in practical time-limits. Given infinite searching time, both algorithms will have the same maximum peaks, while PMCCA will have a better mean value as it searches locally near the peaks. This hypothesis is valid in the coming sections.

Now, the 900-iteration process of independently optimizing all four new morphologies has been replaced by a 450-iteration process - a reduction of 50%. The

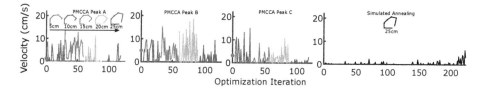

Fig. 4. Comparing a simulated annealing process starting from scratch on $f = 25\,\text{cm}$ morphology with a PMCCA search algorithm that propagates from $f = 5\,\text{cm}$ morphology to $f = 25\,\text{cm}$.

process could be sped up by reducing the number of searches and stopping the refined search once good control candidates have been found. Additionally, the average catastrophic failure rate of the entire process falls from 27.9% to 17.9%, even though it is skewed upwards by the comparatively high failure rate of $f = 25\,\text{cm}$ during the PMCCA search (see Table 2).

Table 2. Comparing the simulated annealing and the PMCCA method catastrophic failure rates

(%)	5 cm	10 cm	15 cm	20 cm	25 cm
Annealing Failures (C)	22.7	15.6	30.7	37.3	33.3
PMCCA Failures A (C)	0	6.7	0	3.3	70.0
PMCCA Failures B (C)	0	0	0	13.3	43.3
PMCCA Failures C (C)	0	0	3.3	13.3	20.0

It is clear from Table 2 that transitioning downwards in foot size is significantly less risky. Of the 180 iterations doing so, only 2 failures occurred: a failure rate of 1.1%. However, Fig. 3 seems to suggest that this direction is associated with a reduction in performance of the 5 cm ft. Though the highest $f = 5\,\text{cm}$ score found during the PMCCA search is only 69.6% of the simulated annealing maximum, the significant increase in safety may prove to justify this in applications where failure of trials carries a high risk and is highly undesirable.

The PMCCA search algorithm is very powerful because of its efficiency. An example is illustrated with scenario shown in Fig. 4, where the method of searching directly on a new morphology ($f = 25\,\text{cm}$) is compared with the method of morphology-controller co-adaptation. The PMCCA search algorithm starts with the $f = 5\,\text{cm}$ morphology and iteratively proceeds to a $f = 25\,\text{cm}$ morphology. This search noticeably led to the development of a range of gaits suited to each morphology, and had high scores averaging 292% that of the simulated annealing maxima, compared to the 204% & 183% of peaks A & C respectively. The PMCCA method not only found superior gaits quicker when compared to the global simulated annealing case, but it also provides valuable information about other morphologies along the 'way'. For instance, the best score achieved among all the morphologies was found on the $f = 20$ cm morphology, through the PMCCA search. Surprisingly, the simulated annealing process performed the worst on the $f = 20$ cm morphology. The top scoring gaits emerging from the simulated anneal were observed to be static, with the sine waves of the two refined peaks having time periods greater than 6 s. In contrast, the higher scoring $f = 20$ cm gaits developed whilst incrementally extending the robot's morphology were observed to be dynamic, relying on the effect of gravity and foot elasticity to achieve faster locomotion.

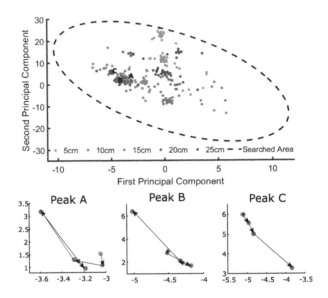

Fig. 5. Clustering of behavioral scores above 2 cm/s compared to the complete search space. Inset shows the shifting of the three peaks in a low dimensional action space representation.

The reason PMCCA performed so well can be understood from Fig. 5. Parameters producing a score greater than 2 cm/s are plotted in the reduced dimensionality control space, in which the axes represent the first two principal components of the normalized 10 dimensional control space. A dashed line marks the boundary of the valid configuration space in the reduced dimensions. On the coarsest of scales, an improvement in search efficiency is quickly deduced from the behavior distribution in the low dimensional representation of the control space. The highest scoring parameters cluster into a central region of the searched area, rarely with a first principal component greater than 5 or a second below -10. Upon further inspection this excluded region largely contains points flagged as catastrophic failures or harmless failures. Efficiency may thus have been improved by eliminating parameter ranges in the 10 dimensional configuration space corresponding to this region of the graph before optimization began. If thoroughness of the search were not a priority, only the densely populated region to the upper left of $(1, -10)$ could be searched. How the peaks shifted with piecewise morphological changes is also quite localized.

The PMCCA search method being evaluated does not prioritise any direction of search over the others, and is equally likely to search any of the physically valid directions. However, it can be clearly observed that peaks have directional correlation. This is most apparent around peak C, suggesting a consistency in the direction of shift of a peak for a directional change in morphology. This indicates that the PMCCA search method can be further extended to include priors from preceding morphologies to also guide the search direction. Further experimentation would be necessary to confirm this hypothesis.

Distinct clusters have emerged for each value of f in the two principal component directions, confirming that optimum control parameters are dependent on the body morphology of the robot. These clusters are often manifested in the form of different gait types, as is seen in Fig. 6. The top half shows four patterns developed during the simulated annealing process. The first and third were somewhat dynamic in nature, whereas the second and fourth were static. Conversely, the final three rows of Fig. 6 contain the gaits developed during the search from peak B. Interestingly, novel gaits, highly dynamic in nature emerged from the refined search even in the 'base' morphology.

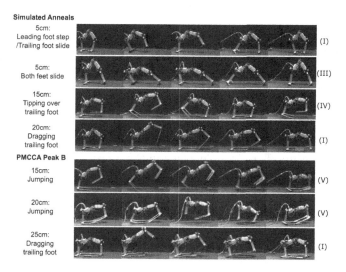

Fig. 6. A range of gaits developed whilst f was varied, from both the annealing and PMCCA searches

Gaits emerging from the PMCCA searches also developed with the morphology: for example, Fig. 6 sees a dynamic jumping gait become a slower, static, gait in which the trailing foot is dragged along the surface. Very few variations of gait pattern observed during the simulated annealing process did not subsequently emerge during the PMCCA search, though some gaits - such as the jumping displayed - only appeared during this search. This occurred most frequently when $f = 20\,\mathrm{cm}$, for which the simulated annealing had the least effect (Fig. 3). However, $f = 20\,\mathrm{cm}$ produced the highest overall score during the PMCCA search - 18.5 cm/s - by developing a jumping gait from the $f = 15\,\mathrm{cm}$ ft. Whilst this morphology would rely on momentum of the fast-swinging links to propel it into the air, the $f = 20\,\mathrm{cm}$ setup used the elasticity of the trailing foot, which would noticeably bend with each step, to spring from the table. Even when searching a small region around the peaks, such noticeably different gaits emerge: if variations in the gait pattern were deemed important to the thoroughness of the search, extending the range and fineness of the refined search can be done.

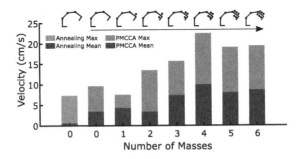

Fig. 7. Results of PMCCA search with incrementally added mass. The simulated annealing results are shown for the 'base' morphology only. (Color figure online)

4.2   Morphological Adaptation by Varying Mass Parameters

In practice, the foot length of a robot may stay consistent whilst another change in morphology occurs. For example, the addition of an arm and manipulator to the top of the robot would not change the size of the action space searched in Fig. 5, but would affect the dynamics of the robot. Such an effect was simulated using the six 33 g masses around the leading leg. The whole robot weighs around 510 g. The results of the incremental addition of masses are presented in Table 3 & Fig. 7. The blue simulated annealing bar corresponds to the optimization

Table 3. Comparing the simulated annealing and the PMCCA performance for additional weight

	Simulated annealing ($M0$)	PMCCA ($M0 \rightarrow M6$)
No. Iterations	225	180
Failures (C) (%)	15.6	6.7
Failures (H) (%)	40.0	7.8

process for the case $f = 10$ cm. The simulated annealing process was not done for the added masses due to the higher risk of damage. Figure 7 shows us that the end of the 180-iteration search using PMCCA had produced a score not only higher than the $f = 10$ cm peak at which it began, but higher than any score seen without the added mass for any morphology, with almost one third of the failure rate of the full $f = 10$ cm optimization. Indeed, the 3 & 4 mass searches were clearly benefiting from the added mass, using the additional momentum to propel the leading foot forwards during stepping. This contrasted with the behaviour when all six masses were initially added at once: the sudden increase in weight tended to pin the leading leg to the surface, achieving very little locomotion. This shows that morphological growth can also be a desirable adaptation strategy for improving performance of the robot, tuned to the real-world conditions.

5   Conclusions

The results presented in Sect. 4 suggest that a naive global optimization, like simulated annealing, of the entire control space is rarely the safest or most efficient way for a controller to achieve high performing behavior when prior knowledge can be extracted from 'neighboring' morphologies and their sub-optimal controllers. Utilising the knowledge of a neighbouring peak along an axis of shifting body morphology enables our proposed PMCCA search to quickly attain, and often exceed the performance of the optimization in considerably fewer iterations. High performing unique gaits were also observed using the PMCCA search possibly because of its finer search process in the regions of high performance. It must however be noted that the stability of the gaits were not analyzed in this study but can also be easily be incorporated in the behavioral score.

This method of piecewise controller-morphology adaptation, in fact, parallels the process of growth seen throughout in nature; developing the controller starting from a stable morphology towards a higher performing but less stable morphology [12]. The proposed methodology is not just limited to shape and mass changes. Other morphological parameters like stiffness, damping and actuator distribution can be be similarly investigated. With advances in soft robotics, morphological adaptations are becoming more prevalent with tunable properties [2,6,13] and hence new and elegant control adaptation algorithms are required.

Although we have restricted our piecewise morphology search to a single dimension, with appropriate automated morphological adaptation mechanisms, the process can be extended to a multidimensional search space. Another interesting observation which was not investigated in this paper is the directional dependencies found in the piecewise morphological changes. This indicates that the control adaptation can be further polished from the current local search to include directional information. The definition and parameterization of the robot behavior is another aspect to be addressed if the method is to be extended to other applications. To extend this procedure to other tasks such as manipulation, appropriate behavioral scores have to be defined and estimated.

References

1. Bongard, J.: Morphological change in machines accelerates the evolution of robust behavior. Proc. Natl. Acad. Sci. **108**(4), 1234–1239 (2011)
2. Booth, J.W., et al.: OmniSkins: robotic skins that turn inanimate objects into multifunctional robots. Sci. Robot. **3**(22), eaat1853 (2018)
3. Brodbeck, L., Hauser, S., Iida, F.: Morphological evolution of physical robots through model-free phenotype development. PLoS ONE **10**(6), e0128444 (2015)
4. Doursat, R., Sayama, H., Michel, O.: A review of morphogenetic engineering. Nat. Comput. **12**(4), 517–535 (2013). https://doi.org/10.1007/s11047-013-9398-1
5. Eggenberger, P.: Evolving morphologies of simulated 3D organisms based on differential gene expression. In: Proceedings of the Fourth European Conference on Artificial Life, pp. 205–213 (1997)
6. Hawkes, E.W., Blumenschein, L.H., Greer, J.D., Okamura, A.M.: A soft robot that navigates its environment through growth. Sci. Robot. **2**(8), eaan3028 (2017)
7. Iqbal, S., Zang, X., Zhu, Y., Zhao, J.: Bifurcations and chaos in passive dynamic walking: a review. Robot. Auton. Syst. **62**(6), 889–909 (2014)
8. Jin, Y., Meng, Y.: Morphogenetic robotics: an emerging new field in developmental robotics. IEEE Trans. Syst. Man Cybern. Part C (Appl. Rev.) **41**(2), 145–160 (2010)
9. Kriegman, S., Cheney, N., Bongard, J.: How morphological development can guide evolution. Sci. Rep. **8**(1), 13934 (2018)
10. Kriegman, S., Cheney, N., Corucci, F., Bongard, J.C.: Interoceptive robustness through environment-mediated morphological development. In: Proceedings of the Genetic and Evolutionary Computation Conference, pp. 109–116. ACM (2018)
11. Lipson, H., Sunspiral, V., Bongard, J., Cheney, N.: On the difficulty of co-optimizing morphology and control in evolved virtual creatures. In: Artificial Life Conference Proceedings 13, pp. 226–233. MIT Press (2016)
12. Malina, R.M.: Motor development during infancy and early childhood: overview and suggested directions for research. Int. J. Sport Health Sci. **2**, 50–66 (2004)
13. Manti, M., Cacucciolo, V., Cianchetti, M.: Stiffening in soft robotics: a review of the state of the art. IEEE Robot. Autom. Mag. **23**(3), 93–106 (2016)
14. Pfeifer, R., Bongard, J.C.: How the body shapes the way we think: a new view of intelligence (bradford books) (2006)
15. Rosendo, A., von Atzigen, M., Iida, F.: The trade-off between morphology and control in the co-optimized design of robots. PLoS ONE **12**(10), e0186107 (2017)
16. Saar, K.A., Giardina, F., Iida, F.: Model-free design optimization of a hopping robot and its comparison with a human designer. IEEE Robot. Autom. Lett. **3**(2), 1245–1251 (2018)
17. Sadeghi, A., Tonazzini, A., Popova, L., Mazzolai, B.: A novel growing device inspired by plant root soil penetration behaviors. PLoS ONE **9**(2), e90139 (2014)
18. Thuruthel, T.G., Falotico, E., Renda, F., Flash, T., Laschi, C.: Emergence of behavior through morphology: a case study on an octopus inspired manipulator. Bioinspiration Biomim. **14**(3), 034001 (2019)
19. Vujovic, V., Rosendo, A., Brodbeck, L., Iida, F.: Evolutionary developmental robotics: improving morphology and control of physical robots. Artificial Life **23**(2), 169–185 (2017)

A Novel Shape Memory Alloy (SMA) Wire-Based Clutch Design and Performance Test

Nan Ma, Xin Dong[(⊠)], Josue Camacho Arreguin, and Mingfeng Wang

University Technology Center, University of Nottingham, Nottingham NG7 2RD, UK
{nan.ma,xin.dong,Josue.camachoarreguin,
Mingfeng.Wang}@nottingham.ac.uk

Abstract. The clutch system is increasingly utilized in a large range of industrial applications due to its working characteristics (i.e. clamping and releasing). However, in conventional design of the clutch, the electromagnet is mostly selected as the actuator to drive the motion, which makes the clutch Bulk and heavy. In this paper, a novel SMA wire-based clutch is proposed to overcome the aforementioned disadvantages of conventional clutches, aiming to reduce the weight and shorten the response time. To achieve this, an SMA wire was selected and twisted around the clutch to drive the motion of the moveable platform. The voltage-displacement response of the SMA clutch was studied, and the appropriate controlling voltage and heating time were obtained. After that, the tracking response of the SMA clutch was checked to study the dynamic working characteristics. It can be found that the proposed SMA clutch can track the given sinusoidal trajectory with high accuracy in the clamping area (i.e. 3.4%). Promisingly, with the studies of the proposed SMA clutch, it can be used in environments (e.g. satellite) where the weight is restricted.

Keywords: SMA clutch · Clutch design · Temperature control · Displacement control

1 Introduction

In recent years, the SMA material is increasingly utilized in the fields of robotics, aerospace and industry. Compared with conventional motor actuated mechanisms [1, 2], the SMA-based mechanisms can have the characteristics of lightweight, powerful output and miniature dimension. However, this new material is sensitive to temperature, requiring accurate control system design, otherwise it is easy to be damaged during the operation. In addition, the strain of the SMA material is usually very small, requiring long material to be used to have the required output [3]. To solve the aforementioned problems, a novel SMA wire-based clutch was proposed, which adopts a long SMA wire and advanced control algorithm to actuate the SMA clutch.

The original version of this chapter was revised: an author that was inadvertently not included has been added. The correction to this chapter is available at
https://doi.org/10.1007/978-3-030-63486-5_44

© Springer Nature Switzerland AG 2020, corrected publication 2021
A. Mohammad et al. (Eds.): TAROS 2020, LNAI 12228, pp. 369–376, 2020.
https://doi.org/10.1007/978-3-030-63486-5_38

SMA based mechanisms are extensively researched among different applications, such as aerospace, automobile, biomedical, and bioinspired applications. In the applications of automobile [4, 5] and biomedical [6], the SMAs are mostly fabricated as a part of a whole device to achieve the required shape set in the original state when the temperature is higher than the phase transformation temperature, while in the mechanical and bioinspired applications the SMAs are traditionally regarded as an actuator to drive the motion of the joints. Kolansky [7] and Guo [8] designed a kind of rotational joint actuated by the SMA wire, and the working frequency can attend to 4 Hz at most with the assisted cooling. The three-link arm robot was designed by Ashrafion [9], and the controllers were designed to realize the position control. The robot bat and robot jellyfish were fabricated by Colorado [10] and Villanueva [11] respectively, where the SMA strip and SMA wire were used as the actuators to drive the motion of the body and wings. The robot hand driven by the SMA wire has also attracted the attention of the researchers [12, 13]. The capsule-type locomotive robot for medical inspection was designed and fabricated by Kim et al. [14] using the SMA actuator, while it will take a long time for heating and cooling. Regarding the clutch research, Menciassi [15] designed a kind of capsule robot using the SMA wire to realize the creeping motion inside the bowels of the animal. Yan [16] designed a gripper using a pair of differential SMA springs. Another kind of clutch is designed by Liang [17] to clamp the cable with high speed and precision similar with this paper, but the clutch is actuated by the stack piezoelectric ceramic in Liang's paper. In this paper, a novel SMA wire-based clutch is developed to realize the clamping and locking functions for constructing the underactuated manipulator.

To address the aforementioned characteristics of the SMA-based mechanisms, a novel SMA wire-based clutch is proposed to improve the clamping performance of clutch with the reduced dimension. For achieving this, the powerful actuator (SMA wire: small size, powerful output) is selected as the actuator to drive the motion of clutch; then the wire twining method was studied to improve the clamping force of the SMA clutch; after that, with the fabricated prototype and developed controlling algorithm, the tests were performed to validate the proposed SMA clutch.

2   SMA Wire-Based Clutch Design

In order to reduce the weight of conventional electromagnetic-based clutch, the SMA was adopted in this paper as the actuator to develop the new clutch (characteristics: miniature and powerful), enabling to be used in special occasions. In addition, the auto-lock function was designed with the clamping function, enabling the clutch to be locked in a fixed position when powered off.

The schematic design of the proposed SMA clutch is shown in Fig. 1. To achieve the reciprocating motion of the moveable platform (Fig. 1), the SMA wire was adopted as the actuator to reduce the size of the system, further to reduce the overall dimension of the system. Based on the working characteristics of SMA wire, the working principle of the proposed clutch can be attributed as follows: when the switch is "on", the moveable platform will be pulled back to clamp with the inner cable; when the switch is "off", the moveable platform will be pushed back (by the internal compressional springs) to contact with the fixed base. Using our novel design, the auto-lock function can be achieved to fix the clutch to a position (by the saw-tooth feature) when the switch is off.

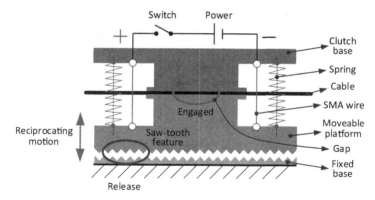

Fig. 1. The schematic of the proposed SMA clutch

Based on the schematic of Fig. 1, the prototype of the SMA clutch can be fabricated (Fig. 2). To actuate the motion of the moveable platform, the long SMA wire (characteristics, power "off": initial length, power "on": shorten the length) is twinned around the clutch base and moveable platform. As the relative motion will occur when the SMA wire changes its length, the large friction will be caused. In order to solve this problem, the miniature grove pulleys were adopted to release the friction and guide the path of SMA with. To have a better motion accuracy between the moveable platform and clutch base, the guide pins and linear bushings were used (assembled on the moveable platform and clutch base respectively). In addition, as the back force is needed to push the SMA wire back to its initial stage/length when power is "off", the compressional springs are used and positioned between moveable platform and clutch base.

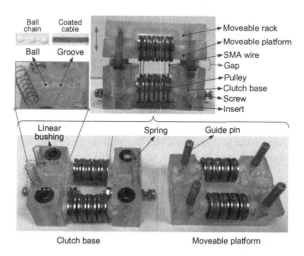

Fig. 2. The Prototype of the SMA wire-based clutch

The working flow of the SMA clutch can be described as follows:

i)   At the initial stage: the moveable platform of the SMA clutch is locked with the fixed base by the compressional springs (Fig. 1) in the initial stage (power is "off");

ii) Clamping stage: when the power is "on", the SMA wire will shorten its length, enabling to drive the motion of moveable platform (clamp with the inner cable);

iii) Releasing stage: when the power is "off", the compressional springs will push the moveable platform back to its initial position (lock with the fixed base, Fig. 1).

In order to achieve the high working frequency of SMA clutch, the parameters of SMA wire and spring should be correctly selected, shown in Table 1.

Table 1. The parameters of the SMA wire used in the clutch

Parameters	Company	Diameter (mm)	Length (mm)	Max strain (%)	Pull force (g)	Temperature
Value	Flexinol, Dynalloy, Inc	0.25	260	4	891	70 °C–90 °C

Four compression springs are symmetrically placed between the clutch base and moveable platform to push the SMA wire to its initial stage when power is "off". The parameters are shown in Table 2.

Table 2. The parameters of the compression springs used in SMA clutch

Parameters	Outside Diameter (mm)	Wire Diameter (mm)	Free length (mm)	Solid length (mm)	Rate (N/mm)
Value	2.997	0.254	10	2.59	0.29

In this section, a novel SMA wire-based clutch, which has the interlock function, is proposed to reduce the dimension of conventional clutches. Based on the schematic and working principle of the proposed clutch, the prototype can be fabricated to test the performance, which will be done in the next section with the corresponding experimental setups.

3   SMA Wire-Based Clutch Design

Based on the previous schematic design of the novel SMA clutch, the prototype was fabricated in this section for the performance test. As the SMA wire is sensitive to the temperature (caused by the imposed voltage in this paper), the voltage response of the SMA clutch is firstly tested before the tracking performance study.

3.1 Experimental Setup

In order to test the performances (i.e. voltage response and tracking response) of the proposed SMA clutch, the experimental setup is built firstly in this section, which includes the SMA clutch and the displacement measuring system, shown as Fig. 3 (a). Specifically, in the experimental setup the SMA clutch is mounted on the base with a vertical plate, where a magnetic scale with 0.244 μm resolution is glued. In addition, the magnetic linear encode (type: RLC2IC) is installed on the moveable rack of SMA clutch, which can feedback the position of SMA clutch to the control system. For adjusting the average voltage on SMA clutch, the pulse width method (PWM) is adopted from the power supply (i.e. 12 V output).

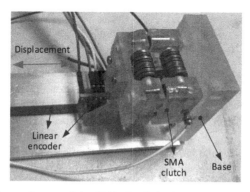

Fig. 3. The experimental setup of the SMA clutch for implementing the model validation

3.2 Voltage Response

By changing the average voltage on the SMA wire, the displacement variation of the moveable platform can be achieved to implement the function of the proposed SMA clutch (i.e. clamping and releasing). Further, by adding a displacement sensor (working principle: relative displacement between the linear encoder and magnetic scale) on a moveable platform, the precise motion control can be achieved to improve the working range of the SMA clutch (e.g. for clamping cable with different diameters). Firstly, the voltage-displacement response of the proposed SMA clutch is shown in Fig. 4.

Figure 4 shows the voltage-displacement response of the SMA clutch under different voltages in a whole working range (i.e. heating and cooling stages respectively). In the heating stage, the output displacement is increasing gradually with the increase of the voltage; then, the SMA clutch will attend to the static balance with the build-in compressional springs, and the stable displacement outputs of SMA clutch under different voltage (i.e. 1 to 6 V with 1 V increment) are about 1.2 mm, 1.52 mm, 1.76 mm, 1.87 mm, 2.32 mm and 2.51 mm respectively. The response times for attending the stable outputs are 5.9 s, 4.3 s, 3.1 s, 2.9 s, 2.0 s and 1.73 s respectively. In the cooling stage, the displacements of the SMA clutch are decreasing gradually. As the real temperature of SMA wire is depended on the heat dissipation speed and initial temperature, the

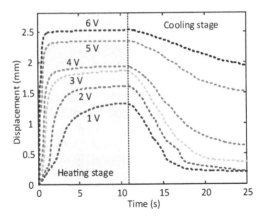

Fig. 4. The voltage-displacement response of SMA clutch under different voltages

displacement variation speeds of SMA clutch are different. After about 15 s of power off, the SMA clutch can almost back to the initial position under the voltages 1 V, 2 V and 3 V. While for the rest of three voltages (i.e. 4 V, 5 V and 6 V), the remaining displacements are 0.63 mm, 1.52 mm and 1.94 mm respectively.

As the SMA wire is very sensitive to the temperature and will be damaged when the temperature is higher than required, the control voltage and heating time should be correctly controlled. From the voltage-displacement response study of the SMA clutch, the parameters (i.e. voltage for SMA wire, heating time and cooling time) can be selected for controlling the SMA wire. This study is also important for the tracking performance test of SMA clutch with the closed-loop controller.

3.3 Tracking Response

In order to test the dynamic performance of the proposed SMA clutch, the sinusoidal trajectory was selected to be tracked with the developed closed-loop controller. To do that, the controller will provide different voltages for the SMA clutch to change the temperature of the SMA wire and read the displacement of the moveable platform by the displacement sensor.

The sinusoidal trajectory used for the performance test is defined as follows based on the characteristic of SMA clutch: 1) the amplitude and cycle are 0.5 mm and 20 s respectively; 2) The amplitude has 0.5 mm offset, enabling the SMA clutch to have positive displacement; 3) the phase has 90° offset, enabling to test the response time/speed of SMA clutch in the beginning. Then the PID control algorithm is implemented on SMA clutch for the trajectory tracking.

Figure 5 presents the tracking response (i.e. blue solid curve) of the SMA clutch for the given sinusoidal trajectory (i.e. Amplitude: 0.5 mm, cycle: 20 s). For the better comparison, the reference trajectory (i.e. red dotted curve) is also plotted. From the beginning, the SMA clutch is trying to track it from 0 mm to 1 mm with the implemented control algorithm, which can be regarded as the step tracking. The step response time for the SMA clutch is around 0.52 s to attend 0.95 mm. It can be seen from Fig. 5

that the lower tracking accuracy is achieved at the following two stages: one is at the beginning of tracking; another is near the bottom of the trajectory (closing to the X axis, tracking error 43.2%). While in the clamping area, the higher tracking accuracy can be achieved (i.e. 3.4%). The reason for the lower tracking accuracy in the beginning stage is that the SMA clutch is trying to track the given displacement (i.e. 1 mm) from the initial position (i.e. 0 mm), where the error is caused. For another reason, as the heating dissipation speed of SMA wire decreases seriously when the temperature of SMA wire is closing to the room temperature, the longer time will be needed for the SMA wire to back to its initial position, where the tracking error is produced.

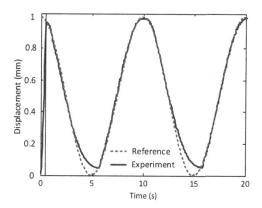

Fig. 5. The experimental results of SMA clutch for tracking the given sinusoidal trajectory (Color figure online)

In this section, based on the fabricated SMA clutch and experimental setup, the voltage-displacement response and tracking response were tested to study the performance of the proposed SMA clutch. From the voltage-displacement response of SMA clutch, the suitable controlling voltage (i.e. 4 V) and response time (i.e. 2.9 s) can be obtained based on the current physical and control system. From the tracking response test, the SMA clutch can be actively controlled to have the required dynamic clamping response (e.g. sinusoidal trajectory).

4   Conclusion

For the first time, a novel SMA wire-based clutch is proposed to reduce the dimension and weight of conventional magnetic clutch. By using the smart material (SMA wire) as the actuator, the dimension and weight of the clutch can be largely reduced, enabling it to be used in some special occasions (e.g. satellite). Based on the proposed SMA clutch and its experimental tests, the conclusions can be summarised as follows: firstly, it was found that the appropriate actuating voltage is around 4 V, enabling the SMA wire to have appropriate response time; secondly, the response time for the SMA clutch is within 1 s to track the given step single, which means the proposed SMA clutch can be used in the rapid operating area; thirdly, it was demonstrated that the proposed SMA clutch can track the given sinusoidal trajectory with the developed control algorithm, which proves the SMA clutch can be used in a wider situation (e.g. clamping the cable with different diameters).

Acknowledgement. The research leading to these results has received funding from the EPSRC project (EP/P027121/1 Through-life performance: From science to instrumentation).

References

1. Ma, N., Yu, J., Dong, X., et al.: Design and stiffness analysis of a class of 2-DoF tendon driven parallel kinematics mechanism. Mech. Mach. Theory **129**, 202–217 (2018)
2. Ma, N., Dong, X., Palmer, D., et al.: Parametric vibration analysis and validation for a novel portable hexapod machine tool attached to surfaces with unequal stiffness. J. Manuf. Process. **47**, 192–201 (2019)
3. Ma, N., Dong, X., Axinte, D.: Modelling and experimental validation of a compliant under-actuated parallel kinematic manipulator. IEEE/ASME Trans. Mechatron. (2020)
4. Hartl, D.J., Lagoudas, D.C.: Aerospace applications of shape memory alloys. Proc. Inst. Mech. Eng. Part G: J. Aerosp. Eng. **221**(4), 535–552 (2007)
5. Bil, C., Massey, K., Abdullah, E.J.: Wing morphing control with shape memory alloy actuators. J. Intell. Mater. Syst. Struct. **24**(7), 879–898 (2013)
6. Morgan, N.B.: Medical shape memory alloy applications—the market and its products. Mater. Sci. Eng. A **378**(1), 16–23 (2004)
7. Kolansky, J., Tarazaga, P., John Ohanian, O.: Experimental implementation of opposed shape memory alloy wires for actuator control. J. Vibr. Acoust. **137**(1), 11007 (2015)
8. Guo, Z., Pan, Y., Wee, L.B., et al.: Design and control of a novel compliant differential shape memory alloy actuator. Sens. Actuators A Phys. **225**, 71–80 (2015)
9. Ashrafiuon, H., Eshraghi, M., Elahinia, M.H.: Position control of a three-link shape memory alloy actuated robot. J. Intell. Mater. Syst. Struct. **17**(5), 381–392 (2006)
10. Colorado, J., Barrientos, A., Rossi, C., et al.: Biomechanics of smart wings in a bat robot: morphing wings using SMA actuators. Bioinspiration Biomim. **7**(3), 36006 (2012)
11. Villanueva, A., Smith, C., Priya, S.: A biomimetic robotic jellyfish (Robojelly) actuated by shape memory alloy composite actuators. Bioinspiration Biomim. **6**(3), 36004 (2011)
12. Price, A.D., Jnifene, A., Naguib, H.E.: Design and control of a shape memory alloy based dexterous robot hand. Smart Mater. Struct. **16**(4), 1401 (2007)
13. Maeno, T., Hino, T.: Miniature five-fingered robot hand driven by shape memory alloy actuators, pp. 174–179 (2006)
14. Kim, B., Lee, S., Park, J.H., et al.: Design and fabrication of a locomotive mechanism for capsule-type endoscopes using shape memory alloys (SMAs)]. IEEE/ASME Trans. Mechatron. **10**(1), 77–86 (2005)
15. Menciassi, A., Moglia, A., Gorini, S., et al.: Shape memory alloy clamping devices of a capsule for monitoring tasks in the gastrointestinal tract. J. Micromech. Microeng. **15**(11), 2045 (2005)
16. Yan, S., Liu, X., Xu, F., et al.: A gripper actuated by a pair of differential SMA springs. J. Intell. Mater. Syst. Struct. **18**(5), 459–466 (2007)
17. Liang, C., Wang, F., Tian, Y., et al.: Development of a high speed and precision wire clamp with both position and force regulations. Robot. Comput.-Integr. Manuf. **44**, 208–217 (2017)

Prototyping Sensors and Actuators for Robot Swarms in Mixed Reality

Alex Murphy[1] and Alan G. Millard[2]([✉]) [ID]

[1] School of Engineering, Computing and Mathematics, University of Plymouth,
Plymouth, UK
`alex.murphy@students.plymouth.ac.uk`
[2] Lincoln Centre for Autonomous Systems, University of Lincoln, Lincoln, UK
`amillard@lincoln.ac.uk`

Abstract. Swarm robotics is an approach to the coordination of large numbers of relatively simple robots with limited physical capabilities. Extending the capabilities of these robots usually requires either purchasing or prototyping new sensors or actuators (a costly and time-consuming process), often before even knowing whether these new sensors or actuators will be able to perform the necessary task effectively. This paper presents a software platform that enables researchers to prototype new sensors and actuators in the virtual world, eliminating the time and resources necessary to prototype physical hardware, and allows for experiments to be run in as many configurations as required in order to determine the efficacy of the proposed sensor/actuator.

Keywords: Swarm robotics · Virtual sensors/Actuators · Mixed reality

1 Introduction and Related Work

Swarm robotics is an approach to the coordination of large numbers of relatively simple robots with limited physical capabilities, typically designed with the space restrictions of lab experimentation in mind. Extending the capabilities of these robots usually requires either purchasing or prototyping new sensors or actuators (a costly and time-consuming process), often before even knowing whether these new sensors or actuators will be able to perform the necessary task effectively. Through necessity (i.e. due to financial/time restrictions), the swarm robotics research community has begun to tackle this problem through the use of mixed reality techniques to create virtual sensors and actuators for individual robots.

Mixed reality refers to a combination of physical and virtual objects acting as one combined version of reality [6]. This is not to be confused with augmented reality [2], which often involves overlaying virtual objects/information onto a view of a physical system. Mixed reality systems for robot swarms typically use a motion capture system in combination with bespoke software to transmit virtualised sensor information to individual robots. O'Dowd et al. [15] and Pitonakova

© Springer Nature Switzerland AG 2020
A. Mohammad et al. (Eds.): TAROS 2020, LNAI 12228, pp. 377–386, 2020.
https://doi.org/10.1007/978-3-030-63486-5_39

[17] have previously implemented virtual sensors for a swarm of e-puck robots [11] performing foraging tasks, using a Vicon tracking system, an external server, and Wi-Fi communication. Similarly, Turgut et al. [21] implemented a virtual heading sensor for the Kobot swarm platform with digital compasses and wireless communication, allowing robots to sense the headings their neighbours while executing collective flocking behaviours. Virtual sensors and actuators have also been implemented for Kilobot swarms through the use of external hardware such as ARK [18] and Kilogrid [1,22].

Reina et al. [19] took a different approach to creating an 'augmented reality' for a swarm of e-puck robots through the virtualisation of their sensor inputs. This was achieved by integrating an overhead camera tracking system with the ARGoS robot simulator [16] to create a mixed reality that was relayed to individual robots wirelessly. Mapping the physical world into a modified version of the ARGoS robot simulator allowed Reina et al. [19] to implement novel sensors and simulate environmental features, such as virtual pollution, which could then be passed to the robots to influence their behaviour. One experimental scenario involved simulating a polluted area and implementing a virtual pollutant sensor. The use of virtual sensors in this manner allows researchers to experiment with real robots in an environment that cannot be replicated easily in the physical world, such as hazardous areas, or to allow for the prototyping of new hardware for the robots. While not part of their research, Reina et al. [19] note that implementation of virtual actuators, such as virtual pheromones, could be done in a similar way, to provide similar experimental benefits for researchers.

Sun et al. [20] present a novel method of virtual actuation in the form of laying virtual pheromone trails behind robots to facilitate indirect inter-robot communication via stigmergy. Their ColCOSφ system integrates an overhead camera and LCD display (in place of an arena floor) with the Colias micro-robot [7], which is able to detect pheromone trails rendered on the dynamic floor with colour sensors mounted to its underside. This mixed-reality approach overcomes the logistical issues associated with implementing 'pheromone' deposition in hardware, thus facilitating research that would otherwise be impractical.

Brutschy et al. [5] take a slightly different approach by abstracting actuation rather than virtualising it. Their Task Abstraction Modules (TAMs) can be placed in the environment at locations where the swarm is required to complete tasks, and individual e-puck robots can drive into them to simulate performing an action. This allows the experimenter to focus on their research question without getting caught up in the implementation of physical actuation, and is less costly than upgrading the hardware capabilities of an entire swarm.

Although virtual sensors/actuators have previously been implemented for robot swarms, there has been little investigation into the effect of different virtual sensors on swarm performance. In this paper we present the results of our experiments that vary the field-of-view of a swarm's virtual sensors, and analyse performance with respect to a simple foraging task. We also detail our mixed reality software platform that enables researchers to experiment with virtual sensors and actuators on a physical swarm of robots. This allows new sensors/actuators

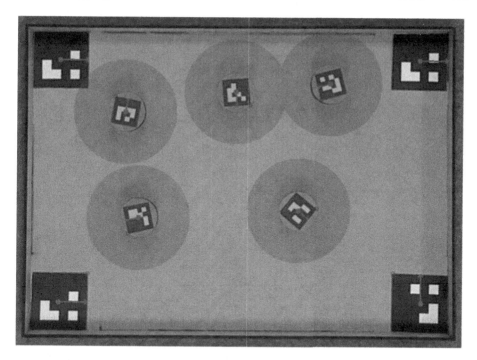

Fig. 1. View of 5 e-puck robots from the overhead camera, with their virtual sensor ranges visualised in green. ArUco tags in the corners delineate the bounding box within which virtual food items are generated. (Color figure online)

to be rapidly prototyped, and their efficacy assessed, before investing time and resources in developing physical hardware. The rest of this paper describes our research methodology and experimental design, followed by a discussion and evaluation of the experimental results.

2   Methodology

In this section we describe our experimental setup, the software infrastructure implemented to carry out the experiments, and the case study foraging task.

2.1   Experimental Setup

The experimental environment comprised a small arena ($600 \times 840\,\text{mm}$) that was free of physical obstacles, as shown in Fig. 1. A Logitech BRIO[1] webcam was mounted in the ceiling above this arena, providing a tracking server with a clear real-time view of the swarm below. The server featured an eight-core Intel i7 CPU and 32 GB of RAM, running Ubuntu 16.04. This server handled all

---

[1] https://www.logitech.com/en-gb/product/brio.

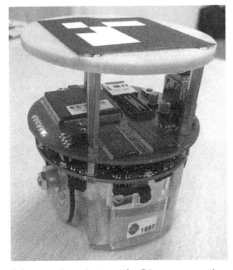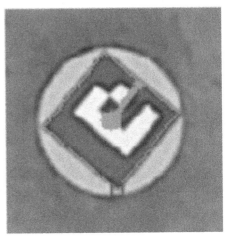

(a) e-puck robot with Linux extension board and ArUco marker.

(b) e-puck robot detected using ArUco markers and `SwarmTracking` module.

Fig. 2. Augmented e-puck robots used for the experimental work.

sensor and actuator virtualisation, using data obtained by the overhead camera to track the location of each robot.

We used e-puck robots with a Linux extension board [8], communicating over the serial port using the advanced sercom protocol[2]. Each robot has a unique ArUco [12] marker on the top of it, as shown in Fig. 2, to enable the camera and server to track each robot individually, and virtualise the sensor and actuator data accurately. Each robot has a static IP address which can be mapped to the unique code from the ArUco tag, allowing the system to transmit individualised data to each robot.

2.2   Software Infrastructure

The software was developed as two separate applications: a tracking system, and a virtualisation system. The tracking system is a standalone swarm robot tracking system developed for this research, which uses the overhead camera to track and identify the robots using their unique ArUco tags. The virtualisation system uses the data from the tracking system in order to simulate sensor data for virtual sensors, and then send this data to the respective robot. Both pieces of software were developed in Python 2.7 using OpenCV 4.0 [4].

`SwarmTracking` [13] locates the ArUco markers on top of the robots in the camera feed, and calculates their positions in the world relative to the camera, then passes this data back to an application in a thread-safe manner. It is capable

---

[2] https://www.gctronic.com/doc/index.php/Advanced_sercom_protocol.

of identifying any ArUco tag that fits within the dictionary of tags specified by the user (either predefined, or custom-generated). ArUco markers provide a simple way of uniquely identifying each robot, as they encode an ID value that can be associated with a particular robot, enabling the system to appropriately track each member of the swarm. The algorithm is also built-in to OpenCV, which means it can be used with any visible-light webcam of sufficient resolution.

Figure 2b shows an e-puck robot being detected by the `SwarmTracking` module using an ArUco marker. Once detected, an outline of the ArUco tag is placed over the camera image, as well as an arrow showing the direction of movement of the robot. Direction of movement is calculated by finding the front point of the ArUco tag, and rotating this point around the centre by the angle that the tag is offset on the robot, specified by the user.

`SwarmVirtualisation` [14] is the software that virtualises sensors and actuators for swarm robots using data from a overhead camera tracking system. The software uses the `SwarmTracking` module to gather its tracking data, as well as connection with the overhead camera. As a result, the `SwarmTracking` module also passes back the frame it worked with when it calculates the position of the robots, so that the frame can be used for virtualisation and for visual feedback to users of the software. `SwarmVirtualisation` supports three distinct types of virtual objects: sensors, actuators, and environment objects. Each of these object types has sub-types that dictate the way that each individual object behaves, and the corresponding data that is generated for each camera frame. These objects are created by the users of the system, and can be written to file to ensure that the users do not have to re-create the objects each time they run the system.

Virtual sensors have three subtypes: circular, conical, and linear. These sub-types represent the different sensing methods that the system is capable of:

Circular: Defined by a range – implements a circular sensing field with the radius of the circle being the range specified, and the centre point being the centre of the robot. The sensor will detect any robots or virtual objects within the bounds of the sensing field, and returns a Boolean *True* when it detects something.

Conical: Defined by a range, field-of-view, and angular offset. The sensor implements a cone shaped sensing area originating at the centre of the robot with a length determined by the range, optionally offset by a specified angle.

Linear: Implements a line-of-sight sensor originating from the centre of the bot, parameterised by its range and width. It also takes an angular offset, calculated and used in the same manner as that of the conical sensor. This sensor will detect any robot or environment object within range and in the line of sight of this sensor, returning a Boolean *True* when it detects something.

There are two sub-types of virtual actuator: placers and grabbers. As with virtual sensors, these sub-types dictate the behaviour and attributes of the actuator.

Grabber: Picks up virtual environment objects when the robot is on top of one, provided that the robot has sufficient inventory space. The grabber picks up an item when the centre of the robot is over an environment object.

Placer: Places virtual environment objects into the world at specified intervals from the robot.

Environment objects have three types: goal, obstacle and item. These subtypes dictate how the robots interact with them:

- **Goal:** Object representing a target for the robots.
- **Obstacle:** An object to be avoided by the robots.
- **Item:** An item that can be interacted with by the robots.

Virtualisation of the sensor and actuator data is separated out into a different thread so as not to impact either the user interface, or the data collection from the `SwarmTracking` module. Each time a new frame is gathered by the `SwarmTracking` module, the simulation thread attempts to calculate whether each sensor on each bot is able to detect an object. Having this run in a separate thread enables the application to continue tracking the robots and collecting data without having to wait for these calculations to be completed.

Communication between the software and the robots is achieved by transmitting JSON[3] packets from the server to the robot. These packets contain the virtualised sensor data, transmitted to the appropriate robot only, to enable the robot to behave as if it had collected the data from an on-board sensor. The networking is handled in a separate thread to ensure that the virtualisation and data collection are not interrupted in the event of network issues.

2.3   Case Study: Foraging

This mixed reality software was used to implement virtual sensors and actuators for a swarm of 5 e-puck robots, which then carried out a foraging task – a typical task for robot swarms [3]. In our particular implementation, each robot moves around the arena at random until it detects a virtual food item, at which point it will move towards it and collect it with its virtual actuator, and then return to randomly searching for more food items. When a virtual food item is collected, another is randomly generated within the arena.

The food items for these experiments were randomly generated within the bounding box of the arena, calculated during a calibration stage when the software starts. One experiment was run for each different sensor using the same random seed, after which the random seed was changed and another experiment was run for each different type of sensor. This process was repeated until each sensor had been tested ten times. Five different virtual sensors were used for the experiments with different fields-of-view ranging from 45° to 360° (as shown in Fig. 3), as well as a control experiment with no sensors at all. The range of each sensor remained consistent throughout all experiments.

---

[3] https://www.json.org/json-en.html.

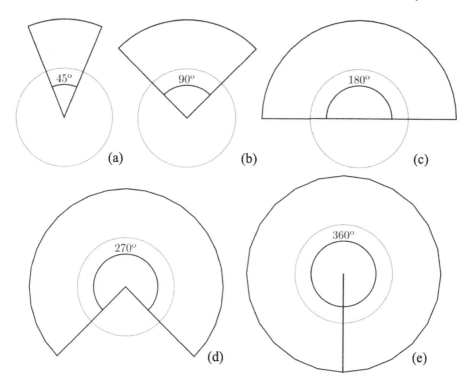

Fig. 3. Virtual sensors used in the experiments. Sensors (a), (b), (c) and (d) are conical sensors, with angles of 45°, 90°, 180° and 270° respectively, while (e) is a circular sensor (equivalent to a 360° conical sensor).

3   Experimental Results

A series of experiments were carried out to assess the efficacy of different virtual fields-of-view for the robot swarm collecting virtual food items. The number of food items collected within 10 min was used to analyse the efficacy of the virtual sensors. 10 repeat runs were completed for each of the 6 different conditions to assess the performance accounting for stochastic behaviour, representing 60 experiments in total spanning 10 h.

Figure 4 shows how effective each sensor was with respect to the total number of food items collected, compared with a control experiment where no virtual sensors were used. Most of the sensors tested show a relatively small amount of variation in the number of food items collected between each experiment, implying that the virtual sensors produce consistent results.

An unexpected result from these experiments is that the use of a 45° conical sensor performed worse than having no sensors at all in almost all cases, implying that the use of this sensor would actually hinder the performance of robots. This is because the 45° conical sensor, and to a lesser extent the 90° conical sensor, had a tendency to overshoot the angle when turning towards the food object.

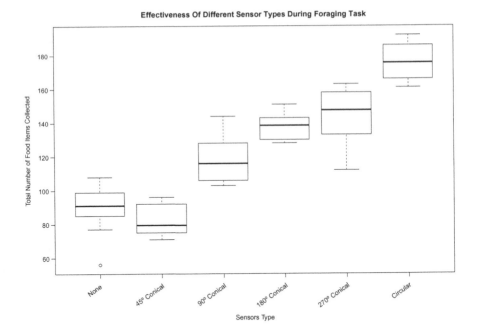

Fig. 4. Performance of each sensor type with respect to the foraging task. Each boxplot represents 10 repeat runs of each condition. The performance metric for each run is the total number of food items collected by the swarm in 10 min.

When the robot overshoots the angle, it does so by turning further than it should have done, often ending up with the food object it was attempting to turn towards now being outside of the range of the sensor. This issue mainly affects sensors with a smaller field-of-view as the larger ones are able to more effectively account for this level of error. All other sensors, outperformed the control experiment, which is to be expected, with the average performance of the sensors improving as the angle of the cone increases.

The results of these experiments show that the use of virtual sensors and actuators can successfully increase the capabilities of swarm robots. In particular, we have shown that the sensors and actuators implemented enabled a swarm of e-puck robots to consistently detect and navigate to virtual objects in real-time.

4   Conclusions and Future Work

The results of these experiments clearly show that the use of virtual sensors and actuators can successfully extend the capabilities of swarm robotics platforms. Through the use of the software developed for this project, a swarm of e-puck robots was able to successfully carry out a foraging task by identifying virtual food objects in real time, navigating to these food objects and collecting them, using a range of different virtual sensor types.

The software developed for this project is relatively limited in its scope, as the virtual sensors/actuators can only interact with virtual objects. Further work on this could include the ability to perform object/edge detection within an image, allowing the software to simulate sensors that can interact with the physical world. Extending this functionality to include detecting physical objects as well would provide a much wider range of possible uses/applications. Modelling the effect of noise would also allows for more realistic implementations of sensor hardware, as physical sensors inevitably have some level of inaccuracy, and is often significant enough to have a noticeable effect on robot performance.

In future, we intend to integrate the mixed reality functionality presented in this paper into ARDebug [10] – an augmented reality debugging system for robot swarms, and to extend the work to support the Pi-puck [9] – a Raspberry Pi extension board for the e-puck robot that is a modern replacement for the Linux extension board used for this research.

References

1. Antoun, A., et al.: Kilogrid: a modular virtualization environment for the Kilobot robot. In: 2016 IEEE/RSJ International Conference on Intelligent Robots and Systems (IROS), pp. 3809–3814. IEEE (2016)
2. Azuma, R.T.: A survey of augmented reality. Presence Teleoperators Virtual Environ. **6**(4), 355–385 (1997)
3. Bayındır, L.: A review of swarm robotics tasks. Neurocomputing **172**, 292–321 (2016)
4. Bradski, G., Kaehler, A.: OpenCV. Dr. Dobb's J. Softw. Tools **3**, (2000)
5. Brutschy, A., et al.: The tam: abstracting complex tasks in swarm robotics research. Swarm Intell. **9**(1), 1–22 (2015)
6. Hönig, W., Milanes, C., Scaria, L., Phan, T., Bolas, M., Ayanian, N.: Mixed reality for robotics. In: 2015 IEEE/RSJ International Conference on Intelligent Robots and Systems (IROS), pp. 5382–5387. IEEE (2015)
7. Hu, Cheng., Fu, Qinbing, Yue, Shigang: Colias IV: the affordable micro robot platform with bio-inspired vision. In: Giuliani, Manuel, Assaf, Tareq, Giannaccini, Maria Elena (eds.) TAROS 2018. LNCS (LNAI), vol. 10965, pp. 197–208. Springer, Cham (2018). https://doi.org/10.1007/978-3-319-96728-8_17
8. Liu, W., Winfield, A.F.: Open-hardware e-puck Linux extension board for experimental swarm robotics research. Microprocess. Microsyst. **35**(1), 60–67 (2011)
9. Millard, A.G., et al.: The Pi-puck extension board: a Raspberry Pi interface for the e-puck robot platform. In: 2017 IEEE/RSJ International Conference on Intelligent Robots and Systems (IROS), pp. 741–748. IEEE (2017)
10. Millard, A.G., Redpath, R., Jewers, A.M., Arndt, C., Joyce, R., Hilder, J.A., McDaid, L.J., Halliday, D.M.: ARDebug: an augmented reality tool for analysing and debugging swarm robotic systems. Frontiers Robot. AI **5**, 87 (2018)
11. Mondada, F., et al.: The e-puck, a robot designed for education in engineering. In: Proceedings of the 9th Conference on Autonomous Robot Systems and Competitions, vol. 1, pp. 59–65. IPCB: Instituto Politécnico de Castelo Branco (2009)
12. Munoz-Salinas, R.: ArUco: a minimal library for Augmented Reality applications based on OpenCV. Universidad de Córdoba (2012)

13. Murphy, A.: GitHub - SwarmTracking (2019). https://github.com/amurphy4/SwarmTracking
14. Murphy, A.: GitHub - SwarmVirtualisation (2019). https://github.com/amurphy4/SwarmVirtualisation
15. O'Dowd, P.J., Winfield, A.F.T., Studley, M.: The distributed co-evolution of an embodied simulator and controller for swarm robot behaviours. In: 2011 IEEE/RSJ International Conference on Intelligent Robots and Systems, pp. 4995–5000. IEEE (2011)
16. Pinciroli, C., et al.: ARGoS: a modular, parallel, multi-engine simulator for multi-robot systems. Swarm Intell. **6**(4), 271–295 (2012). https://doi.org/10.1007/s11721-012-0072-5
17. Pitonakova, L., Winfield, A., Crowder, R.: Recruitment Near Worksites Facilitates Robustness of Foraging E-Puck Swarms to Global Positioning Noise. In: 2018 IEEE/RSJ International Conference on Intelligent Robots and Systems (IROS), pp. 4276–4281. IEEE (2018)
18. Reina, A., Cope, A.J., Nikolaidis, E., Marshall, J.A., Sabo, C.: ARK: Augmented Reality for Kilobots. IEEE Robot. Autom. Lett. **2**(3), 1755–1761 (2017)
19. Reina, A., et al.: Augmented reality for robots: virtual sensing technology applied to a swarm of e-pucks. In: 2015 NASA/ESA Conference on Adaptive Hardware and Systems (AHS), pp. 1–6. IEEE (2015)
20. Sun, X., Liu, T., Hu, C., Fu, Q., Yue, S.: ColCOSφ: a multiple pheromone communication system for swarm robotics and social insects research. In: 2019 IEEE 4th International Conference on Advanced Robotics and Mechatronics (ICARM), pp. 59–66. IEEE (2019)
21. Turgut, A.E., Çelikkanat, H., Gökçe, F., Şahin, E.: Self-organized flocking in mobile robot swarms. Swarm Intell. **2**(2–4), 97–120 (2008)
22. Valentini, G., et al.: Kilogrid: a novel experimental environment for the kilobot robot. Swarm Intell. **12**(3), 245–266 (2018)

ROSMonitoring: A Runtime Verification Framework for ROS

Angelo Ferrando[1(✉)], Rafael C. Cardoso[1], Michael Fisher[1], Davide Ancona[2], Luca Franceschini[2], and Viviana Mascardi[2]

[1] Department of Computer Science, University of Liverpool, Liverpool, UK
{angelo.ferrando,rafael.cardoso,mfisher}@liverpool.ac.uk
[2] Department of Computer Science, Bioengineering, Robotics and Systems Engineering (DIBRIS), University of Genova, Genova, Italy
luca.franceschini@dibris.unige.it,
{davide.ancona,viviana.mascardi}@unige.it

Abstract. Recently, robotic applications have been seeing widespread use across industry, often tackling safety-critical scenarios where software reliability is paramount. These scenarios often have unpredictable environments and, therefore, it is crucial to be able to provide assurances about the system at runtime. In this paper, we introduce ROSMonitoring, a framework to support Runtime Verification (RV) of robotic applications developed using the Robot Operating System (ROS). The main advantages of ROSMonitoring compared to the state of the art are its portability across multiple ROS distributions and its agnosticism w.r.t. the specification formalism. We describe the architecture behind ROS-Monitoring and show how it can be used in a traditional ROS example. To better evaluate our approach, we apply it to a practical example using a simulation of the Mars curiosity rover. Finally, we report the results of some experiments to check how well our framework scales.

1 Introduction

There are many different techniques that can be used to provide reliability assurances for software applications. Formal verification allows us to verify the correctness of a software application against some kind of formal logic specification, for example Linear Temporal Logic (LTL [12]). Using formal verification, the system can be analysed at design time (offline) and/or at runtime (online).

Verification at design time, such as model checking [13], exhaustively checks the behaviour of a system. This is done by generating a formal model of it and then performing a state space search looking for the satisfaction of the formal properties in all possible executions.

Runtime verification (RV [10]) is a more lightweight approach which is usually more suitable for examining "black box" software components. RV focuses on

Work supported by the UK Research and Innovation Hubs for "Robotics and AI in Hazardous Environments": EP/R026092 (FAIR-SPACE), EP/R026173 (ORCA), and EP/R026084 (RAIN).

© Springer Nature Switzerland AG 2020
A. Mohammad et al. (Eds.): TAROS 2020, LNAI 12228, pp. 387–399, 2020.
https://doi.org/10.1007/978-3-030-63486-5_40

analysing only what the system produces while it is being executed and, because of this, it can only conclude the satisfaction/violation of properties regarding the current observed execution. Since RV does not need to exhaustively check the system behaviour, it scales better to real systems, since it does not suffer from state space explosion problems that can be commonly found in model checking.

There are many techniques and implementations of RV that use different formalisms, such as LTL [4] or finite automata over finite and infinite strings [11]. One of the most common approaches to perform RV of a system is through monitoring, where monitors are used to check the system execution against formally specified properties. This check can happen incrementally at runtime (online RV), or over recorded executions such as log files (offline RV).

Even though many frameworks and libraries exist that support RV of software systems developed across many different programming languages, there are only a few suitable for monitoring robotic applications in ROS. One of the most promising is ROSRV [9], a general-purpose runtime verification framework for ROS. ROSRV uses the Monitoring-Oriented Programming (MOP [6]) paradigm. However, one of the main drawbacks of ROSRV is that it has very limited portability, in fact, the latest version available at the time of writing can only be used with the ROS *Groovy Galapagos* distribution, which stopped being supported in 2014. This lack of portability in such dynamic and evolving context leaves a significant gap, and it is one of the main motivations for developing our new framework, called ROSMonitoring.

The ROSMonitoring RV is a general, formalism agnostic (i.e. does not depend on using only a specific verification formalism to represent and check properties), runtime monitoring framework that can be used with multiple ROS distributions (tested in Melodic and Kinetic). It is designed for the automatic verification of the communication between ROS nodes by monitoring topics and checking against formal properties expressed using the user's formalism of choice. Because of this, ROSMonitoring can be applied to any kind of ROS-based robotic application, with no limitation on how each communication endpoint is implemented.

2   ROSMonitoring

ROSMonitoring[1] is a framework for runtime monitoring of ROS topics, and to do so it creates monitors that are placed between ROS nodes to intercept messages on relevant topics and check the events generated by these messages against formally specified properties.

Our framework has three main components: (a) *instrumentation*, used for automatically creating a monitor and inserting it in the middle of the communication among ROS nodes; (b) *oracle*, used for checking whether the events that are observed by the monitor conform to some formal specification or not; and (c) *monitor*, the implementation of the ROS monitor, it is responsible for intercepting messages between nodes and communicating with the oracle.

---

[1] https://github.com/autonomy-and-verification-uol/ROSMonitoring

In Fig. 1, we provide a high-level overview of ROSMonitoring. From left to right: we create the monitor nodes and perform node instrumentation according to a YAML configuration file customised by the user; as output we obtain the new instrumented nodes (with the communication gaps), and the ROS monitor implementation as a Python node; and we run ROS with the instrumented nodes and the monitor nodes, which performs RV either online or offline, depending on the configuration file used.

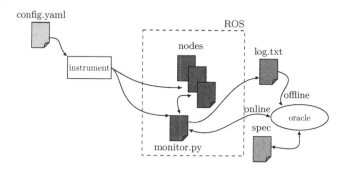

Fig. 1. High-level overview of ROSMonitoring.

2.1   Instrumentation

First, let us consider a common publisher/subscriber example that can be found in ROS tutorials. The example comprises two nodes communicating on a specific topic. One node is called *talker*, and continuously publishes the message `"hello"` in the topic *chatter*. The *listener* node subscribes to the *chatter* topic.

We use a YAML configuration file to guide the instrumentation process. ROS users should be familiar with YAML, as it is also used for configuration there. Within this file, users can set the number of needed monitors, and then for each monitor can set the topics that have to be intercepted, including: the name of the topic, the ROS message type that is expected in that topic, the type of action that the monitor should perform, which side (publisher or subscriber) is the monitor intercepting the message, and the names and launch path of the nodes that are going to be remapped. After preferences have been configured in *config.yaml*, the last step is to run the *generator* script to automatically generate the monitors and instrument the required ROS launch files. By default, the monitors so generated can perform two different actions when intercepting a message: *log*, the monitor will simply log the observed events into the log file specified in the monitor's `log` attribute; and *filter*, the monitor will filter out all the events inconsistent with the specification (requires an oracle).

For instance, in Listing 1 we have the configuration file for the chatter example. Note that we need a unique id for each monitor, and that the monitors always log the events received (thus, we also need to specify a log file for each of them). In this example, the list of topics we want to intercept only contains *chatter*. In general, we can have more topics that we want to monitor in our application, and with this field we are able to add as many as necessary. It is important that the ROS message type is exactly as it is specified in ROS (i.e. ROS is able to find the given message type), in this case it is the primitive ROS message type *String*.

```
monitors:
  - monitor:
      id: monitor_0
      log: ./log_0.txt
      topics:
        - name: chatter
          type: std_msgs.msg.String
          action: filter
          side: publisher
            - node: talker
              path: /chatter/launch/chatter.launch
```

Listing 1: Configuration file for the chatter example.

```
oracle:
  port: 8080
  url: 127.0.0.1
```

Listing 2: Extra configuration lines for adding an oracle.

By passing the path to the file that contains the launch code for the *talker* node we can automatically instrument the node by remapping the *chatter* topic to *chatter_mon*. Note that this is done only for the specified side, the publisher (*talker*) node in this example. The following is automatically added to the appropriate section of the *chatter.launch* file:

$$< \text{remap from} = \text{``chatter''} \text{ to} = \text{``chatter\_mon''} / >$$

Remapping topic names allows us to create a gap in communication. In this example, the two nodes are now unable to communicate directly anymore, because the instrumented *talker* publishes on a different topic from the one subscribed by the *listener*. We fill this gap by adding our monitor, which is automatically generated during the instrumentation step. The monitor subscribes to *chatter_mon* and publishes to *chatter*. Then, the monitor has to decide if it wants to propagate the message or not with the help of an oracle, further described in Sect. 2.2.

There are some applications where this type of invasive monitoring is not desired, such as when it is not required to intercept incorrect messages (e.g. in offline RV), or when dealing with proprietary code. In such cases, we can omit the last part of the configuration file (side, node, and path). By doing so, the monitor no longer intercepts messages between ROS nodes, but it still has access to the relevant messages and can log them or do another appropriate action.

2.2 Oracle

One of ROSMonitoring aims is to be highly reusable. The best way for achieving this result is being formalism agnostic, and we obtain this by introducing the notion of oracle. The oracle is an external component, which can be produced by third-parties, containing the logic and implementation of a formalism.

The oracle must be listening on a specific URL (specified in the *url* attribute) and port (specified in the *port* attribute). These attributes are specified in the instrumentation configuration file. If we wanted to add an oracle to the previous example from Listing 1, then we would add the snippet in Listing 2 between the *log* and *topics* attributes.

In the offline scenario, the oracle is used for checking the log file produced by the ROS monitor node. In the online scenario, each time an event is intercepted by the ROS monitor, the latter is propagated to the oracle, which has to check it and to reply with a verdict accordingly to the current satisfaction or violation of some formal property (specified in the oracle side using the formalism supported by the oracle). Upon the reception of this verdict, the ROS monitor decides what to do with the event.

ROSMonitoring requires very few constraints for adding a new oracle. We use *JSON* as data-interchange format for serialising the messages observed by the ROS monitor. The ROS messages are first translated into their JSON representation, which are then logged (offline case) or sent to the oracle (online case). The oracle must be listening and ready to receive the JSON messages using the *WebSocket* protocol. We chose WebSocket because of its real-time bi-directional point to point communication between client and server, which does not require a continue polling of the server. For demonstration purposes, we describe two default oracles available.

Runtime Monitoring Language (RML) Oracle. This oracle supports RML[2] for the specification of properties. RML is a rewriting-based and system agnostic Domain Specific Language (DSL) for RV used for defining formal properties and synthesising monitors from them; it is inspired by trace expressions [2], a formalism adopted for RV in several contexts, such as Multi-Agent Systems (MAS) [8], Object-Oriented programming [7], and Remote Patient Monitoring (RPM) [3]. We chose RML because it imposes no restrictions on how events are generated, and is completely system agnostic. Thanks to this, RML monitors and specifications can be reused in many different contexts, and since RML is based on the data-interchange format JSON for representing events, its synthesised monitors can easily interoperate with other JSON compatible systems, such as ROSMonitoring. The RML oracle is implemented in SWI-Prolog, along with the event calculus on which the semantics of RML is based. Given an RML specification, it is first compiled into its intermediate language representation implemented in SWI-Prolog (trace expressions [2]), then the SWI-Prolog oracle starts listening on a WebSocket for checking incoming JSON events intercepted by the ROSMonitoring monitor.

---

[2] https://rmlatdibris.github.io/.

Reelay Oracle. Reelay[3] is a header-only C++ library and set of tools for system-level verification and testing of real-time systems. Reelay implements state-of-the-art runtime verification techniques to construct runtime monitors that check temporal behaviours of the system against system-level requirements. Reelay supports definition of temporal properties, extended with past operators, such as LTL, MTL, and STL (Linear, Metric and Signal Temporal Logic respectively). Since the Reelay library does not expect JSON messages as input to the monitors, we integrated the latter inside a Python oracle implementation which takes care of this message translation.

2.3   The ROS Monitor

When the instrumentation program analyses our configuration file, in addition to the resulting instrumentation launch files, it also produces the ROS monitor code. Each monitor is automatically generated into a ROS node in Python, which is a native language supported in ROS. By default, the monitor can log or filter the intercepted messages accordingly to the configuration chosen in the instrumentation step.

ROSMonitoring always logs the events generated by the messages in the monitored topics. The best option if we are only concerned in logging messages and not intercepting them, is to employ an external monitor (i.e. not interfering with the messages).

There is an extra configuration attribute that can be set during instrumentation called *warning*. Warning is a flag that determines when the monitor should publish a warning message containing as much information as possible about a property that has been violated. This message is published on a special topic called *monitor_error* and has its own message type *MonitorError.msg*. Information in this message includes: the topic that originated the event, the content of the message that was intercepted in that topic, the property that was violated, and the ROS time of when the message was intercepted.

The algorithm for automatically generating the monitors is fairly straightforward. We report the pseudo-code for the offline (Algorithm 1) and online (Algorithm 2) monitors that would be generated for a chosen set of topics T_1, ..., T_n. In the offline scenario, we first subscribe to the topics we want to keep track of. Each time a message is received the callback in lines 6–9 is activated and the ROS message is translated to JSON. This translation can be easily achieved using the *rospy_message_converter* package. We assume that the oracle can read JSON messages, a fairly common message format. Then, the converted message is logged, ready to be used by an oracle when the system is offline.

In Algorithm 2, we create a publisher for each topic (just *chatter* in our example) and a subscriber for each instrumented version (*chatter_mon* in our example). When the subscriber is created, we pass the corresponding publisher that will be used to eventually republish the message. Then, we have two callback functions that are activated when receiving messages. The first callback (lines

---

[3] https://doganulus.github.io/reelay/.

Algorithm 1. Offline monitor generated for topics $T_1...T_n$.

```
1: function OFFLINE_MONITOR
2:     for i = 1 to n do
3:         CREATE_SUBSCRIBER(T_i, receive_msg)
4:     end for
5: end function
6: function RECEIVE_MSG(ros_msg)
7:     json_msg = CONVERT_ROS_MSG_TO_JSON(ros_msg)
8:     LOG(json_msg)
9: end function
```

7–10) is called upon the reception of a ROS message on an instrumented topic. Inside this callback, the ROS message is first translated to JSON and then propagated to the oracle. On line 9 we also inform which callback has to be called when the response from the oracle arrives (`oracle_msg`).

Algorithm 2. Online monitor generated for topics $T_1...T_n$.

```
 1: function ONLINE_MONITOR
 2:     for i = 1 to n do
 3:         pub_T_i = CREATE_PUBLISHER(T_i)
 4:         CREATE_SUBSCRIBER(T_i_mon, receive_msg, pub_T_i)
 5:     end for
 6: end function
 7: function RECEIVE_MSG(ros_msg, pub)
 8:     json_msg = CONVERT_ROS_MSG_TO_JSON(ros_msg)
 9:     SEND_TO_ORACLE(json_msg, oracle_msg, pub)
10: end function
11: function ORACLE_MSG(res, pub)
12:     verdict = EXTRACT_VERDICT(res)
13:     json_msg = EXTRACT_JSON_MSG(res)
14:     ros_msg = CONVERT_JSON_TO_ROS_MSG(json_msg)
15:     if verdict then
16:         pub.PUBLISH(ros_msg)
17:     end if
18:     LOG(json_msg)
19: end function
```

The `oracle_msg` callback (lines 11–19) extracts the verdict and the JSON message from the oracle's reply. Next, it converts the JSON message back to a ROS message. This is needed if the oracle can change the contents of the message in any way, such as when it is equipped to perform failure handling. Then, if the verdict is valid we republish the message on the corresponding topic name.

After receiving the response from the oracle, the first thing the monitor does is to check for the presence of the attribute *'error'* inside the JSON answer. This is used by the oracle for communicating the validity of the current event. In case of error the event is logged and if the monitor is set to filter wrong messages then it does not propagate the message. When the message is consistent, the monitor simply logs the event and republishes it to the correct topic.

3   Evaluation

We evaluate ROSMonitoring through two separate experiments. First, we apply
it to a case study based on a simulation of the Mars curiosity rover. We use this
practical example to demonstrate the different features in our framework. In the
second experiment, we stress test the delay that can be introduced by adding
our monitors in the chatter example.

3.1   Simulation: Mars Curiosity Rover

Curiosity is a rover sent by NASA to explore the surface of Mars. Its main
objectives include recording image data and collecting soil/rock data. Although
in the original mission the software used in Curiosity was not ROS-based, a ROS
version has been developed using official data and 3D models of Curiosity and
Mars terrain that were made available by NASA.

```
monitors:
  - monitor:
    id: monitor_0
    log: ./log_0.txt
    oracle:
      port: 8080
      url: 127.0.0.1
    topics:
      - name: wheels_control
        type:
        curiosity_mars_rover_description.msg.Move3
        action: filter
        warning: True
        side: subscriber
          - node: wheels_client
            path: /curiosity/launch/wheels.launch
```

Listing 3: Configuration file for the first curiosity example.

We applied our framework to the Curiosity case study by using the filter
action to intercept external messages sources (e.g. human or autonomous agent)
that violate our property. Due to space constraints and their simplicity, we do
not show examples based on the log action, but source code with these examples
are available in ROSMonitoring repository.

As an example of the filter action, consider an action library in ROS that
controls the wheels of the rover. Action libraries are similar to ROS services,
both can receive a request to perform some task and then generate a reply. The
difference in using action libraries is that the user can cancel the action, as well
as receive feedback about the task execution. ROSMonitoring can only monitor
messages that are sent through topics; however, in complex ROS applications it
is common to have external commands (e.g. human control for semi-teleoperated
movement, or an autonomous agent that sends high-level commands), and these
are usually received on a topic that an action client subscribes to.

In this setting, a human sends movement messages to the *wheels_control* topic. The content of the message includes: the *speed* of the wheels, the *direction* for the rover to move (forward, backward, left, or right), and the *distance* that it should move (for how long it should move before it stops). The configuration file for this example is shown in Listing 3.

Note that since the message is being published by a human (i.e. it is not coming from a ROS node), we have to instrument the subscriber side in this example. Our instrumentation does so by remapping *wheels_control* to *wheels_control_mon* in the launch file of the *wheels_client* node.

Due to the gravity and rocky/difficult terrain in Mars, the Curiosity has to be careful with its speed. Thus, when we intercept a message in the *wheels_control* topic, the message is sent to the oracle to verify the following property:

```
left_speed matches {topic:'wheels_control', direction:'left',
    speed:val} with val <= 10;
right_speed matches {topic:'wheels_control', direction:'right',
    speed:val} with val <= 10;
forward_speed matches {topic:'wheels_control', direction:'forward',
    speed:val} with val <= 15;
backward_speed matches {topic:'wheels_control',
    direction:'backward', speed:val} with val <= 15;
Main = (left_speed \/ right_speed \/ forward_speed \/
    backward_speed)*;
```

That is, if the direction is left or right (i.e. a turn action) then the speed can not be greater than 10, and if the direction is forward or backward then the speed can not be greater then 15. These are arbitrary numbers that were defined based on testing to prevent Curiosity from rolling over. If the verdict from the oracle comes back as an error, then the message is discarded. Otherwise, the message is propagated to the *wheels_control_mon* topic. This filtering monitor correctly prevents any messages that could cause the rover to crash due to a high speed turn.

3.2 Scalability

We stress test ROSMonitoring in a scenario with multiple nodes, multiple topics, and different frequency of messages sent/received per second. The structure of the nodes is very similar to the *chatter* example discussed previously; each node publishes only on one topic and subscribes to the topics on which all the other nodes publish. The goal of each node is to receive a preset number of messages, once received the node can stop. The delay introduced by the presence of the monitor(s) determines the monitor(s) overhead.

In our experiment we set the number of nodes to 10 and varied the frequency rate (i.e. messages published per second). We chose three different values: 100, 500 and 1000 [Hz]; since we have 10 publishers which publish on only one topic each, the total number of topics is 10. Thus, we can reach 1000, 5000 and 10000 messages published per second, respectively. Since we were interested in the overhead introduced by the presence of the monitors, in all the experiments we kept the property to be verified as fixed. More specifically, we chose a property which analyses each event in constant time, and is always considered satisfied. In Fig. 2 we show the overhead introduced by the monitor(s) for the different frequency rates; these results have been obtained using ROS Melodic (Version 1.14.3), on a machine with the following specification: Intel(R) Core(TM) i7-7700HQ CPU @ 2.80 GHz, 4 cores 8 threads, 16 GB RAM DDR4.

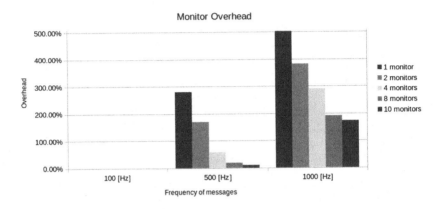

Fig. 2. Overhead introduced by the monitors.

In the first case, having 10 nodes, 10 topics and a frequency of 100 [Hz], the number of messages sent is 1000 [msg/sec]. For such a low number of messages, the presence of one or multiple monitors is practically transparent to the system. This means that the workload is low enough for the monitor(s) to keep up with the message rate. By increasing the message rate we observe a performance decrease introduced by the monitors. In the second case, with a frequency rate of 500 [Hz], we can observe how with only 1 monitor the system becomes almost 4 times slower (~270% overhead). This is due to the high number of messages that the monitor has to intercept, 5000 [msg/sec]. The results we obtained for this second case shows the importance of distributing the workload on multiple monitors; in fact, we observe the monitors overhead dropping, reaching ~9% with 10 monitors (1 monitor for each topic). Naturally, if the number of messages to be handled is too high, even distributing the workload on multiple monitors can not be enough, as we may observe in the third case when the frequency is set to 1000 [Hz] (10000 [msg/sec]).

It is interesting to note that the monitors are more influenced by the higher number of messages to receive, rather than messages to send. The reason for this can be found in the monitor implementation. For each received message, the monitor propagates the information to an external oracle, through web sockets. This communication is sequential in order to preserve the order of the messages that the oracle has to analyse. Increasing the number of messages at this side can cause bottleneck problems, and it is the main reason for the performance decrease. On the other hand, increasing the number of messages to send (propagate) to the other nodes has less influence on performance. We obtain this result because, once the monitor receives the message back from the oracle, it can propagate the latter in parallel exploiting the ROS API.

Besides analysing the monitor's overhead, we evaluated how the presence of monitors delay the communication. As in the overhead analysis, the distribution of the workload on multiple monitors reduces the delay per message, but, when the frequency of messages to intercept increases too much and the monitors become bottlenecks for the communication, the messages start being queued and this causes the increasing delay. We noticed that with a slow frequency (100 [Hz]) the delay is negligible (<1 [ms]), and can be limited to few seconds (<5 [sec]) with a high frequency (500 [Hz]). Frequencies higher than that can not be realistically analysed by the monitors.

We also evaluated in our experiments the latency of the error messages. This aspect is mandatory to determine the reaction time of the system in the presence of errors. Also in this case, for reasonable frequencies the reaction time is low, but when the frequency is too high, the nodes would know about the occurrence of an error with too much delay.

4   Related Work

ROSRV [9] shares some similarities with our framework. Both use monitors, not just for passively observing the messages exchanged among the nodes, but also for intercepting and possibly dealing with incorrect behaviours. The main difference between ROSRV and ROSMonitoring is how they create and insert the monitor in the system. More specifically, ROSRV achieves this by swapping the ROS Master node with a new one, called RVMaster. By replacing the Master node, all node communication has to pass through RVMaster; the latter then establishes peer-to-peer communication by adding the monitor as the man-in-the-middle. In ROSMonitoring we do not change the ROS Master node in any way, instead, we add the monitor through node instrumentation.

In [1] the authors present DeRoS, a DSL for describing safety rules. DeRos provides automatic code generation to integrate these rules with runtime monitoring by generating a ROS safety monitoring node. The logic of the monitor and its integration in ROS are merged. They use the specification to derive the ROS monitor. Unfortunately, this causes a high coupling between the formalism and ROS. In ROSMonitoring instead, the logic of the monitor is external to the low-level integration of the ROS nodes.

Performance Level Profiles (PLP) [5] is an XML-based language for describing the expected properties of functional modules. They provide tools for the automatic generation of code for runtime monitoring of the described properties. Their approach is very close to ours, and goes in the direction of a more general purpose verification process for robotic systems. However, they focus more on a performance checking viewpoint. As in ROSMonitoring, they generate monitors for ROS trying to decouple the monitor's logic from the ROS implementation. Their approach is flexible with respect to the target system (does not have to be only ROS), but requires the specification formalism to be fixed; on the contrary, in ROSMonitoring, the target system is fixed (ROS), but the specification formalism can change.

5 Conclusion

In this paper we presented ROSMonitoring, a new framework for RV of robotic applications in ROS. We showed how, starting from a set of ROS nodes, we can build a ROS monitor node to intercept all the topics related to the properties we want to verify. We described how we implemented ROSMonitoring and its main differences with the state of the art tool ROSRV. The strength of ROSMonitoring lies in its portability and being formalism agnostic, resulting in a framework that is completely decoupled from ROS distribution and oracle implementation.

Future work includes a quantitative comparison against ROSRV, and applying our framework to more practical applications. An interesting extension of ROSMonitoring would be enriching the information exchanged with the oracle. Instead of only communicating the verdict for a single event, it would be interesting to add the global verdict on the trace. Then, it would be possible to simplify the ROS monitor to automatically republish everything, because, if the monitor knew that the property checked by the oracle has been already satisfied, there is no point in propagating the messages to the oracle anymore.

References

1. Adam, S., Larsen, M., Jensen, K., Schultz, U.P.: Towards rule-based dynamic safety monitoring for mobile robots. In: Brugali, D., Broenink, J.F., Kroeger, T., MacDonald, B.A. (eds.) SIMPAR 2014. LNCS (LNAI), vol. 8810, pp. 207–218. Springer, Cham (2014). https://doi.org/10.1007/978-3-319-11900-7_18
2. Ancona, D., Ferrando, A., Mascardi, V.: Comparing trace expressions and linear temporal logic for runtime verification. In: Ábrahám, E., Bonsangue, M., Johnsen, E.B. (eds.) Theory and Practice of Formal Methods. LNCS, vol. 9660, pp. 47–64. Springer, Cham (2016). https://doi.org/10.1007/978-3-319-30734-3_6
3. Ancona, D., Ferrando, A., Mascardi, V.: Improving flexibility and dependability of remote patient monitoring with agent-oriented approaches. IJAOSE **6**(3/4), 402–442 (2018)
4. Bauer, A., Leucker, M., Schallhart, C.: Monitoring of real-time properties. In: Arun-Kumar, S., Garg, N. (eds.) FSTTCS 2006. LNCS, vol. 4337, pp. 260–272. Springer, Heidelberg (2006). https://doi.org/10.1007/11944836_25
5. Brafman, R.I., Bar-Sinai, M., Ashkenazi, M.: Performance level profiles: a formal language for describing the expected performance of functional modules. In: IROS, pp. 1751–1756. IEEE (2016)
6. Chen, F., Roşu, G.: Towards monitoring-oriented programming: a paradigm combining specification and implementation. In: Workshop on Runtime Verification (RV 2003), ENTCS, vol. 89(2), pp. 108–127 (2003)
7. Ferrando, A.: The early bird catches the worm: First verify, then monitor!. Sci. Comput. Program. **172**, 160–179 (2019)

8. Ferrando, A., Dennis, L.A., Ancona, D., Fisher, M., Mascardi, V.: Verifying and validating autonomous systems: towards an integrated approach. In: Colombo, C., Leucker, M. (eds.) RV 2018. LNCS, vol. 11237, pp. 263–281. Springer, Cham (2018). https://doi.org/10.1007/978-3-030-03769-7_15

9. Huang, J., Erdogan, C., Zhang, Y., Moore, B., Luo, Q., Sundaresan, A., Rosu, G.: ROSRV: runtime verification for robots. In: Bonakdarpour, B., Smolka, S.A. (eds.) RV 2014. LNCS, vol. 8734, pp. 247–254. Springer, Cham (2014). https://doi.org/10.1007/978-3-319-11164-3_20

10. Leucker, M., Schallhart, C.: A brief account of runtime verification. J. Log. Algebr. Program. **78**(5), 293–303 (2009)

11. Pinisetty, S., Jéron, T., Tripakis, S., Falcone, Y., Marchand, H., Preoteasa, V.: Predictive runtime verification of timed properties. J. Syst. Softw. **132**, 353–365 (2017)

12. Pnueli, A.: The temporal logic of programs. In: 18th Annual Symposium on Foundations of Computer Science, Providence, Rhode Island, USA, 31 October - 1 November 1977, pp. 46–57. IEEE Computer Society (1977). https://doi.org/10.1109/SFCS.1977.32

13. Visser, W., Havelund, K., Brat, G.P., Park, S., Lerda, F.: Model checking programs. Autom. Softw. Eng. **10**(2), 203–232 (2003)

One-Shot 3D Printed Underactuated Gripper

Jordan Cormack[1]([✉]) [iD], Mohammad Fotouhi[2] [iD], Guy Adams[3],
and Anthony Pipe[1] [iD]

[1] University of the West of England, Bristol, England
`jordan.cormack@uwe.ac.uk`
[2] University of Glasgow, Glasgow, Scotland
[3] HP Inc. UK Ltd., Bristol, England

Abstract. Underactuated gripping mechanisms allow a wide range of objects to be grasped, with relatively simple control and input. Current 3D printed underactuated grippers are often composed of multiple parts that need assembly before use. Consolidating many of these parts allows the gripper to be manufactured more quickly for less money, and allows custom gripping devices to become more accessible. A novel one-shot printed underactuated gripping mechanism was developed, which was manufactured using HP's MJF 3D printing process. The conventional tendon lines were replaced with a band which was 3D printed as part of the gripper. Finite Element Analysis was used to model the gripper behaviour, and 3D printed prototypes were manufactured and tested, which were to grip a range of objects.

Keywords: 3D printing · Underactuated · Gripper

1 Introduction

In the context of robot grippers, underactuation is where there are fewer sources of actuation than degrees of freedom [1], or joints. This can enable objects to be gripped with relatively simple control, as there is not a dedicated actuation device for every joint. Existing underactuated grippers usually feature rigid sections which are connected with flexible joints which act as springs [2]. A tendon line is then passed through the rigid digits, which causes the digit to bend once it is pulled [3]. Figure 1 shows tendon lines on the underside of a robotic hand [4]. As the arm casing is already 3D printed [5], if the tendon line could also be 3D printed in place, time could be saved during assembly.

2 Digit Design

Initial prototypes were manufactured on a Prusa i3 MK3S [6] which uses the FFF (Fused Filament Fabrication) 3D printing process. This process requires

---

This work was supported by HP Inc. UK Ltd.

© Springer Nature Switzerland AG 2020
A. Mohammad et al. (Eds.): TAROS 2020, LNAI 12228, pp. 400–404, 2020.
https://doi.org/10.1007/978-3-030-63486-5_41

Fig. 1. Tendon Driven Hero Arm [4] Used with permission from Open Bionics

a support structure to be printed below hanging regions, but it is possible to 'bridge' certain straight line distances without support [7]. Figure 2 shows a basic underactuated digit design. The large blocks are the rigid sections, attached to each other by a thin flexible/compliant base. The tendon line is then printed from the end digit, through a channel in the others, to a pull tab within the main gripper body which can be attached to a linear actuator or similar. Pulling the tendon will create a bending force on the thin regions, causing the whole digit to flex. As there is only a single tendon line and actuator, this force causes bending in the regions with the least resistance [8], allowing the gripper to conform to whatever shape it is grasping. In an FFF process, the print orientation plays a key role in the performance and manufacturability of such geometry. Due to the individual layers and lack of support, bridging can only be done parallel to the print bed. Printing digits perpendicular to the bed would be possible, but as the strength in this direction is much lower, the tendon and compliant regions would fail much more easily. In compression the tendon line can still transfer force to the tip as, even if it buckles, limited off-axis movement is possible within the digit channels. This allows the digit to bend in both directions.

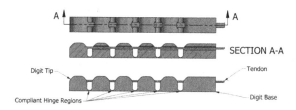

Fig. 2. Underactuated Digit

Finite Element Analysis (FEA) simulations within Ansys 2019R2 have been used to simulate the deformation of the underactuated digit to an applied load. Figure 3 shows the total deformation for a 4N load acting on the tendon. The maximum deformation is 39.6 mm at an angle of 49°.

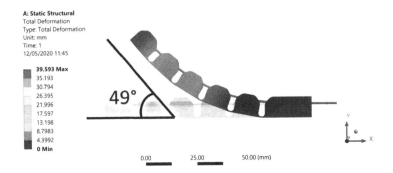

Fig. 3. Underactuated Digit Finite Element Analysis

3   Digit Testing

Figure 4 shows two prototype digits, complete with integrated tendons. The left design requires the tendon to be cut at the back (rightmost) wall before it can be pulled to bend the digit, the right design was printed with two independent base sections, allowing them to be pulled apart without cutting. The compliant region thickness in these prototypes was chosen based on the first layer thickness of the FFF machine, 0.2 mm in this case. This allowed the sections to flex easily, whilst still being relatively strong.

Fig. 4. Prototype FFF Digits

Another prototype digit was manufactured using HP's MJF (Multi Jet Fusion) process, shown in Fig. 5. In this powder based process the un-fused powder provides support for the parts, removing the need for a solid support structure. This allows geometries to be printed which would be either impossible or require a complex, difficult to remove, support structure if printed using FFF. An FFF prototype with three digits has been manufactured and once connected to a linear actuator, it can be opened and closed to grasp a range of objects, as shown in Fig. 6. Objects up to 200 g have been successfully lifted using this setup. The possibility of gripping a wide range of objects is key for general purpose gripping applications such as for prosthetics, or where objects are in an unknown orientation.

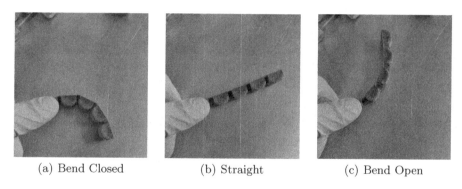

(a) Bend Closed   (b) Straight   (c) Bend Open

Fig. 5. MJF Underactuated Digit Bend Test

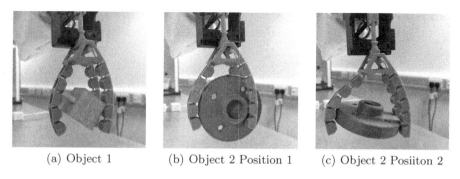

(a) Object 1   (b) Object 2 Position 1   (c) Object 2 Posiiton 2

Fig. 6. Underactuated Gripper Grip Test

4 Conclusion

3D printing tendon lines as part of the digit allows time to be saved in the assembly process, and the initial results show relatively good performance. Considerations must be taken depending on the selected manufacturing process, as support structure may be required to print the tendon line successfully. Part orientation on a FFF process is key, as the thin sections will break easily if printed perpendicular to the bed. Processes such as Multi Jet Fusion produce almost isotropic parts that can be printed in any orientation, and do not require any support structure for the tendons. The isotropic parts also more easily allow the gripping mechanism to be simulated using finite element analysis. This means different gripper configurations can be tested and the best chosen for manufacture.

References

1. Birglen, L., Laliberte, T., Gosselin, C.: Underactuated Robotic Hands. Springer, Berlin (2008). https://doi.org/10.1007/978-3-540-77459-4

2. Montambault, S., Gosselin, C.M.: Analysis of underactuated mechanical grippers. J. Mech. Des. **123**(3), 367–374 (2001)
3. Ozawa, R., Hashirii, K., Kobayashi, H.: Design and control of underactuated tendon-driven mechanisms. In: IEEE International Conference on Robotics and Automation, pp. 1522–1527. IEEE (2009)
4. Open Bionics Hero Arm - User Guide. https://openbionics.com/hero-arm-user-guide/. Accessed 24 Jan 2020
5. Open Bionics: 3D printed prosthetic limbs. https://ultimaker.com/learn/open-bionics-3d-printed-prosthetic-limbs. Accessed 11 Feb 2020
6. Original Prusa i3 MK3S. https://www.prusa3d.com/original-prusa-i3-mk3/. Accessed 11 Feb 2020
7. How to design parts for FDM 3D Printing. https://www.3dhubs.com/knowledge-base/how-design-parts-fdm-3d-printing/#bridging. Accessed 10 Feb 2020
8. Wu, L.C., Carbone, G., Ceccarelli, M.: Designing an underactuated mechanism for a 1 active DOF finger operation. Mech. Mach. Theory **44**(2), 336–348 (2009)

A Cable-Based Gripper for Chemistry Labs

Lupo Manes[1,2]([⊠]), Sebastiano Fichera[1,2], David Marquez-Gamez[1], Andrew I. Cooper[1], and Paolo Paoletti[1,2]

[1] Leverhulme Research Centre for Functional Materials Discovery, Material Innovation Factory, University of Liverpool, Liverpool L69 7ZD, UK
{LManes,Seba84,David.Marquez-Gamez,aicooper,Paoletti}@liverpool.ac.uk
[2] School of Engineering, University of Liverpool, Liverpool L69 3GH, UK

Abstract. This paper presents the design of an end-effector for handling of supplies commonly found in chemistry labs. The system uses a cable loop capable of providing an effective grasp of any prismatic or cylindrical object, making it ideal for handling vials and other containers commonly used in laboratories. When compared to the more common parallel jaw gripper design, the proposed cable based end-effector is able to handle a larger variety of objects without interfering with the surrounding objects even in a crowded environment (minimal footprint). The payload capability of the gripper have been tested on a load test apparatus with different materials, demonstrating its effectiveness.

Keywords: Robotic gripper · Cable-based manipulator · Chemistry automation

1 Introduction

The current trend in industry and research is pursuing effective human-robot interaction and cooperation, where the two would participate to the same workflow both efficiently and safely. This would make for easier set up and inspection of automated plants, since the safety features and procedures would be embedded in the robotic system. Currently, robot manufacturers provide cooperative robots in the form of low-power robotic arms (<35 kg max payload), sometimes mounted on mobile bases. These systems come equipped with collision detection and avoidance and compliance features to avoid harming humans or damaging themselves or the surrounding environment [4].

Chemistry research, and more specifically material discovery, relies on exploring a large number of chemical combinations. Artificial intelligence trained for the task can skim most combinations through simulation and narrow down the possible solutions to a few hundred composites. This software combined with a robotic system makes a robotic scientists that can run the reactions in a lab and has provided some great results [1]. Current systems require a highly controlled environments and can only perform specific tasks [2]. As a result, a significant

© Springer Nature Switzerland AG 2020
A. Mohammad et al. (Eds.): TAROS 2020, LNAI 12228, pp. 405–408, 2020.
https://doi.org/10.1007/978-3-030-63486-5_42

amount of resources goes into the design and possible modifications of a physical system. The creation of a robot that can work in any chemistry lab with the available supplies is extremely appealing to reduce the set-up costs of chemistry automation and improve its accessibility.

In order to be effective in an environment with variable features, like position of supplies or layout of the lab benches, the robotic system needs to be extremely robust. Specifically, when it comes to manipulation, a balance needs to be struck between computation (the software) and embodiment (the hardware). Computation has traditionally been the main focus for manipulation task because of the quicker turnaround when compared to mechanical design. However, thanks to the advance in rapid manufacturing technology, the hardware can nowadays be updated at similar pace to the software [5]. This has lead to further exploration of potential mechanical designs in an effort to find the right tool for the job instead of finding a workaround for sub-optimal equipment. This is particularly true for the development of end-effectors, where many of the newer designs have become better adapted for their work environment [3]. The end-effector proposed in this paper aims to outperform current designs in their flexibility, footprint and ease of grasping. The use of a cable loop mechanism allows for all of these requirements while also keeping costs low.

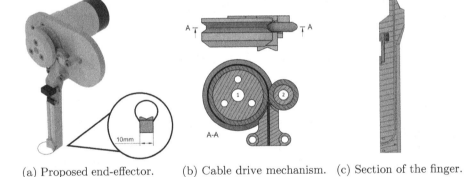

(a) Proposed end-effector.   (b) Cable drive mechanism.   (c) Section of the finger.

Fig. 1. Render and key design elements of the proposed gripper.

2   Proposed Design

The proposed design, shown in Fig. 1a, consists of a main body containing the drive components and a vertical beam (finger) with a cable loop at its end. A 0.5 mm polyamide cable is used to envelop objects and pull them against the finger. To keep the object aligned to the end-effector, the contact surface on the finger is concave. One end of the cable is fixed at the end of the finger while the other can be pushed or pulled by a two wheel arrangement, shown in

Fig. 1b, with wheel 1 driven by a geared DC motor and wheel 2 used to keep the wire in contact with wheel 1. Both wheels use a 3D printed flexible material (Ninjaflex^{TM}) external cover with a V groove to better grip and feed the cable. The cable is fed into a channel, shown in Fig. 1c, that guides it to the desired position. All the mechanical components for the design have been 3D printed.

An embedded capacitive force sensor (SingleTact^{TM}10N) mounted behind the contact surface collects information about the grasping force, and a rotary encoder mounted to the motor shaft is used to estimate the radius of the cable loop. A closed-loop control system, implemented on an Arduino^{TM}Mega board, allows the grasping force to be stabilised at a specific user-defined set-point.

The key parameters in the design are the motor torque (τ_m), the width of the finger (W_f) and the pulley radius (r_p) which can be used to calculate the maximum ideal gripping force (F_g). A simplified relation between such parameters and vial radius (r_v) can be obtained by neglecting friction and reads

$$F_g = \frac{2r_v W_f^2 \tau_m r_p}{r_v^2 - \frac{W_f^2}{4}} \tag{1}$$

The minimum vial diameter is given by the cable bending radius, i.e. a few millimeters for the polyamide cable. The maximum diameter is determined by excessive deformation of the loop under self-weight, i.e. 45mm in the current setup.

3   Testing

The gripper has been tested by grasping cylindrical objects of different diameters attached to a load cell to check the maximum payload weight, see Fig. 2a.

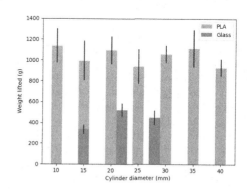

(a) Assembled test rig.

(b) Maximum weight lifted as the diameter of the samples increases. Error bars represent one standard deviation.

Fig. 2. Test apparatus and results

The tests were conducted with both glass and plastic cylindrical vials, performing 5 runs for each test sample to insure reliability. For each test, the cable loop was tightened around the cylinder until a grasping force of 5 N was registered by the sensor in the end-effector. The drive wheel was then locked in place and the end-effector was slowly lifted using the linear actuator of the load test apparatus shown on the right of Fig. 2a.

The results of these tests are summarised in Fig. 2b. The end-effector could lift more weight with plastic specimens because of their higher surface roughness and therefore extra friction. In spite of the lower friction of glass, the end-effector was still able to reliably lift 400 g of payload. Tests with both materials show no significant decrease in performance as the diameter increases, which suggests that the design could prove to be highly versatile. The maximum load exceeds the requirements for use in a chemistry lab: the largest commercially available vial would only weigh 50 g when filled with water.

4   Conclusions

The proposed gripper provides a small footprint and can handle variable payload sizes, thanks to an unconventional grasping mechanism. The cable loop design compromises on the type of shape the system can grasp but has potentially unprecedented flexibility for payload size. The compact design can be easily fitted to commercially available robotic manipulators.

To improve its reliability, the prototype will require better selection of materials and electromechanical components, alongside further prototype testing. Later, software integration with a robotic manipulator will need to be developed for testing in a realistic environment.

References

1. King, R.D., et al.: Towards robot scientists for autonomous scientific discovery. Automated Experiment. **2**, 1–11 (2010). https://doi.org/10.1186/1759-4499-2-1
2. Pan, J.: Engineering chemistry innovation. ACS Med. Chem. Lett. **10**(5), 703–707 (2019). https://doi.org/10.1021/acsmedchemlett.9b00096
3. Tai, K., El-Sayed, A., Shahriari, M., Biglarbegian, M., Mahmud, S.: State of the art robotic grippers and applications. Robotics **5**(2), 1–20 (2016). https://doi.org/10.3390/robotics5020011
4. Vysocky, A., Novak, P.: Human - robot collaboation in industry. MM Sci. J. **2016**, 1066–1072 (2016). https://doi.org/10.17973/MMSJ.2016_10_201640
5. Wade-McCue, S., et al.: Design of a Multi-Modal End-Effector and Grasping System: How Integrated Design helped win the Amazon Robotics Challenge (2017)

Magnetic Force Driven Wireless Motor

Cameron Duffield[✉] and Shuhei Miyashita[ID]

Automatic Control and Systems Engineering, The University of Sheffield,
Portobello Ln, Sheffield S1 3JD, UK
{cduffield1,shuhei.miyashita}@sheffield.ac.uk
https://sites.google.com/site/shuheidotnet/

Abstract. A wirelessly actuated motor has wide potential application in in-vivo mechatronic devices, due to the absence of power and control cables from outside the device. This paper presents a magnetically actuated wireless motor with no net force acting on the device. The developed motor has a double crank; each connecting rod accommodates a 5 mm neodymium magnet, actuated using a magnetic field produced by an electromagnetic coil system located nearby. The magnetic field aligned parallel to the direction of the magnet produces a magnetic force. The magnets are oppositely oriented, so experience attraction and repulsion forces, the crank converts this into a rotational motion. By altering the direction of the magnetic field, these forces are switched, and by using a ratchet a rotational motion in a single direction is produced.

Keywords: Magnetic control · Wireless motor · Dual-crank mechanism

1 Introduction

Recent advances have been made with implantable medical robots. These implants often have electrical connections to the outside of the body [2], or in the case of soft robots pneumatic or hydraulic connections are used [6]. Magnetic induction based wireless power transmission is a promising approach, however, it necessitates the presence of electronics and a receiver coil within the device [1]. Magnetic direct drive mechanisms, where magnetic force or torque are transmitted in a non-contact manner, offer an alternative to on-board energy source or tethers. Small magnet on-board microrobots are one of the examples, where a magnetic field provided by an electromagnetic coil system directly actuates the robot [5]. Locomotion of magnetically controlled robots involves the entire body moving. Hu et al. developed a soft robot that exploits multiple modes of actuation including, rolling, walking, and swimming [3]. The method removes the energy source from the robot, allowing them to be smaller and lighter. However,

Supported by the Department of Automatic Control and Systems Engineering, The University of Sheffield.

© Springer Nature Switzerland AG 2020
A. Mohammad et al. (Eds.): TAROS 2020, LNAI 12228, pp. 409–412, 2020.
https://doi.org/10.1007/978-3-030-63486-5_43

this approach does not allow for the driving of mechanisms within the robot as a net torque is applied to the robot body, causing it to rotate [4].

This paper presents a novel magnetic drive mechanism using a double crank. A magnet in each connecting rod is directly actuated by a magnetic field, producing a rotational motion. Thanks to the opposed directions of magnetic forces, the motor experiences zero net force, thus minimising the impact on the local environment where it is situated.

2 Method

The developed motor consists of two counterweighting cranks, with $180°$ phase difference, on each of which is a 5 mm cubic neodymium iron boron (NdFeB) magnet at the end (Fig. 1).

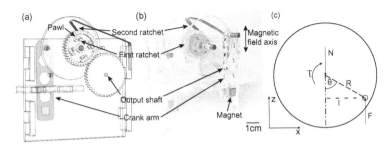

Fig. 1. The developed magnetic force driven wireless motor. (a) CAD section view and (b) Photograph. (c) Force analysis.

The magnets are vertical, with opposite orientation, this ensures there is no net magnetic force acting on the motor from the external magnetic field. The magnetic field gradient $(0.14\,\text{T m}^{-1})$ is applied vertically from a 200 mm diameter electromagnetic coil embedded 40 mm below the workspace, and can periodically switch the orientation. A crank converts the linear motion of the crank arm to rotary motion. To remove the singularity at top dead centre the crank is designed to oscillate $45°$ either side of horizontal. A double ratchet mechanism is used to convert this oscillating rotation to rotation in a single direction and prevent the load back-driving the motor. The first ratchet consists of four pawls within a saw-tooth ring gear. The second ratchet uses a combined pawl and pawl spring against the involute tooth driving gear.

For the driving stroke the magnetic field gradient is applied in the negative z direction, moving the crank clockwise. The geometry of the design prevents the crank from rotating past $\theta = 135°$. The field gradient is then reversed, the first ratchet disengages and the crank moves counter-clockwise for the recoil stroke. The maximum torque is given when the crank is horizontal $(\theta = 90°)$ and the minimum is at the two extremes of motion $(\theta = 45°, \theta = 135°)$. The control of the magnetic field is open loop. The angular position of the output shaft can be calculated for open-loop position control from the number of driving strokes performed.

The magnetic force on a magnet with moment $\boldsymbol{m}$, $\boldsymbol{F}_m$, in a magnetic field $\boldsymbol{B}$ is given by

$$\boldsymbol{F}_m = (\boldsymbol{m} \cdot \nabla) \, \boldsymbol{B}$$

$$= \left(\frac{\partial \boldsymbol{B}}{\partial x} \frac{\partial \boldsymbol{B}}{\partial y} \frac{\partial \boldsymbol{B}}{\partial z} \right)^T \boldsymbol{m}. \tag{1}$$

Referring to Fig. 1 (c) which shows the relation of a free body diagram of the system, with (1), The producible torque about the output shaft, τ, is

$$\tau = 2\,n\,\frac{\partial \boldsymbol{B}}{\partial z}\,\boldsymbol{m}\,R\,\sin\theta - Fr, \tag{2}$$

where the coefficient 2 represents the use of two magnets, n is the used gear ratio, R is the crank radius, and Fr is torque loss to friction in the mechanism.

The housing parts were laser cut from 3 mm, and the connecting rods from 2 mm, sheet acrylic using a CO_2 laser cutter. The gears and ratchet parts were manufactured from Formlabs clear resin using a Form 2 SLA printer. The 3 mm diameter shafts were cut from brass (CZ121/CW614N) rod and 2 mm diameter stainless steel rod. Small pieces of Ecoflex 00–10 were used for the pawl springs in the ratchet mechanism. The second ratchet was cut from a 0.1 mm thick steel sheet (full hard, cold rolled, low carbon 1008–1010) and bent to shape. The mechanism was assembled using acrylic adhesive and cyano acrylate.

3   Results

The experimental setup for the measurement of torque is shown in Fig. 2 (a).

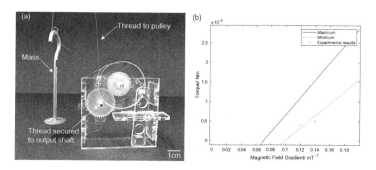

Fig. 2. Measurement of torque. (a) The experimental setup, (b) Theoretical and experimental plot of torque τ.

The output torque of the motor was measured using a simple hoist mechanism. A length of mono-filament nylon thread was secured to the shaft, passed up over a pulley, and down to a known mass to provide the load. The friction in the mechanism was measured by removing the crank arms, winding the thread around the output shaft and adding mass until the mechanism rotates. This gave $Fr = 0.15 \times 10^{-3} \pm 0.01 \times 10^{-3}$ Nm. Figure 2 (b) shows the measured and calculated motor torque for a given magnetic field gradient. The maximum line represents the point when the crank is horizontal and torque is greatest, while the minimum line shows where the crank is at its lowest or highest point (45° from horizontal) and the torque is at its minimum. The experimentally measured values are the greatest load at which the motor could complete the full cycle, so correspond to the minimum torque line. The provisional experimental results in Fig. 2 (b) show the model being a reasonable fit for the data.

4   Conclusion

A magnetically actuated wireless motor driven by a magnetic force has been presented. Because of the force and weight countering mechanism, the device experiences net zero force and thus exhibits stability in operation. Initial values for output torque were measured. Future work includes further data collection and improvement of the design to reduce the torque lost to friction.

References

1. Boyvat, M., Koh, J.S., Wood, R.J.: Addressable wireless actuation for multijoint folding robots and devices. Sci. Robot. **2**(8), eaan1544 (2017)
2. Damian, D.D., et al.: In vivo tissue regeneration with robotic implants. Sci. Robot. **3**(14), eaaq0018 (2018)
3. Hu, W., Lum, G.Z., Mastrangeli, M., Sitti, M.: Small-scale soft-bodied robot with multimodal locomotion. Nature **554**(7690), 81–85 (2018)
4. Lien, G.S., Liu, C.W., Jiang, J.A., Chuang, C.L., Teng, M.T.: Magnetic control system targeted for capsule endoscopic operations in the stomach–design, fabrication, and in vitro and ex vivo evaluations. IEEE Trans. Biomed. Eng. **59**(7), 2068–2079 (2012)
5. Miyashita, S., Guitron, S., Ludersdorfer, M., Sung, C.R., Rus, D.: An untethered miniature origami robot that self-folds, walks, swims, and degrades. In: 2015 IEEE International Conference on Robotics and Automation (ICRA). pp. 1490–1496. IEEE (2015)
6. Perez-Guagnelli, E., et al.: Characterization, simulation and control of a soft helical pneumatic implantable robot for tissue regeneration. IEEE Trans. Med. Robot. Bionics **2**(1), 94–103 (2020). https://doi.org/10.1109/TMRB.2020.2970308

Correction to: A Novel Shape Memory Alloy (SMA) Wire-Based Clutch Design and Performance Test

Nan Ma, Xin Dong, Josue Camacho Arreguin, and Mingfeng Wang

Correction to:
Chapter "A Novel Shape Memory Alloy (SMA) Wire-Based Clutch Design and Performance Test" in: A. Mohammad et al. (Eds.): *Towards Autonomous Robotic Systems*, **LNAI 12228, https://doi.org/10.1007/978-3-030-63486-5_38**

The original version of this chapter was revised. Mingfeng Wang was inadvertently not included as a coauthor. This has been corrected.

The updated version of this chapter can be found at
https://doi.org/10.1007/978-3-030-63486-5_38

© Springer Nature Switzerland AG 2021
A. Mohammad et al. (Eds.): TAROS 2020, LNAI 12228, p. C1, 2021.
https://doi.org/10.1007/978-3-030-63486-5_44

Author Index

Printed in the United States
by Baker & Taylor Publisher Services